KU-739-537

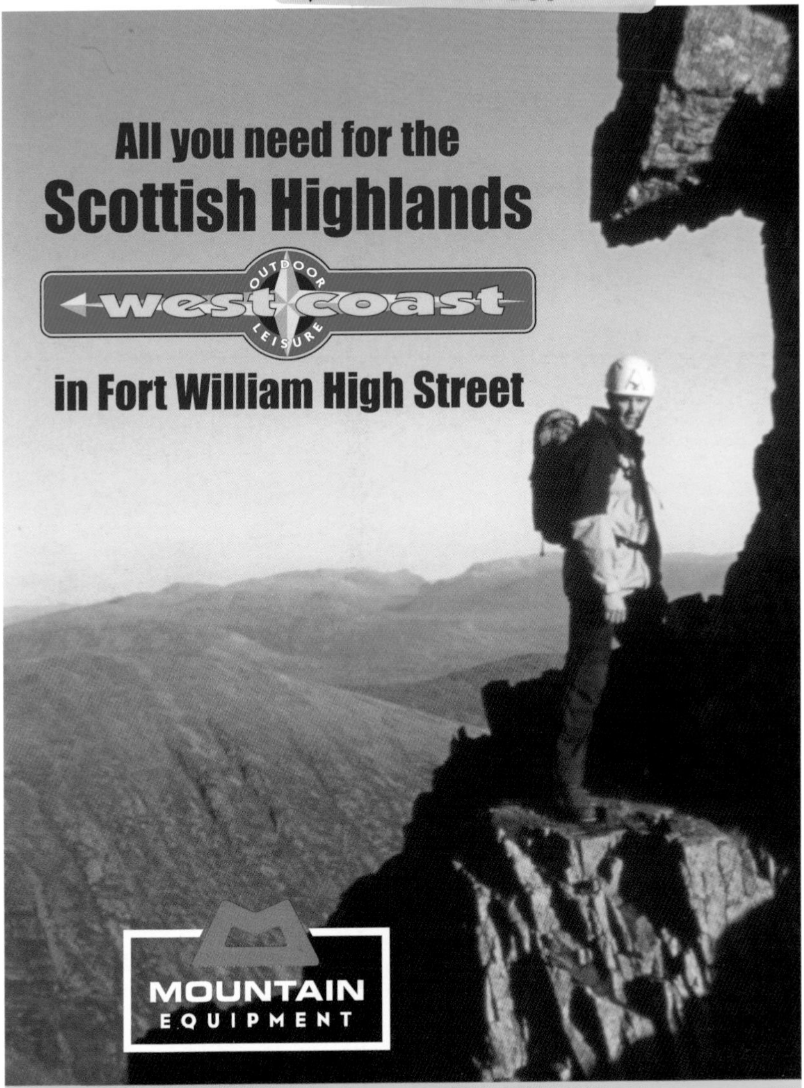

THE SCOTTISH
MOUNTAINEERING
CLUB JOURNAL

Vol. XXXX **2006** **No. 197**

UNDER THE WEATHER

By Simon Richardson

Why is Scotland such a good training ground for much higher mountains? Perhaps because an average winter day in Scotland offers more adventure than a week of storms anywhere else.

IT WAS past two in the afternoon, blowing hard and snowing heavily. Roger climbed up to the stance and we took stock. We were attempting a new route up the crest of Mitre Ridge, deep in the Cairngorms, and were battling on in a rising storm. It had taken six hours to climb the first three pitches. Scottish winter days are short, and we had fewer than three hours daylight, but the line was just too good to give up. Logical and elegant, a succession of steep corners and unclimbed turfy grooves slotted together like a jigsaw puzzle all the way up the spine of the ridge.

I took the rack and continued straight up the crest, grateful that Roger had insisted I take a warthog, as this was the only protection below one particularly awkward bulge. The natural winter way was a steep right-facing inset corner that had accumulated a huge quantity of powder snow. The crack at its back was devoid of turf, so I laybacked up it on torqued ice tools with my crampons skating on the smooth rock. I badly misjudged it near the top, and was on the point of falling when I found a crucial foothold. Panting heavily, I pulled on to the platform above just as the rope came tight. The next pitch was the last difficult one. I struggled up a steep corner, hand traversed on wilting arms to the crest of a tower, and stumbled along the sharp ridge to belay in a col below a second tower in the gloom. By the time Roger arrived it was dark and the urgency of the last few hours dissolved into the icy blackness.

Six hours later, we had finished the route and I trailed head down behind Roger as he kept us on the correct bearing. Conditions on the plateau were extreme with gale force winds and blinding spindrift. Our world was limited to the pools of light from our headtorches and the ever-shifting snow around our feet. We counted our paces to track our progress against the map and shouted out every hundredth step into the screaming wind.

Niall McNair on In Profundum Lacu (E5 6a), Pink Wall, Pabbay. Photo: Iain Small.

When we bumped into a prominent boulder we'd passed on the approach the relief was immediate. We stumbled back down the glen, and elated, we collapsed into our tent after 22 hours on the move.

The Scottish Winter Experience:

Our ascent of *The Cardinal* in the remote Garbh Choire on Beinn a'Bhuird is typical of many Scottish winter adventures. The 200m. climb had seven pitches of sustained mixed climbing, but technical difficulty was just one aspect of the experience. The 16km. approach, the short eight-hour winter day, the wild and unpredictable weather and difficult navigation all provided equally important ingredients to the challenge. Overall it was more like doing a major alpine route than climbing on a roadside crag.

At just under 1200m. altitude, Beinn a' Bhuird is one of the highest Cairngorm summits. In summer the Cairngorms are a range of flat-topped grassy hills, but like the rest of the Scottish Highlands they are transformed in winter and take on a seriousness out of proportion to their size. Their summit plateaux collect huge quantities of snow that are swept by the prevailing westerly winds into deep-sided corries that were carved out by glaciers in the last Ice Age. Their granite cliffs are cracked and vegetated and made for on-sight climbing. The cracks take protection readily and frozen turf has the consistency of plastic ice. When conditions are good, ice dribbles down corners and powder snow and hoar transform the dark granite walls and buttresses into white frosted fantasy castles towering up into the sky.

Scotland is a small country and more than half the landscape is mountainous. The mountains range from the rolling schist hills of the Southern Highlands, to the spectacular sandstone summits of the North-West Highlands. The Central Highlands comprise the rugged volcanic peaks around Glen Coe and Ben Nevis, while the Cairngorms lie in the centre of the country and include the largest group of high mountains in Scotland. The Hebrides Islands on the western seaboard are mountainous too, and in a hard winter they can give spectacular climbing overlooking the sea. Most of these areas are accessible from Glasgow and Edinburgh after a two or three-hour drive, and are within weekend range of the English cities. On a good day in peak season during February and March, the popular areas can take on a cosmopolitan air and you are as likely to meet a climber from Slovenia or Spain on the summit plateau of Ben Nevis, as you are someone from Glasgow or Manchester.

Unlike the Alps, there is very little fixed gear on Scottish cliffs and bolts are shunned. Every route you climb is like doing a first ascent. Protection has to be placed on the lead and belays can sometimes take half-an-hour to find. On the harder routes, three-hour leads of 30m. pitches are common, as the leader fights to clear the rock to find gear placements. This ground-up approach maximises the challenge from the cliffs, and the harder routes are always a race against time and the short winter day. Most ascents are made in weather that you would not consider leaving the valley when in the Alps. The wind blows almost continuously, it is often raining in the glens and snowing on the tops, and despite modern clothing and materials one is nearly always damp. On longer routes a single push is far more effective than a multi-day ascent as the weather is too poor to consider bivouacking. The sub-Arctic climate is unforgiving and it is always better to stay moving rather than stop.

It is the mental dimension that makes Scottish winter climbing so compelling. Solving the frozen puzzle of leading a pitch and finding protection is one aspect, but predicting conditions and selecting an appropriate route is the underlying challenge. Conditions change daily, and historically the most successful Scottish winter climbers have not been the strongest or most technically gifted, but those who have the knack of being in the right place at the right time. While many Scottish climbs are reliably in condition most winters, others take a particular sequence of snowfall, wind, thaw and freeze to form, and many climbers will wait for years for their chosen route to come into condition.

A Brief History:

Scottish winter climbing has a long history. The Victorians pioneered winter ascents of the great 500m. ridges on Ben Nevis before the end of the 19th century using long unwieldy alpenstocks, clinker-shod labourer's boots and short lengths of hemp rope. Even today, *Tower Ridge* (IV,4 1894) and *North-East Buttress* (IV,5 1896) are respected climbs, with the latter sporting a short M4 crux near the top of the route. Step-cutting skills were similarly advanced and Harold Raeburn took ice climbing levels to WI3 levels with his ascent of *Green Gully* (IV,4) on Ben Nevis in 1906. It was another 50 years before ice climbing standards advanced significantly again, when Jimmy Marshall and Robin Smith brought step-cutting to its pinnacle in 1960 with a magnificent series of ascents on Ben Nevis culminating in the first free ascent of *Point Five Gully* and the 400m. *Orion Direct* (V,5). These climbs were the preserve of the elite. Marshall and Smith wore crampons, but step-cutting was still a slow, dangerous and exhausting process where a short single axe was used to cut a ladder of handholds and steps in the ice. Farther east on the powder-covered rock of the Cairngorms, Tom Patey used nailed boots and a single axe to push mixed climbing standards up to M5 levels with *Eagle Ridge* (VI,6 1953) and *Parallel Buttress* (VI,6 1956) on Lochnagar and *Scorpion* (V,6 1952) on the Shelter Stone.

Throughout the 1970s, the 'curved axe revolution' concentrated winter activity on climbing ice – mainly on Ben Nevis. British climbers, well practised on Nevis ice, applied their skills with great effect in the Alps and elsewhere throughout the 1970s. Perhaps the best example is the

Colton-MacIntyre Route on the North Face of the Grandes Jorasses (ED3 1976). This very narrow couloir, totally Scottish in character, was undoubtedly the hardest ice climb in the Alps at the time. Another example was the application of Nevis-style thin face climbing to the North Face of the Pelerins (ED2) by Rab Carrington and Al Rouse in February 1975. Towards the end of the decade however, the focus began to slowly turn back towards mixed climbing and during the early 1980s the art of 'torquing' was developed. Mountaineers have jammed axe picks into rock cracks for centuries, but ironically, it was the reversed curve 'banana' picks, developed on the Continent for steep ice climbing, which proved to be perfectly suited to the technique of levering shafts to cam picks in narrow cracks. The vegetated cliffs of the Cairngorms are ideal for this type of climbing, for the deep cracks and rough rock hold the picks well, and there is a liberal supply of turf on all but the very steepest of routes.

During the mid 1980s, the Aberdeen-based team of Colin MacLean and Andy Nisbet forged one of the strongest partnerships in the history of Scottish winter mountaineering. The bulk of their new routes were in the Cairngorms, but their first Grade VIII was away from home territory, 100km. to the west, in Glen Coe. Their winter ascent of the prominent corner line of *Unicorn* (VIII,8) in Stob Coire nan Lochan in January 1985 proved controversial, as the local West Coast climbers doubted whether a hoar-frosted ascent really counted as true winter conditions. The line of *Unicorn* occasionally forms as a thin ribbon of ice, but MacLean and Nisbet were applying Cairngorms techniques and attitudes developed over the previous few winters where the key requirement for a route to be in winter condition is that it should be frozen and have a wintry appearance. These criteria are now accepted as the norm for high standard mixed climbing across Scotland.

Three weeks later, the MacLean-Nisbet team went on to climb their greatest route, *The Needle* (VIII,8) on Shelter Stone Crag. It took two weeks of continuous effort, scoping the best winter line and waiting for a settled spell of weather, before they made a two-day ascent with a bivouac. Twenty years on, the 250m. climb still rates as one of Scotland's most demanding winter routes in terms of length and sustained difficulty, and only last winter saw its first one-day free ascent.

The way was now open for the other great challenges to fall. The following season, Kenny Spence succeeded on his third attempt to climb *Centurion* (VIII,8 1986) on Ben Nevis with Spider MacKenzie, and Nisbet and Sandy Allan linked up an ingenious line on the front face of the Central Gully Wall of Creag an Dubh Loch to give *The Rattrap* (VIII,8 1986). As more people became aware of the new techniques such as hooking edges and torquing, attention in the early 1990s shifted to the easily accessible Northern Corries of Cairn Gorm. Brian Davison, Graeme Ettle and Nisbet were all involved in the action, resulting in a series of short technical routes including *Big Daddy* (VII,8 1991), *The Vicar* (VII,8 1992) and *Prore* (VII,7 1992). The late 1990s were primarily a time for consolidation, and these climbs introduced dozens of climbers to Grade VII routes. As climbers became fitter and more skilled, many of the big winter routes of the 1980s were repeated, and the one or two points of aid often used on the first ascents were eliminated.

State of the Art:
Until the mid-1980s, many of the harder mixed routes were winter ascents of summer lines, but as confidence has grown there has been an increased emphasis on seeking out winter-only lines. These are typically vegetated, wet and dripping in summer, but they are transformed by winter's grip into inspiring mixed climbing possibilities. *Diedre of Sorrows* (VIII,8 1986) on the Tough-Brown Face of Lochnagar was an early example of a cutting edge winter-only line, and more recently routes such as *Magic Bow Wall* (VIII,8 2001) and *The Godfather* (VIII,8 2002) in the North-West Highlands have expanded this concept to create 300m. routes of alpine proportions that have significant technical difficulty.

Today, two distinct styles are emerging. The first is a continuation of the traditional approach with an emphasis on climbing routes on-sight and ground-up. Attitudes to aid have now hardened, and ascents using rest points or direct aid are considered seriously flawed. As a result perhaps, Scotland can lay claim to the most stylistically pure form of mountaineering in the world. Some routes require multiple attempts over many seasons such as Brian Davison's ascent of *Mort* on Lochnagar (IX,9 2000). This took 18 attempts over 15 years and is widely considered to be the hardest traditional winter route in Scotland. The three-pitch climb involves technical and very strenuous icy mixed climbing with poor protection and serious ground fall potential.

The second style is to pursue technical difficulty by applying modern rock climbing techniques such as pre-inspection to shorter (often single pitch) climbs. Dave MacLeod, one of Scotland's most talented rock climbers, is at the forefront of this development with routes such as *The Cathedral* (X,11 2004) on The Cobbler to his name. MacLeod climbed this 30m. roof problem by placing the gear on the lead, and suggested that the overall difficulty was similar to a pre-protected M12 route. Some climbers are questioning whether *The Cathedral* represents the limit of what is possible using traditional Scottish winter ethics, and for standards to progress, routes need to be pre-protected or practised on a top rope. Although these techniques will drive up technical standards, the difficulty of the bigger traditional routes will always be dominated by the mountaineering challenges of longer approaches, lack of daylight, exposure to weather and a strong determination to preserve the on-sight ethic.

The Fowler Influence:
Mick Fowler, one of Britain's most successful alpinists, has had a prolific Scottish winter career.
"The appeal of Scottish winter climbing is not something readily understood by the average person," he wrote in the 2002 SMC Journal. "I have to admit that I struggled to come to terms with it. Conditions are fickle, early starts wearing and success comes only to those that persevere. Perhaps these are the attractions. Successes that are won too easily are inevitably those that are the least rewarding."
Fowler made his Scottish new route debut in 1979 with the first winter ascent of *The Shield Direct* (VII,7), a soaring line of icy chimneys on the Carn Dearg Buttress of Ben Nevis with Victor Saunders. Fowler went on to climb a superb string of sensational icy mixed routes in the 1980s, mainly in the North-West Highlands. Routes such as *Tholl Gate* (VI,6 1984), *Gully of the Gods* (V,6 1983) and *Great Overhanging Gully* (VI,7 1984) are among the most sought-after winter routes in the country, and climbs such as *Ice Bomb* (VII,7 1988) on Beinn Dearg, *Against All Odds* (VII,7 1988) in Glen Coe and *Storr Gully* (VII,7 2000) on the Isle of Skye are still unrepeated. All these climbs take strong natural lines of daunting steepness, and are predominately ice or icy mixed.

It was natural that Fowler should take his Scottish skills to the Greater Ranges. The first ascent of the technical South-West Buttress of Taulliraju in Peru with Chris Watts in 1982 was his first major success, but the Golden Pillar of Spantik in the Karakoram climbed with Victor Saunders five years later was an eye-opener. Unquestionably, this was one of the finest Himalayan routes of the decade and was very Scottish in character. Intricate route finding, poor protection and tenuous mixed climbing on powder-covered rock all contributed to the difficulty.

Fowler told me recently: "Prior experience of hard climbing in grim conditions helped enormously with this ascent. Scottish winter gave us the confidence to be bold and push on for pitch after pitch knowing that we could find protection in snow-blasted situations."

Spantik led to a series of outstanding first ascents on Taweche, Cerro Kishtwar, Changabang and Siungang. These routes shared several common factors. They were mainly icy mixed climbs, the hard climbing was below 6500m. and they could be climbed relatively fast in an alpine style single push. But most importantly perhaps, they were all intelligently chosen objectives that in many ways could be described as 'super-Scottish' climbs.

Scottish Style in the Greater Ranges:
The current generation of British alpinists has grown up with Mick Fowler's exploits, and his style very much defines the current British approach to climbing the Greater Ranges. There has been a shift of emphasis away from 7000m.+ peaks or attempting technical rock routes

at altitude. The recipe is simple. Combine Grade VII Scottish winter skills with good alpine experience, then go and attempt a mixed climb on a moderate altitude peak. Ian Parnell and Kenton Cool's near-free repeat of the Denali Diamond (2002), Nick Bullock and Al Powell's bold route on Jirishanca (2003) and Rich Cross and Jon Bracey's rapid ascent of the North Face of Kennedy (2004) all point to the success of this approach.

One of the finest British successes of the 1990s was the first ascent of the North Face of Changabang by Andy Cave and Brendan Murphy (1997).

"Undoubtedly, having climbed hard mixed routes in Scotland helped us dispatch sections of the Changabang climb more quickly," recalls Cave. "We'd often made similar technical moves on previous climbs up north, and the ability to climb a long way above protection is also something that you learn in Scotland. New routeing in Scotland also breeds essential route finding skills – a sense of where the line is going to lead. Climbing through bad weather is *de rigueur* in Scotland too, something we did a lot of in India."

It would be simplistic to claim that Scottish winter climbing is the underlying basis for these ascents (proximity to Chamonix, good libraries and sharing of information and an excellent expedition funding system also play their part), but many British climbers passionately cite Scottish winter experience as a key ingredient of their success.

Ian Parnell says: "The weather and conditions even novice Scottish winter climbers take as part and parcel of heading out into the hills really is unusual in world mountaineering. While we miss out on the scale and terrain, everything else about Scottish winter climbing is very close to the big mountain experience. A hard day in Scotland is as tough as any you'll ever spend in the mountains. Even an easy day in Scotland you have to commit, whereas Continental ice cragging you can amble up and decide when you get there whether you can be bothered or not."

The variety of climbing encountered on a Scottish winter route is another key factor, as Malcolm Bass, author of several new routes in Alaska, explains: "In an average Scottish winter season you climb all sorts of white stuff. Water ice, névé, powder, rime, verglas, lovely plastic squeaky ice, wet snow plastered on rock, turf and all sorts of intermediate material. If you waited for routes to be in perfect condition, you'd wait for decades. Winter climbing in Scotland is done, almost by definition, when the routes are 'out of condition' in the traditional Alpine sense. You do your best to make a good choice of venue, walk in, and if it's white you climb something. You climb what you find in the corrie and on the route. I think this gives Scottish winter climbers an advantage in the big hills. When it snows all over your rock pitches you can go on. When the ice pitches melt out you can climb the running rock beneath, and powder-covered slabs come as no great surprise."

But it is not just the technical skills that are important. "It is your will that is most tested when climbing in Scotland," Patagonian winter expert Andy Kirkpatrick told me. "Conditions are never assured. The mountains can strip before your eyes as warm winds push north, and even when you find good conditions, climbing can prove impossible with hurricane winds and metres of rime and verglas. Once the top is reached – usually in the dark – there is the descent, testing the navigation skills of even the professional orienteer, especially in a white out with no pistes to follow or cable cars back to the valley. This means we Brits are optimists. We'll give any climb a go if we have fighting chance."

The Ben Nevis Playground:

Although there are hundreds of corries and winter cliffs across the Scottish Highlands, the great North-east face of Ben Nevis is the best known, and has had the greatest influence on successive generations of British alpinists. It is reliably in condition from January onwards and has the CIC Hut conveniently situated at its base. Climbing on the Ben is unique. Its cliffs are alpine in stature, and by virtue of their height and position on the west coast, they are exposed to the full force of Atlantic weather systems. The resulting high level of precipitation, and frequent changes in temperature and wind direction, allow ice to build rapidly and produce a winter climbing ground without equal in the country. While the mountain is best known for its Grade V gully climbs such as *Point Five* and *Zero*, it is the thin face routes such as *Galactic Hitchhiker* (VI,5), *Albatross* (VI,5) and *Pointless* (VII,6) that climb the blank slabby walls in between, which have the monster reputations.

Thin face routes rely on a build-up of snow-ice on steep slabs and are normally climbed when the covering is only two or three centimetres thick. Rarely does the pattern of freeze-thaws allow the snow-ice to form thicker than this, and once committed to the route the climbing is a delicate game of mind control while balancing on tip-toe up thinly-iced slabs far above protection. The transitory nature of these climbs adds to their attraction, for it only takes one quick thaw to strip the routes, and they can disappear in a few hours.

Dave Hesleden, one of Britain's finest all-round climbers, says: "Climbing on the Ben has had a big influence on my climbing. There's no fixed gear. You have to find protection and set up belays yourself. Routes like *Orion Direct* are big adventures – far more so than doing a Grade V+ icefall in the Alps where you can use screws and Abalakovs. The Ben is the most exacting climbing I've ever done. I would never dream of falling off. I'd be prepared to go for it and fall off in the Cairngorms, but never on Nevis."

Hesleden's comments reminded me of the time I met French climber Catherine Destivelle in the CIC Hut. Catherine was making a reconnaissance trip with her husband to check out some climbs for a photo feature in *Paris Match*, but the weather had been poor and they had failed to do a single route. The hut was full and Catherine joined in the general banter with grace and charm, but underneath you could sense that she was disappointed with her week. She visibly brightened when Robin Clothier, the hut guardian and renowned Nevis ice climber, suggested they follow him and Harvey Mullen up *Orion Direct* next morning.

It was a preposterous suggestion. The mountain was very snowy and it was too early in the season for snow-ice to have formed on the upper slabs of the route. Next morning was dark and grey with low cloud and blowing spindrift and most climbers in the hut sensibly chose icefalls or mixed routes low down on the mountain. Robin was undeterred, however, and soon after breakfast the four of them set off for the Orion Face. That evening when I returned to the hut, everyone had got back down safely and were now recounting the day's adventures over steaming mugs of tea. Catherine's eyes danced with delight as she described their climb.

They had followed Robin and Harvey up into the murky gloom of Observatory Gully and when the slope steepened they roped up as two pairs and started climbing. There was no ice, just a 15cm. thick layer of barely consolidated snow covering smooth slabs. There were no runners or belays. Route finding was desperately difficult in the mist, but the marginal conditions meant it was critical they took the easiest possible line. Blindly, they followed Robin and Harvey across the delicate traverse that led right from the Basin and up into the maze of exit gullies above. Every so often they could hear avalanches hissing down *Zero Gully* somewhere to their right. When they got to the summit, Robin pointed instinctively through the swirling snow with his axes and they plunged down through the whiteout towards the Carn Mor Dearg Arete and the descent route.

Catherine said: "It was like nothing I've ever done before. It's a climb I'll never forget."

International Perspective:

For international visitors, the most practical way to experience Scottish winter climbing is to attend one of the International Winter Meets organised by the British Mountaineering Council every other year. The meets are based in Glenmore Lodge, the Scottish Mountaineering Centre in Aviemore at the foot of the Cairngorms. Guests are paired up with local climbers who have the necessary Scottish winter skills to direct their partners to the routes, swing leads and then get them back down the glen.

The meets have attracted many top climbers from around the world. Interestingly, it is the Slovenians such as Janez Jeglic, Andre Stremfelj and Marko Prezelj, who have been most at home in Scottish conditions. Prezelj first climbed in Scotland in March 1999 and notched up eight big routes, almost a lifetime's worth of hard Scottish classics in a mere five days. The following summer he made a rapid alpine-style repeat of the Golden Pillar of Spantik.

He told me: "There's no doubt that my Scottish experience has improved my approach to mixed climbing. Scottish routes are quite short compared to those in major areas, but the experience is very strong. It's a complex thing, but after experiencing the long approaches in Scotland, clearing snow off routes to place gear, climbing in bad weather and coming back in the fog and wind, I now believe that many things are possible in the mountains. On Spantik I had the technical experience from Scotland so I wasn't scared to make interesting moves without protection close by, and my Himalayan experience meant I wasn't scared about the altitude and size of the mountain. It was really good."

The meets have also given Scottish climbers a greater understanding of what makes Scottish winter climbing unique compared to the rest of the world.

Coast Range guru, Don Serl, told me recently: "You get great training in Scotland for big mountains. You tend to be out in all weather, so bad weather is not unsettling. You know how to dress for it and how to cope with it. Most success in the big mountains depends first and foremost on being able to 'live' in the mountains, in any and all conditions. Here in the Coast Range and the Cascades, the problem is one of consistently bad weather coupled with extremely heavy snowfalls and long approaches. If you get two mountain routes in over a winter, you're doing really well."

When you live in Scotland, the accessibility of the Scottish winter experience is easy to take for granted. Keen climbers will climb routes every weekend. There are probably few other places in the world where you can leave your own bed early in the morning, have a full mountaineering experience, and be back in time for dinner

But Scottish winter is far more than just training for big mountains. Some of the finest Scottish winter climbers rarely climb elsewhere because Scotland gives them all the adventure, challenge and commitment they need. The Scottish winter game can be frustrating and uncomfortable for much of the time, but when it works nothing can compare. As I write this in early January, a warm south-westerly is howling outside, the ice is falling off the crags and the hills are being stripped by a deep thaw. I've failed on every route I have tried in the last month, but I know I'll be back on the crags as soon as it freezes again.

Andy Kirkpatrick understands: "Every season, countless climbers make the pilgrimage to the Highlands, believing that it's better to take a shot and miss than never take the shot at all. Every now and again you'll score, and when you do there's no better place on the planet to climb."

This article first appeared in The American Alpine Journal and I have taken the unusual step of including it here in order that the excellent writing can be appreciated by a wider audience and that it can stand as a record of both the antecedents and the current state of Scottish winter climbing. (Ed.)

MAN-EATER

By John MacKenzie and Ken Crocket

Now my old mate, Ken Crocket was really only semi-retired from the winter climbing scene and I thought it was time for him to go for a gentle potter up some local crag that would be encouraging and not too taxing. He had arrived the day before and now February 23, 2005 promised to be a good winter's day with a keen east wind that promised a classic mixture of sun, snow showers and cloud. Just right for a nice Grade III, suitable for not too long a day since we had to be back by 6pm as we were invited to a dinner party.

The last winter climb I had done was several years ago now, fading as fast as the synovial fluid in my knee joints. So it was in anticipation of a pleasant Grade IV on John Mackenzie's local mountain that I ambled up the A9, waving cheerfully at the Ballinluig speed camera which has caught out so many sleepy club members. The forecast was, for once, wintry, and in deference to my increasingly larger comfort zone I had packed my best winter clothes. There were, naturally, several bottles of comfort too, for his castle, though brimming with hospitality, was usually about 10° cooler than my lowland home. But I had also packed my silk shirt in anticipation of a dinner party.

The lower end of Glen Strathfarrer has the famous locked gate that deters the casual driver, but rewards the seeker of the Combination Lock with entry into a magical and remote kingdom. All the birches were snow laden, frosted and heavy; the road deep in powder and the hills quite markedly more snowy on the eastern part of the glen than farther west. This is what we were banking on, that the forecast was sufficiently accurate that our choice of climbing venue on the east faces of Sgurr na Muice and Sgurr na Fearstaig would be snowy but not buried under a metre of useless powder. The mantra of all winter climbers, indeed the Holy Grail, is the word 'Conditions.' Would they be at least sort of okay, the powder hard packed by the recent easterly gales into a climbable medium, even with ice in places, or would it be a white devil of deception, hiding everything and holding nothing save a ptarmigan's weight? Indeed we had the choice of two crags to look at, both very different in appearance and structure but one usually less snowy than the other.

I had forgotten one of the few and debatable benefits of a cold bedroom – one does not hang about on waking. The evening meal had been sociable and afterwards, as John fed the sitting room stove with wood, he entertained me with stories of his father, back when it was really, really cold. Breaking the ice on the face bowl in the bedroom for example. In the morning I whipped on my long johns faster than a Highlandman downing a free dram and faced a brave new day.

So we drove the long miles to near the top of the glen, past the large herds of stags so tame that we had to stop the car so they could shuffle out of the way, hoping that every car that came was full of fodder. By the time we had reached the burn and the start of the track uphill the snow was a quarter the depth it had been 10 miles back. It was freezing and the ground hard with frost but it had been a dry winter to date and I was not expecting any 1980s style build up of 'perfect conditions' but just something climbable.

The track after half-mile or so turns into a stony path that winds its way up quite gently, gaining a farther 300m. in height as it does so. The burn was only partially frozen lower down but now, higher up, quiet and banked with snow and our path grew less distinct with every gain in altitude. The brisk wind promised a raw day that brought in rapidly passing snow squalls and blinks of sunshine that suddenly lit up the hills to a glaring white and equally suddenly hid them within purple brown clouds.

We stomped up the track, John in the lead. I was fit through hillwalking, but the weight of a rope and jangly stuff was slowing me slightly. Besides, John was a master at 'allowing' others to break the trail, and today I was content to learn from a master. Or rather, I was content to use lessons hard earned from him in the past. He gave me one or two glances between narrowed eyes as I graciously allowed him to take the lead.

At a prominent stone where the track crests a rise before the loch, the sun came out and revealed both faces; that of Sgurr na Muice above us looking pretty white but with rock showing through, and that of Sgurr na Fearstaig a mile or so farther on uphill and totally white, not unexpectedly as it is usually the snowier of the two faces. Now to be completely truthful I was nursing an ambition, shared only with Andy Nisbet and Dave Broadhead, which, though hardly falling into the 'gentle potter up a Grade III' category, I rather wondered if, after 15 years of never finding suitable conditions, might be realised sooner rather than later. It just so happened that at that very moment, as I was standing in the direct line of sight to it, it was lit by a shaft of sunlight that showed it in seemingly better and fuller cover than I had ever seen it before.

Some years ago I had done an easy route here with John – one of his routes. It had been enjoyable but I had come away feeling slightly disappointed as there had been nothing stretched. Today looked more promising, and there had been a certain air about my host which, with hindsight, I should have recognised. After all, when a young man myself, I had led several companions up the garden path in search of adventure. I feared I was about to experience what my faithful friends of the past had suffered at my hands. The worm was turning.

John led through snow-covered bogs in what seemed to be an illogical route. In fact, he was casting about for the best spot from which to spy out the crag. A two-legged setter. He stopped. Looked up. Looked at me. There was definitely something going down. I hoped it wasn't going to be me.

Dave Broadhead and I had been up to the foot on several occasions, always thwarted by the overhanging wall that bottomed a steep and uncompromising groove line which led straight up to the summit. Though we had climbed the major line of that part of the face, *The Boar*, some years back, the groove to its left, the object of my ambition, was never possible. Now it looked white and complete, either an illusion of false promises or the gateway to the promised land. Unfortunately, standing 300m. below it and some distance back neither confirmed nor denied my hopes. More to the point there was Ken to consider, my friend and guest, so in as dulcet a tone as I could muster I asked casually whether he had any preferences for choice of route today.

"No," he said. "As long as its new."

Hoping that the inner tiger was still alive within him, I was gratified with the answer. I pointed out that since he had last climbed on the face all the major lines had been done save one.

"Where is it?" He asked pretty quickly, which didn't sound like the answer from a hesitant man at all. So I pointed out the line to him and suggested that it might be a little harder than a Grade III, but this too seemed absolutely fine and since it was a lot closer than Sgurr na Fearstaig and less snowy, it would be the sensible choice for a climb today.

John could not conceal his body language as he gently probed my mood. I thought quickly before answering. He was easily the most enthusiastic climber I knew. He was also, as I was learning quickly, very modern in his analytical and calculating approach to routes. If he wanted to try something, I would be happy to accompany him. Whether I would lead any of it depended on how horrible it looked. I was in his capable hands. I was also aware that something big and important was driving him today; I could either step aside, or help him along.

There are two major couloir lines running up to the base of the cliffs plus several minor gullies. To get to the right-hand side of the face we took the right-hand couloir and started up its 200m. height gain of Grade I snow and short icy steps. The powder snow was indeed compacted into a hard slab, well bonded to the hillside and giving easy climbing. Now, I have often noticed that good conditions on the approach mean rather poorer conditions on the face and vice-versa, unless a perfect freeze – thaw – freeze cycle has happened, which was not the case here. Plenty of freeze but no thaw.

The easy access, exposed but straight-forward, led us to the great slab beneath the various grooves. The massive central groove, *The Boar*, had taken several winters to finally form, while the groove to its right, *The Wolf*, formed most winters, albeit briefly. The groove we were now looking at had never formed until now, with the barrier wall sporting a fat free-standing icicle running from the apex of a slab to the base of the groove above.

My eyesight has been slightly myopic for decades – never really a handicap, in fact it has helped on many an adventure, as I often fail to see the gory details of a route in advance, instead picking out the general line. So if it looks elegant and defined from a distance, it's probably worth looking at. Grasp the nettle, get stung later.

Now it's a curious thing that when standing on an already steep slope the steeper ground above you always seems reasonably friendly. This optical illusion plays down just how bloody steep it actually is. If suspended icicles hanging from the undersides of rocks above are hanging out into space then that normally suggests the angle is close on vertical. But all I could see was this great fat free-standing icicle, the 'open sesame' to the promised land. We were drawn to it, two moths to a great big flame.

The slab we were now climbing up can be a pleasant Grade II dance up thin ice, leading under normal conditions to a rock wall. Today, it was thickly covered in not very substantial snow, adequate for purchase – just, so we soloed up and across its top to arrive at the icicle. This at least did not disappoint, no more than 5m. high but really thick and juicy, spanning the barrier wall and ending below a little icefall that ran up to a sizeable overhang just to the right of the groove line I coveted.

The icicle gave a solid belay of two longish slings, after which it was time for tea, that fine British tradition that no battle could start without. Though not exactly expecting a 'doddle,' at least I was buoyed up by the warm liquid into thinking that what lay above looked challenging but fun, just the thing for Ken to get back into the swing of things again.

The axes bit into the ice well, the sudden transition from the relaxed 50° inclination of the slab below to an arm wrenching 90° of the ice making this a blessing. This was quick to climb though and very soon the ice above thinned to a thickish dribble. Just above me was the overhang I had spotted from below and some rather tenuous moves up the diminishing ice led to it. I noticed, rather clearly from this close-up point of view, that the fringe of icicles hanging off its lip were well out into space. Looking down, Ken was huddled up against his icicle and below him the slope fell swiftly and without interruption to the loch a long way below. I felt in need of a little protection at this juncture. The overhang had, curiously in such massive rock, a very thin square flake that took, with some careful manoeuvring, a very thin sling. The rock and sling were evidently well suited to each other. Just being attached to the mountain made a huge difference – better than seeing the ropes hang into space uselessly, as the icicle belay from up here looked a great deal thinner than it did from down below.

The first pitch looked reasonable; there was ice. The view was great, into the peaceful bowl of the corrie. There would be deer calving here in the summer, skylarks above. Today it was cold. Too cold to lace up my boots properly. My left boot was a bit loose. While not a bad handicap, on what was to come up today it certainly reduced my motor skills slightly. As John huffled and puffed upwards, lumps of ice battered downwards. I had to carefully judge where to stand and when to glance up, though I did end up with a small nick on my face from an ice shard.

Stepping left from below the overhang led into the groove; initially this was okay, quite thick snow-ice led up to the start of it giving me some hope of success. However, the angle of the groove immediately turned up a notch to just less than vertical and, worse, there was only pretty poor snow masking it. Time to take stock and have a considered think. Firstly, clear away the useless snow and look for hidden cracks and turf. The groove was a perfect 'V' in profile and turned out, surprise, surprise, to be completely crackless and smooth. This was a bit of a blow but not entirely unexpected as schist can sometimes be like that. So, no cracks. How about some nice frozen turf to get the tip of an axe and crampons into? Not much luck there either. Oh dear. I'd have to think a little bit harder. The right wall of the groove however did hold a bit of a promise. Blobs of ice ran down it and they were well frozen blobs as far as blobs go; certainly not ideal but something to go for. So with a right axe and right crampon delicately tapping 'blobs' on the right wall of the groove and the left neatly shearing off the thin slabs of snow in the back of the groove, some kind of upward progress was beginning to materialise.

As I was edging up this Braille trail of ice a wee voice rang up from below: "How's it going, is it about Grade III do you think?"

My answer was, inwardly, a little whimper but outwardly "Probably that sort of thing, bit tricky and delicate in places but quite fun", being careful not to breathe too heavily while talking in case it upset the teetering balance I was holding. By now I was more than 20m. above the thin sling runner and was getting a little anxious. However, the Gods sometimes provide where least expected and I found a thin but deep vertical slot just wide enough to take a No.1 wired nut, in other words rather on the small side but well in. Phew. Soon things took a turn for the steeper. On the left wall of the groove was more ice and even an isolated 'dod' or island of turf. Both were too far away across blank rock to be of any use and so the only option was straight up on totally vertical ground. However, more good things were being revealed. The promise of well frozen turf was above me and though obviously somewhat uphill as they say, did suggest a viable way to reach what looked like an easier angled continuation of the groove just above another overhang.

I'm not only here to hold the belay rope, I'm here to encourage. John was running into something hard, even I could sense that this was not going to be a pleasant IV, never mind a fun III. "You're looking good," I shouted up, before ducking down again.

My little nut runner was now well below me and further protection highly desirable. One more teetery move and I struck turf. Initially, this was a bit disappointing as it simply exploded beneath my axe, so cold and dry that it had no substance. A longer reach sunk my axe into something that would have held the weight of ten men. Better still, despite the steepness I could relax, feeling the sudden departure of the nervous tension that had coiled up within me for the last 25m. There were still no rock cracks around but I did hammer in a 'turf hook', now worth its weight in platinum, and quite capable of holding a short fall. Less tentative now and feeling bolder, some powerful and reachy moves led rapidly to the next overhang which I judged marked the end of the immediate difficulties. A crack appeared and a tied-off peg and good nut runner greatly enhanced life expectancy and even allowed a bit of banter with Ken, now cold and far below and no longer believing that this was going to be a pleasant wander up a Grade III.

Above the overhang the angle fell back, and rather than being a groove was in fact a narrow shelf that ran up along the edge of the much bigger and deeper groove of *The Boar*; definitely not a good place to fall into. The day being what it was, nothing but nothing was going to come easily. The shelf rapidly thinned of any visibly useable turf and instead provided a delicate exercise in looking for the isolated bits of turf hidden beneath a crust of useless snow. Of course, there was no further protection but at least it wasn't too steep. I was hoping to head for an obvious snow bay, still a long way above, but to my great joy found, shortly before the rope ran out, a deep crack that took one good peg belay. There was no stance and standing was tricky as the slabby rock encouraged a slither, crampon points hovering on the point of shooting away from under you and staying put on some unseen rugosity.

It was my turn, and after a routine bash up the ice all hopeful expectations disappeared and turned into featureless rock, covered in distinctly unfriendly snow. I had stiffened in the cold and a forgotten and unmissed painful hot flush did little to cheer me. Worse, the Dachsteins I had chosen as being the best pair turned on me and a pink thumb began wavering in the wind. Luckily, I had a pair of thin liners, but even so it added to a cold experience. My brain began to turn up the flow of life-enhancing drugs, we were definitely into something interesting. And John was doing a great job in front.

Ken came up expostulating and taking some time. His thumb had come through his mitt and his hand was rather cold in consequence. He had long ago put aside the 'Grade III' and was now in full battle mode. The wind blew in freezing eddies and spindrift came and went. It was a full on Scottish winter's day with the outcome anything but certain.

With Ken tied back on to the belay peg I headed up to the snow bay up to my right. A thin icefall ran down the right wall of a deep groove that itself seemed to end in another overhang. The icefall had been the scene of Dave Broadhead's bold lead that had ensured success on *The Boar* and I was certain that if the groove to the left was climbable today then we

Sgurr na Muice NE face. Photo: John Mackenzie.

Ken Crocket celebrating his survival of Maneater. Photo: John Mackenzie.

probably had the climb 'in the bag'. However, as I climbed higher towards the groove, so the snow got, if anything, worse. The groove once reached was plumb vertical and crackless as before with no turf being immediately evident. I retreated to a shelf about 12m. above Ken to see if I could climb the left wall of the groove instead. There was ice, but rotten until about 4m. or so above me. This would have reached uncertain snow covered slabs which may or may not have been climbable. Would I be able to retreat if they were not?

I was tied on again to an imaginary stance, fighting both the cold and the ropes. They were united in making my belaying as uncomfortable as possible. The ropes kept twisting and jamming, my feet were only just on some hidden nick in the rock, one edge at a time. And above, John had run into a real dilemma. Time to dig in and grit teeth. Oddly enough, I was beginning to enjoy moments. I would raise my face and feel the spindrift. To know a familiar discomfort was to be more fully aware. To be aware was to be alive. And the view continued to calm the mind.

There were no runners between Ken and me. A fall of more than 20m. on one peg was not, in my estimation, advisable. So I down-climbed the horrid snow and rejoined Ken. Another hour of precious daylight gone. The one remaining option was to somehow traverse left a short distance into the direct continuation of the groove below, the intervening rib looking characteristically blank. Mild farce then followed as I untangled the rope from Ken's sack – my feet shot from under me and I began a graceful slide downhill, soon brought to an abrupt halt by Ken. A more successful re-arranging of the ropes then followed, plus a cup of tea which immediately improved both the weather and our chances of success.

By down-climbing about 5m. I thought I could see a way across the rib to the groove beyond. Some moves not dissimilar to the crux of *Zero Gully* then followed, which I have to say seemed pretty straight-forward compared to what had just been climbed and what indeed might be awaiting higher up. Being established in the groove felt good; on closer acquaintance it was obviously the line of choice. Straight as a die, it led up to yet another overhang, a narrow steep groove above that, and then it went out of sight. Good turf led to some speedy climbing as far as the overhang and I was just starting to feel optimistic. A good peg runner helped even more and then, of course, came the proverbial slap in the face. Some tricky traversing under the overhang led into the narrow groove ahead. It soon steepened into a vertical, smooth and in every damn way a mirror image of the ghastly groove above the snow bay. There were no obvious signs of cracks for protection and I was now a long way above the sole piece of gear. A solitary turf foothold provided a respite to take stock and think. Hope, in the form of a huge 'dod' of turf lay about 3m. above me. Do I go hell for leather up the groove hoping to make it by sheer momentum or do I retreat and see if I can find another solution to this baffling climb? Given a rock

Climbing at the Ice Factor, Kinlochleven. Photo: Gavin Newman.

solid piece of gear I might have risked it, but by now the fall potential was huge and unacceptable.

So, once more I down-climbed the wretched groove, not that easy, and surveyed the left bounding wall closely. At a point about 6m. below my high point I could see a good but small island of turf isolated in the middle of the slabby left wall of the groove. It was about a metre-and-a-half away and offered the one slender chance of completing this climb which was rapidly becoming anything but 'fun', let alone a 'Grade III doddle.' How one eats one's words at times like this.

How often had I been in the lead on some desperate pitch, way above a solid companion stuck on a miserable belay ledge, calculating the chances of survival. The roles were now neatly reversed. More than that, there was no way I could see me leading such climbing. It was not only difficult and serious, it was really technical. I had never experienced such rock; where a corner would normally be cracked, it was not, where a wall might show a weakness, there was none. At one point I found myself bridging up a corner with nothing for the picks and nothing for the points. "I have absolutely nothing here," I shouted up. "Just climb," the Master replied. Recalling past climbs, I breathed in, deliberately kicked the points onto the left wall, and stepped up. It worked, a few crystals grating in protest. Another desperate pitch. Another great lead.

Grateful for long arms and leaning left with the desperation of salvation at hand I hooked the solid, dependable and blessed piece of turf. Trusting in what I had at hand, a long swing across the groove plus a simultaneous pull up brought the other axe next to the left one. There was still nothing for feet but, and it was a huge but, a ribbon of turf followed the crest of the groove and it was but one more move to reach it and I could stand in balance for the first time since the base of the route. Wasting no time, this was done and better still a big horizontal crack gobbled up a large nut and life looked and felt ever so sweet. A short distance above a small stance and perfect belays compounded the feeling of well being and I brought Ken up. He was now firing on all cylinders and the light of battle was in his eyes; could I detect a hint of the old Ken of *Minus One Gully* and other heroic sorties? I thought I could.

It was good to be united again as both of us were feeling the strain. The wind was still eddying and swirling, bringing gusts of spindrift that hit both from the front and behind, finding, as it always does, the tiniest chinks in clothing and depositing little granules of extra cold snow. However, on the positive side our prospects were improving; if I could get into the wider, squarer groove ahead of me I think we had a good chance. On a darker note it was distinctly late afternoon-ish and our groove appeared to end at an undefined barrier much higher up.

The first few moves were very thin but then much friendlier ground arrived with cornucopias of turf. Inevitably all this sudden speeding up came to a halt at the next blocking overhang. However, this was not nearly as bad as I had feared, being turfy over its crest and even having some gear. I was very much banking on previous knowledge of this crag which is geologically a bit of an odd-ball. The entire face is a concertina of grooves that are massive and often crackless for the initial pitch or two but then the rock, which is always near perfect, becomes more broken and turfy higher up. Some parts of the face are steeper than others and this right-hand section the steepest of all. Banking on the hope of easier ground above I had a bit of a shock when I had run out the rope to arrive at a most definite *cul-de-sac*. Another perfect belay on the left wall of the now totally enclosed groove allowed a grandstand view into what followed.

Ken came up rapidly and a council of war followed. Above lay a steepening slab, boxed into a perfectly rectangular amphitheatre of vertical rock. Thick ice flowed down the slab and this ended abruptly at the headwall which appeared to overhang. Surely we wouldn't get defeated at this late stage, there must be a way through this headwall. Resisting another cup of tea, I found the ice perfect, plastic in consistency and a sheer pleasure to climb. If only the rest of the climb had been like this it would have been a different story. From the left wall sprung a remarkable yardarm of rock, very similar in appearance to those old fashioned car indicators. Perhaps it was telling me to go right but it certainly was reassuring to drape a sling around its considerable length.

The ice thinned as it approached the headwall, the yardarm now well below. I moved right, as indicated, and found a crack that promised safety. Hammering in a large nut made whatever I was about to do relatively secure. The headwall indeed did overhang, was about 5m. high at most and was capped by turf on the right where it was a little lower. However, overhanging pull-ups well right of my runner seemed less attractive than the higher central portion of the wall which sported a little groove ending in a bulge. This was directly above the nut runner and looked rather intriguing. A deep horizontal crack lay just below the top bulge and if I could reach it then I could probably move left and out onto what was definitely easier ground. Avoiding a very loose block it was no big deal to climb the groove and reach the crack. This perfect feature allowed the entire axe pick into its depths. It was now a slightly strenuous but relatively straightforward manoeuvre to pull up on this and bury an axe into deep turf out left. Hey presto, salvation; we had escaped the jaws of The Man-eater.

We were not about to be beaten. At this point I felt that the rocks, if not exactly lying back yet, were at least showing signs of having been softened by the weather. By now, we had been hardened by the weather, especially my thumb. I scratched up to bump into the overhang where John had gone left. A large nut marked his saving grace. It was new, and my newly-found position as faithful second would not allow me to readily abandon it. I had to shout several times above the roar of the wind before John gave me some slack and I went back a bit to attack the nut. Unfortunately, he had hammered it in as a sacrifice to the Gods of Survival, and there it will stay until long after we've moved on. I reluctantly, but happily, went back left and pulled over the final bulge.

This had been another long pitch and Ken took ages to follow. This was not due to idleness on his behalf but to my hammered-in nut placed in the crack below the headwall. Being a good Scot, waste is never an alternative when a good hour's hammering and prising would release the jammed item of gear from its rocky home. Unfortunately for Ken, despite his enthusiasm to remove the nut, my enthusiasm to place it securely outweighed his. The nut would remain firmly wedged in its rocky crack, its yellow tape gradually fading into a bleached white.

We were now nearly at the summit of the hill, the wind had fortunately abated somewhat and Ken set off to climb to the top. Time-wise the sun was now sinking in the west, the full glory of the evening light was upon us and the dinner party (remember the dinner party?) was about to begin. Part one of the day was ending, part two was just beginning. Ken was belayed about 20m. left of the summit cairn, so we walked on over, shook hands and remained pretty subdued. It had been a little too cold, too windy and too hard to fully enjoy. More to the point we still hadn't had lunch and it was gone 6pm. We had started the first pitch before 11am and a degree of fatigue was now evident. I tried to phone home to apologise for being so late, but for the first time, at this location I could get no signal. Ken tried as well, but failed. Suddenly, a more serious aspect was emerging in this day of trials. We were still a good hour from the car and it was at a point 13 miles along a snowy glen with no mobile phone reception. Folks would start to get worried.

We were up. And out. And down with hunger to boot. I was seriously famished. Only now did I take in the full majesty of the scene. To the west the sun was behind a bank of dull red cloud, lighting up the sky above and the loch beneath. To the east a superb full moon filled the corrie with its ghostly light. As we finally gained the easing under the crags snow crystals winked in the moonlight. We had to push on but I tried to save my knees from the worst.

A hurried bite to eat, a couple of photos that I hoped would capture both a knackered Ken and the wildness and beauty of the area, and then down. There is a good easy descent down a broad gully a little way south west from the summit, so we took crampons off and stumbled over the slithery boulders towards it. Expecting a quick descent in soft snow we were not amused to find the best and hardest snow of the day. Back on with the crampons again, more time passing by and by almost running we reached the car in 50 minutes. Still no reception. Today was obviously just one of those days when the Gods twist and turn at opposing angles to yours.

Anxious not to crash the car and to avoid the deer, the journey was slower than the incipient panic within would have liked. At a point less than halfway down the glen I met another car hurtling towards us. Both of us stopped just in time. It was Scott Russell, a good friend whom Janet had phoned and here he was looking for us. Oh dear, time to get to a phone. With Scott leading the way back to his house in the glen, I wasted no time phoning. We reckoned on being back home well before 9pm, so we had a little time in hand. Scott's wife Julia put on the kettle, home-made cakes came out and Scott hugged me with relief.

There were one or two moments hurtling down the glen when I thought how silly it would be to die now, but my trusty leader retained a grip on reality and the road. It was good to find a local out looking for us. We were not late by many an epic standard, but John has a good reputation and his friends were worried. By stages, the evening just got better and better. Tea and cake in the house kept us going, and once on the safer roads I began to probe John regarding the climb's grade. "Definitely too hard to be a IV," I ventured. "Must be a V," I guessed. "Pretty sustained, and serious too," I dropped in. All the time John was agreeing. "That route, I ventured, was a man-eater."

"That route was a Grade VI," replied my host. And so the route was pinned down.

Well fortified and with less troubled consciences we drove home. I even got a hug from Maureen at the gate. So, well hugged and with the roads now black, the journey back was a winding down process. Of course, the irony of it all was that two of the other guests at the dinner were even later, so by the time we reached the party, everyone was extremely well oiled and Ken and I had a bit of catching up to do. One of the more interesting sides of climbing is managing the huge gap of reality between being 'up there' and now down in a dinner party, separated by only a few miles and hours but of a different realm. Two entirely enjoyable situations (give or take) and somehow one enhancing the other, the rare chance to mix and match opposites. It had indeed been a strange day.

Back at the castle we were met by my concerned hostess. On learning from Janet that in 25 years John had never before been later than his estimated return time, I understood the level of concern. A quick hot shower worked wonders externally, a large glass of wonderful red wine internally, and conversation over a fine dinner in their friends' house worked the usual magic of gently landing us back on firm ground. But all the time, listening to the gently relaxing susurrus of polite conversation, in the background I could still hear the wind on the rocks and the shifting snow in the gully. It made it all the finer, having been there. Having tussled with, and escaped, The Man-eater.

HOT ICE

By David Adam

THE writhing gondola swayed between the darkness and the dawn on a cable that stretched forever into the blown mists of the mountain. It slowed with trepidation and then, with a sickening lunge, plunged from the giant pylon into suspended space out across the corrie. Stunned faces bravely tried to ignore instincts to clench, with whitening knuckles, anything that felt solid. Fearful missed heartbeats dissolved into euphoric, fairground whoops of delight as the cable took the vertiginous strain and the veil of cloud ripped apart to reveal the cliffs of the North face. The lichen covered rocks, 300m. down, stood still in their perpetual silence and waited for their next age to come. They had been free of snow and ice for a long time now, some say 50 years. Yet others can still recall climbing there, on the real stuff, during the good old days.

The hot cappuccino took the March chill from his fingers and Mac looked up towards the gondola from the hotel balcony. The tiny capsule moved slowly towards the Tower like a spider on glistening gossamer and then merged again with the morning haze and disappeared. As the gondola wafted its way through the rainbow tinged vapour he could hear the faint, echoing drone of the cryogenic gear working high up on the mountain. Inside, his room was clad in a warming, knotty pine with a grand view towards the arête. Dramatic photographs of climbers on extreme ice routes, with details of the last known winter ascent printed below, pronounced the sanctity of the place. Mac poured over them again and again, absorbing the real moments when ice stuck to rock and snow actually fell. Many of the pioneers had started their ascents from this very location years ago. The stone from the ruined hut was used to fashion the hotel entrance and even although they had arrived by funicular, visitors became aware of a bond with the past as they crossed the threshold. Over the door hung a crossed pair of ancient Piranha axes belonging, it is said, to the greatest hero of the mountain and underneath them, the old hut's plaque.

On the cliff, a viewing gantry with 300 seats was nearly complete for this evening's extravaganza. Speaker systems spat out screechy static, spotlights were positioned and tested. Trickle pipes, alongside the air-blast freezers, had the ice forming up nicely into a row of ten free-hanging icicles, each, being eventually some 20m. long. The tip of each icicle dripped ominously into the void. Sponsors' slogan banners were gently flapping where they dangled from the climb platform, teasing the depths of the empty space between the two opposing buttresses. Live broadcast crews set up satellite dishes. The busy stir was eerily paused for a moment as another packed gondola clattered into the top station, disgorging a gaggle of giggling corporate guests into the summit bar. The bar was built like an earth-house covered in rock slabs, with its form emerging rather beautifully from the rocky plateau like an eye-lidded crescent moon but, most importantly, it was filling up with thirsty spectators, hungry for thrills.

Sitting on the edge of his bed, Mac methodically filed his crampon points and fitted the step-in bindings against the boots. He fiddled about with the cords on the chute, then felt the balance of the axes and adjusted the cams to suit the technical report which stated that this evening's ice would be a poor quality four. The air humidity had affected the formation of the ice early on, making it 'mega-crystalline' and this was bad news for Mac. He, unlike the others, didn't have technicians on hand to design and fettle gear to suit different conditions, his entry was on a 'wild card.' The quietness of his room was blasted by the chopper coming in to land and the intercom telling all competition climbers to proceed to the embarkation point. Mac rushed his gear together and gorged it into a sack that always seemed too small, then crashed through the door leading to the heli-pad. A hand grabbed his sack and pulled it in, chucking it in the tail-stow. Mac teetered across the deck and strapped in.

"You boys got to be mad," shouted the deckhand as he pulled more gear inside. "And you have to be nuts to fly around the hill in this crate," replied Ben, the American ace, who grinned confidently from the deepest corner of the draughty fuselage. He gave everyone a knowing glance and for Mac it was a reassuring one. The chopper rose in a spiral over the burn and then pulling its tail up, headed for the cliff at speed and circled around the summit buttress.

"Gee, look at those diamond-drops," Ben was peering out between the battered joints of the chopper's tin plates at the row of icicles that hung like beast's teeth from the top of the venomous one. "That is something else, wow." Nobody stirred or spoke as the chopper bellied down to the plateau like a burst balloon and the first 10 climbers, relieved to be out of that 'bucket of bolts' spewed out onto the rocks. It buzzed off to pick up the others before darkness fell.

A timeless calm washed over the mountainside with the setting of the sun. Mac let every last ray of light and colour soak into his mind, as if it might be his last, until, when he closed his eyes, the burning disc was still there, changing from ferocious white orange to electric blue. He waited. Ben was behind him trying to share the moment and confided: "You just can't beat a Scottish sunset." Mac opened his eyes in surprise, trying to bring them into focus, still seeing the after glow of the sun razoring across his vision: "Aye, you're right, some things don't change." There was a nice chill to the air up here, but not enough to keep the ice right. The chopper arrived and soon it would be time to start.

At the corrie edge they rock-hopped down onto the buttress crest and grabbed their first close up view of the rigging. The alloy climb platforms were suspended, like a web, from cables anchored on the rocks below their feet to the buttress facing them – 40m. away across the gully. The top platform was the business end of things where the icicle roots were and all the mechanisms for the cryogenic gear. About 20m. below this and level with the ice tips was slung a narrow, retractable platform where the climbers geared up and launched themselves onto the ice. Mac stopped on the walkway leading to the platform and peered into the depths below the ice. There was about 75m. of space between the ice tips and the steep gully scree boulders.

"That might be kind of tight down there," warned Ben, as the rig creaked and wallowed under the strain, "barely enough drop to rip your chute in".

Preceded by a huge round of foot stomping and applause from the spectator's gantry the spotlights were finally switched on, bringing to life a darkening place full of gravity and foreboding. A vivid amphitheatre for a spectacular sport was unveiled. The first-round climbers took up their positions on the lower platform and double checked their gear. The scrutineer slowly examined all backpack cords and tools and waved up to the adjudicator.

"Ladies and Gentlemen, welcome to the British Hot Ice Competition, 2075. We present 20 international climbers, please welcome them and give them all your support in this, the most dangerous and exhilarating sport in the world and I hope that you have an enjoyable evening," the compere announced with 'sponsored' eloquence.

The climbers had already drawn for position and were stationed below their respective icicles, restlessly clattering their crampons on the platform, like race horses in the stalls. Life or death betting on 'Hot Ice' was common and many critics had compared it with the most heinous of blood sports, but the prize money was good, very good and sponsors loved the media exposure. The fastest 10 of the bunch went through to the final. Mac looked up at the 20m. of overhanging ice and then down towards the scree, which was stunningly highlighted by spotlights, trying to fix the distances in his mind. He had climbed Grade 10 indoor ice before and had done a few free-falls before but this was his first time on 'Hot Ice.' Here, there were no ropes to stop a fall and no wrist loops on the axes to ease the strain, just you and the ice.

"Climbers, take your positions," came the command from the starter. Mac looked along to Ben, three places away, for a lead. Ben gingerly pecked his first pick into the ice – it seemed all right – followed by the second and hung back on them. Letting his weight do the work, he screeved his crampon points into the ice as high as possible, not kicking yet in case the icicle tip sheared off. He hung there, backside pushed out ready to go. Like tree climbing cats all 10 climbers clawed tenuously into the ice, suspended with cavernous space below their feet. The stage was set and each climber was highlighted against the rocky darkness. Wisps of steam rose from their sweating hands. Their last refuge, the platform, was hoisted up. For Mac, seconds turned to hours and blood drained from static arms. Space between his knees was occupied by the see-sawing rocks of the scree seventy-five metres below. Down was just a step away and for some, this is as far as it goes, they ditch out on the wait.

"Wait for it," shouted the starter and then blasted the air horn. The crowd went wild when Ben lost it and was left hanging on one pick. Crampons daggered into black space, squirming himself up in vain, trying to sink into the target icicle. A long reaching shot with his right pick whacked into the ice as his points finally hit home. Mac had 5m. under his belt and was keeping level with his neighbour, Marie from Chamonix. Higher up things get better, where the ice becomes kickable, the overhang angle reduced and the pace could be quickened. Cranked grips on the axes helped to fight fatigue as fingers 'dumbed out,' then, the nip in the air could become a serious factor. Thumping in a pick is easy, getting it out again uses up lots of energy. Mac had found a happy medium by tapping the picks into the ice by just a couple of centimetres, leaning back on them and trusting in positive crampon work. Calves and forearms were in agony now, forced breathing essential to keep muscles from cramping up, the heart missing or adding a beat amidst the manic palpitations. The patriotic crowd, as always supporting the underdog, repeated and repeated, "Come on, Mac." He was there, grabbing the rail, finished and safe, crumpling up, stress waning, dryness, retching, trying to swallow and nothing there. The 'easy' bit was done and he had gained third place in this heat. Mac watched from the viewing gantry, with a certain undefined feeling of pride in himself, as the other group of competitors lined up for their heat.

"Looks like really scary stuff from here, eh?" said Ben.

"Aye, well it is I suppose and the ice is crap too. Then if we ditch out there's that bloody awful landing," something that had been worrying Mac for a while.

"Try steering off to the left into the breeze away from the drop zone and pull the chute round into the slope above as you go down, stops you from tumbling too much. Hell, he's quick." Ben had just clocked his main rival on the ice, the Norwegian champion. On the climb platform they waited anxiously for the climbing time that would set the pace for the final – this is usually the fastest time of the day minus 10 seconds.

"Ladies and Gentlemen, this evening's target time has been set at an incredible two minutes, fifteen point three seconds and the fall time is two seconds."

Mac knew that he stood little chance of winning or even finishing. He dreamed through the jet darkness towards the pin-points of light coming from the hotel, to his room and the photographs of the cliffs smothered in snow and ice, real winter climbing in Scotland and just to be back then.

The 10 qualifying climbers made their way down to the icicles, deep breathing all the way, adrenaline surging to the point of sickness and all going through the blind motion of finding and pulling the ultra fast rip. They stepped out onto the platform and once again assumed their positions. The French lass, doing a Joan of Arc, kissed the icicle's tip and crossed herself. Mac clenched and thrust his mum's lucky Ptarmigan foot deeper into his pocket and Ben slurped the last of his Coke. The Norwegian shook himself down constantly and jumped up and down on the spot several times, unbalancing the platform and the others, in a display of utter defiance to the ice and the exposure.

"Climbers take your positions."

To Mac this was the real thing now, as pertinent now as it was way back then: Simply life or death. Get up this icicle before it melted or lose the tools, bale out and rip. The icicles' internal heating elements, that could be seen glowing fiery orange in the roots, were set for two minutes, fifteen point three seconds after which all of the icicles would drop to the screes, like crashing chandeliers regardless of anyone on them or below them. The draw for positions had Mac sandwiched between Ben and the Norwegian. They all mounted the ice and hung.

"Wait for it," screamed the starter and, keeping them on hold until he could see arms and legs begin to shake, he finally blasted the horn. Marie peeled off immediately as her first placements dinner plated. The other climbers wanted to watch for her chute but just had to keep bashing on, ignoring her diminishing screech of, 'Sacre-Bleu.' The crowd went silent as her axes ricocheted like dropped pins onto the rocks below and echoed around the cliffs with a savage loneliness. And then, as if lit by candles, the flickering of blue and red stripy nylon was caught in the spots and the instant cheering told all that her chute had miraculously deployed. Ben was in the lead, climbing beautifully with grace and speed. Long measured stretches out for placements and then crampon run up a metre. Mac was learning by the second and amazingly was keeping pace with the Norwegian who, for once, showed that he was human after all by glancing nervously down at the screes as he struggled to withdraw an overdriven pick. Mac's confidence was brimming and he was actually savouring this like a home-made stew. Ben was now a matter of inches in the lead from Mac, who in a blaze of determined ferocity launched himself higher. Then, in too much haste, crampons scratched out, a pick slipped the ice and time stood still for Mac as he floundered around trying to regain one crampon point on the ice. His arm stretched in shivering weakness, with the pick chattering in its slot anticipating failure. As a last resort he crimped the icicle between his ankles and let loose a massive lunge with the other axe. Ben was nearly at the top platform and had hooked into the metalwork to scramble up, victorious. Mac had 10 metres of climbing left and half-a-minute to do it in. His rhythm returned and soon he had completed five of those metres when the diamonds began to flaw. First a creaking judder ran down the ice into the tools, the only warning of imminent collapse. Mac's icicle started to move like some animated, mythological statue and shunted dramatically over to the left before parting and falling. He jettisoned the tool grips and kicked himself farther away from the diamond drop. The black void between him and the ice became the birth place of shear fear. It fell with him, sucking him down into the death zone.

"Rip.... Mac.... Rip," an awakening shout of desperation came rocketing down from Ben above. A third of his fall time had passed and he was still in the legendary and dreaded 'faller's dwam'. The cold wind hurtling past at 140km. an hour flipped him up with his arms flapping over his helmet. Spinning, star-spangled lights from above and below confused him along with the relentless chanting of the screaming crowd: "Rip, Rip. Pull the chord."

He grabbed wildly at the parachute release handle and caught a finger in it. The canopy, with a blue and white saltire design, snapped open and thumped sensation back into his numb, free-falling body. The icicle silently plunged down past him like a rocket sent from space and then thundered into the boulders. The crowd went wild as six other climbers baled out into the depths, chutes banging open in a myriad of colours. The massive explosion of ice on rock sent shards across the corrie and peppered the hotel roof several hundred metres below.

Pulling at the chute lines, Mac managed to manoeuvre through the turbulent breeze and moved slightly away from the fall area. Filled with a satisfied excitement and the sudden realisation that he had actually survived, he released the most enormous, ear-splitting, thrill-filled screech of: "Yee-Haa," that resounded, over and over again with the spirit of youth and life across Echo Wall, over the Tower, up Hadrian's Wall and onto the Orion Face. The grin on his face grew as he thought about the old pioneers grumbling about the sanctity of their hill and then turning in their graves. The tumbling ice had created a huge downdraught that headed directly for Mac. It was only then that the scree rocks rushed up at an incredible rate, forcing a desperate, inexperienced bid to control his turn into the hill. Pulling hard on both brake lines the canopy stalled, then collapsed and fell.

An hour later Marie, making her way down, found him.

THREE HITS AND A MISS

By Phil Gribbon

THE faint moaning filtered round the edge of the crag. It thrust a wedge of tension into the peace of a still summer evening.

We had come out to scramble about on the minor problems of our local outcrop. Nothing serious or demanding, just the delights of moving freely on warm rock, up one line, then down another, and so on. Working confidently through little facile sequences of moves but ignoring other options that required more commitment. Cut out the risk factor, and have fun, man. This was all about personal satisfaction. It was the capture of a sense of freedom, the pleasure and *joie de vivre* of moving in control along a linking series of random rocky blemishes on smooth little walls. However, it was too easy to switch off and dream, in an imagined world of anticipation and enjoyment with an afterglow to store in the memory of a route well done. I was lost in the mythological realms of the Osnabergs. Come down to earth and concentrate on the moment.

Here I was, belayed on the top of a pinnacled block trying to talk my son up a move that would be tricky for the wee lad. His pal on the end of the rope awaited his turn with innocent impatience. Time would have to pass before I could get down and venture round the corner.

I had heard the swish of brushed bushes and the dull thump on the ground. What had my companion done to himself? On a crag which was never more than 25ft. high. Don't dwell on it, but nonetheless, that noisesome sound had been tinged with pain when it came drifting across the face.

The rock was pleasantly warm, the yellow was on the broom, and the sickly scent of the elder flowers wafted over my pinnacle. Tiny insects idly hovered in the slanting sunlight, all here today and gone tomorrow. Close by towards the Howe of Fife were gentle hillocks patterned with neat fields and along the road from Dairsie the quiet cars were slowly strung towards Cupar. All rural idyll with a distant pantheon of well kent hills stretching in blue silhouettes along the horizon. Those upthrust twin volcanic bumps in the Lomonds floating on their upland moorland raft, dipping down and rising into the cramped swelling hummocks of the Ochils, down again to wide strath before up the Chonzie Munro framing the cutout funfare target pair of Stuic a'Chroin and Vorlich at the end of the line. More low ridges and then the Lawers range beyond and the indistinguishable Glen Lyon hills, and then the classical mountain of the fairies, Schiehallion, with its old path scars now healing but with fresh hordes tramping ever upwards. Come now, not more hills, yet afar the Farragon hill, then Ben y Gloe and the merging masses of a glut of Grampians that lurk behind the tower blocks of Dundee.

This is a fine reward to get from a little Fife hillock where a few miles from home the mountains were gathered around to murmur of myriad distant hills. Dream away boy.

We were on the crag of gray metamorphosed mudstone that caps and rings the crest of Craiglug hill. Its old baked rock held a grayish green patina of dry lichen rings and its sharp curving edges and furrowed blocks offered a welter of lines to follow but with no names and no words in guidebooks. The crag was in its development stage and not every possible line had been climbed, neither had its gorse prickles been clipped nor its vital holds been tested. Brown rusty blotches were spattered incongruously on little open walls, a sure sign of former holds that had parted company with the bedrock.

My scrambling companion was being given his introduction to the joys of Craiglug. I kept wondering what had happened to him. It was all much too quiet for comfort. It was time to walk round the corner.

He lay sideways on the slope and pushed up against an evil long-fallen block that was half buried in the grass. A fresh dark scar some 10ft. up marked his point of departure. He was a twisted shrunken gnome beside the acute harsh brown boulder into which he had toppled and spun with his thigh impacting into its immutable bulk. His face betrayed his sense of shock, his skin drained to faint pallidness with drops of moisture filming his forehead, his brave stiff upper lip deadened with an adrenaline rush that held his fear and pain in check. His hand stroked at his thigh, his eyes averted to his plight. Something, he claimed, had snapped within his leg.

This was serious stuff and how the heck was the casualty going to be got off the hill by one adult male and two open-mouthed small boys? My car was parked at the bottom of the sloping field 400 yards across the cow pasture, but for the wounded warrior to reach the field he had to be negotiated down a scuffed path, through a jungle of rank tussocks and over a very compact stone dyke. The car could be brought up to the wall, but would he make it there on one hip-hoppity step and jump leg? We got him upright, I embraced him round his shoulder, he mumbled, groaned and hopped, once, twice and that was all. What was to be the next option in our personalised rescue service? Abandon him to his suffering and go search the ambulance?

However, this was unnecessary, some help was on its way. It was the lang Dougie and two pals from furth the Tay coming up to play on the rocks. More support plus brain power was to solve our quandary: we would manhandle him downhill in a home-made seat stretcher devised from a mat of old carpet normally laid flat on the back floor of my station wagon, hoist and push him over the dyke, plonk him on the floor and take him to the hospital.

Three months later he was discharged from Dundee Royal Infirmary. He had missed out in participating in the first attempt to be made by the members of a climbing club to climb all the Munros in a period of 24 hours. He had intellectualised his enforced stay in bed to tax his mind with Proust's *Au temps perdus*, Tolstoy's *War and Peace*, and other mentally-demanding tomes. He came out on a pair of crutches with a wasted limb and an attractive limp, and a store of thoughts of deep significance.

That was the hit on someone else, poor fellow, and now years on it was my turn. Gravitational attraction drags loosened items towards lower potential energy states, or given the chance, what is up wants to go down.

It was another peaceful summer's day on the coast of the Solway Firth. The tide had shrunk back across the mired mud at Kipford and the wind found it hard to raise the slightest force, two factors that ruled out a spin in the little sailboat to circumnavigate a minor island.

Forget the granite cliffs at Clifden, he said, and let's look at some bouldery sandstone stacks down by the shore. We parked above the beach and trotted over to the stacks to find that a conventional nuclear family, full of noise and chaos, were picnicking in joyful confusion on the sand beneath the best routed wall. We did not wish to have our public scrambling exhibition performed in front of the seaside paddlers and castle makers. We continued on, our frustration contained by our gentle coastal strolling in search of some alternative piece of climbable rock.

Within a stand of sycamore trees an irregular indentation cut back from the high tide mark and in their shade was a decaying sandstone face split by a weathering vertical groove and all of 15ft. high. It showed a sad lack of holds, its edges were rounded curves in muted orange tones, but it was the sole testpiece on show, and moreover directly above there was a reassuring tree trunk for a top-rope runner. We rigged up the rope by an outflanking wander through ferns and campions and returned to the base.

I tied on and addressed the unresponsive rock. A wiggle, a squiggle, some pushing and then levitation and I was standing on a feeble horizontal ripple with a tight pressure finger grip on another identical feature. A hand brushed the rock above and dust peeled off and trickled down on my head. On the ancient aeolian eroded right wall with undercut scoops and hollows was a hefty column half-propping up the sky. This was fragile territory where everything had to be stroked with the merest touch to assess any help it might provide to get up the groove.

I touched the topless column. I can't recall feeling any sensation when my exploratory fingertips stroked it or whether it just didn't like me when I looked at it. There was little time to react while everything started to go into slow motion in my brain. It was sliding off its base and gently coming at me. This was where my instinctive old-fashioned training began to betray me. I belonged to the school in which one does not consciously part company with the rock but remains as securely attached to the face by as many points of contact as one can muster. The prime rule for ancient climbers was that the leader must never fall off, and even more improbably jump off. Anyway the average personal reaction time of a quarter of a second was the same time it took for the descending column to crunch onto my left hand as it pinched onto the thin ripple and kept me on the wall. I had been hit and fell off so close to the start of the groove that I reached the ground on the extra extending length of the stretching rope.

I looked at my bloodied floppy index finger held up for inspection. Hadn't I once seen a similar unpleasantness many years ago? Yes, my thoughts went back to an outing up *Ravens Gully* on the Buachaille when a falling stone had hit, and then, more disastrously, chopped the identical finger off my leader. With a lack of foresight we then had precipitately abandoned the route, quickly abseiling down and leaving the lost digit lurking somewhere in the pebbles under an overhanging chockstone. We fled towards Belford Hospital in Fort William, the victim sitting in the passenger's seat with his injured appendage sticking up visibly in the air to help us negotiate our priority onto the Ballachulish ferry. Our doctor was not impressed that we had omitted to bring the errant object with us for reattachment.

This time my finger remained stuck on but there was some urgency to leave for the Crichton Hospital in Dumfries. We wrapped it in a grotty old green sock, walked it passed the relaxing beach parties, took it to the hospital, waited ages while a real emergency was handled, got a jab and drifted double quick into oblivion to wake up for breakfast in a cosy bed.

Later, back at work I was able to amuse my companion of the broken-thigh episode with my tendon-strengthening crane attachment that could be wiggled back and forth like the miniature dipping duck device that pumps up oil from the depths of the earth, but really I don't think he was too amused.

This time a veritable *chute de pierres* threatened a lethal finale for us when the big brutal boulder and its diverging shower of scattering baby missiles headed our way, tumbling down the final abseil pitch. We had enjoyed the 20-plus pitches on excellent rock with a subtle variety of features that traced a serpentine route up to a virgin summit. The return descent down the exposed ridge to the glacier had all the snags expected from abseiling and climbing down, with the ropes conjuring up their frustrating fankles, their jams on anchor blocks and snags on projecting spikes. This was the penultimate rope retrieval and soon we would be coiling up the ropes and wandering down to our bivouac site at the desolate col.

My partner started tugging on the rope but it remained fixed at the unseen abseil point. Another tug, but again nothing happened. A stronger pull and the rope runs and falls free but snags on its downward flight. I sensed that directly above our ledge, but out of sight, was that unstable patch of loose gravel and stones that ended at the lip of the wall.

I spoke too late: "Don't pull until we're out of the way." But as the rope came snaking down, there followed a horrid rattling, grating sound of moving stone, and over the lip came a cascade of deadly rocky detritus. The largest lump, shaped as a headstone with our names on it, and its attendant swarm swept towards us fanning out like those images of speeding asteroids seen from a spacecraft in a sci-fi film. There was nothing we could do but watch its line of flight and wait until the last moment and think that we could dodge the ill-starred consequences of our unthinking folly. With luck this big 'un would not hit us. Sparks of ignited, vapourised rock were flying off the wall. When it was unbearably close I ducked instinctively, wishing to shrink and disappear into another dimension of space and time. Out of mind I never saw it whistle past us a mere metre away while wee pebbles and shreds of gravel slithered off my bone dome.

This was a very scary and hard lesson to put into our experience. We were also out on the proverbial limb, miles from anywhere and the nearest link with the outside world several days of travel away. There were the high glaciers to cross with the surface snow soft in the continuous daylight as the sun circled on its daily round.

What might have been our fate didn't bear thinking about. We just carried on as if nothing had happened, slipped off our slings, packed the ropes, hitched up our sacks, and staggered erratically down to the col.

There was only the glacier to cross to the tents but the little crevasses would be lurking below the surface and waiting to snap at an ankle. The problems never ceased but we had become blase beyond the point of self-preservation. We were riding on the high crest of fulfilment.

You missed us, thank God, and we now live to climb another day.

IN GOOD HANDS, 1955: A TRIBUTE TO ERIC LANGMUIR

By Ted Maden

In 1955 the Cambridge University Mountaineering Club held its annual Alpine meet at La Berarde. I was 19-years-old and had completed my first year at Cambridge. Almost the first thing I had done on arriving at the University was to join the Mountaineering Club. Previously, I had been a keen hill walker but had had few opportunities for real climbing. Most of my limited knowledge had been gained vicariously by reading Smythe and Kirkus. With the Club I climbed on meets, made friends and had some cautionary incidents which I heeded but lightly. In the summer a small group of us went to climb in the Pyrenees before continuing to the Alpine meet. For most of our Pyrenean stay we had an excellent time, but on our last day I had a narrow escape when I was persuaded to lead a steep rock pitch that was much too hard for me and the only way out was up.

A few days later we had made our way to La Berarde for the Alpine meet. Smythe's *Mountaineering Holiday* had started in La Berarde, It was exciting to be following in his footsteps to this wild valley, even if our climbs would be different from his. Wildness is one word that characterises the Dauphine. Looseness is another, as we were to discover.

Fifteen of us had assembled for the start of the meet, including three successive Club presidents: Geoff Sutton (1953–4), Eric Langmuir (1954–5, outgoing) and Bob Downes (1955–6, incoming). There was one other experienced alpinist (Ian Hughes), so the rest of us were divided into groups with those four as group leaders. I was with Eric and Geoff Horrocks. Eric was extremely fit by nature, and had only narrowly missed a Half Blue for Cross Country. My diary spells out his five day start-of-meet plan for the three of us.

July 6, to Refuge Pilatte.
July 7, Col du Sele, nearby peak, Refuge Sele or Lemercier.
July 8, Sialouze Arete of the Pic Sans Nom (D sup.).
July 9, Traverse of Mont Pelvoux.
July 10, Les Ecrins; if the Sialouze goes well, by the South pillar (TD inf.); if not, then by the Voie Normale.

Some itinerary! The weather was good. The Refuge Pilatte was crowded. On the ascent of the glacier to the Col du Sele Geoff and I had to ask Eric to moderate his pace. He acceded graciously, and we had a pleasant climb to the Col and to Les Bouefs Rouges. This minor rock peak above the Col afforded a magnificent panorama, especially of the great group of peaks comprising the Ailefroide, Pic Sans Nom and Pelvoux nearby to the east.

The ambiguity of plan regarding the Sele or Lemercier refuges was because Eric knew that one of them had been destroyed by an avalanche. It turned out to be the Sele. In fact the Lemercier was much better placed for the Sialouze Aràte. However, getting there entailed a long haul, down the Sele Glacier and a stony valley with a rock band, then a considerable re-ascent to the hut. Geoff opted out of the Sialouze plan for the morrow, but Eric considered that I was up to it. The hut was small but was magnificently situated, perched high above the rocky valley from which we had climbed, with the Pelvoux group rising gauntly behind. There were only three other occupants in the refuge beside ourselves. It was a stark contrast from the Pilatte, and an aura of seriousness did not promote a good night's sleep. Eric and I set off at dawn, diagonally up a glacier, at first beneath another, hanging glacier. Gradually, peaks around us and in the distance were touched by the sun.

The Sialouze Aréte is the south ridge of the Pic Sans Nom. It starts with the spectacular Aiguille de Sialouze, where the main technical difficulties were expected, and then continues past gendarmes and for quite a long way to the summit of the mountain. Based on guidebook times, we planned about 2hrs. 30mins. to the foot of the route, 8h on the route, and 3hrs.–4hrs. for descent by the Voie Normale. The weather remained set fair, but if we were to get back to the hut before dark the schedule did not allow much margin for the unexpected.

We reached the col at the foot of the Aiguille de Sialouze on time, and relaxed briefly in the warm sun and kitted up. Eric led off. The climbing was superb, much of it up slabs and shallow cracks, delicate rather than strenuous, with continuous pitches of up to V. We made good progress to where the route temporarily quits the ridge and traverses beneath the summit of the Aiguille on its west flank. Here a relatively easy looking line led above the steep west face, and we started to move together. I was behind, and carried much of the 120ft. rope as coils in one hand. I had the two axes tucked between our small rucksack and my back. Once my foot made a slipping noise and Eric instantly responded to the alert. I assured him that I was OK. That is the last thing I remember, except, possibly, a dim, fleeting impression that something was not OK. Or did I imagine that afterwards?

I woke up gradually. It was not like waking from sleep, but, rather, from the edge of oblivion. Someone, Eric, was calling down to me from a long way above. I was groaning, and starting to ask questions. He answered patiently. I wanted to know the name of a wicked looking rock gash that I could see on the skyline across a glacier. I must have been pointing at it. He answered that it was the Coup de Sabre. There was an ice axe on a patch of snow a long way below me. Gradually, my state of consciousness improved, and we addressed the central questions. Where was I? How was I? What had happened?

I was on a ledge, on a shaded rock face, about 100ft. below Eric, held by him on the rope. I could move my arms and legs, but my chest hurt, and there was blood around. I had fallen off the traverse with a large mass of rock, about two tons Eric thought, which had immediately fragmented. I had probably been hit on the head by a fragment and concussed at the start of the fall, so I had had no chance to hold onto the rope coils. Eric, unbelayed, had managed to jam himself into a crack and save both of us from falling to the bottom of the face 1000ft. below. Then, holding on with one hand, he had managed to hammer in a piton with the other and so secure us. He asked me to get myself belayed so that he could climb down to me. He did not expect me to belay him but wanted me to be tied to the mountain while he climbed down. I managed to find something to which to belay a few feet up. It was my first action towards our self rescue.

When Eric joined me we took stock of the damage. This was miraculously light. My limbs were functioning. The pain in my chest had suggested a broken rib, but was subsiding, and was probably due just to bruising. I had surface cuts on the hands and face and a partly split lip. I put on ski mitts and a Balaclava. Crucially, I was capable of supervised movement.

Even so, Eric did not try to coax me back up to the ridge. Escape from that section of the ridge would have been difficult. He judged that it would be easier and safer to get me down the west face. The face was broken for several hundred feet. He belayed me down for some rope lengths and we did one abseil. Eric collected the axe from the snow slope, and luckily, found the other axe nearby. The sun had now reached us. This meant that we were warm, but also that time was ticking away. Then the face below steepened to vertical for several hundred feet to the Coup de Sabre Glacier. The cliffs were of very wide extent and there seemed to be no way down. Eric searched with great determination and patience, guiding me back up a bit, across a bit, down a bit, across some more. It was beginning to look as if we really would have to climb back to the ridge. Eric admitted this possibility, adding that he had a bivouac sac. The prospect of a night out struck the beginnings of despair into me. Then, when the sun was starting to sink in the west, we reached the one breach in the defences, where only 100ft. of partly overhanging rock separated us from the glacier.

Eric very briefly considered making a single abseil and abandoning the rope, but a crevasse was visible on the glacier, and he almost immediately rejected forfeiting the rope as too dangerous. Instead, he abseiled 40ft. down a groove that slanted diagonally through the overhang, taking great care not to swing beneath the latter, and reached an extremely awkward ledge where he placed a belay piton. He called me down. I joined him and he pulled the rope through, with great relief. He placed another piton so that we could stay belayed to the first one while preparing the second abseil. At last, all was ready and we made the abseil to the glacier, which we were then able to descend safely roped.

It was dark when we reached the stony valley that we had descended the previous day. We were above the rock band. In fact, Geoff had found the path down this band while Eric and I had taken a rougher line. Now Eric managed to locate the path that Geoff had found. It was quite steep, with some metal cables, and we stayed roped until we were down. It was our last obstacle, but it was still a long way down the valley to civilisation at Ailefroide. We arrived there after midnight, hammered on a hotel door, were admitted, fed, wined and given a bed. Next morning, Eric took me to the doctor, who declared I was all right but was to rest for four days. Eric then speeded back up to the Lemercier Hut, to the relief of a worried Geoff.

During the split seconds of my fall Eric had reacted with athletic swiftness and precision to avoid disaster. Throughout our difficult self rescue he had acted with great mountaineering skill, calmness, kindness and resolve, qualities that presaged his future distinguished career in outdoor education and mountain leadership. I had been in outstandingly good hands.

Footnotes:

On the meet there were other incidents with loose rock, though none as serious as that which befell me and Eric. After the meet Eric, Bob Downes, Geoff Sutton and recent Oxford president Alan Blackshaw enjoyed an outstandingly productive continuation of the season based on the Ecole Nationale de Montagne et de Ski at Chamonix. Their routes together included the SSW Face of the Gugliermina (ED, second British ascent) and the NE Face of the Badile (ED, first British ascent). (Also climbed was the N Face of the Triolet, TD, Blackshaw and Downes, first British ascent.)

The substance of this article was adapted from a more wide ranging article, *Dangerous Learning Curve,* which has been submitted for publication in a planned Centenary volume of Cambridge Mountaineering. Eric read the manuscript of that article with pleasure. Following Eric's untimely death through illness I hope the present article will be of pleasure and interest to many readers of the *SMC Journal.*

WITH MIDGES IN HIGH PLACES

By Malcolm Slesser

THE responsibility of climbing a hard route with someone much less able and/or experienced than oneself is not of itself unpleasant, or even dangerous, if the climb is well within the leader's ability and there is adequate protection. Nonetheless, there is a very different tenue, as the French would say, about the outing. It is not quite as carefree as climbing with a partner of equal skill. Normally, a well-balanced climbing pair take each pitch alternately. They share the decisions, they share the risk. They share the ambition. If one partner cannot find a way, often the other will succeed, not necessarily because he or she is a better climber, but in the same way that one player will read a hand of cards differently from another. But climbing with your inexperienced wife or girl friend completely changes the nature of the game. It not only places an enormous responsibility on you – especially if either of you have family responsibilities – but generates a strain for the leader that must be totally hidden from the other party. Moreover, the chances are that the tyro may be little adept at belaying, unable to hold you were you to peel. Mountaineering is a practical sport. You have to have held a fall to know how to prepare for one. But to shove your dearly beloved companion off a cliff just to demonstrate the technique is not a good way to warm a relationship.

I got to know Jane quite late in my life and hers. She was over 50, and though she was an adventurous quine, high standard rock climbing was not one of the skills she had honed in her youth or been exposed to subsequently. But she was at home among mountains and, to my joy, was very willing try her hand at rock. I tried her out on *Route One* on Carn Dearg, a steep, severe, route of impeccable rock. Because one is cossetted within two walls the sense of exposure is limited, something that can be very intimidating to a beginner. She kept her cool, but climbed jerkily. Several years later, now in her 60s and quite a polished climber, I thought she was ready for a really challenging route. I was determined it should be of the very best, offering exposure, position, views, aesthetic sensations and, of course, good sound rock. I settled on *Shining Cleft* on Sgurr a'Mhadaidh in the Cuillins of Skye. The name alone has allure. I had climbed it before, though not for some time. It is a long route – 270m. – and takes one way out over a sheer bulging vertiginous wall, home to the extreme climb *Thor*. It had been pioneered by three undergraduates of the Cambridge University Mountaineering Club in 1952. They must have been in great form for it is truly a bold line. I consider it to be one of the finest of the early post-war routes in Skye, even today reckoned to be Hard severe. In those days a first ascent was always led from below on the basis of a perceived line on the cliff face. There was no prior rappeling down the face to check for holds and belays. You started at the bottom.

You judged the potential for ascent by examining the rock above you, and worked out a set of moves. On every pitch at the back of your mind was the possibility that maybe it wouldn't go, and then what? A perilous climb down if that was possible, it being a fact that it is much harder to climb down than up. Sometimes retreat was impossible, then the route had to be forced either taking you beyond your ability, and in so doing possibly releasing talents and self-control you never knew you had. And to add to the prestige of that Cambridge first ascent, rock boots had yet to reach the UK. Wrangham's party did the ascent in hill-walking boots!

The Gods dealt Jane and me a peerless, windless, August day for our ascent. It started in our tent on the greensward below the bridge over the Allt Coire na Bruadaram, at the head of Loch Ainort in Skye. As experienced campers we had gone to bed with everything needed for breakfast within the tent, and just as well, for outside the midge-proof gauze door there pulsated a black cloud of ravening beasties. They were doubtless maddened by the succulent scents emerging from our unwashed bodies. These were not mere foot-soldiers here to challenge the human invader, but female impis with their assegais ready drawn charging upon the tent utterly fearless of the might of our flyspray. The death of 10,000 seemed of no account even to the hordes following the first wave. Here was an entire army, brigade upon brigade of perhaps hundreds of thousands of *Culicoides Punctati*, armed and passionate, ready to puncture our skins and draw forth our life blood while inserting a maddening itch.

A few kamikazes had worked their way in, and were incinerated by our Primus stove. We observed the fruitless battering of our door by the restless horde with serene detachment while we prepared breakfast. Then came the call of nature! With socks pulled over my trousers, midge cream on wrists, ears and nose, hat jammed over my ears, I made a high speed exit and ran like a deranged dervish to the edge of the sea. It was low tide. I took refuge among the seaweed in the belief, false as it turned out, that midges do not invade sea water. But just as a sailing boat cannot outrun the wind, no human can out pace the midge. No sooner had I my trousers down than the hellish horde surrounded me. It reminded me of that wonderful line in Tam O'Shanter at Kirk Alloway "As bees bizz out wi' angry fyke." In moments my face was swollen, my backside aflame. Pulling up my breeks I tore back to the sanctuary of the tent, while Jane cremated hundreds of midges by playing the Primus flame around my face, hair and backside. The smell of cremated midges mingled agreeably with singed hair. Dead bodies accumulated on the tent floor in a tousled heap.

We decamped in haste. Everything was hurled into the boot of the car any old how. In moments we were speeding at 50mph, the windows wide open blasting out the little brutes, and soon approached Sligachan Inn. My bowels were in torment. Something had to be done quickly. The Inn seemed closed. Jane drove to the adjacent campsite, to the very door of the loo, where a queue of patient campers scratching their bare legs were awaiting their turn. As a door opened, I ruthlessly (did I have an alternative?) dashed in, locked it and dropped my pants (and much else) as howls of rage and beating of fists on the door told me what sort of reception awaited me on my exit. Swiftly relieved, I emerged to find a campsite manager purple with rage. I placated him by paying for a night's camping, and, amid boos drove out of the campsite.

Now detoxified, I was ready for the day. We hastened along Glen Drynoch, one of Skye's bleakest glens, towards Talisker, where we embarked upon the equally dreary moor road by Satran with its deadly boring conifer plantations on each side. Then as the road dips towards glen Brittle, the plantation abruptly peters out. Here the Cuillin ridge etches the skyline, as bold and exciting as any mountain range, and one's heart beats that little bit faster. The view is straight into Coire na Creiche, dominated on the right-hand (south) side by the cliffs of Sgurr a'Mhadaidh – hill of the fox. For the most part one can find a way up through these cliffs without serious climbing to gain a notch on the North-west ridge. On the right, however, the cliff is sheer, broken only by the line of *Shining Cleft*. The face was in shadow enhancing its sense of steepness. Against the morning light we could not pick out the exact line of our chosen route.

We parked. The day resonated with the gentle hum of insects going about their business. It was now seriously hot and muggy – ideal midge conditions. We scraped together all the gear we could dig out of the boot and with two 11mm. 45m. ropes headed down the slope to join the track to the coire along the bank of the Allt a'Mhadaidh. This is the most delightful of all the Cuillin burns. The beaten way holds to the north side of a ravine, and passes a succession of waterfalls creating frothy pools of peat brown water reminiscent of home brew. We identified one deep pool for our swim on the way home. The occasional rowan clung to the side of the chasm, garnished with tufts of heather. The vegetation was the familiar couch and cotton grass illuminated by pink asphodel, yellow tormentil and blue-flowered butterwort. Jane was picking bog myrtle leaves, crushing them to release their oil, which is well known to repel midges. I contented myself with the folklore that midges can't stand the heat and shack up till the evening and that we would, anyway, leave the pests behind as we gained the vertical heights.

The rock face of Sgurr a'Mhadaidh faces north west, offering a complex array of cliffs, ledges and basalt dykes 600m. high. Once in the shade we were able to pick out detail on the cliff. A leftward slanting gully detracts from the purity of the face, but offers a way of gaining an entry to the vertical wall, which was not climbed till 1967, the Cuillin's first E2 route by Bolton and Cain. *Shining Cleft* starts to the left of the slanting gully, using as an approach two pitches of steep slabby black-brown gabbhro as rough as a pot scrubber but, as we discovered, offering no placements for protection. I enjoyed the climbing, eventually finding an indifferent belay after 30m., Jane joined me finding it well within her standard. I continued to the point where the route crosses the slanting gully. Deep within it I thankfully found a good belay crack.

At this point the climb becomes not so much hard as serious. A basalt dyke offers a line of weakness that leads out into space. I was now unaccountably nervous. At this degree of exposure I was accustomed to having an experienced companion belaying me. Was I justified in bringing Jane here? Was this within her scope? She evinced no qualms, and as is so often the case when a cautious reappraisal is called for, the momentum of the day's plan brushes aside prudence. I am dripping with nuts, friends and slings. If there is the remotest possibility of a running belay I will take it, every few feet if the opportunity presents itself. I am determined to make this climb safe for her. But as I climb no such opportunities appear. By the time I have led out 35m. I am 100m. above the screes with nothing but space between my feet and feeling distinctly nervous. Eventually, I find a meagre stance and something to hook myself onto. Jane arrives at my side in good form. I supervise her belay with all the attention of an anxious mother strapping her infant into a car seat.

The route is obvious – a gangway, leading out and upwards to the centre of the vertical cliff. It is steep but the rock is sound. But it is also devoid of cracks for running belays. Long lead-outs without protection are not appropriate for one of my age, I am thinking. Soon I am on slabby rocks under an overhang. About 10, 20m. out and I still haven't found a runner. I can only press on. I worry that the exposure will unsettle Jane. It is certainly getting to me. At last I reach a place where I can place a belay. Its not much of a stance, just somewhere to brace the feet. I place two nuts, neither of which look like having much holding power. I comfort myself that so far the climbing has not been that hard. The rock is dry and we wear rock boots with sticky soles. Jane joins me with accomplished elegance.

Swapping positions isn't too easy, but finally she is tied on, and ready to handle the rope as I press on. She asks if I think the belay is good. I pretend it is. The route now leads into an amphitheatre. It is a severe move, but uncomplicated, yet desperately exposed. No opportunities for runners emerge. My gear is useless weight hanging from my waist. In due course I reach a stance, and look for a belay. The position is good, but I have to explore 10ft. above me to find anything into which I may insert a nut and hook on my rope. As an anchor it is about as irrelevant as bottled water. I descend back to the stance. I am worried. This is not my recollection of my previous ascent, then I recall that on that occasion there had been three of us, Bill Wallace and his inexperienced son. Bill had led followed by his son with me as his adviser. At the tail end I hadn't had to worry about looking for protection.

Anyway, this belay is good enough to bring someone up, but quite inadequate to hold a falling leader. I seriously consider calling it a day till I reflect on the nature of the descent. No protection, and, for Jane, a downward traverse which means I cannot really give her real support from the rope. In truth, we are already past the point where retreat is attractive. We cannot rappel down for not only are we at least 130m. above the deck and have but 45m. of rope, and there is nothing I would trust my life to. I have lost two friends from failed abseils. Better go on. I tell Jane not to hurry. What I really mean is for God's sake don't slip. While I am slowly bringing in the rope I become conscious of midges dancing in front of my eyes. Where one moment there was one, there are soon 10 and within minutes many more. They home in on my face and wrists. I am raw meat laid out to entice the lion. I am cold meat for maggots. My hands are entirely taken up with attending to the rope at the end of which Jane is working her way towards me, so I cannot scratch to rub off the offending beasties. They zoom in and out like dive bombers assaulting a battleship. By the time Jane gets to me I am in desperate straits, torn between care for her welfare and a desperate need to beat off the enemy.

We juggle the belay around, and when satisfied that she at least is reasonably firmly attached I set off. I am now conscious of the fact that even if she were the finest belayer in the world, she could not hold me. Hence, I must not fall. Desperately, I hunt around for runners, now for my sake as much as hers. Nothing. The route steepens, nothing desperately difficult, but needing skill and care. I might as well be climbing solo. I am not happy. I cast my mind back to the last time I climbed this route. I recall there being a really good stance farther up. We are truly committed to the climb. I begin to long for the days when we carried pitons.

I continue to climb. The basalt dyke is smooth, not rough like gabbhro. I do not have the guide book with me. Guide books can seriously detract from adventure. I did indeed read up the route before I left home. My memory of that description did not tally with what I now saw around me. Later, when I returned home I checked. Three editions of the guide book faithfully copied the original description in the Sligachan climbs book, which later was published in the SMC journal of 1953. I concluded that the guide book editors had never climbed this route, and subsequent inquiries confirmed this. This is like the Internet. Once bad or false information gets recycled often enough it takes on the aura of authority and truth. Then I recalled the fate of the original pioneers. Two had since died (one by being hit on the head by a falling rock on Pillar in the Lake District). Ted Wrangham, with whom I had expeditioned to the Pamirs 30-odd years before was very much alive, but with a dim memory of the event. He, too, had been a number three on the rope and so had simply followed his mates. Back to the climb.

Looking up, I sense that the angle eventually relents. Up there should be the ledge. One further rope length brings me to it. A genuine commodious ledge! A resting place with room to manoeuvre. Above me soars vertical rock split by a crack, which provides an ideal location for nuts. Soon I am attached to the first reliable belay since we left slanting gully. A1, first class, bomb-proof! All anxiety vanishes. Momentarily, relieved of the stress of such exposed climbing I can again enjoy our situation. It is a spectacular spot. If it weren't for the midges life would be perfect. I take in the sunlit sea. Not a breath of wind stirs its surface. The isle of Canna squats like a huge vessel on a pewter ocean. This is perfection.

Jane arrives and we examine the way ahead. The route is now not at all obvious. I wondered what the Cambridge pioneers must have thought when they reached this point. Were I a limpet, I could traverse a holdless slab to some quite hold-worthy rocks about 20m. away. But I am not a limpet, so I turn my gaze elsewhere. Above me, in the crack, is an old peg, and above it, a tattered weathered sling. So someone has been up there, however that doesn't prove it is the route. It might be a false trail. On the other hand we could see no other options. It is clearly necessary to climb the crack to see what prospects it opens up. You never know till you rub faces with the rock. That's climbing for you. That's what makes it so exciting. I cast a critical eye over Jane's belay so assiduously attached that she looks like Houdini's assistant on a bad night.

Comforted by such precautions, I climb the crack rejoicing in the frequent opportunities to place nuts. The climbing, though technically harder, is mentally more relaxing. And 20m above me the crack disappears into a blank overhanging wall. An ancient sling hangs from a pebble jammed in the crack. Signs of pre-nut climbing technology? There is no further way upward. If there is a route it has to be across a sheet of smooth rock, not steep enough to be called a wall, but rather too steep to be termed a slab. 15m across this slab-wall rises a rib of seemingly climbable rock. The obvious procedure is to make a tension traverse. This would involve my bracing my feet against the slab while Jane paid out the rope in accordance with my commands. Secured by my sling placed beside the ancient one, if I slipped, I would come to no great harm. But when it came to Jane's turn, no such tension was possible. I would need to climb really high above her to be able to give her adequate rope support, and if she slipped, she would swing through an arc and crash against the rock rib. What decided me against this manoeuvre was that a slick of water ran over part of slab. No boot could grip on such a surface. It might have been a defensible strategy with another climber of my own experience and ability, but not with someone of Jane's limited experience.

Very unhappily I descend the crack, inordinately grateful for the various runners I had placed. What now? Looking around I see that if I can descend, negotiate some rather bald bits of slab, it may be possible to gain a climbable rib of rock 30m. away. Because I would be descending, Jane could afford me quite a bit of support through tensioning the rope. Grimly aware that this was our only hope, I set off, climbing with the delicacy of a cat on a slate roof, aware that its claws are useless. I found some running belay points, but couldn't put them in since they would hold me back when I started to climb. Finally, I embrace a substantial hold like a drowning man grabbing a life-belt. A huge exhalation of breath reveals the tension that has built up within me.

The sun has come round making the scene less awesome. Now the only way is up. No matter what I encounter I have no choice but to ignore the deficiencies of the rock above me. Whatever little it offers, I have to accept. In these situations the key is to plan ahead. Just as a sentence has a grammatical order the rock imposes a specific sequence. A false line can spell disaster, for in retreat, moves that are just in balance on the way up are distinctly 'iffy' on descent when it is often impossible to hold one's self in balance. After a few metres I feel confident that the passage will go. I move more fluently. At last, with myself well above Jane with 20m. of rope stretched between us, I find a ledge, a stance and a belay. The issue is no longer in doubt.

I am lathered in sweat, no doubt partly from the intense mental effort of the climb, but also due to the speed with which my anxiety has driven me. Nothing could be more attractive to the midge. One by one they call in their pals to join the feast. So much sweat is streaming off me I am surprised they aren't drowning. My first act is to cool off. I dearly want to strip to my waist but the thought of them devouring my lily-white body stayed my hand. Jane meanwhile is scratching away at her face and wrists, while nobly continuing to belay me in the appropriate manner.

I call her to climb downwards. Gingerly she descends. Down-climbing is not something of which she has experience – few have! I give her a tight rope. I admire the way she keeps her cool. She crosses the smooth slab with commendable delicacy, and soon has her hand on the 'Thank God!' hold. There she pauses. She knows she has to follow my line. I can see she is not relishing it. I am glad of my excellent belay. I pass this news to her. Sensibly, she takes her time. Eventually, she joins me on my large and comfortable platform.

The way ahead is now easy, and in two pitches we are on easy ground and unroping. A light breeze caresses us and is accepted as a just reward for our efforts. The midges, reduced in number, are still circling like sharks round a bleeding swimmer. What was needed was to really cool off. Midges don't attack cold skin. There is no-one in sight. We strip naked. Absolutely stark naked, except for boots. The evening sun sheds its golden rays over our bodies, making them seem bronzed and luscious. It is a handsome sight. If Courbet had been here, he would surely have painted us. We linger over the view, for as the sun dips the Outer Hebrides stand out like a pencil drawing. It has been a good day, a testing day, giving the sort of satisfaction that only comes when overcoming odds rather greater than expected. The final treat will be our swim in the Allt a' Mhadaidh. Donning our clothes we pick our way down the ledges and cliffs of the coire. At our chosen pool we again divest our clothing, and revel in the coolth and cleansing of the peaty bubble bath. As we dress, we glance back. The coire wall is rose-red. The line of *Shining Cleft* is easily picked out. We relive the climb, recalling the best bits, discarding the worst, before picking up our sacks and returning to the banality of everyday living. The wind was up. The midges were in hiding.

THE WEE TRAIN ROBBERY

By Morton Shaw

"It would never work!"

"Aye it would, I spent a long time today thinking about it on that manky belay waiting for you to make the move. You were forever."

"What do you expect, at my height it wisnae easy, I had two choices and the second choice was you letting the rope go as I hit the deck."

"Aye whatever. Anyway it would work, these guys have been carrying the cash for so long they don't know what they've got and couldnae care less. After Tyndrum they go up to the driver's compartment and share a glass or two."

"Awa and bile yer heid ya stupid loon."

"The Chemist and the Counter slouched in the corner morosely listening to the conversation wondering only if this evening would end like so many with the Shipbuilder and the Engineer being held apart on the long road back to the doss with insults being traded at high volume, only stopping when one or other of them landed in a ditch.

The summer passed into autumn with the usual litany of failure and drink, compounded this year with rumours from the south of a band of schoolkids blitzing the Rock at a standard we could only boast about. It was only a matter of time before they appeared in person and made our lives even more unbearable.

The weather had the October miseries, work was a pain and, in the total absence of what is euphemistically described as a personal relationship, there was little alternative to the usual hitch up the loch, a wet Saturday and the drink again in the bar.

The fifth or sixth pint was on the table with the conversation going round in a circle when the Shipbuilder raised the subject again.

"Look I'm no saying it would be easy but they're just asking for it, it's almost criminal the way they treat that money." This time there was a spark of interest.

"So how are you going to take it from them."

"Stop the train just after Corrour, grab the cash and leg it."

"As easy as that eh?"

"Nae quite, but we can block the line both sides, take out the telephone wires and disappear into the Moor. If we hide out in the CIC for a few days by the time we come off the hill they'll be searching the slums of Glasgow."

The walk back to the doss that night was no more enjoyable than usual but by the time we rolled into our pits all the problems were solved and the only thing left to do was to drift off into a drunken slumber dreaming of spending the Mill's payroll somewhere warm.

Sunday was as useless as Saturday had been and eventually we struggled out of the bunks bad tempered and sore. Even the rats had the good sense to keep quiet. We drifted over to the other side of the road trying to look upright and made our way home. The year had turned, and for once the snow had come, when the phone rang.

"It's on, we meet next Tuesday in the Coe."

"But..."

"Nae buts, take some holiday, you cannae drop out now. The others are in, you're needed and what's more – you know." The last said slowly.

The hint was taken and on Tuesday night we assembled in the doss. The Shipbuilder laid out his plan.

"They shift the money on the Wednesday train, count and sort it into the paypackets at the works on Thursday. I drive up to the Fort with the Wee One, dump the climbing gear in the CIC and come over the col and down to Staoineag. You pair meet us at Loch Treig where the track from the Blackwater comes in. Keep your packs light with plenty of space. They've been working on the line just past Corrour and there are lots of sleepers to block the track. I wave down the train with a light to stop it before it hits the sleepers, the Chemist piles some more behind the train and you cut the telephone wires. The Wee One gets on board and dumps the cash over. If we get it right and stop them at the bridge, we duck under the bridge, down to the loch and then up the path and over the CMD arete and down to the CIC.

"How do you stop them just laughing at us?"

"The Dhu left their guns under the boards at the Ville, they didn't think anyone would be stupid enough to steal them. We won't have to use them."

"They'll just lift the sleepers and head off to the Fort."

"No way they won't, not after the Wee One uses the gelly he has left over from the hydro he was working on last year."

"And if there's someone in the CIC?"

"We dump the gear in the shelter in Coire Leis and pick it up later."

The next morning the Shipbuilder and the Wee One left in the car that the Shipbuilder said he had bought –"And I'll be wanting the cash back first before the split." – their sacks piled high with our gear. We left a little later, travelling fairly light, cutting straight across to the dam, though straight was not how it would appear on a map if our course had been drawn. Up and down and in and out of bogs with a light wet snowfall adding to the pleasure. The track beside the Blackwater was more in the imagination than real and we eventually stopped for a rest in the bothy beside Loch Chiarain. The Chemist, a dour man at the best of times, slumped in a corner steam gently rising from his wet trousers.

"I don't like this," I said.

"Neither do I but I don't see an alternative. The Shipbuilder would do us good and proper if we pull out. I'd rather face the cops."

"Aye."

Silence reigned again.

It was getting dark as we reached Loch Treig and we sheltered under the bridge leaving a sack on the track to get the others' attention. Half-an-hour later they appeared.

"No problems, there is no one in the hut."

"Right let's get on, the train passes at about nine. Don't forget to wear your Balaclavas."

In the event it all went smoothly. The train came to a halt at the pile of sleepers, I cut the wires, sleepers were piled behind and while the Shipbuilder held the driver and guards in the cab with his gun the Engineer tossed out the three bags of notes. We scuttled under the bridge and down the track to the loch with the hills still resounding to the noise of the gelignite going off on the track and the shotgun blast that the Shipbuilder had let off to remind the guards not to follow. The night was black, the only light being the glow of the quartz on the track but we didn't stop until the bridge where the track bent left towards Staoineag. The railway line was well out of sight as we put on the torches and struggled up to the bothy where we stopped just long enough to share out the weight of the cash more evenly and then set off again into the face of a bitter wind with the snow dancing and whirling in the light of the torches.

It was a long struggle from then, up past Luibelt, through the boggy flats at the pass and down to Steall. Another rest in the limited shelter of the ruins, everyone lost in their own thoughts, our breath frosting the edges of our balaclavas. Then we turned and set up the coire in the darkness, down to only two working torches. The snow gradually hardened and steepened until just below the CMD col we started to cut steps. On the other side of the col the snow in Coire Leis was rock hard and our crampons bit as we nervously found our way down under the face and into the coire, rarely able to make out our feet in the flowing spindrift.

The CIC eventually loomed out of the dark and we quickly unhinged the corner window and slid in over the basins to the quiet of the hut. The fire was lit, a brew on and the Shipbuilder set to work on the padlock on the trapdoor to the loft. Once free we removed the cash from the bags and separated it into four piles – nearly £20,000 each – but I for one was too knackered to care. We wrapped each pile up in an identifiable item of clothing and passed it up to the Shipbuilder in the loft. He secured the padlock as best he could and we collapsed into the bunks. A ghostly light coming in the one open shutter in the corner signified the coming of dawn.

The next day was fortunately horrible. Gale force winds and low scurrying cloud kept anyone with any sense off the hill and we rested in the bunks, only occasionally braving the wind to crawl through the snowdrift at the window for water and relief.

"Bloody hell," the chemist said, as he appeared over the sink, snow cascading from his clothes. "With this money we could build the old farts a toilet and do everyone a favour."

"They still wouldn't give you a key though."

Friday dawned calm and bright and we were away sharp trying to give the impression of being real climbers. The Engineer and the Shipbuilder headed for Tower Ridge while the Chemist and I cramponned round under the Douglas Boulder to the area right of Vanishing Gully. The Chemist claimed that he had seen possibilities of an easy line or two on one of his rare forays to the Ben. As usual his optimism outweighed our ability and after scratching about at the bottom of two obvious grooves we settled on the right-hand chimney which had the advantage of being shorter in difficulty than the other two, with the difficulties well within retreating distance if, as normal, failure loomed. A pillar of steep snow led to the chimney and the Chemist quickly disappeared. I stood paying out the ropes in short bursts as steps were cut and moves made. It seemed like forever, but eventually, the rope came tight. Despite his steps it was a struggle and I left dirty marks of Rannoch mud as I, in my usual style, kept as close to the ice as possible. We changed places at the belay with only a "I don't think this has been done before," to speed me on my way. Eventually, the angle eased and in the early afternoon we approached the ridge just below the little tower.

The other two's steps were still visible and we made fast time to the Eastern Traverse. As I edged out on the traverse faint cries could be heard and in the distance a figure could be seen descending Observatory Gully. I looked at the Chemist and was met by a shrug of the shoulders.

As I rounded the corner below the chimney the reason for the cries became clear. A rope was tied off to one of the blocks and hung over the edge absolutely taught. My shouts elicited no sensible response, the curve of the ground, distorting the words but there was real anger in the sounds. The Chemist joined me and after rigging up a pulley system we managed to slowly raise the weight on the end of the rope. As the body came closer the noises become more intelligible but consisted mainly of Glasgow patois interspersed with an amazing range of swear words. The Engineer was a mess, blood everywhere and his clothes in tatters. His anger overcame any pain he may have felt and we felt lucky that he had lost his axe.

"He pulled me off then scarpered – I'll kill the bastard."

After a few minutes things calmed down and we edged off leftwards into Tower Gully and down Observatory. By the time we reached the hut we were reconciled to what awaited us. He hadn't even bothered to shut the trapdoor behind him and not a note had he left. We packed up and struggled down the glen with the Engineer complaining so loudly that I for one began to wish that the rope had not been tied off so securely. By the time we met the police as we crossed the golf course it was patently obvious that there was hardly enough competence in the group to climb a hill far less rob a train and so, after we morosely answered a few questions, they gave us a lift to the Belford where the Engineer was patched up with their usual incompetence and sent on his way with a patronising lecture.

And what of the Shipbuilder? It was quiet for a few years then rumours floated around of sightings in the Far East, of a business venture going wrong and a partner who was there one day and gone the next. Once in Bangkok I thought I saw him in a bar but I left my drink – and town. The memories are still there though. And, of course, the 'new' route had been done before by some ignorant students from Glasgow.

THE SHELTER STONE SAGA

By Julian Lines

June 1989:
THE HARD smooth sheet of crystalline granite gives away none of its secrets – it is blank, unforgiving, and once again tosses me down its cruel rough surface. I let out a yelp and close my eyes until I feel the elastic security of my two ropes tugging at my harness, rendering me safe once again. My first basic instinct is to shoot a glance up the line of ropey tension; I spy the rust-weary downward pointing peg from which I am suspended without fear, for this is the third time that blade of rust has held my 30ft. fall in the last hour.

Sunlight has disappeared from the surrounding plateau, the night stealing in at the same rate as my confidence leaks out; I begin to realise that I have bitten off far more than I could chew, on attempting my first E4 lead. I glance down to my belayer, searching for an expression of reassurance on Mike's face. The blonde haired, cherub-like face that stares back at me shows signs of bemusement and anxiety at my cloth ripping falls. "Are you ok," he asks with a grin.

"Yeah, I'm fine," I reply as I climb hand over hand up the rope to the peg, ready to forge another attempt.

I sigh heavily as I look around, quickly absorbing my predicament among dusk-coated mountains; the vista is authenticated by the sound of tumbling melt water that roars with perpetual echo over bare granite. On the one hand I feel demoralised but on the other I feel free and happy, testing my limited technique on the Shelterstone's unorthodox and flawless granite. Once again I find myself at the 'blank bit' 15ft. above the security of the corroding artefact and my body is channelled yet again into the same compulsory sequence of moves as before. My parched throat gulps with anxiety and tension as I anticipate being propelled down the granite sheet in yet another skin tearing arc...but wait, my hand reaches a hold at the far side of the 'blank bit' and for an instant I am overjoyed, before realising that I am in fact lonely, committed and now on unfamiliar ground. I manage to secure a big nut before shakily scampering along a rattling hollow flake with youthful spirit, hoping there aren't going to be any more difficulties before the belay. In gathering gloom, I release Mike from the torment of his semi-hanging belay, he follows rapidly and we abseil from the *Missing link* into the silhouettes of darkness.

We bivy on the beach at the head of Loch Avon, under a star-infested sky, it is windless and the midges are a nuisance which makes for a restless night. At some ungodly hour I prop myself on my elbows and gaze at the charcoal-black shapes of the mountains silhouetted against

Shelter Stone Crag. Photo: Andy Tibbs.

an inky blue and lacklustre orange sky. The serene surface of the loch is reflected through the night air like an ethereal mirror – a varnished image of nature that no lens could ever fittingly reproduce. Within an hour the sun emerges like a blood apricot and, as its light intensifies, the mirror shatters and the image is lost forever.

The heat of the morning brings on apathy as we sunbathe on the beach's coarse granite husks, cooling down when required by foolhardily diving into the loch's heart-pulsing melt-water. Every now and again I look up at the huge turret of the Shelter Stone Crag, rearing up like a formidable geological sentry at the head of the loch. What steals my attention is the circular sweep of flawless slabs, bang in the centre of the Shelterstone, like the centre-stone of a tiara. Ever since, I have become fascinated by that jewel – an obsession.

Late that afternoon, after the sun's eccentric powers have drifted from the beach, we stir, gather our gear and head for *The Steeple* – a stunning 800ft. line of corners up the right edge of the crag which, at E2, is perhaps the finest mountain climb at its grade in the country – Scottish heritage at its best.

At gone nine o'clock, Mike sets off on the penultimate pitch. From out of the dusk golden shards of sunlight sparkle into the corner, illuminating us in the surrounding darkness.

"Mike, look at that – the sun is out!" I shout in high spirits, as I crane my neck backwards to find Mike absorbed in wide bridging manoeuvres 80ft. above me. He makes effortless work of the chisel-featured corner as I struggle to pay out the disobedient rope in rhythm with his upward movement. Within minutes he is out of sight, the rope snakes out and it is my turn. We both sit on top spellbound – the view down the loch, the peace of the mountains, the company, the fun, the challenge – everything is perfect, a memory that will last my lifetime and one which would stoke the desire for many return visits to my favourite 'spiritual home' – 'The Shelterstone'.

June 1992:

Even the words in the guidebook intimidated me – 'a modern desperate'. I had read the description of *The Run of the Arrow* in the Cairngorms guidebook over and over again, along with Kev Howett's account, detailed in *Extreme rock,* naively thinking that the more I read, the easier the route would become. My University Finals start tomorrow and if only I could revise my Geo chemistry like I do the guidebook, then I would surely attain a first class degree – if only.

I climb out of the confines of the *Thor* diedre onto the slab, losing sight of Matt and all other securities. I look up at the blank sweep of rock above, wondering why I didn't stay in Aberdeen to revise for tomorrow morning's exam. After slotting a number of uninspiring RPs

Climbing on Skagastolstind. Photo: Carl Schaschke.
Ben Alder during the 2006 Ski-mountaineering Meet. (See page 442).

in a sinuous crack, I begin to wobble uncontrollably in fear as if I had just been thrown into a coliseum full of lions. I now know that any attempt is pointless.

Matt and I had returned for a further attempt on *The Run of the Arrow* after my Finals. Matt who we all knew as 'Matt the cat' with his agile build and long unkempt brown hair is one of the most understated rock climbers I have ever known. It was hard to determine how keen a climber Matt was, as he is soft spoken, affable, and at times, apathetic, but he always climbs fluently and with flair.

I offer Matt the lead, and cocoon myself comfortably into my belay alcove. Matt oozes past the lower section and then boldly climbs out to the flake, he doesn't find the crucial large nut for the crux and proceeds to take a few 20ft. whippers off the crux on marginal gear, somewhat casually. On reaching the belay he abseils off, strips the gear and pulls the rope for my attempt. Matt's chalk dusted holds, instill confidence in me as I sketch my way past the tenuous lower section to reach a salvational line of natural carved steps – the climbing is no more than Severe standard for 40ft., albeit with no gear. The steps peter out at a large handhold and with frightening reality, fear envelops me as my dangerous predicament dawns.

Bloody hell – my mind goes into spasms of horror at the thought of Dougie Dinwoodie on his first-ascent attempt, reaching this point, unprepared, with no chalk and a pair EBs. I myself was now reliving that horror – albeit with sticky rubber, chalk and the knowledge that it was climbable. I awkwardly spy a perfect, parallel nut slot that spits out everything that I try to secure in it. Luckily for Dougie, he managed to smash a couple of nuts in with his peg hammer and lower to safety, unscathed. The 'welded' nuts have now gone, and a blank 5c slab needs to be addressed before gear can be placed in a flake that drools downwards like a blood-hound's jowl. Spillage of nerves here would lead to a 120ft. fall. My mental state was still in tatters due to my exams, and my commitment only went as far as emptying the contents of my chalk bag on the one good hold. After half-an-hour I felt it was wise to down climb 40ft. followed by a 30ft. jump onto RPs.

Having climbed down the 40ft., the idea of jumping started to haunt me. I now felt humiliated, vulnerable, scared and stuck. I find a tiny crack in the granite that takes a Rock 1, half in. Once seated, I tug it numerous times to make sure it is firm. I have Matt take up the tension in the rope and I spread-eagle myself on the rock, close my eyes, let go and shout down to Matt to lower me. I was shit scared, I waited for the wire to pop, but it held and I escaped, thoroughly traumatised. When I returned in 1996 to lead *Run of the Arrow* with Sue Harper, I couldn't even find this Rock 1 placement – an illusion forged in desperation perhaps.

1995-1997:

Ever since my first visit to the Shelterstone, my eyes always focused on the beautifully curving sickle and its smooth powerful architecture. I could never understand why no one had climbed it. Was it because it curved into *The Missing Link* and had no true finish?

I left Scotland in 1992 after University, but I kept obsessively staring at the crag photo of the Shelterstone in *Extreme Rock*, dreaming of ways to link up the sickle with a blank top pitch above *Thor*. My dreams of an ascent, slowly became an obsession, but not living in Scotland and not having the time, tormented me. In 1993, I hear on the grapevine that Rick 'The Stick' Campbell had climbed the line of the sickle and named it *Realm of the Senses* known as *Realm* for short. Rather than being frustrated at missing out on the first ascent, it was quite the contrary – I was happy, as I now knew it was possible and this urged me to return to Scotland.

In 1994, Rick returned to climb the top pitch independently calling it *L'Elisir d'Amore*. Rick had frightened himself on the ascent, and when he arrived back down at his tent, among boulders in the alpine style meadow, he proposed to Sarah – now his wife – and gave up bold slab climbing. A romantic ending. Along with his swansong, *Aphrodite* – which he attempted 'on-sight' in dramatic nail-biting fashion in 1990, when, run-out above the crux, he found himself in a frightening position with no runners and little rope. He eventually 'escaped' into *Cupids Bow* and completed the clean lead in the morning – Rick had now completed a trilogy of E7 routes on one of Scotland's purest pieces of rock; not to mention the first free ascent of *Thor*, quite possibly Scotland's most coveted E5 mountain route. I was envious.

I returned to Scotland in 1995 to take up residence with my adopted family at 'Muir of Knock.' I wrote, asking Rick for his route descriptions and he happily replied, however I never managed to secure climbing partners for the Shelterstone during the perfect summer of 1995. So in frustration I soloed a sack-full of routes in the Cairngorms, including *Firestone* on Hells Lum Crag. Rick's comment on this, writing in *Climber* magazine, "Gritstone psycho routes reach the Gorms," made me smile, and gave me inspiration for greater things to come.

In 1996, even Rick accompanied me to the Shelterstone, we dabbled with a few variation starts and finishes to existing routes, one of which Rick mockingly named 'Hard Lines' – possibly a jibe at me. One morning on waking up to the noise of the burbling stream, I poke my head out of the tent, glance past the flat meadow grass, up past the beautifully carved boulders, past the infamous Shelter Stone – a large rectangular boulder 12ft. high and 30ft. long, there was a doss underneath it, but sadly it has been rodent infested for years and not used during the summer. My eyes drift forever upwards to the jewel, glistening in the sun and I become excited about climbing on such immortal stone once again. I make subtle noises to try and stir Rick from his tent, and luckily Rick stirs, he is a morning person too.

At more than 6ft. in height, with a frame like a skeleton, I couldn't understand how Rick had developed into a bold slab climber as he has the physique of a 'sport' climber. Initially, I was slightly unnerved by Rick, due to his legendary ascents on the slabs, but this soon wore off as his quick wit, freshness and perverse sense of humour smothered any hints of arrogance or ego that he may have had.

"Which of the three routes do you want climb today Julian?" Rick asks in well-spoken tongue, like me, Rick had gone to public school.

"Err...I don't know," I replied, knowing damn well deep down that I wanted to climb the amazing sweep of granite architecture of *Realm* and link it with *L'Elisir.* Rick was a little disappointed with my decision, he had hoped I was going to repeat his most coveted route – *Aphrodite.*

With Rick on belay, I set off up the beautifully twisting groove of *Realm.* I feel unfit and a little intimidated at the fact that Rick is obediently holding my ropes. I struggle with the puzzling awkwardness of the groove and I become scared of falling off inches above the belay. Rick makes comment at my pumped and oversized forearms, which breaks the tension and makes me relax a little. After an awkward rest halfway up the groove, it fizzles out and into more intense technicalities. Rick shouts some numbers and, after many body contorting manoeuvres, I peel off the rock onto a brace of RPs.

"Julian your rock boots are in pieces. You can't climb tenuous routes in those." Rick shouts up in incredulity

"These are my favourites, I don't want to bin them," I reply, knowing that Rick's right and my boots are in pieces. On my second attempt, the flyaway groove pushes me into a sequence of levitation moves, before reaching the overlap utterly stunned and shaken by the experience. The overlap lends a meagre rest, chunkier gear and a little time to reflect on the impossibilities to come.

"Pinch the lip of the overlap and traverse left on miniscule footholds," Rick advises, trying to be helpful. However, this doesn't work for me, I am too short to dangle from the lip and secure any footholds at all. "There aren't any footholds." I shout down rather pissed off. Having managed to clip a sturdy down-pointing peg, I try to climb entirely on the slabs crystalline surface, but I fall numerous times, become deluded, tired and eventually lower off.

"Perhaps it is 7a." Rick bursts, with a smile on his face.

"I don't know, perhaps I am being useless," I reply, in a subdued manner.

Later that afternoon, I decide to accompany Rick on an ascent of an 800ft. route – *The Stone Bastion.* Only the top two pitches were of worth, so Rick and I race up the lower pitches of *The Needle* another of the Shelterstone's timeless classics – a Robin Smith route from 1962. I sit on a ledge, below and right from the 'Crack for thin fingers' and pull the ropes in for Rick to start climbing. In the distance I can hear the familiar deep-bass roar of turbines and chopping rotors as the wasp-coloured Sea-King emerges at the head of the valley and heads plum for us.

"Bloody hell, the chopper's coming straight for us."

The pilot pulls along broadside, below me, and I can see the winch man baring his teeth in a broad smile as he claps his hands in the open doorway. The chopper then turns and disappears back down the glen. When Rick arrives on the stance, I ask: "What's all the clapping about?"

"The helicopter came in close, so I decided to perform the Highland fling on the belay ledge," Rick replies with a grin, somewhat pleased at his performance.

Rick's main climbing partner over the years was Paul 'The Stork' Thorburn, their climbing partnership gelled into a Scottish *tour-de-force.* Their new-routes list was endless, routes of E5 to E7 fell thick and fast, when one failed the other would succeed – symbiosis in harmony. They were commonly dubbed 'Sticky' and 'Storky'. Stork, similar to Rick, is far more than 6ft. tall, and again has a physique such that he could get a stand in part for the skeleton in a human biology class. He has a quiet but intellectual manner and is unusually practical for an academic – a Dr of Chemistry too. Although at 30 years old he still didn't drive a car. I always thought he was called Stork due to his slender shape but later it transpires that the term was coined on a climbing trip years ago, when he used to stand on one foot, stoop down and pull his rock boot onto his other foot, making him look like a stork standing in the shallows. It was my great fortune that Stork was keen to climb the Shelterstone routes too, so we teamed up to link *Realm* and *L'Elisir* before I had to leave the country for the heat, humidity and toils of a bustling shipyard in South-east Asia.

I sit on the belay watching Stork smoothly cruise into the crux section, for a moment I think he has done it, but without warning he slumps onto the rope – even Stork was human after all. I follow on a tight rope, tearing at the uncompromising crystal surface, not wanting to fall, how embarrassing that would be. Eventually, I join Stork on the *Thor* belay – an assortment of pegs, banged into the cliff's granitic hide, it makes me think of a dying bull, laden with matador daggers. I leave Stork dangling on the belay, among the graveyard of rotting iron carcases. My head is a bag of nerves at the thought of the unknown *L'Elisir* run-out above me. Climbing out of *Thor* is an awkward, swear-spitting, energy-sapping affair before reprieve arrives at the deserted 'peg in the pocket'. At this point, *Thor* drifts easily off rightwards along a line of shelving holds to *The Pin* and easy ground, but not so my destination. The streaks that follow directly above look appealingly reckless and thoroughly dangerous, but annoyingly, they are seeping with water, which puts an end to our attempts.

The day before my departure for Asia, Stork and I turn our attention to *Aphrodite*. We had come to the arrangement that Stork was to lead the fiercely overhung initial overlap and I was to lead the mega run-out slab, which incorporates the infamous soul searching section on *Run of the Arrow*. I climb quickly on familiar ground and spend little time dwelling on the consequences of a hundred foot fall. I grab at the flake with pulsating heart, I fumble in gear, relax slightly and then proceed to place the large dovetailed nut at the top of the flake. The crucially tenuous crux of *Run of the Arrow* traverses left from here via a move of utmost imbalance or technical mastery. My path was on the right. Discreet edges and a set of topless and bottomless seams suck me upwards via a sustained sequence of moves. I claw bravely at the rock noting there may be a 6c move ahead, my whole body pumped and shaking with the anxiety of the unknown. I look up, and there it is, inches above me, a large hold and slender ledge that marks the end of the crux, I reach up for the hold, the mix of fear and excitement is unbearable at the thought of success, my fingers touch the hold, my body turns to rubber and I rattle 35ft. down the rock and end up bouncing up and down like a puppet on a string! "You useless piece of shit!" I shout at myself, as pissed off with falling as I was surprised to find that the moves were easier than *Run of the Arrow,* although there were more of them. On the second attempt, I make no mistakes and as I attain a standing position on the ledge, I look around to see a sea of unblemished rock. I am absorbed, anxious and frozen to the security of my foothold. In ten minutes I haven't moved but I have to commit soon before all commitment evaporates. The slab above me is covered in positive brick edges, I know it is easy, just a game of mental trauma. After twenty minutes I committ to the glassy curbs, my senses alert to every move I make. I join into the final holds of *Cupids Bow* and the closer I move towards the finishing holds my involuntary shaking becomes intolerable as if I had just popped out of a frozen loch.

August 1999:

Light filters through the fly sheet of the tent, I cautiously creep out into the beautiful morning scene, the boulders are radiating heat, the grass is luscious green and the alpine flowers are vibrant with colour. I look up to see the Shelterstone glowing pristinely in the morning sun, the slabs look brazen like a Centurion's shield glistening in bronze. I can feel excitement well up in me – this is the day. Now if only I can get Stork out of his sleeping bag – Storky unlike Sticky isn't a morning person.

It had been crap in 1998 for climbing. It was also the year that Stork had found himself a girlfriend, taken up paddling, took work more seriously and had his bum-tickling locks of hair cut off. So when Stork led the introductory pitch to *Realm* he was faffing.

"Come on," I mumbled, as the Samson and Delilah scenario sprang to mind.

"Stork if you don't hurry up, I will untie the ropes," I called over, laughing at his lack of nerve. On the belay beneath *Realm* I was brimming with confidence, anything less wouldn't be enough for the challenge that lay ahead. This confidence was due to the fact that I had mastered the required sequence of moves while attempting the line a week before with Wilson Moir, my mentor and friend.

The moves along the sickle fitted together with such ergonomic simplicity, I felt I was floating, but once again anxiety makes me take another fall at the end of the hard section, but soon I am back onto normal sized holds. The crux of *Missing Link* passes without thought before latching onto the flake at the base of the *Thor* belay by the skin of my teeth, *Realm* was complete! Stork follows, ties into the belay of decaying iron and lets me get on with the awkward passage of *Thor*. The white streak above the 'peg in the pocket' looks innocuous enough, but it hasn't any holds, attention to detail is called for, dot to dot between clusters of crystals leads to a flat hold, which offers two perfect nuts in opposition. I take a deep breath, pull at the ropes to make sure they are running smoothly, and without hesitation launch up the slab, the flake hold soon disappears, and I have to quickly study the moves required to gain the pocket, I tweak a crystal like a grit pebble and technically shuffle leftwards into the pocket. I am committed now, comfortable in my self-inflicted environment, my adrenaline rushes me through the moves, my feet pop and my wide eyes start to dramatise my inevitable 60ft. fall just as my hands lustfully secure themselves onto a good flat hold, I scrabble into the groove and secure some modest gear. I boldly climb up to reach the final impasse. I can't reach the wire placement that Rick had utilised, years previously – at this moment I feel emotionally drained from the physical and mental duress that the route has exacted from me. In desperation I search for hope, and find an RP placement, I bash at the tiny brass cube with my nut key, pleading for it to seat itself as tears begin to roll out of my eyes. I have difficulty staying calm as I launch out with trepidation to grab the final flake, I scuttle up it dangerously, not stopping or looking down until I reach the turfy finishing ledge, my sentence finally over as I slump on the belay, empty of all emotion.

June 2001:

Since I had repeated all Rick's routes, I was eager to try a new line of my very own on the Shelterstone – a slice of history for myself. My idea was to link up the direct version of *Realm* with a top pitch, following the red streak in its entirety.

I had difficulties with the weather and more so with climbing partners, but as the summer of 2001 arrived, everything was set. I had managed to talk Lawrence Hughes into a trip to the Shelterstone. Lawrence, like Stick and Stork was tall and spindly, yet unlike them he was a young, rampant, red-blooded male, that liked to drive fast, go to all night parties and play music at a billion decibels. I first met Lawrence in the local climbing shop in Aviemore where he was manager. I groomed him with Shelterstone stories and eventually he became keen to accompany me – 'The Judge' – to attempt my line.

My legs start to buckle under the sheer mass of two climbing ropes, climbing gear, a tent, a sleeping bag and food for four days, but it all seems worthwhile when I reach my perfect camping spot down the far edge of Loch Avon, a tight pitch with a beach and a boulder on the edge of the loch, which I term my diving board. I loose my baggage before wandering over to the boulders and acclimatise myself to the nuances of the granite once more. Lawrence turns up in the twilight after work. "How's it going Judge?" Lawrence inquires through the door of the tent in his usual laid-back tone.

"Cool man," I reply, thankful that he has turned up.

"Got something for you to release your stress," as he pokes a couple of girly mags through the porch. We both laugh in hysterics.

The morning is peaceful, the crag glints in the sun's early rays as I dive off my boulder into the cool water of Loch Avon, refreshing myself of all inhibitions. I feel alive and ready.

Once at the foot of the slabs, I foolhardily start climbing directly up the steep wall left of *The Pin,* it is totally devoid of gear, and I find myself in an inescapable position, with no protection and an unknown rounded mantelshelf to complete before the belay. I know I have to commit now, the only other option is to fall 50ft. onto ledges, and smash myself into bits. Lawrence reaches the belay, wide eyed.

"Judge, you mad bastard, that was awesome!" he announces in high praise. I laugh, feeling pleased that my hunch had paid off. We sort the belay and Lawrence pulls out some Mars Bars and cracks open a tin of Red Bull. In a glucose overdose, I climb the *Realm* groove before laying on a frenzied attack on the overlap. The finger holds in the slab above are miniscule, there are no tangible footholds and I am casually spat off, not once but 15 times. Frustration is starting to mount as I try many different sequences, all to little effect. It has to be possible, I did it on a top rope years ago. I tell myself. Reality starts to dawn on me, perhaps it was impossible after all, and I only climbed it on a top rope because the rope was taking half my weight. In defeat, Lawrence climbs *The Pin* – I follow and then have a quick practice, in hope of finding a solution to the overlap, which does materialise.

Lawrence and I were back within the fortnight but, with wet streaks dribbling down the top pitch, we set our sights on *Thor*, the original and most lucid route of all – a diagonal line of diedres that make for a perfect granite experience and the only route I hadn't climbed on the slabs. It was first climbed on aid with bongs, angles, leepers, blades, rurps and even a sneaky bolt – enough steel to sink a battleship. However, when Mike Rennie and Greg Strange reached the end of their adventurous ordeal, I was still only an embryo clawing at the walls of my mother's womb. Today, most of the rust-ridden relics have disappeared, producing a brilliant modern day extreme – tortuous, awkward, forever interesting but never too bold.

Within two days I return my attention to my new line. Back at the overlap, with leg tucked high and hands scratching at crystals, I commit to a heinous move that leaves me stranded on the upper slab feeling like flotsam, alone on the swell of a ruthless ocean. It takes a moment to comprehend my fragile situation, just as spits of rain tinkle down and evaporate on my forehead. With curses mixing with my fears, I focus on my only hope, the hidden slot 15ft. above me. I sketch my way up the damp 6a slab and fix my 00 friend lifeline, at the same time as the clouds release havoc. I hang from the friend, like a freak-child from an umbilical cord, as miniature waves of water ripple their way down the granite-plane.

"Why?" I shout in desperation, as the thought of another failure starts to sink in. In a mad rage, I repeatedly bang my head on the hard granite slab in front of me, shouting "I hate Scotland," over and over again. I then watch my blood drip from my head into the torrents of water and disappear into the void below.

June 2003:

The gods had at last given me a good hand. A fine forecast – the Ace, and Stork, keen to hold my ropes – the King. I was ready to play my hand, and win.

At the overlap, the tension becomes unbearable, the thought of failing floods back through, I have not been on the route for two years, but I have been practicing one-legged squats almost every day in that time, to ensure I have the ability for the next 15 seconds of muscle searing madness. I tear at the blank slab in panic and bewilderment, then wobble my way into the heart of the slab to find my only security in that tiny slot. After regaining a little composure, I tip-toe daintily leftwards into another holdless arena, where faith, hope and keeping cool are my only allies. I relax as I join easier rock, at the crux of *The Missing Link.* My mind then recalls that this section was once my Nemesis, spitting me off three times, those 14 years ago, but today I am glad to have reached the safety of its holds. I spin a web between four rusty relics at the belay and shout down: "Climb when ready," to the ever-patient Stork.

I want to chill, relax and celebrate after success on such a brilliant pitch, but I am only halfway there. I have a super run-out pitch above me to complete first, a pitch that I had inspected on an abseil rope, five years before, but a pitch, which I had never practiced and because of this I feel intimidated by the unknown. Stork follows smoothly until the overlap, where his long spindly legs and bad knee are of absolutely no use; soon he is up on the belay, tangling himself in my uncouth assortment of ropes. I certainly didn't want to leave the web I had spun myself, but words rolled round my head like a tumble drier – it's now or never.

The actual thought of failing after what I had just climbed below spurred me into action. I left Stork dangling in the web and rushed through the awkward section of *Thor* to reach security at the crescent shaped crack, the crucial ring peg reminds me of a bull's nose, I clip it and feel safe. Knowing that this is the last safe place, I step into the crescent-shaped crack, lean my forehead against the rock, close my eyes and take a few inspirational deep breaths before stepping into a selection of pockets that run out. I begin to stare at the steep blank slab in front of me, thinking what a fool I had been to believe that this line was possible. I have no choice other than to commit, so I spend a few minutes dusting all the crystalline curbs with chalk as I try to read a plausible sequence of moves that will work. I curl my fingers round quartz crystals and edge upwards, shuddering all the while. I reach a Thank-God hidden hold, 30ft. above the ring peg, from which I desperately stretch blindly to push in a cam, for this was all I had for a farther 40ft. The red streak was now the line. I cautiously follow its path into the pocket and then it's right edge to a foothold. I stand here for eternity weighing up my mortality, before gazing down the slab to see nothing but two tiny ropes that look like spaghetti – two moves – two moves, I tell myself. They didn't look hard but they were to be the most precise and important moves of my life. Eventually, I smear and dart up into the termination scoop, where the top of the slabs rear up into the vertical. Yet again, I curse myself for not placing a blade peg in the edge-ridden vertical wall, now I feel ridiculous attached to ropes – I may as well be bloody soloing. I secure an RP and reach some holds before moving left and then up onto another slab. I hadn't noticed the clouds swirl in, until I noticed specks of rain making invisible holes in the backs of my chalked hands. I hadn't a piece of gear below me for 100ft. worthy of holding a dead pheasant, so I switch off and rush at the final 6a slab in the drizzle without care. I heave onto the belay and sit on my throne, regal, my mind lost in a world of chaos and aspirations – the *Icon of Lust* set in stone forever.

RAMBLES IN THE ALPS

By Cairns Dickson

I HADN'T been to the Alps in October before and was full of anticipation about my visit to Chamonix. Three days is a pretty short alpine season I suppose, but never mind. The distant snowy white domes were bathed in sunshine as our bus sped through the suburbs of Geneva.

By 1pm. we'd checked out the weather, (good but with a fohn wind on the way) bought some food and were leaving the valley heading for the Argentiere hut. It was so picturesque, I could almost imagine the smell of wood smoke but my early enthusiasm was quickly subdued by the steepness of the path leading to the Refuge de Lognan.

Later, teetering about on moraines and ladders, I knew that despite my assiduous planning my pack was too heavy, and it was dark as we trudged wearily across the glacier spending a happy hour, shuffling around in the snow, trying to find a way into the hut.

The comfort of the winter rooms did not disappoint. We slept in and left the hut at 10.30am. A pathetic alpine start even by my own dismal standards. We picked our way through the moraine and staggered on up to the Milieu Glacier.

Too hot, too tired and too late – I knew even at this early stage that the Aiguille d'Argentiere would not be ours today. We sat down and I allowed my eyes to wander around the awesome circle of peaks that lay before us, so big, so cold and so, so scary. Sitting here, wretched, heaving for breath in this thin and unfamiliar air, it was hardly real, I could scarce believe I'd been on these faces – neither could my companion, Magnus.

So, what had changed since my last visit in 1979? Well sure, I had, not just my flabby and arthritic frame but also my frame of mind. No more the joy of youth, the thrill of unmixed play, the unquenchable drive to succeed, but the measured compromise of experience. Discomforts and dangers weighed against the fear of failure and more frighteningly the fear of missing the pub. Had I spent too much time on the couch in vacant or in pensive mood, allowing icy spires to flit across that inward eye instead of under foot?

And what about the climbers – have we changed? Is Chamonix in summer still heaving with Brits on everything from the *Freney Pillar*, the *Eckpfeiler* and the *Dru Couloir* to the Petit Clocher and the Aiguille d'Argentiere? I doubt it and why should it, new climbers – new games, harder, better? And the mountains themselves, what of them? Summer temperatures and thawing permafrost have brought new dangers and completely removed some icefields. The old sport of summer ice climbing is not as appealing so climbers adapt and develop to face the greater challenges of climbing in winter. And what of these Argentiere peaks, much, much less ice but still the same – immense, austere, brooding in the shadows.

I couldn't climb them now, but what about then? What thoughts still come to mind over the long and twisting decades that separate me from that distant past?

August 1979:

Not a terribly alpine start, even then I'm afraid, left the hut about 9am not that we stayed in the hut, rather too hot I think? Strode with great purpose across the glacier, the face looming ever more menacingly above us. Try not to feel small. The Bergschrund – hmmm! Bad memories from Les Courtes, this one not so bad. Our little hearts flutter as we scuttle rightwards across these enormous crenellations. Desperately steep sides, they were apparently garbage shoots, making one feel uneasy about resting in them. It's not too late I could still go home! Enormous packs (mandatory) and an unending ramp of ice, although not technically difficult, still steep enough to concentrate the mind. We had a long way to go and I suppose it gave us a chance to acclimatise to our new vertiginous world and familiarise ourselves again with our equipment.

We had both spent a busy year doing nothing so we were as rusty as our gear. And what magnificent equipment it was, Joe Brown helmet, Whillans harness, Deadmen, Salewa drive in ice screws (three each!), Moac nuts, Mountain Equipment Snowline duvet, Galibier Terray Fitzroy boots of which I was justly proud, two Terrodactyls – prehistoric ice tools designed to macerate fingers, Chouinard crampons, an ice axe and some slings, all stuffed into a capacious Tiso sack.

The névé on the ramp was superb, hastening our progress. The Salewa drive ins working well, sometimes too well. This was our first day on the face, going fairly smoothly. I look up, Neil's Terrodactyl hammer is flying directly towards me. I'm reminded of another idiot mate whose 'Quick release' crampons were always coming off. Fear for lost tool, fear for myself. Splat, sticks straight in the ice right beside me, I thank the presiding deity. We'd done about 2000ft. of this and felt we had front pointed enough by this time, the steepening rocks of the upper section were assuming gigantic proportions in the failing light. Don't be intimidated! Lovely, a little platform just big enough to sit on, we sat on it and had our tea.

The sun had already dropped behind the Verte, the rock spires of the Chardonnet glowing fiery red in the evening light. The sense of exposure was very grand as we looked down between our boots to the thread like bergschrund and the ripples of the crevasses on the glacier. I was enjoying the peace of the moment that comes after a good days climbing, everything was fine. The moment passes, weather, route finding, the conditions conspire to rob me of my rest. Something else was just starting to tug at my consciousness, I couldn't place it at first then it dawned, I was freezing.

Promptly rearranging my seating I look over to my companion, he was still there. I regale him with pleasant tales of the *Forbes Arete* and its suicidal descent! He had dosed off. The day had gone well, memories of our first encounter flickered through my mind.

February1977:

One last effort that must not fail – he's out. I've made my point, who the hell is he anyway? Dave, my other passenger looked on with disinterested hauteur. Well petrol bills were an issue back then and my Mini 850 used more oil than petrol and it had to be paid for. Neil Harding-Roberts re-entered the car, we continued our journey to Beinn a' Bhuird after our brief altercation in Perth. Well there was no one else. Money, work, resits, he would have to do. We'd survived our first alpine trip and here we are again, happy as can be, 2000ft. done 1000ft. to go. Another late start, very poor.

The climbing was harder now, quite sobering, an awkward pitch leading rightwards beneath a slightly overhanging rock wall led to a nasty little bulge – 100ft. of rope out, nae runners, why am I here? Anyway, that pitch connected us with a series of grooves and chimneys that would take us through the most difficult part of the face. Neil leads on through and up into a steepening groove, disappearing into swirling mist and flurries of spindrift. He was climbing quite well I thought – good choice after all. The next few pitches were similar and needed some care. Sustained steep climbing, well iced up, good belays, favourable conditions, (Scottish 4/5 maybe?). We were starting to feel the altitude a little by now despite our training – a leisurely saunter up the *Gouter Ridge* of Mont Blanc. The mist made our position seem more serious but we had lost the exposure of the ramp. We were so committed by now that there were no decisions to make, just keep climbing.

We were supposed to be on the *Axt Gross* variation, which is to the left of the *Cornuau Davaille* route on the North face of the Droites. I'm pretty sure we were on the Droites but there were so many grooves, chimneys, slabs and couloirs all fitting the guidebook description. The mist was clearing and we were catching some afternoon sunshine which warmed our hearts as well as our bodies. The climbing difficulties had eased a little and we were heading directly for an obvious lentil shaped rock very high up on the face.

I found myself on steepening water ice that was starting to dinner plate. I whapped in my 'terror' hammer and off comes this large scab of ice. I leaned in on it to stop it but it knocked my front points clean off. I was hanging from the wrist loop of my elegant and beautiful 55cm. ash-shafted Chouinard Frost ice axe, the shapely curve of its long pick securely embedded in better ice. Our day could have been spoiled. I recovered hastily and, but for a little more detritus coming his way, Neil seemed unconcerned.

We moved quickly up and round to the left of our lenticular rock, the summit now lay at the end of a long snow cone. Neil opted for a shorter, but quite spectacular, rock pitch to get us directly on to the summit ridge. We pulled on our duvet jackets and settled down for another bivi, the tensions of the day giving way to the delightful and the mundane. Very stupid to have ejected food earlier to reduce weight.

Anxious now about the weather, a much earlier start saw us scramble onto the summit of the East peak of Les Droites (4000m.). We had conquered the useless and set off hastily along the East Ridge towards the Col des Droites. Frustration with our pitiful progress persuaded us to opt for a more direct descent down the East Buttress, abseiling from ice bollards, then on towards the Talefre Glacier inadvertently glissading over a small bergschrund. Our antics had cost us time and it was long dark before we staggered into the Couvercle Hut. The guardian produced some wine, which we absorbed immediately. It was many years later I learned that he had in fact expected us to pay for it.

Magnus, unimpressed with my fitness was now showing signs of impatience and boredom with my story. Fear of this 'Fohn wind' sent us scurrying back to Chamonix and the pleasures of Les Vagabonds.

Our midday departure from the Midi teleferique station was another disgrace, perfect weather and no fohn wind.

We were heading up Mont Blanc du Tacul, but of course, we were too late, I sat down in the snow, my mind wandered back to 1978 and my last visit to this mountain. Neil and I were descending, this serac above us collapsed and...Magnus yawned.

Well maybe another time.

CHANCE ENCOUNTERS IN NORWAY

By Carl J. Schaschke

WE WERE on our way through the Jotenheimen mountains of central Norway, heading for our 20-year anniversary rendezvous on the Romsdalhorn a bit farther to the north. Lasse was behind the wheel of a camper van he had hired. Complete with its foldaway chairs and indoor toilet, the vehicle was not the most conventional mode of transport for a seasoned Norwegian climber. But then conventional is not exactly Lasse's style. Who else fills in his lottery ticket without paying and then sits in front of the national TV show hoping his numbers don't turn up?

"At the end of the programme you haven't won and you haven't lost any money either," he says. Lasse has been around long enough to have seen and done just about everything there is to do in Norway except make a successful ascent of Norway's highest alpine peak– Store Skagastolstind. I've collected a good number of Norwegian peaks in my time too, but not this one either. The mountain is very much the benchmark for all others, and frustratingly, for us both, had remained a dream.

I first met Lasse, 17 years my senior, in 1985 on the Romsdalshorn. Climbing alone one day that July, I chanced upon the Norwegian, also alone. For Lasse, this particular block-shaped mountain, which stands on the other side of the valley from the Troll Wall, had been a family taboo after a relative was avalanched off the lower slopes and seriously injured some years before. Unbeknown to his wife, the unauthorised sneaky visit – which apparently had not been his first – resulted in a great day together and the start of our 20-year friendship. Over the intervening years, and many Norwegian and Scottish mountains, rock climbs, cross-country ski trips and sails around the Norwegian islands later, it was time to return to the Romsdal. Any excuse for a fun time.

Having crossed the high mountain passes, Lasse parked for the night in front of the Turtegro Hotel – a well-known starting point for aspiring ascensionists of the big peak. With roughty-toughty folk milling around outside the hotel, the camper van gave us remarkable invisibility. It reminded me of Billy Connolly's comic sketch about the Glasgow drunk on a bus whose outrageous behaviour is completely ignored by other passengers; the magic of whisky thereby making him invisible. So camper vans (or 'Toilets on Wheels,' as Lasse so elegantly puts it) it seems, are not what climbers drive about in. Lasse may not be conventional but he is wise in his own country. Think of Scottish weather and then multiply by 10. They say that if it's not raining it has just finished or it is just about to start. Camping in Norway can be very miserable indeed. Camper vans are very comfortable and dry.

The old climbers' hotel accidentally burned down in 2001 and was replaced almost immediately by a modern purpose-built climbing centre. The character of Turtegro is much changed but, because of its location, it remains as popular as ever. The new front porch faces out towards the mountain which confusingly (but more conveniently) is also known as Storen. When we arrived, a couple of climbers were sitting outside with a beer – reward indeed for an ascent. What else can possibly justify parting with one's life savings for a glass of øl?

Staring up towards the peak, they ignored Lasse in the immediate foreground busying himself unfolding his chairs and table outside his 'Toilet on Wheels.' Other washed-out blond-haired climbers began to appear as the evening lengthened. The hurdy-gurdy tales of the day's adventures were lost on me. Lasse leaned back nonchalantly in his chair without a care in the world. Not exactly the picture of the master alpinist.

I had been past the old hotel several times in previous years, but only once ever caught the slightest glimpse of Storen. Worse for Lasse, he had actually been to Storen on three separate occasions with a view to climbing it and had once sat at the bottom for a week waiting for the rain to lift. With no joy, he had gone home, like so many others with great expectations, frustrated and disappointed.

Although we had intended only passing by Turtegro, the weather forecast claimed to be reasonable so the deal was done. By 5.30 the next morning we were packed and off up the verdant valley following the milky melt water towards the glacier. We weren't alone. Two teams had beaten us and were already some way ahead. It could have been a trip up to the Ben from the golf course. The pace between the teams quickened, culminating in an outright race to the foot of the mountain. One team eventually veered off up a different route, and we overtook the other that turned out to be a Norwegian Guide and his paying clients. Lasse is no newcomer to powering his way to the bottom of routes in Glencoe and the Guide eventually conceded defeat, passing comment to Lasse as we cut our way past: "Your mate might have the youth but you'll have the experience."

At the strangely striped turquoise glacier, we steered a course away from the crevasses and passed over the years of glacial flow underfoot to the bergschrund. Beyond, signs of vegetation ended and the sterile arctic world above began, relieved by the delicate pink and white flowers of the perennial mountain buttercup *Ranunculus glacialis*. In spite of the forecast, the upper reaches of Storen remained lost in cloud. All we could be certain of was being on the right mountain. The snow-clad lower flanks were beginning to get uncomfortably steep the higher we ascended. The thought of a slip was a bit worrying. I kicked over-sized bucket steps through the crusty snow until we reached the start of the solid rock band, a blessed relief that couldn't have come soon enough. The rock above was reminiscent of Coir' a Ghrunnda. From below, the rocks had appeared small but now, up close, the blocks and cracks belonged in the Land of the Giants. I felt very small.

Cairns Dickson climbing on the Droites North Face in August 1979. Photo: Neil Harding-Roberts.

By good fortune the mist was lifting, slowly unveilling Storen's upper walls. That was a help for our navigation. The guidebook, on the other hand, was not. The Norwegian text didn't make sense and we could make neither head nor tail of the illustrations. The walls appeared massive. Slingsby had impressively made the first ascent of Storen, solo, well over a century before but it wasn't from this side. We cut a diagonal line across the lower face until we could go no farther. This was definitely wrong. So now upwards. Even though we couldn't find any sign of a route, there was evidence that we had not been the first to reach this particular point. Karabiners hung ominously from pegs. We found ourselves on a belay that appeared to have been used as an unscheduled escape route. Stinking evidence of rapid bowel movements suggested it had been an epic.

From nowhere, the Guide magically reappeared some way overhead, minus one of his clients who, apparently intimidated by the shear enormity of Storen, had opted for the relative safety of the glacier below. Lasse and I had traversed too low and been unwittingly overtaken. While the Guide busied himself on 'The Corner' securing his remaining clients, we climbed up to join them. Now on route, we collectively traversed 'The Gallery,' an open ledge high over the Slingsbybreen glacier 2000ft. below. We were in danger of tripping over the Guide and tying ourselves in knots with his clients. I recognised that even by my usual low standards of climbing etiquette, carving past on this occasion was going to be poor form. The Guide could see this, too. In no uncertain terms he made it clear that they were taking the left-hand *Andrews Renne* (AD-) and that our options were either directly above up a deep crack known as *Heftyes Renne* (AD+) or to follow another groove farther to the right. However, dripping melt water from the bottom of this as well as its disappearance from view narrowed the choice down to *Heftyes Renne.*

Launching off the belay proved a bit of a challenge. Before disappearing upwards, the Guide briefly filled us in on the historical details of the first ascent. In time-honoured tradition, Heftye himself had apparently stood on the shoulders of his companion to gain access into the crack. Forget the rock ballet, this was down to pure unadulterated brute force and ignorance. It was a desperate scuffle into the crack and a fumble to clip into a peg embedded some way overhead. Squirming farther into the crack, the pack on my back restricted mobility in a way not dissimilar to the upper section of *Sassenach.* God, how I wish I'd left it behind at the bottom as the Guide had done. Smart guy.

Popping out of the crack above to belay, I was now in a position too high to see down below or to communicate with Lasse. I tugged on the rope a couple of times. I could feel movement as my friend sorted himself out below, then suddenly I was drawing in the rope, he was on his way up. He had watched the inelegant thrutching and reckoned that he would have to perform the move spontaneously or face the prospect of perhaps never getting off the belay (or so he claimed.)

Jason Currie climbing on Coire Ghranda Upper Cliff. Guy Robertson.

Some more rope lengths led to the summit – a clean sweep of granite of humongous proportions. There we rejoined the Guide and his clients. By chance, the third team appeared from Mohs Scar over the other side of the mountain. From my pack, I offered Lasse a dram of Scotland's finest to celebrate but he barely condensed the vapours in his nostrils.

"We have only done half the job, Carl," he wisely reminded me. Straddling the summit block, the views over the Jotenheimen were magnificent. Our heads were clear.

With the thought of that shitty belay down below fresh in my mind, the escape was something I wasn't particularly relishing. Like a roll-on, roll-off ferry, the team that arrived last left first followed by the Guide and his team, and then us. I was beginning to appreciate the fact that the Guide knew the mountain like the back of his hand and that keeping behind him might have its advantages.

About 100m. or so below the summit he nipped off around an innocuous looking corner. Lasse and I tagged along behind to find him with a jumble of multi-coloured slings hung around a block. We would never have found this abseil point in a million years. Threading the rope through one of the *in-situ* steel karabiners, we all descended. I was chuffed that I'd brought a 60m. rope. It was plumb vertical downwards. We used all of it. More abseils followed until we were back at the edge of the snowline. Making our way to the top of the bucket steps I'd kicked earlier, we descended down to the glacier. Then, safely away from the reaches of Storen, we quaffed the whisky. Looking back up I still couldn't fit the guidebook's topo to the rock that lay in front of us. Our heads were no longer clear.

A few days later, Lasse and I were on the top of the Romsdalhorn, this time having carved our way past a Swedish team on the North Face. It was yet another great outing in the hills with Lasse. For 2005, the Romsdalhorn was always going to be the reality but Store Skagastolstind? Well, that was the dream come true.

THE LAUGHTER OF THE BIRDS

By P. J. Biggar

MAC raised himself and looked out of the window but the hillsides were obscured by low cloud and it was starting to drizzle. He remembered casting for sea trout in the river and lying out in the early morning sun on the green sward. Harvey was snoring peacefully. He was a couple of days into his holiday and starting to look less haggard. At breakfast time it was raining properly. Mac rigged up a can under the downspout and they had no need to go to the river for water.

Camasunary was full of shoreline creatures, French, Dutch, German – Mac particularly liked the Spanish waiters with their guitars and flutes. He cooked a large breakfast and sat in a rickety chair with his feet on an old orange box watching the weather. Away out on the grey sea a bright line was forming under the clouds. In mysterious gaps torn by the jagged rocks the Island of Rum took shape. Harvey moved purposefully from one pile of gear to another. "We should be able to go out about two," Mac said.

They forded the river in warm sunlight. Mac had chosen his old green boots and almost at once he felt the left heel start to rub. The tide was out and the beach by Loch na Cuilce was a gleaming field of bladder-wrack, by going over it they could avoid the awkward slabs on the hillside. Mac forged ahead and slipped, his feet shot into the air and his head narrowly missed a large rock. "That was close," said Harvey and turned up the hill.

At the highest trickle on Garbh Bheinn they filled their water bottles. Mac recalled doing that with Mike back in 1988. Big climbing days left a bookmark in the year. Now the reflection in the pool had grey hair. The hill had changed too – it was getting steeper. Then Harvey, who was already ahead, made one of his blunders. The way seemed so obvious to Mac, avoid the slippery slab by the easy crack on the right. Why make things difficult?

"Och Harvey," he yelled in amused frustration, "They will be calling you Mr Harvey of the Slabs!"

Harvey said nothing for the next few minutes while he extricated himself. He always did, at least he always had. Mac remembered a *cul-de-sac* on Tower Ridge and gleaming ice-sheets in Coir'a'Ghrunnda. He never seemed to learn, but indignation was vain. Every companion had some niggling defect, the trick was to live with it.

Silently, they surveyed the great sea-serpent uncoiling towards Sligachan. Harvey got ahead again. Mac could feel his heel rubbing. He manoeuvred up the huge rough blocks of Sgurr Dubh an Da Bheinn. Light evening cloud was drifting around sharp teeth which came and vanished like ghosts. Mac wondered if he should have brought his sticks, but the ground was too difficult. His hands were starting to feel the sharpness of the gabbro.

Harvey stood by the cairn, he looked slightly chilled. He spent a lot of time nowadays waiting for Mac. The night's rain had left pools. They siphoned enough water to cook their dinner.

"Mike's trick," said Mac, "Works a treat."

He leant back comfortably against the slab while the little stove hissed under the pan. Pink vapour clung about Sgurr Alasdair high above them and swirled across their vision of Rum far out to sea. From where he lay among the rocks, Mac looked up towards the rocks of the Thearlaich-Dubh Gap. His attention was caught by two little figures. As the mists cleared for a moment he could see them quite clearly but there was something odd about them, although he couldn't quite say what, and yet they were moving well. Mac thought he heard them shout with delight as they vanished upwards. The mists moved over the peaks again obscuring everything.

He turned to Harvey: "Did you see those guys up there?" "No Mac, when?"

"Just now."

Harvey started violently as their quiet conversation was shattered by a hideous burst of mocking laughter.

"Lord, Mac it sounds like fiends in the air!"

But Mac, recovered from his own shock, knew the answer.

"Birds Harve, birds. They nest high up on Rum. Always make that bloody racket when they come back to their burrows, so I'm told. Manx Sheerwaters."

He laughed: "No wonder the Vikings called that hill Trollval eh! I didn't know they nested here as well. We're privileged to hear that. Talking of Rum," he continued, "D'you remember that wee plastic bottle I had in the Alps? I think I've got it here somewhere."

Working in the construction industry, Harvey never had trouble sleeping. Now, despite sharp stones and the biting of the midges, Mac heard his breathing turn into the familiar snore. He smiled to himself in the dark.

"Now Mac," he quoted the familiar words, "If I should start to snore, you be sure to give me a good nudge."

To which he always replied: "You know I like to hear you snoring, makes me feel comfortable."

How long had they been climbing together?

Mac himself was far from sleep. The chill of the night was creeping down and the thought of the Gap made him apprehensive. Late on a June evening more than 30 years ago he had learned to abseil there. Youth! Adventure! It had all passed in a blur of effort and they had been up and away to King's Chimney, the Pinnacle and a few hours sleep on Beinn Dearg. Mac wriggled farther down into his plastic bag.

And 15 years ago it had started to rain as Mike was leading. Two English climbers had arrived just as he was setting off. A top rope had been requested. Mac remembered the relief when he got his boot into the crack, pressed up and gained a decent hold above. Jim had come up well but Linda had had a slippery struggle as the rain got worse. They had all ended up in a dripping cave on Sgurr Sgumain.

Mike reckoned Jim and Linda weren't married – "... much too fond of each other."

They'd cooked Pitta bread and sardines with a blowlamp and heated water in an old enamel mug. Mac remembered the revelation of the morning as black peaks rose through an ocean of cloud, but that was then.

Like polished pewter the north wall of the real Gap rose before their eyes, its rocks cold and damp under their fingers.

"Don't feel you have to," Mac shouted.

"I don't think I can come back!" shouted Harvey, teetering on the crux. Mac gazed at the yellow lichen on the jagged boulders and held the rope. At long last it came tight. Mac lurched forward. He hadn't remembered it being this hard! Every move took every scrap of energy. With gasps and grunts he hauled himself over the final lip.

Harvey grinned: "I couldn't have gone back and told Proudfoot we'd failed there." (Proudfoot was the club super-hero, he'd done everything.)

"I couldn't have led that Harve," said Mac. He looked at his friend with added respect, he was fast outstripping him.

In ecstasies they climbed Thearlaich and Alasdair and then delighted in the spiral staircase leading to Collie's Ledge. While they sauntered across, the day started to turn towards heat. On the brown slabs of An Stac the heat really struck them. Harvey got well ahead. Mac's boot was chaffing his heel into soreness.

He needed rest. "I have a plan," he said.

Mac sat by the cairn while Harvey climbed the Pinnacle alone. Mac photographed him abseiling. They took water and food and went on. The day grew hotter. The charcoal of the Bannachdich ridge slow-cooked them.

Mac knew that Harvey must have been waiting for half-an-hour when he got to the summit. He slumped heavily beside the cairn. His legs were tired, his hands were raw, his left heel was badly rubbed. He had reached a decision. Harvey knew him better than to argue and they divided the food and water. Mac watched him out of sight before turning away and beginning to retrace his steps along the dusty flanking paths.

Mac was alone on vast, loose, stony slopes and the winding mirage of the river never seemed to come closer. Everything seemed to be in motion as he descended. He noticed that Time itself was going faster, for whenever he looked at his watch it was an hour and a half later. He dislodged a huge boulder which smashed into bits with a whiff of cordite. Farther down, he fell and cut his hand. The effort of getting plasters from his pack was too great and bright drops of blood spattered on the rocks and stained his dirty trousers.

Down in the valley, the heat became intense and scree gave way to delusive sheep tracks amongst bog-myrtle scrub. Time accelerated even more, but at last Mac lay in meadows among clear springs, greedily drinking the cold water. At length he came to a blue river pool flowing over white rocks. He took off all his sweat soaked clothes and edged into the water. He lay for a long time as the current washed him gently round and round while his swollen toes traced patterns on the jagged peaks. He hoped Harvey had made it. He was sure he would have, he really deserved to. He needed a younger fitter partner. Maybe Proudfoot was the man? But he was in the Alps as usual.

Mac remembered finishing the Ridge himself. Screw top bottles of pale-ale at Sligachan and the Election result crackling over the radio in the tent at Glen Brittle – Heath for Wilson – then, years later, the smell of flowers as he and Mike came down from Gillean.

On the slabs near the stepping stones Mac had to stop to lie down. The path along the coast, which they had hardly noticed yesterday, went on and on forever. Just as he came in sight of the white walls of Camasunary a smir of rain brought out the midges, but try as he might Mac found he could not hurry. As he approached the building he could hear music, even the sound of castanets.

Harvey lay in his bag in the little back room. Mac stirred him gently. "Did you make it?" but he hadn't. After all their efforts, the heat had sucked him dry and he had quit the ridge at Bidein.

"I'll bet you didn't drink enough," said Mac covering the guilt he felt.

"Maybe not," said Harvey ruefully. "To tell the truth Mac, I was a bit worried about finding my way back here in the dark."

Mac shook his head and busied himself with the stove. The laughter of the birds had foretold something after all. He opened the wine.

As food and drink revived him, Harvey began to talk. "You know you thought you saw some guys ahead of us at the Gap?" Mac nodded. "Well, just as I got near the end I think I saw them."

"What were they like?"

"There was a little guy who seemed to be in the front most of the time, then the other bloke was taller. Funny old gear they had, Mac – breeches and old rucksacks and that. I tried to catch them up. I must've been pretty tired by that time, but know what? I couldn't get anywhere near them. I couldn't get a right look at them either – even though it was clear and sunny. They kept vanishing among the rocks. I reckon they must have finished the Ridge some time ago."

Mac nodded thoughtfully as he poured more wine.

"I think you're right," he said. In his mind's eye he could see them climbing past the Gendarme and whooping their way over the moor as the rain started to fall. Down the corridor the Spanish waiters played a slow and rhythmical refrain.

FINAL DESTINATION

By Guy Robertson

THE two of them sit there, all hot air and comfy. Like a brace of stubborn pupae, they try to ignore the inevitable metamorphosis that will eventually extricate them from the car. Straight off the back of a long working week, and four hours of warm stasis is about to crumple under the staggering load of two overnight winter packs. Their task is substantial – two hours to camp, at least – and the lateness of the hour induces sleepy second-thoughts into their lazy minds. But there's no escaping it.

Four burning legs power down big-booted on four tiny pedals, the first steepening of the track melting slowly into darkness behind them. Sweaty uphill first-gear grunts and twitchy front wheels, torch beams dancing under monstrous loads. They slither out-of-control through icy puddle glitches, rectified only by more effort and downward momentum. And then, in a jolt, the unthinkable arrests them, their jaws dropped slack like a pair of wooden puppets. A mighty Gulf Stream fist has driven unchallenged across the great stand of pines through which they toil. And now, up ahead, great wooden bastions lay slain and slaughtered across their way, all twisted and crumpled, 5m. deep in all directions. And more, the moss of damp on dead bark has cunningly frozen to sheath each calloused carcass in a slippery veneer. At once their wheels are rendered useless – crampons may well be required.

A few tentative probes at the main massif are convincingly rejected. Each stepped branch may be a ladder, but each hulk of trunk is an icy snake-back, creeping up, across, then down and sideways, this way and that, always onwards and somewhere, but never forward. The stumbling, prickled pair soon wearily retreat to diverge and meander through unknown, but at least, less precipitous outliers. Their rapid, wheel-assisted approach is presently transformed into a complex and demanding approach of energy-sapping proportions.

Once through; moonlight, stillness, and the hot slow steam of frosted breath. No more dead trees to wrestle. A clear path ahead and at last two clear minds. The West Buttress stands guard like a million miles away or more, its 1000ft. of cracked rock and turf and ice made small by the trick of Midwinter's dim. And so they crunch on, a second start, through a fresh frozen carpet of snow, towards an uncertain destination, finally.

Tented and togged up, cocooned in feathers and fibres and fabrics, the two of them soon lie silent in wait of dreams. Legs still throb from the endless march. The tent skin flaps briskly in a gathering breeze, and one of the two ponders the undeniable advantages of not being born a ptarmigan. A few words of quiet optimism are exchanged passively, before the slight touch of snowflakes tickles falling minds off to sleep.

Nokia bleeps, the repetitive strain. A quiet, but sufficiently, insidious and narking irritant that ensures that both parties are infected with a blurred awareness. First things first – coffee *in-situ* or straight up and at it? A turgid bladder makes one decision, while the other is forced shortly after, through a combination of guilt, and paranoia that time is warping against them. For the Clock – as ever – ticks loudly in the silence.

Back to the future again, and the dull memories of sleep evaporate in the sudden heat of an uphill stomp. With monotonous whiteness once more they engage, as a biting easterly swells up and tears away any chance of conversation. Two little flecks of silent torch light edge forward on the map, each hosting its own little hooded world of hopes, fears and dreams. Step, step, step, crunch! Stop, leg out, breathe, step, step, step, crunch! Stop, leg out, step, step, crunch! Partners in purgatory, taking it in turns, but it won't last forever.

The angle relents and they scuttle now, relieved and wind-assisted over ice-scoured flats towards the col. And there they sit, crouched in the drifting lee of the ancient dyke, gorging snappy, crunching, chewy bars and salt-sugar drinks. A strong grainy wind whips the air with a sharp bite and few words are spoken. And then, right there, straight above, a window is opened, the thick morning clouds are cleaved into blue, and two hearts start to pound. Some more and then more and then more is revealed, unfolding in great sweeps from sky down to loch. Cold and unmentioned apprehension is replaced with sharp excitement in the tight snap of a krab. To their right, and across, their Buttress emerges slowly, glistening and festooned with great icy shards. A dragon in waiting. Decisions are made and minds are prepared and weapons are drawn. They move off together, spitting hope into the wind, two hot-faced jangling fools with spikes and cranked-up boots. The clock ticks louder still.

Side-stepping carefully out and down and left, one of the pair now scans the wall – a great icy canvas, devoid of art. His eye traces keenly up, through familiar territories, to a previous impasse where it all ran out. The undisputed blankness that black schist often presents. Dwelling briefly on that point of return, of sure and sudden failure, he shrinks back quickly from memories of defeat. Tracing left now, across and away back down, he finds a subtle snow cone flirting with sheer rock; a weakness, a quick decision, and a flicker of his fire.

The ropes are unleashed at the base of the line, and the signs are good. A cooperative fault quite bristles with vegetation, slanting left to a bulge, from where a line of tenuous icy tears weeps back across right. And so on into a groove, it would seem, and the start of a battle unknown. A quick knuckle-numbing punch up the fault yields blood to the bones, then a sinker belay, and the second man soon flights up behind to kick out his place.

Into the fray now, teetering out on the tears, to where a searching grope right for the groove is rewarded with a pick in a crack. Both feet swing in tandem to settle on creases, and the unknown groove is now shedding some light. Nuts tumble from the rack like coins from a slot machine. A thin seam yields a high torque on the left wall, for a high step up with the right foot, then the same again, rocking over, to both picks in good turf. A scrabble, a puff and a manteling heave, and the turf sits solidly under his crampons.

Above is a corner – smooth, black and steep. There's no hint there of turfy goodness, and there's no faint slot for a pick to keep. So he swings back out left, blindly, popping up onto the crest, to where an eyrie and dragging ropes force out a second stance. Good cracks, good belay, and some good progress for sure. Safe? – Enough, at least, to stave off the ridicule of the bulging wall barring access above. This is steadfastly ignored, as coils of rope are rushed in, and the shivering second is yanked from his bubble to hack and claw his stiffened limbs up the groove to the stance.

Their words of uncertainty are brief and in agreement; they are only mild in hope. Our second now leads through, from defence to attack, struggling with the sudden shock of the transformation. Soon he's 10ft. or so up, axes dangling hopelessly from his wrists, spread-eagled, underclung it seems on verglas, and looking quite the limpet. With nothing stopping him below, their stance becomes a target, a human bullseye. The belayer concentrates intensely, hounding every twitchy move, surely wishing he was leading and out of the firing line. But the limpet sticks, and slithers haltingly upward, nothing breaking the shared apprehension but the frightened, lurching gasps of his frozen breath. Until a pick is thrown suddenly, repeatedly, and with conviction overhead. C'mon! C'mon! C'mon ya bastard! The pick finds a slot.

Several great gasping puffs, and an all-or-nothing heave confines their 'impassable wall' to the history books – for now at any rate. Watch me here! Not hard, but bugger all gear! No worries, it'll save some time, and it's running out for sure. A quick snack. Stomping feet and bouncing shoulders, as the rope feeds quickly out and the second's eyes gaze out into the murk, questioning the depth of the grey, and the lateness of the hour. Then the ropes go slack. Aye, slack, take some in then. What? But that's no…WHAAHOOOOAAAAAYYAAAA! The Banshee howl booms heavily round the bowels of the Coire, both the ropes are struck tight, and there's metal clashing metal. Delayed impact….WHHHHHHHUUUMP! Jeeezus man, you OK?! Oh man, oh man, I don't know, I think so, give me a minute. Any blood? When does falling become flying?

The clock's tick now echoes tangibly, such is the hour, and the white murk is turning brown towards the sunset. At this, the third stance, their prospect is undoubtedly the grimmest yet. Any weakness above is reliably short-lived, and not a line to take seems logical in any way. The grooves all fade to walls, all the walls are capped by bulges, and there's no glinting crack to catch the eye. But with battered pride set aside with such stalwart valour below, who would they be to shy away now? Take a look at least man, take a look. So he looks, and he looks, and he looks again. Each time he probes tentatively higher, each time he is more committed, and each time the intensity of his awareness of that commitment grows, until he knows; there's no going back. A move up on more frozen moss than turf, with no bite for crampons, arms locked at the elbows and feet smearing an uncertain balance on the smooth blank shist. Protection still eludes him, and his need becomes acute. The leader must not fall. Fate hangs like a guillotine, sharp and taught around him, as his moves become more frequent, more sure, but less cognitive. It's climbing by instinct. The belayer stares silent at the clean sweep of the rope, momentarily punctuated by a solitary peg, tied off and tokenistic.

The first bulge is beaten trending left under the worst of it, the second succumbs to a more head on approach, cranking hard towards the sanctuary of what appears to be a decent crack at last, praying for mercy. And brief mercy there is, in the form of a nut, but the crack turns blind and forces wild swings out right, crampons all smearing again until a tiny spike accepts a sling. Then right again, and down. Down? He realizes now that there is no line, only the desperate and chaotic clamberings of a man who seeks escape. And there, at last, it appears, out of nowhere – a slim groove laced with ice. Once more the cracks all disappear but it doesn't seem to matter; there's a way out up ahead, and the trimmings of ice and turf have returned sure grip to both feet. Head down, into high gear, engage the exit ramps, and they're out of there.

Staring out into the giddying, amorphous expanse of a winter's dusk up high, he feels the clammy cool of relief on frosted cheeks. The *Final Destination*. It's over, and he knows it, but he's spent of any passion. Sleep whispers in his ears as he slowly heaves the ropes. Real Life is a galaxy away – driving cars, tapping keyboards, drinking beer, sitting on sofas, watching telly. For a while up there it's just hot blood and wind and grey space and frozen ropes, until the faint jangle of the second becomes louder from below. And then the two are united, slapping backs and shaking hands, sorting the compass, the map and the who-goes-first as the slow grind down dawns wearily upon them.

The two of them sit there, all damp but comfy. Like two fat cats by the fire they embrace the car's warmth and settle in for their journey. Straight off the back of a 16-hour epic, four hours of food, music and warm stasis beckons them homeward. Their task is substantial – three hours to bed, at least – but the rich zest of their experience fires crazy ambitions and new dreams across their lazy minds. They'll be back for more, there's no escaping it.

This article relates to the first ascent of the unclimbed wall left of *Ice Bomb* in Coire Grandha on Beinn Dearg, near Ullapool. The route was climbed in January 2005, and was named *Final Destination* (VIII,7).

NEW CLIMBS SECTION

Corrections and comments on descriptions and diagrams in the new Scottish Rock Climbs guidebook are to be found on the SMC web site at: http://www.smc.org.uk/books/books_scottish_rockclimbs.htm. Opinions on grades are not necessarily in the majority as opinions were collected in preparation of the book and these are not reproduced. Further corrections and comments are welcome to anisbe@globalnet.co.uk.

OUTER ISLES

LEWIS, AIRD MHOR BHRAGAIR, Arch Wall:
Sea an Enema 20m E2 5c *. G.Latter. 10th August 2005.
The overhanging right-slanting crack above the right end of the upper ledge (left of Children of the Sea).

Lagoon Wall:
Sleight of Hand 20m E1 5b *. G. & K.Latter. 10th August 2005.
The shallow hanging groove in the centre of the wall. Start up a short left-slanting crack, then the groove, finishing up an easy short crack above a ledge at the top.

UIG SEA CLIFFS, AIRD UIG AREA, Screaming Geo:
Whirlwind 20m E8 6c **. D.MacLeod. 6th May 2005.
The 'YY unclimbed crack' shown in the crag topo in the guide. The first section of crack up to the horizontal is serious with poor gear and snappy holds. Above, the climbing gets steadily harder towards the top but better protected, culminating in a tricky crux right at the top. F8a climbing and awesomely exposed. FA headpointed.

SANDRAY, The Galleries:
The Galleries are situated at a geo on the south-west coast of Sandray (NL 635 909). There are three main walls described from the north. The Tait Gallery is the first tapering wall with many short routes. The Burrel Gallery is the next wall, reached by walking past the Tait. The back wall gains more height and is tidal towards the right side, where an inlet separates it from La Louvre. La Louvre is reached by descending to the south.

Tait Gallery:
Art Deco 15m E2 5b. G.Lennox, K.Howett, G.Little. 1st May 1999.
Climb a groove to a roof below a flaky crack. Move right round the roof and back left to finish up the flaky crack.

Art Nouveau 15m E3 5b. G.Lennox, K.Howett, G.Little. 1st May 1999.
Climb to the small roof left of Art Deco. A thin crack on the right provides runners for moves up left to a good quartz jug. Finish straight up.

Clean Sheet 15m VS 4c. G.Lennox, K.Howett. 5th May 1999.
Climbs the wall right of the corner, moving out near the arête.

Burrel Gallery:

Finger Painting 15m E3 5c *. G. Lennox, K. Howett, G. Little. 2nd May 1999.
Climbs a short wall at the left end of the back wall. From the block ledge follow breaks up rightwards and make tentative moves up square edges.

Muscular Art 25m E6 6b ***. G.Lennox, K.Howett. 4th May 1999.
This spectacular route climbs up the largest section of the continuously overhanging back wall. Start where the lip of the cave is closest to the slab. Hard moves lead to a flared crack. This is climbed to a juggy ledge in the centre of the wall. Move out left and up to jugs. Climb up right passing a rounded edge and finish straight up.

Pastiche 35m E5 ** K.Howett, G.Lennox. 6th May 1999.
Abseil nutting in to gain the a small ledge towards the right edge of the back wall.
1. 15m 6a. Climb up left using breaks to gain the open groove above.
2. 20m 6a. Follow ledges rightwards to the arête. Climb this and then the right wall on big holds.

La Louvre:

Tormented Textures 20m E4 5c ***. G.Lennox, K.Howett. 2nd May 1999.
Climb up the rounded grey wall, following a crack which becomes a corner before the roof. Pull over the roof and climb the orange wall above.

Creag Mhor:

Creag Mhor is a long cliff on the west side of the south-west tip of the island (NL 639 903). The routes described are situated towards the north end of this cliff, where the rock is cleaner. The first routes are approached by descending slabs from the north which run round the base of the cliff. Farther south the routes must be approached by abseil. The crag reaches only approximately 50m above the sea, but many of the routes involve significant amounts of traversing to turn the many roofs and overhangs. The following three routes are situated on the initial wall above the descent slabs, before the start of the huge cave.

Creag's Big Break 25m E3 5c **. C.Adam, G.Lennox. 25th July 2005.
Start right of the blocky corner at the far left of the wall. Gain the obvious break and climb this almost to its end before pulling up rightwards across to and up a right-facing corner. (Think this route was climbed previously by Kev Howett).

Nurse Ratchitt 13m E4 6b *. C.Adam, G.Lennox. 25th July 2005.
Start as for Creag's Big Break to gain the start of the break. Layback up to holds leading left, then traverse right to a flake hold (crux). Climb up to the block and gain the ledge above. Finish straight up.

Trap Door 15m E6 6a/b **. C.Adam, G.Lennox. 25th July 2005.
Climbs directly to Creag's Big Break, then finishes straight up the wall above. Start at a small right-facing corner and up on layaways with poor RPs on the right. Move up and right to more layaways and make committing balancy moves to gain the break (serious). Pull straight up to obvious jugs and follow the faint groove above with more balancy moves to a slight niche. Make a difficult move up and left to a good flat hold and pull through the short V-corner to finish (very run out).

Crowbar Corner 20m E1 5b **. C.Adam, G.Lennox. 31st July 2005.
Climbs a black corner above the big cave. Abseil down to the hanging ledges. Traverse left, move diagonally left up a short wall to gain the black corner and finish up this passing some rattling flakes.

Central Reservations 20m E1 5b *. C.Adam, G.Lennox. 26th July 2005.
Abseil down the central fault, nutting in to a birdy ledge. Climb a wide crack above the ledge and continue steeply up the fault on huge holds.

Tangoed 30m E5 6b ***. G.Lennox, C.Adam. 26th July 2005.
Abseil down the central fault, but continue to a semi-hanging stance above the lower overhangs. Climb up the fault and out to a spike on the left. Move up and left passing cracks through a black band to a shake-out flake in the centre of the wall. Climb up to the overlap and cross it rightwards to below another small overlap (crux). Turn the small overlap on the left and finish straight up.

Pissin' in the Wind 30m E4 6a ***. G.Lennox, C.Adam. 30th July 2005.
Follow Tangoed to the black band, then traverse left to the juggy ledges at the left arête. Move up and right to gain the thin cracks in the leaning headwall (crux). Finish up these.

The Don Mac Highway 30m E4 ***. C.Adam, G.Lennox. 27th July 2005.
Abseil down the central fault to the semi-hanging stance as for Tangoed.
1. 20m 6a. Climb the fault swinging out left to a large flake. Sling the flake and traverse horizontally left with difficulty and continue boldly to a good square jug. Step down to foot holds at the lip of the roof. Move left to gain a thin crack and climb this with difficulty to gain better holds. Continue up round the arête to a stance.
2. 10m 5c. Climb the bulging crack above.

Orangoutang 55m E6 **** G.Lennox, C.Adam. 27th July 2005.
Abseil down the main corner right of the southerly orange wall, nut in at the big slab and continue down to lower ledges (the abseil is 50m if rigged close to the edge, but a buried rock well back gives the best anchor).
1. 10m 5b. Traverse left along breaks for 10m to gain a semi-hanging stance at foot ledges.
2. 25m 6b. Take a rising leftwards fault heading towards an obvious block. Swing round this and continue in the same line to a second block and do the same. Move left and up to the main roof and climb through this rightwards. Pull through on the incredibly formed rock and climb up the birdy ledge of Central Reservations. A wildly steep pitch.
3. 20m 5c. Cut across the steep fault to a square roof, turn this on the left and continue up a steep groove at the right edge of the north orange wall.

The Gift 30m E5 6a ***. G.Lennox, C.Adam. 30th July 2005.
Abseil down the main corner and belay at the left end of the ledge. Traverse out left onto the south orange wall, then up to gain sloping ledges. Move up left to a line of edges. Follow these until they peter out. Make a move out right to a quartz hold and climb up to a pocket. Trend left to flakes, and finish more easily up to follow the huge break left.

One Flew Over The Kittiwake's Nest 55m E5 *. C.Adam, G.Lennox. 29th July 2005.
An adventurous line weaving through the enormous roofs right of the main corner. Abseil down the main corner to the big birdy slab.
1. 20m 5b. Scramble up right across the birdy slab to a ledge and climb the break back left across the first roof. Move up to a stance.
2. 20m 5c. Traverse the grey wall rightwards to jugs on the arête where the roof above recedes. Climb up steeply to belay at a short corner in the black rock band, below the final capping roof (more belay anchors can be found in the harder yellow rock up right).
3. 15m 6b. Traverse left with increasing difficulty along a narrowing corridor, in an incredible situation, until the capping roof is passed.

MINGULAY, Trevor's Hole:
(NL 573 848) Alt. 40m SE-facing
A small sheltered cave which is a real suntrap, at the right end of a terrace.
Approach: Continue north along the coast past Haunted Geo, to scramble down the left end of a small band of crags to gain a terrace leading north to the base. 45mins from the beach.

Liposuction 20m E5 6a **. T.Wood, G.Latter. 11th June 2005.
The prominent left-rising crack along the lip of the cave. Move in from the right using a dubious pegmatite lump to gain good flakes. Continue into the niche and some gear. "You should have shed a few pounds by now." Continue traversing to gain easier ground, then step left round the arête and finish direct on good holds. Descend by traversing off left.

PABBAY, Pink Wall:
Huffin' 'n' Puffin 75m E6 ***. T.Wood, G.Latter. 5th June 2005.
Another excellent sustained main pitch.
1. 30m 6b. Start up a short crack between The Bonxie and I Suppose a Cormorant's Out of the Question, Then? Climb the crack to a break, stand on this and reach a small flake. Make hard moves up the wall to reach another flake, then trend left following flakes. Atop the second flake/plinth, make hard moves up a shield to a break. Traverse left to the original hanging belay on The Bonxie.
2. 45m 6b. Follow The Bonxie until the jugs after the undercuts. Then direct through a black niche and bulges until below an obvious weakness. Pull through this on slopey holds (crux) and continue more easily to top.

Note: The Bonxie was climbed several times omitting the hanging belay at 25m, to give a superb sustained 35m pitch. First climbed this way by P.Thorburn and R.Campbell in June 2005. The grade remains at E6 6b,5c.

Guarsay Mor – The Undercut Wall
Between The South Pillar and Cobweb Wall, just left of the latter, is an impressive undercut wall, capped by a band of large roofs at the top, with a convenient non-tidal shelf at its base. Bird Restrictions. Routes at the left side are unaffected by birds, though the centre is heavily birded; avoid May to August.

Note: Rayburnt, E4 6a,6a,5b *** and Burning Desire, E5 5c,6b,5c,6a. Both take lines up this wall, the former starting up the fantastic right-facing corner bounding the left side, though the whereabouts of *Burning Desire* are still unknown, as the routes have never been formally recorded.

Descent: Make a 100m abseil, from a good block in a recess about 40m south of The South Pillar abseil point (in line with a smaller white stone 50m back from the edge), to gain the centre of the shelf at the base.

Taking the Hump 135m E5 6a ***. T.Wood, G.Latter. 10th June 2005.
A line breaching the centre of the wall, spectacularly breaking through the capping roofs.
1. 35m 6a. Climb a prominent right-facing capped groove. Break out right at a roof and continue up to a prominent horizontal break. Move up left through bulges and continue to a good ledge.
2. 35m 5c. Continue straight up to the first small roof, move right and follow a rising right-trending line to a commodious ledge.
3. 30m 5b. Continue right along the ledge until a weakness in the bulging wall. Climb this then move right to a block belay on a ledge below roofs.
4. 35m 6a. Pull through the roof using a quartz rail clump, then follow crazy runnels to a second roof. A long stretch reaches good holds. Continue to a third roof which is surmounted via a diagonal left-trending crack. Traverse right along an easy break (birdy!) under final large capping roofs past a lichenous yellow hanging corner. Climb a groove right of this on good holds to the top.

Banded Geo:
Treasure Island Mild VS 4b. J.Preston, G.Ettle. 7th June 2004.
Start midway between Silver Fox and Grey Cossack, below a small roof. Climb a black slabby wall to the roof (a ragged crack on the left). Pass the roof on the right and continue up to a superb flake-crack which is followed to the top.

RUM, Barkeval, South Crags:
Note: D.F.Lang and D.Guild climbed Broad Buttress from bottom right to top left, with a Severe exit up a slightly overhanging crack. The length was 150m not 120m as in the guidebook.

Slab of Tranquillity 130m Severe. D.F.Lang, D.Guild. 14th May 2005.
Descend an open grassy gully to the east of Honeycomb Arête and Aficionado to arrive at the base of an area of slabs.
1. 45m. Ascend a raised red coloured slab (with lower dark slabs either side). Climb directly to a triangular niche.
2. 35m. Exit the niche on the left and ascend a fault-line for 4m until able to gain the right-hand fault-line which is ascended passing two largish blocks. Go up a steeper groove, move left and up to large ledge with a conspicuous block at its extremity.
3. 50m. Continue scrappily to cross a grassy rake, ascend a prow and continue to finish near the top of Honeycomb Arête.

MULL, Port Langamull:
Take the B8073 west from Dervaig for about 5km. At a left-hand bend take a dirt road right (Forestry Commission signed) into the forest for approx. 2km. Go through a gate to a small parking area on the right just before a building at

Langamull. Walk left down a track through three gates to the beach (10-15mins). Head north-east over a wide sandy area across a stream draining into the sea and over towards a small cliff-line that becomes visible. Head to a very large black rock in the sea. The climbs begin on the cliff behind this rock.

Buttongrass Crack 12m VS 4a. D.Eckstein, J.Croft. 1st September 2003.
Climb a right-facing corner to an awkward move as the crack veers right. Pass a large loose flake to a much larger flake on the right. Go up to the next ledge and the top.

Ewan's View 22m HVS. J.Croft, D.Eckstein. 1st September 2003.
Start right of a sharp nose.
1. 14m 5a. Pull up a steep wall and move into an S-shaped crack. Go up towards the slabby headwall, then traverse left around the nose to a good ledge.
2. 8m 4a. Move left and mantel up onto the corner of a large block, then continue easily to the top.

Ardtun, Waterfall Wall:
Jimmy Heron 20m E3 5c **. G.Latter, C.Moody. 12th May 2005.
Climb the finger crack left of Little Red Rooster. Step right, then climb a bulging right-facing corner-crack.

Ardtun, Yellow Block:
That's Horrible 12m HVS 5a *. C.Moody, C.Grindley. 15th October 2005.
The crack right of Caterpillar.

Soaking Staffa 12m HVS 5a *. C.Moody, C.Grindley. 15th October 2005.
Start to the right and climb the left side of the short pinnacle, then the crack above with a bulge near the top.

Rally Carnage 12m E2 5c **. C.Moody, C.Grindley. 15th October 2005.
Climb the crack on the right side of the short pinnacle to gain the top. Step right and climb an awkward finger crack, go over a bulge and finish at a chockstone. Easy for the grade.

Ardtun, The Blow Hole:
Kinetic 9m VS 4b *. C.Moody, C.Grindley. 6th August 2005.
The crack left of Kiribati.

White Stuff 12m E1 5b *. C.Moody, C.Grindley. 29th June 2005.
The awkward finger-crack between Bunty's Ducks and Oot Ma Rays, going slightly left at the top bulge.

Erraid, Asteroid Chasm:
Solar Collector 20m E2 5b ***. C.Moody, C.Grindley. 7th August 2005.
Twin cracks up the corner across from Asteroid Groove. There is a big boulder at the start.
Notes: Space Traveller is 28m; Black Hole is 26m E1 5c (SMCJ 2003).

IONA, Raven's Crag:
Note: A large block has been moved to the start of Passage in the last two or three years changing the grade from VS 5a to VS 4b.

SKYE

SGURR NA H–UAMHA:

Left Hand Route 295m III. M.Shaw, D.Paterson. 30th December 2000.
This is the left-hand of the two parallel gullies in the middle of the south-east face. Approach from An Glas-Choire until below the climbs on the east face and continue traversing leftwards around a terrace until the left-hand gully is reached. Climb the gully that is mainly easy angled up and over some steps for 150m, until a short steep section is reached. Climb this and continue until the gully ends. Climb slabby rocks above bearing right for two pitches and move over easier ground to reach the summit ridge.

Note: The route recorded as Cuill Climb (SMCJ 1999 p77) follows the lower section of the original summer route of 1887 but has a direct finish. It is now recorded in *Skye Scrambles* pp91-92 as North-East Face.(diagram p92). Cuill Climb is much of North-East Face but was finished more directly and ignored both the Original and Right-Hand finishes. Perhaps this would be better recorded as North-East Face – Direct Finish II/III. Here is a clearer route description.

Start 20m right of the gully on the North-East Face face. Climb a short icefall and continue up a left-slanting groove to join a broader part of the gully after 30m. Climb this until it swings to the right and as it turns upwards again follow it past an exit left towards the eastern flank. Continue until the gully makes a small diversion rightwards. At this point climb up the slabs ahead, moving slightly left to link up the two right-facing overlaps above, before finishing more directly to the summit.

SGURR NAN GILLEAN, Knights Peak, West Face:

Synchronicity 210m Hard Severe 4b *. S.Kennedy, R.Hamilton. 15th September 2002.
A prominent corner/groove runs almost the full length of the buttress just right of centre (right of West Face Direct). Start at the foot of a slabby corner system just left of the foot of Subsidiary Gully. Climb the initial easy angled corner to a wide ledge beneath the main corner (cutting across West Face which comes in from the right) (40m). Climb the corner directly, surmounting a bulge near the top, to a ledge (40m). Continue directly up a groove and corners to the top of the pinnacle in three pitches (130m).

SGURR AN FHEADAIN:

What have I Becombe 80m E6 ****. D.Birkett, M.Edwards. May 2004.
The obvious overhanging off-width crack to the right of The Rent.
1. 40m 6b. Climb the crack with a bold start leftwards past a peg runner and continue rightwards up the crack.. Make hard moves over a bulge to a big flake ledge to the right.
2. 40m 6a/b. Continue up the crack with a hard start leading to easier climbing over ledges to a big grassy ledge. Descend by an easy walk off left.

SGURR A' MHADAIDH, North West Face:

Day Tripper 400m IV,3. E.Brunskill, D.Morris. 19th February 2006.

A fine mountaineering route taking a rising rightwards traverse from Foxes Rake to join the top section of Deep Gash Gully. Start at the foot of Foxes Rake and climb snow grooves, ramps and icy slabby steps on the right edge of the rake aiming for a ramp system and ledge below the prominent tower at the top of Pye and Mallory's Route (300m). Traverse rightwards along the ledge until it stops at an area of slabby ground. Traverse boldly rightwards across the slabs in an exposed position following the line of least resistance (poor but usable snow on the slabs on this ascent, may be easier or harder depending on snow conditions) to reach a shallow gully, which is the top of Deep Gash Gully (50m). Climb the gully to join the NW ridge (50m).

COIRE NA BANACHDICH, North-West Buttress:
Toolie Grooves Direct Finish 20m VS 4c **. J. & D.Preston. 23rd April 2005.
Climb the crack immediately above the notch. Steep but on good holds and well protected. The route with the normal finish was also thought to be VS 4c **.

Hippocratic Oath 70m HVS **. J. & D.Preston. 23rd April 2005.
A fine direct line on the wall well to the right of Valkyrie corner gives steep climbing on perfect rock. Start from the scree ledge at a broken dyke slanting right. The start is probably as for Aesculapius but going straight up where this traverses left.
1. 40m 5a. Climb up easily to steeper compact rock. Continue boldly up the steep open face to a hanging corner-crack high up. Pull through to a ledge on the left.
2. 30m 5a. Step right and climb a vertical 3m wall. Squirm behind a huge block to mantel on to a sloping shelf below a final corner-crack, climbed to the top.

SGURR SGUMAIN, West Buttress:
Note: In an ascent of Sunset Slab and Yellow Groove on 24th April 2005, J. & D.Preston climbed both the grooves with yellow left walls (30m 5a, 30m 4c; HVS 5a ** overall). In the current guide, Yellow Groove seems to be to their right and The Klondyker to their left. The first groove seemed to have been climbed before but not the second.

Tam's Corner 45m VS 4b. S.Kennedy, T.Hamilton, R.Hamilton. 16th May 2005.
An alternative finish to The Slant. Follow The Slant to a wide ledge beyond the vertical wall. Instead of following the chimney finish climb a corner system on the undercut buttress to the left. Finish up rough rock to join the final rocks of The Slant.

SRON NA CICHE, Crack of Doom Area:
Pillar Crack (Rib of Doom Direct Start) 35m HVS 4c. A.Glasgow, J.Bankhead. 6th June 2005.
Start from the Terrace. Go left to gain and climb the centre of a long smooth slab via a thin vertical crack-line and two thin horizontal breaks, then a crossing a short terrace to reach the top of the slab. Move right to join the normal route.

The Cioch:
Lowlander 45m E2 5c. C.Pettigrew, T.Cooper. 25th June 2005.
Located to the right of Erotica and just left of Cioch Nose on a vertical wall with

a faint crack-line. Start where the slab dropping from the Cioch meets the Terrace. Climb an easy angled slab to the steeper wall of the Cioch, just right of an obvious corner. Climb the faint crackline to a slab. Follow the crack left below an overlap on the slab. Join and finish up Cioch Nose.

SGURR NAN EAG, North-East Face:
Reverse Thrust 80m VS 5a. R.Archbold, B.Findlay. G.Strange. 31st May 1997.
On the face well right of The Chasm is a recessed area. This route follows a big corner bounding the right side of the recessed area and finishes just right of a prominent white scar. Climb the corner over a basalt bulge at 10m and continue into a recess (30m). Continue up a crack-line, climb a bulge into a V-groove (crux) and go up to a glacis (20m). Climb slabs, then trend left below a monster block to easy ground.

BLA BHEINN, Winter Buttress:
Where Eagles Dare 50m Severe. P.Mather, R.Mather. 12th June 2005.
Climb the slabby buttress a few metres left of Escape from Colditz more or less directly (Difficult climbing but no gear) to a grassy ledge (20m). Climb awkwardly through the crux bulge above the ledge (bold) heading towards a left-slanting diagonal crack underneath an overlap. Climb the crack then follow the line of least resistance to the top. A pleasant route, largely on immaculate rock, though very bold, the crux is Severe with no gear above a poor belay.

South Buttress:
Il Dort dans les Choufleur 195m Severe. P.Mather, R.Mather. 12th June 2005.
This climbs the arête high up between Birthday Groove and Virgo. Climb Birthday Groove to the large grassy ledge. Climb the slabby arête above to a large roof, turn this on the right with considerable exposure and climb steeply to a large ledge. Climb a short corner above then a slabby wall above directly.

Clach Glas:
Sickle, Variation Finish E1 5b *. S.Brown, G.Smith. 8th September 2005.
An imposing steep wall directly above the stance at the base of the final pitch. From the belay, traverse left around a corner to reach a vague weakness. Follow this firstly up to a small roof (protection) and then traverse left on small holds (crux) to more positive holds on the left arête which is followed to the summit and belay.

Clach Glas to Blaven Traverse:
The terminal tower of Clach Glas is usually taken by the chimney/gully right of the crest or by a Mild Severe wall leading to a loose chimney above the crest. The following offers a more pleasant if bold alternative.

The Groovey Alternative 45m Very Difficult. J.R.Mackenzie, J.C.Mackenzie. 25th June 2005.
1. 25m. Start just left of the chimney/gully and go up shelves to step left into a groove overlooking the gully below. Follow the groove up and left to a block in the loose chimney above the crest.

2. 20m. Move up right and traverse around a steep nose to a shallow cracked corner. Climb up just left of this to a groove below the final slabs of the ordinary route to the summit. A nice exposed pitch.

NEIST, Lighthouse Wall:
Rising Tide 16m Mild VS 4b *. B.Barnard, T.Allman, S.Chislett. 23rd May 2005.
An interesting, sustained and strenuous route with good protection. The route is best reached by abseil and is located opposite the small island with the squat sea-stack, a few metres right (facing) of Horny Corner. Here is an obvious plinth, just above barnacle level. Start on this. Climb the corner-groove to an overhanging block. Move up and slightly right to gain a continuation groove. Climb this to its end. Belay here or scramble to the top.

The Upper Crag, Financial Sector:
Maggots 55m E1. C.Moody, C.Grindley. 31st July 2005.
Between Worm's Eye View and Bad Dream is a straight crack split by heather ledges above the left side of a grassy bay. Start below and left of the grassy bay at a right-facing corner.
1. 30m 5a/b. Move up the corner, then the rib on the right to gain the grassy bay. Climb a crack on the left side of the bay; belay after a wide section.
2. 25m 4c. Continue up the crack, then more easily up the shallow corner.

Have a Nice Day 30m E3 6a **. G.Latter, J.Rabey. 8th September 2005.
Sustained well protected climbing up the prominent right-facing groove just left of Wish You Were Here. Climb the groove with increasing difficulty, moving rightwards at the top past a triangular flake to pull over the capping roof spectacularly on good holds at a large thread.

Down and Out Wall:
This is between Poverty and Destitution Points. Abseil in from a stake.

The Wind of Freedom 15m Severe. C.Moody, C.Grindley. 5th June 2005.
The right-facing corner at the left side of the crag.

The Wind of Change 15m VS. C.Moody, C.Grindley. 5th June 2005.
The easy looking crack left of the right-facing crack at the right end of the crag.

The Euro Zone, Fulmar Wall:
This is the wall at the north end of the zone. Near the top is a ledge which has a number of nests. Near the left end of the wall is a deep crack forming a slot.

Death of a Parrot 20m VS 5a *. C.Moody, C.Grindley. 22nd October 2005.
Climb a crack right of the deep crack. Move left, then back right high up, and finish up the continuation crack, which is left of a rib.

Death Flock 20m Severe *. C.Moody, C.Grindley. 22nd October 2005.
A crack just right. Step right at Fulmar Ledge and continue to the top.

Maybe a Dead Whale 20m Hard Severe *. C.Moody, C.Grindley. 22nd October 2005.
A crack to the right. Finish up Death Flock after Fulmar Ledge.

Zig Zag 20m Very Difficult *. C.Moody, C.Grindley. 22nd October 2005.
At the right end of the wall is a left-facing corner with an obvious crack just left. Climb up, moving back and forth between these features to gain Fulmar Ledge. A short section leads to the top.

A Non Parrot 20m VS 4b *. C.Moody, C.Grindley. 22nd October 2005.
From the platform of the previous route, step right and follow the crack and corners to Fulmar Ledge. Step left and finish up the previous route. A direct start would make a longer route. Still Wet (SMCJ 2005) is just round right.

Sinus 22m VS 4c **. C.Moody, C.Grindley. 30th July 2005.
Climb the corner on the left side of the pillar left of Staircase (SMCJ 2005).
Note: Rope Gripper (SMCJ 2005) is probably undergraded.

Broozez 18m VS 4c *. C.Moody, C.Grindley. 30th July 2005.
Start 2m right of Rope Jammer (SMCJ 2005) and climb a steepening crack.

The Key 20m VS 4c *. C.Moody, C.Grindley. 30th July 2005.
Start 3m right and climb a fault-line through the wall.

Echo 22m VS 5a *. C.Moody, C.Grindley. 30th July 2005.
Just to the right, make thin moves to gain a left-facing corner and continue up corners.

Fish out of Water 25m VS 4c *. C.Moody, C.Grindley. 30th July 2005.
Start up a wide crack round to the right. Continue up, then follow a fine ramp left, below the yellow headwall.

Silence 25m Severe. C.Moody, C.Grindley. 30th July 2005.
Climb a rib just right of Fish Out of Water and continue up right-facing corners.

Optimum Snore Time 25m E1 5b ***. C.Moody, C.Grindley. 31st July 2005.
The left-facing corner, a fine line.

Cumhann Geodha:
Curry Island 15m E1 5a *. C.Moody, C.Grindley. 23rd October 2005.
The rib left of The Old Warden. From the big ledge, step down onto a sloping foot ledge. Climb up a rib and wall just right, finishing on the rib, protection could be better. This is probably the same as Low Potential (SMCJ 2001) without the "rightward rising traverse".

Note: The Old Warden (SMCJ 1999) was climbed finishing directly up the corner with no change of grade.

The Old Hex 15m HVS 5a *. C.Moody, C.Grindley. 23rd October 2005.
The crack between The Old Warden and Quite Fatigued (SMCJ 1999). Climb the crack and pull left onto a ledge, continue easily up (next to The Old Warden) then step right and follow the continuation crack.

Bagpipe Deadline 15m Severe. C.Moody, M.MacLeod, B.Taylor. 18th February 2006.

About 10m right of Quantum Tunneling are three lines, the middle line has a short chimney just above high tide level. Abseil to a tidal ledge (or start on a smaller ledge higher up). Climb up through the short chimney to a bulge, move left then back right above the bulge and continue up the rib.

Clam Dredger 15m VS 4b. C.Moody, B.Taylor. 19th February 2006.
Well right is a detached pillar. Climb the crack on the right side of the pillar with a bulge to start.

Wall Between Bay 4 and Cumhann Geodha:
Headless Chicking 15m VS 4b *. C.Moody, B.Taylor. 13th November 2005.
Round left of Curry Island is a finger crack in a right-facing corner. Climb it passing a large block. The grade is unsure, being cold and damp.

G&T Shocker 12m HVS 5a *. C.Moody, M.MacLeod. 18th February 2006.
Start at the same ledge as Headless Chicking. Climb the right-hand corner crack, steep low down.

TROTTERNISH, Old Man of Storr:
Note: L.Houlding made a free ascent of the Portree Face in 2004 at E4 5c.

KILT ROCK, Gully Wall:
Joik 40m E2 5c **. G.Latter, C.Pulley. 5th October 2005.
The obvious line between Brazen and Secret Service. Start just left of a large flat boulder, beneath twin intermittent cracks high in the wall. Climb up onto a small protruding ledge and a wee left-facing corner. Continue up the cracks which soon lead to easier climbing up hand cracks and a flake to a ledge. Finish up a short sporting off-width forming the left side of a huge flake at the top.

NORTHERN HIGHLANDS NORTH

BEINN DEARG, West Buttress:
Niccy's Rib 205m III,4. P.Macpherson, D.Williamson. 22nd February 2006.
An enjoyable mountaineering route with varied climbing. Start right of Inverlael Gully at a small gully/snow bay left of Inverlael Buttress.
1. 30m. Go up the gully for 5m, step up and right onto an icy ramp and pull over its top on turf; continue on easy ground to a left-facing wall.
2. 45m. Move back right 2m onto a rib and continue up via grooves and short steps to below an obvious steep corner/groove.
3. 35m. Go up a ramp to below the corner/groove. Climb the helpful corner/groove (crux) and continue on easy ground.
4. 45m. Go up grooves to a slabby wall below and left of a square hole. Climb up and left to a perched block. Step on to the block, pull over and exit onto easy ground.
5. 50m. Continue for 50m on easy ground to the stone dyke at the top.

Note: J.Workman repeated the Right-Hand Finish to The Ice Hose on 17th March 2006 with good ice and thought it worth V,5 at most, maybe IV,5.

RHUE SEA-CLIFFS:
Rhue-Barb 25m E5 6a/b **. I.Taylor, T.Fryer. 20th August 2005.
Lies between Perestroika and Rhue-Rhapsody. Start at a big corner that leads to a huge roof. Ascend the corner easily to its top, then hand traverse a break rightwards to the end of the roof. From here take a thin crack up the wall above to an easier finish. A Friend 4 is useful for the traverse. Strenuous, sustained climbing with good protection.

Notes from I.Taylor: Rhue-Rhapsody is underplayed in the current guide. E4 6a *** and a wild trip. One the best routes in the area (but not ****).

Notes from N.Morrison: Firing Line is harder than E1 even with a very large Cam for the top break. Also unpleasant rock and vegetation. Midget Gems (Gem Walls) is a nice route but not three stars; we thought one star would be more appropriate.

ARDMAIR, Arapiles Wall:
Maralinga 15m E5 6a **. I.Taylor, T.Fryer. 2nd July 2005.
The deceptively steep pillar at the right end of Arapiles Wall. Start just right of Biological Warfare at a short crack. Follow a line slightly rightwards to a big flake hold below a dubious thread. Go diagonally left past the thread to reach good holds and a big break. Finish by easier climbing up the left arête of the pillar.

Beast Buttress:
Tinsel Town 20m E6 6b *. I.Taylor, T.Fryer. 26th December 2005.
A route between Market Day and On the Western Skyline. Start just left of the Direct Start to On Western Skyline at a thin crack. Boulder up the thin crack, then easier climbing leads to the good ledge. On the wall above, just right of Market Day, is a short flake. From the flake bold and insecure moves up and rightwards lead to better holds. Step left and climb directly to easier ground. Head pointed without any side runners in Market Day.

Timorous Beastie 25m E6 6b **. I.Taylor, T.Fryer. 21st April 2005.
Start as for Beastmaster. Where that route takes a short diagonal crack into Unleash the Beast, reach up and left to a good hold and make hard move through a poor break, to gain a flake. Finish up and right to gain the top of Unleash the Beast.

CAMUS MOR:
Blitzkrieg! 60m E5 6a. J.Clark, N.McNair, I.Small. June 2005.
Walk another 20mins beyond Camus Mor to an obvious headland. Descend to the right. The route takes the middle and deepest open groove, roughly in the centre of the crag at the bottom of the descent gully, above a grassy bay. Start in a broken corner, then traverse out on purple rock boldly to better rock and gear just to right of a square-cut roof. Take this on the right, then step left to gain slanting grooves (crux). Go up these to a shelf, then right to gain a ramp and belay at the bottom of a corner. The second pitch is up a corner and wall on the left (5b). Comes with a health and safety warning – very loose!

STAC POLLAIDH, North Face:
Pollaidhstyrene 140m IV,6 *. I.Taylor, T.Fryer. 6th March 2006.
Climbs the buttress left of North Gully. Based on a summer Difficult not in the

current guide (First Rib 1945?). Good though escapable climbing. Start at the lowest rocks at an obvious turfy gully.
1. 30m. Climb the gully to a ledge on the left.
2. 40m. Using a wide crack on the right, climb the arête above to a ledge. Continue up the arête to gain a level ridge below the upper buttress.
3. 40m. Climb turfy grooves, then broken ground before a short descent gains a col.
4. 30m. Finish up easier ground to the top.

West Buttress, South Face:
Original Route 100m IV,5. A.Tibbs, M.Shaw. 13th March 2005.
Start about 10m right of Baird's Pinnacle.
1. 15m. Follow ledges up leftwards to beneath a 5m corner (directly above the pinnacle).
2. 20m. Climb a short corner and move right with difficulty to easier ground. A V-corner with a thread runner leads to a ledge.
3. 20m. Go directly up easier ground until it steepens.
4. 25m. Follow a right-slanting turfy line towards the buttress crest and a good ledge.
5. 10m. Leave the ledge on the right by a short crack, then follow a right-trending crack at the top of a slab to disappear round the buttress edge.
6. 10m. An awkward pull leads to easy ground.

Note: The well protected corner-crack 3m right of the second pitch of Enigma Grooves gives a good pitch (25m E2 5b, A.Tibbs, I.Blackwood, 10th September 2005).

REIFF:
Notes from I.Taylor: Headstrong at Stone Pig Cliff is E4 5c ** and Great Black Back at Black Rocks is E4 6a *.

Mechanics Geo:
Sump 8m HVS 5b *. I.Taylor, T.Fryer. 31st October 2005.
Start right of Shifting Spanner. Climb the bulging right-hand crack, finishing rightwards up a short hanging corner.

Black Rocks, Orange Wall Area:
Autumn Colours 8m E2/3 5c/6a *. P.Mather (unsec). 15th October 2005.
Climb the distinctly overhanging wall between Hanging Groove and Slanting Corner. Climb onto the ledge at the bottom of Slanting Corner, then launch up the left side of the wall heading for two deep horizontal breaks. Move right and climb the headwall centrally (crux). The grade was hard E2 or easy E3.

ACHMELVICH, Clean Cut:
Flawless 16m E7 6c ***. J.Lines. 22nd August 2004.
Scotland's answer to Master's Edge, and not a bad attempt too! The second arête from the left, the first being bottomless. Climb this most prominent arête first on the left and then on the right to a big jug and gear just above. Deep breath and layback the arête with commitment and technical finesse. Superb! Headpointed.

Unnamed 8m VS 5a. A.Nisbet, D.McGimpsey. 22nd August 2004.
At the top right end of the cliff are two clean corners above a slabby platform half-way up the cliff. The route starts from the platform (reached by abseil) and climbs the left corner, which has a crack on its right wall. Just when it starts to get hard, a ledge on the right arête can be reached.

Hed Kandi 8m VS 4c *. D.McGimpsey, A.Nisbet. 15th August 2004.
At the seaward (north) end of the easy descent shelf, there is a short wall facing the main crag and with a corner on its right. This gains and climbs the left arête.

Loch Roe West Crag (NC 055 241):
Eye Spy Corner 12m VS 4c. D.McGimpsey, J.Lines. 14th August 2004.
Climb the central corner.

OLD MAN OF STOER:
Original Route, No Comfort Variation 25m HVS 5b. A.Wallace, R.Wallace. 27th March 2005.
Traverse onto the landward face on the fourth pitch, but after a few metres climb a short chimney to an evil looking overhanging off-width. Go up onto a ledge on the right, then swing back left into the off-width and gain a big ledge and a possible belay. Climb diagonally right over large ledges to join Original Route at the top of the V-chimney.
Note: A large block has fallen off near Diamond Face Route but it is not known whether it has affected the route.

QUINAG, Barrel Buttress:
Note: G.Robertson and P.Benson repeated the direct version of the Raeburn, Mackay and Ling Route on 4th March 2006 and thought VII,7.

FAR NORTH WEST CRAGS, Creag an Sgriodain:
Note: Friends Essential. J.Lyall notes that the line described in *Northern Highlands North* is not the same as the original line. The Variation Start is the original line and therefore should be 1996, not 2002. The described line was climbed by A. & G.Nisbet on 30th June 2000, by accident! Pitch 2 of Scavenger is only 5a if climbed on big holds immediately right of the corner.

TARBET SEA CLIFFS, Balmy Slabs, White Slab:
Jeepers Creepers 30m E1 5b *. S.Kennedy, R.Hamilton, T.Hamilton. 5th June 2005.
Follows a corner-line starting about 15m right of Writer's Cramp at the right end of a series of small overlaps on the right side of the White Slab. Start from a small pointed block just below the high-water mark. Step off the block and make some thin moves on the wall just right of a small corner. Move up to better holds on the left arête of the corner, then move back right under a small roof into the large upper corner. Finish up the corner.

Cornucopia, Rooftop Finish E1 5b **. S.Kennedy, T.Hamilton, R.Hamilton. 5th June 2005.
A fine airy finish to Cornucopia taking the hanging slab left of the finishing

chimney. From a point a few metres below the chimney move left and climb diagonally left following the lower edge of the slab in a sensational position.

Geo an Amair (NC 161 506):
The next narrow geo north of Acarseid Mhic Mhurchaidh Oig. The sea-cliff on the north side of the zawn consists of a large south-facing slab containing a number of vertical crack-lines running from an overlap in the lower section. The slab is bounded on the right by a large corner (Loan Shark) and right again by a long tapering slab with a bulge at about half-height. Right of the tapering slab is a steep overhanging red wall with a prominent right arête (Marinator) which contains the crack-line of The Boardmaster. Approach as for The Grey Slabs. An abseil approach is necessary to reach the base of most of the routes. A 60m rope is useful.

Loan Shark 45m Hard Severe 4a *. R.Hamilton, S.Kennedy. 18th June 2005.
The corner defining the right edge of the main slab (looking up). Abseil to small ledges on a narrow rock tongue which stands proud of the slab just above the high-water mark. This is just left of a dark recess at the foot of the corner. From the top of the tongue step onto a thin slab, then move rightwards above a dark recess into the main corner. Climb the corner.

Prawn Stars 45m Hard Severe 4a *. S.Kennedy, R.Hamilton. 18th June 2005.
The slim corner in the upper slab a few metres left of Loan Shark. Start from the tongue and climb the initial thin slab of Loan Shark. Instead of moving up rightwards into the main corner, climb the cracked slabs directly above and climb the slim corner.

Prawn again Christian 45m Very Difficult *. S.Kennedy, R.Hamilton. 18th June 2005.
The first obvious crack-line running up the slab just left of Prawn Stars. Start from the tongue and step left into a small recess in the overlap at the foot of the crack-line. Climb the crack and slabs directly above.

Prawnography 45m Severe *. S.Kennedy, R.Hamilton. 25th June 2005.
The next obvious break through the overlap about 4m left of Prawn again Christian. This and the following routes on the main slab start at small ledges left of the tongue just above the high-water mark. Climb the slab to a small right-facing corner breaking the overlap. Surmount the overlap and climb the slab left of some small overlaps, then step right and finish directly.

Prawnconnery 40m Severe *. R.Hamilton, S.Kennedy. 25th June 2005.
The crack-line breaking through the overlap about 6m left of Prawnography by a small left-facing corner. Pull through the overlap, then step right and take a line up leftwards under some small overlaps finishing up a slab above a corner.

Creelman 30m Very Difficult *. S.Kennedy, R.Hamilton. 25th June 2005.
The left-facing corner near the left edge of the main slab.

Save the Prawn 30m VS 4c **. R.Hamilton, S.Kennedy, A.MacDonald. 5th July 2005.

The leftmost edge of the narrow slab just left of the corner of Creelman. Start at the foot of the corner and take a line as close to the left edge as possible.

Curse the Trawlers 47m VS 4b *. R.Hamilton, S.Kennedy. 25th June 2005.
An atmospheric route up the tapering slab right of the main slab. A long abseil leads to a promontory by a large cavern. Start up a left-facing corner come groove on the left edge to a steepening which is climbed via a small recess near the left end. Move right and climb the middle of the slab to the top. Block belay available well back up the slope.

The Red Wall:
The Boardmaster 40m E3 5c **. S.Kennedy, R.Hamilton, G.Reid. 20th August 2005.
A fine and sustained route taking the striking left-trending crack-line in the middle of the Red Wall. Steep and very exposed but well protected. Abseil to the rocky promontory at the foot of the crack-line. Pull into the crack by an airy step left off the promontory, then make a series of strenuous moves up the crack until a small black sloping ramp is reached. An awkward move leads left onto the ramp. Continue up leftwards by cracks, then move back right onto a steep slab and easier ground. Finish in the same general line bearing leftwards up much easier cracks. Possibly E2.

Marinator 40m Hard Severe 4b *. S.Kennedy, R.Hamilton. 25th June 2005.
The prominent right arête which is accessed by abseil. Start up a slabby left-trending ramp to a black chimney. Step left onto the exposed edge which is followed directly to the top.

Right of Marinator is a smaller buttress characterised by a small but prominent quartz pinnacle just right of some steep crack-lines.

Quartz Pinnacle 35m Very Difficult *. S.Kennedy, R.Hamilton. 24th July 2005.
Start just left of the quartz pinnacle and traverse rightwards via the pinnacle to the edge which forms the right side of a large flake. Climb the outside wall of the flake then directly to the top.

Crack of the Ancient Mariner 35m E1 5b **. R.Hamilton, S.Kennedy. 24th July 2005.
A couple of metres left of Quartz Pinnacle is an overhanging crack with an undercut start. Surmount the short overhang to reach the base of the crack then make strenuous moves up the crack to a ledge. Finish directly up a short wall which leads to easier ground.

At the back of the narrow inlet well right of Quartz Pinnacle are two south-facing slabs. Approach at low tide by scrambling down easy slabs from the base of Q.P.

Minnow 30m Very Difficult. R.Hamilton, S.Kennedy. 24th July 2005.
The left edge of the left-hand slab. Disappointing.

Sea Wasp 25m VS 4c *. S.Kennedy, R.Hamilton. 24th July 2005.

The left side of the black right-hand slab. Start by some boulders and move out left to the edge. Climb the slab close to the edge and finish via a crack.

Piranha 25m Severe. S.Kennedy, R.Hamilton. 24th July 2005.
Takes a direct line up the right side of the right-hand slab starting from the boulders.

Orchid 40m Very Difficult *. A.MacDonald, S.Kennedy, R.Hamilton. 5th July 2005.
The dark north wall of the geo contains an obvious right-trending fault line low down. This route starts at the left end and follows the initial section of the fault before taking a steeper and higher line where the fault splits at about halfway. Steep and juggy. Reached by abseil.

Queuing Up 20m Very Difficult *. C.Grindley, W.Hood, C.Moody. 24th July 2005.
At the left end of the traverse of Orchid is a crack that goes up slightly leftwards to grass high up. Start at another crack just left of it. Climb up and step right to cross the other crack, then continue up to a ledge.

Another Tiger Beetle 20m Very Difficult **. C.Grindley, W.Hood, C.Moody. 24th July 2005.
To the right is an overhanging left-facing corner. Climb the prominent crack on the left to the ledge. Steep and juggy.

Upper Tier:
Above the Geo is a long wall of good quality containing a number of grooves and with a slabby right edge. The right edge offers a convenient descent down slabs (Difficult in ascent).

Son of a Pitch 25m Severe *. S.Kennedy, R.Hamilton, G.Reid. 20th August 2005.
On the left side of the wall is a prominent chimney-groove and right again is a rib with pockets. This route takes the corner right of the rib. Climb the corner, then move left onto a sloping shelf. Finish directly up from the left end of the shelf.

Sundance Kid 25m HVS 5a *. R.Hamilton, S.Kennedy, G.Reid. 20th August 2005.
The rib starting 3m left of the above route. Climb the rib using large pockets, then steeply up a crack to pull awkwardly onto a sloping shelf. Finish up Son of a Pitch.

Creag Cnoc Thull, Pygmy Slab (NC 250 500):
A pink slab lies to the right of the overhanging crag on the south shore of Loch na Thull, 10 mins from the road. The slab has an inset wall and overhang to the north and a more benign western facet.

Sugar Pygmy 20m E1 5c *. J.R.Mackenzie, R.Brown. 27th July 2005.
Guaranteed to put a smile on your face. Climbs the overhang and groove at the inset base of the slab. Climb the overhang cleverly and groove above; step left and up the broken wall to the top.3

Sweet Nothings 15m Very Difficult. R.Brown, J.R.Mackenzie. 27th July 2005.
The left side of the slab right of a wider crack or via a short crack to the right.

A Little Something 12m Hard Severe 4b *. J.R.Mackenzie, R.Brown. 27th July 2005.
The straight thin crack to the top, quite good.

Something for a Pygmy 10m Severe. J.R.Mackenzie, R.Brown. 27th July 2005.
The crack and scoop at the right end.

Ridgeway View Crag (Guide p250):
Starry Saxifrage and The Silk Glove Memorial Route (SMCJ 2005) are the same route. The routes in the guide are overstarred for a small crag.

Notes from I.Taylor. Creag an Fhithich: A bit over-starred; The Swirl E3 6a ***, Ruby Wall E3 5c **, Sapphires E3 5c **, A Diamond is Forever E4 6a **, Honey Monster E2 5c *. Rayfish (Fisherman's View Crag) E4 6a **.

Notes from N.Morrison: Sapphires is good but felt more like E2 5c than E3 while The Swirl is pretty stiff at E3. Ruby Wall is fairly redundant with the other two described as they are.

SHEIGRA, Na Stacain:
The following routes were climbed by C.Grindley, W.Hood, C.Moody on 22nd and 23rd July 2005.
Swirl 12m Severe.
This is on the south-east (?) wall that faces Tall Pall. Traverse right to a barnacle ledge that slants down right into the sea. Move up right under bulges, then climb a cracked wall.

Just west of the southern tip of the island is a deep chimney, Very Difficult.
Garlic Wall 15m HVS 5a **.
About 12m left (north) of the Very Difficult chimney is a block before a small pool. Start right of the block. Move up, then rightwards up a steep wall.

Gannet Squadren 15m Severe **.
Start up Garlic Wall, then climb a crack up leftwards.

One Blind Mouse 15m HVS 5a *.
About 5m left are two blind corners. Start up the left corner, then climb a cracked wall above and pull out left at a flake.

Unusual 15m VS 4c *.
Just left are two shallow corner-cracks. Climb the right corner, then a flake-crack.

Bizarre 15m Severe *.
The left corner, then move easily left and climb another short corner.

Arête Crack 15m E1 5a **.
Climb the arête, starting slightly right of it.
A Difficult crack was climbed on the wall to the left. Left of it are easy descent

ramps. Left again is a tidal wall (perhaps containing Diff Crack, Mod Crack and VS Wall – *Northern Highlands North* p281).

Vienneta 18m Very Difficult **.
Climb the right side of the wall past a ledge and small overlap.

Unnamed 15m Difficult *.
To the left is a shelf above the barnacle line. Climb a crack straight up from the right side of the shelf.

Unnamed 15m Severe **.
A wall just left.

Unnamed 15m VS 4b **.
Start right of Left End Corner. Climb small right-facing corners, go over a bulge and continue up.

Left End Corner 15m Very Difficult **.
A corner at the left end of the shelf. Continue up a chimney.

Squeek Severe *.
Traverse left above the sea to a sloping shelf. Move up right, then continue just left of the rib overlooking Left End Corner.

MEALL HORN, Creag an Lochan Ulbha:
Goldie Horn 90m VI,5. M.Edwards, D.McGimpsey, A.Nisbet. 2nd March 2006.
An icefall which flows down the big hanging slab at the left end of the cliff and which would, given cold enough conditions, form down the overhanging base. Start 10m right of the icicles at the base. Serious, but with fully frozen turf on pitch 1 and thicker ice, the grade would drop.
1. 15m. Gain and climb a turfy groove to reach a ledge on the left.
2. 30m. Return to the groove and gain a higher ledge above. Climb thin ice above and traverse left to the main icefall. Follow this to under the left end of a big roof (ice belay).
3. 45m. Traverse right under the roof and pass its right end (thin ice). Go leftwards up the hanging slab in a superb position, then up ice to easy ground.

FOINAVEN, Lord Reay's Seat:
Pobble 220m VII,7 **. M.Bass, S.Yearsley. 3rd March 2006.
A sustained and varied route with strenuous and helpful chimneys and delicate slab climbing. Start at a large right-facing flake 10m right from the toe of the buttress, well right of the summer start.
1. 50m. Climb the flake, then the wall above for 2m. Traverse left, aiming for the block on the skyline. Continue horizontally left, then up to the base of the first chimney.
2. 25m. Follow the summer second pitch, direct through the overhanging chimney.
3. 20m. As for the summer route, but belay directly below the chockstone.
4. 25m. Climb the chockstone direct, to the bottom of the crinkly slab, move out onto a rib on the right and follow this to a belay below an obvious large crack in

the right wall below the line of the direct finish.
5. 35m. Descend to the top right of the crinkly slab. Follow the top edge of the slab delicately leftwards and then climb the steep rockfall scar to the ill-defined arête. Move easily leftwards then up to a bay below the steep corner of Breakaway.
6. 35m. As for the summer route.
7. 30m. Climb direct to the summit of Lord Reay's Seat.

BEN LOYAL, Sgor a' Chleirich:
This impressive crag dries quickly and receives sun in the afternoon. Walking in from the south is the most straightforward, following a faint Land-Rover track from the A836 bridge at the south end of Loch Loyal (NC 598 444) and then contouring around the hillside near the 450m level, to reach Loch Fhionnaich. Note that the existing routes, Marathon Corner and Priests Rake take the most vegetated lines; the intervening areas contain plenty of good rock.

Milky Way 210m E2 5c **. K.Milne, S.Helmore. 18th April 2003.
Takes the clean slabs at the left-hand side of the crag. Approach by walking up about 80m in elevation from the toe of the crag, opposite the north end of Loch Fhionnaich. The start is where a tongue of grass leads back right to the base of the slabs. The first part of the route follows the left hand of two clean crack-lines. The small left-facing corner on pitch 3 is also visible from the ground and provides another reference point.
1. 40m 4c. Climb somewhat vegetated slabs to reach the crack proper. Belay just above a horizontal weakness where the rock steepens.
2. 45m 5b. Continue up the cleaned hand-jam crack to a grassy groove and ledges. With good protection here (optional belay), move back on to the slab and make a rising traverse leftwards, almost reaching a slanting blank groove on the left. Continue up the slab boldly to a triangular heather ledge and a small flake.
3. 45m 5b. Traverse 2m right easily to a prominent flake and up to reach a thin crack. Continue up the crack, climbing through a short left-facing corner. Where the crack fades into slabs above, traverse delicately left 4m to easier ground and up on to a small low angle slab. Traverse left 3m to a wide grassy ledge.
4. 40m 5c. Walk along the ledge for 5m and climb the gritstone-like overhang with difficulty into a cracked groove. Move leftwards out of the groove to reach a line of interesting flakes. A sloping heather ledge leads up and right.
5. 40m 4c. Step on to the grey slab on the right and continue up the right-trending weakness to a good horizontal crack 5m below the summit (664m).

Mars 230m E3 5c *. M.Atkins, K.Milne. 11th September 2005.
Tackles the walls and slabs on the impressive right-hand side of the crag. Start 75m right of the grassy gully of Marathon corner. Scramble up steep heather to belay 20m below the left hand side of a prominent line of overhangs.
1. 35m 5c. Climb a poorly protected vegetated slab (5a) to reach a grassy gully. Step right on to a rib and climb this pleasantly until the rock steepens. At a line of overhangs, a tricky step right leads into a clean groove. Climb this for 4m and move back left with difficulty. Go steeply up flakes and then left on to a spacious ledge.
2. 35m 5c. Climb the left side of a black lichen covered corner (a good marker from the ground) through a bulge (thread) to a difficult exit on to a sloping ledge.

Continue more easily via clean slabs trending left to a groove-line and huge block (passing a suspect block below this).
3. 30m 5b. Step on to the rib on the left side of the block and continue in this line for 15m until it is possible to traverse right and slightly down to reach a heather patch (a more direct alternative may be to climb unprotected slabs to reach the same point). Climb up the easier slabby groove to good cracks.
4. 45m 5b. A system of grassy cracks leads to a small ledge. Step right on to slabs and then trend back left up a series of interesting steps. Move right and up a groove in slabs to reach the prominent grassy section of Priests Rake.
5. 45m 4a. Make a rising traverse along the rake and climb up a heathery groove to clean rock on the right.
6. 40m 5a/b. Continue the rising traverse, taking in a grooved slab, to finish about 20m right of the crest of the buttress.

Note: A better more direct finish looks feasible, but darkness was approaching on the first ascent.

AUCKENGILL, Orange Wall:
The Happy Pineapple 6m Severe 4b. G.Richard, R.Wallace. 8th July 2005.
Entering the quarry one is faced with the left edge of the Orange Wall. Climb the deep crack through ledges and red bands of rock to a shaky finish.

Auck and Gull 8m S 4b. R.Wallace, R.Christie. 13th September 2005.
Climb the corner at the left edge of the Orange Wall bridging through a roof and onto the top.

Push up to the Bumper 8m E1 5a. R.Christie, R.Wallace. 13th September 2005.
Tackle the thin crack 2m right of Turbodiesel and awkwardly overcome the roof above.

SOUTH HEAD OF WICK:
King Tubby and the Fat Boys of Lard 10m E2 5c. N.Morrison, P.Allen, W.Moir. August 2005.
The next line left of Wick and Feeble (SMCJ 2005). Left of Wick and Feeble is a left-facing corner at the base of the cliff. Start on the wall just right of this and climb up to the main bulge. Surmount the bulge and follow the cracks to the top at a notch. Strenuous but very well protected. Cleaned on the lead then redpointed.

Left of The Darkness of Lard (SMCJ 2005) is a vicious overhanging roof crack with corner systems to its left. Left of these and at a slightly lower level is a long wall characterised by the compacted shale band low down and the sandstone band at the top. The following route lies several metres along the wall where a shallow right-facing groove leads to a vertical crack in the sandstone band.

Spaced Out Lardboys On The Road To Obesity 10m E1 5b **. W.Moir, N.Morrison, P.Allen. August 2005.
Climb the groove on to its left edge, then pull slightly right into the crack.

Scott Muir red pointing Jedi Mind Tricks, God's Crag, Colorado. Photo: www.scottmuir.com
Margherita from the Elena Hut in the Ruwenzori Mountains, Uganda. Photo: Derek Pyper.

SARCLET, Cave Bay Area:
Note from N. Morrison: Occum's Razor, grade confirmed. The part in the description about using the right arête is a red herring. It should read: "Climb directly up to roof and follow the crack-line through the roof to gain the big jug on the right, continue up the crack using the wall on the right to a rest before the final headwall. Climb this to an exciting top-out."

Big Buttress, East Face:
Notes from N.Morrison: Sarclet Pimpernel is one of the best single pitch routes of its grade that I have done on a sea-cliff. We thought E1 5a appropriate. Well protected, sustained and continuous. Groove Armada is equally good but we felt VS 4c was the grade and straightforward at that.

Djapana Buttress:
Note from N.Morrison: Djapana is a great route, starting from the chimney at the base it is about 28m long not 20m.

The left-hand edge of the buttress is bounded by a magnificent arch. At the base of the buttress is a sloping ledge at its left and on the right, a pink platform separated from the buttress by a gap. At the middle is a small platform. Access by abseil from a tombstone-like rock.

Arch Rival 25m HVS 5a *. R.Wallace, B.Tosh. 20th August 2005.
From the small platform make easy moves up a shallow groove over a horizontal break to the base of a left-facing curved flake. Surmount a large ledge at the top of the flake and tackle the groove and flake above until forced into some delicate moves on the left wall, then pull back onto the top of the flake and scramble to the top.

Like it or Limpet 25m Very Difficult. B.Tosh, R.Wallace. 21st August 2005.
Step across the narrowest point between the pink platform and the buttress and ascend grooves and blocky ledges aiming for a jutting nose. Ascend the left side of the nose, mounting its bridge and continue easily to the top.

Oily Buttress:
This small buttress sits at the north end of the entrance to Oily Geo (ND 345 424). Access is by abseil onto a non-tidal ledge.

That Petrel Emotion 15m E1 5b *. R.Wallace, R.Christie. 7th August 2005.
Climb a shallow left-facing corner 2m right of a roofed corner on to a ledge below hanging flakes on the right and an arête on the left. Move up the smooth wall using a forearm brace between the flakes to bridge between the arête and flakes. Make a few steep moves up and left to a break below a small roof. Turn this to the right on to the top of a small pillar, then a short wall.

Cold Halo 15m VS 4b. R.Christie, R.Wallace. 12th July 2005.
Start at the left end of the ledge, 2m left of That Petrel Emotion. Climb on to a rectangular block, then up a short shallow left-facing corner to the base of a big left-trending flake. Move up the wall and flake to a platform on top of the flake. Continue on the same line up a short groove.

Guy Robertson on the First Ascent of Where Eagles Dare (VII,8), Lochnagar. Photo: Simon Richardson.

Fancy Dancing with the Fleas? 15m VS 4c. R.Christie, R.Wallace. 15th July 2005.
From the left edge of the ledge traverse 1m left onto the top of a flake. Climb a shallow left-facing corner and move up right onto a ledge on the arête. Continue up the corner to a ledge on the right. Traverse along the ledge across Cold Halo to a small roof below an open groove that is tackled directly.

Oiled Up 15m VS 4b. R.Wallace, R.Christie. 15th July 2005.
From the left end of the ledge traverse 3m left into a left-facing corner. Climb this to a small roof, then move left to another corner and climb this by a roof on the left onto a sloping slab overhung with a roof. Climb the corner formed by the roof and the right-hand wall, then continue up an open corner to the left and top.

At the northern arête of the buttress, 20m north of That Petrel Emotion, is a large corner with a non-tidal square platform at its base, accessible by abseil. The next three routes depart from the square platform.

I Heard it Down the Pub 15m Severe 4b. R.Christie, R.Wallace. 7th August 2005.
Start from a ledge on the front of the face 3m left of the square platform. Diagonally down climb 3m left to the base of a crack. Follow the crack up the fine wall to a small overlap then move right and follow the edge of a flake to the top.

I Saw it in a Picture 18m Severe 4a. R.Wallace, R.Christie. 7th August 2005.
Climb the open corner to a small hanging arête. Move right into an opening groove and finish straight up the short wall above.

I Smelt it on the Breeze 18m Severe 4b. R.Christie, R.Wallace. 7th August 2005.
Teeter up the arête bounding the right wall of the corner and follow it as it curves away and peters out. Continue directly up the open crack above to the top.

Black Lagoon (ND 346 246):
Ten metres north of Oily Geo Buttress, beyond a broken buttress and arête, is a rocky bay with ramparts leading up to a black oily pool. Just north again from the rocky bay is a large open corner atop a triangular platform. The next three routes can be accessed by abseiling from a jutting boulder above the corner.

Sartorius Stretch 20m VS 4c *. R.Christie, R.Wallace. 31st August 2005.
Superb bridging up the open corner to a tricky move at mid-height leading to more delicate moves towards the top.

Nag's Head 20m HVS 5a *. R.Wallace, R.Christie. 14th September 2005.
Starting from just above the black pool, this route climbs the left corner of the rocky bay, initially following a large flake to a horizontal break. From the break, bridge up a black open groove to a narrowing and gain a hanging corner. Climb past the black horse-head shaped jammed boulder (this can be made to nod up and down, but not removed) to a hanging arête. Move up a short groove to the left and surmount ledges on the left wall to gain the top.

Geezer from the Black Lagoon 16m HVS 5a. R.Wallace, R.Christie. 28th September 2005.
From the north end of the black pool, surmount a couple of blocks to gain access to a crack. The crack steepens through a bulge leading to a niche, then some broken climbing to the top.

Hidden Bay (ND 342 420):
Access is via abseil to a massive ledge that stretches as far north as Djapana Buttress, giving great views of the impressive arch.

Hard of Herring 25m Severe 4b. R.Wallace, G.Richard. 7th July 2005.
Start at the right-hand base of the triangular pinnacle and climb to the apex. Continue up and right under flakes and through a narrow chimney to the top.

On the Rebound 25m HVS 5a *. R.Wallace, R.Christie. 16th August 2005.
At the left-hand base of the triangular pillar is a short chimney. Bridge up the short chimney exiting at its top to the right into a narrow corner passing a small roof on the left. Mount a sloping slab above the roof and follow twin cracks through a pair of steep overlaps until it is possible to step right into a corner. The corner has an interesting leaning pillar in it that is tackled directly.

Tilted Ledge:
In the middle of the bay north of the Tilted Ledge is a jutting headland (ND 341 419) with a non-tidal ledge running along the southern edge of its base. Access by abseil.

Tug of the Tide 35m Severe *. R.Wallace, R.Christie. 22nd July 2005.
A deep tidal pool splits the ledge and its rear juts against the base of a wide cracked pillar. Start on a ledge at the base of a chimney and climb the left edge of the chimney to an overlap. Follow a crack by the overlap that leads to a pedestal in another short chimney with a deep shaft in its rear. Bridge the chimney and follow a crack up left to a grassy ledge. The slab above has a right diagonal crack running up it. Climb straight up the slab, crossing the crack and up onto the arête that is followed to the top and a surprising block belay.

Kaleidoscope 30m HVS 5a *. R.Christie, R.Wallace. 22nd July 2005.
Start from the ledge directly below the prow of the headland. Use an overlap and edge to pull up onto a sloping ledge at the base of a diamond shaped niche in a groove. Continue up the groove until it peters out then follow the crack till it stops. Make a wee jiggle over to the right using some side pulls and continue up into a shallow groove and an easier angle. Finish up the open blocky corner above.

Directly landward from the north end of the Tilted Ledge is a grey slabby pillar with corners on either side of it (ND 34150 41855). Access by abseil.

Donnie Darko 35m VS 4b. R.Christie, A.Wallace, R.Wallace. 5th September 2004.
To the left of the grey slabby pillar is a large non-tidal platform with an open book corner at its left end. Climb the corner, then move right under spikes and up a black chute.

WHALIGOE, Neapolitan Buttress (ND 327 407):
This huge south-east facing buttress lies directly to the south of Ellens Geo.
Approach: From the Whaligoe Steps car park, walk 1km north along the cliff tops through a few fields until some small rocky outcrops are reached. The main buttress lies below these and its northern end is marked from above by a large block at the cliff edge just before a grassy gallery.

Layer Cake 40m HVS 5a ***. R.Wallace, R.Christie. 5th July 2005.
At the northern end of the high cliff, a steep tidal ledge runs south into the sea. From this ledge start by climbing a brown sandstone corner with ledges to a good belay ledge at 12m. Continue through the red sandstone up steep corners to a large ledge at the start of the conglomerate. The right-hand wall of the layback corner above overhangs.

The following routes are reached by scrambling down to a grassy gallery at the north end of the big wall, then abbing off a large block northwards down big ledges to a non-tidal ledge. The next routes start on the wall to the right (facing inland).

Razorbill Redirection 20m HVS 5a. B.Tosh, R.Wallace, R.Christie. 3rd July 2005.
Start below and right of a triangular niche. Climb on to the wall and traverse right to an arête. Make some shaky moves up on to a ledge. Climb a right-facing corner on to a ledge, then follow a short crack to easier ground.

Akimbo 20m HVS 5a. R.Christie, R.Wallace, B.Tosh. 3rd July 2005.
Start to the right of Razorbill Redirection around an arête. Bridge up a steep open corner to a roof that is awkwardly turned to the right. Continue up the middle of the broken slabs above.

Escape from Misery 15m Difficult. R.Wallace, B.Tosh, R.Christie. 3rd July 2005.
Move right around the next arête and follow a stepped chimney and crack against the right wall.

After the abseil, the following route is the corner right of centre of the crag, clearly marked by white Razorbill droppings near the top.

Pilot Whale Play Time 35m E1 5a. B.Tosh, R.Christie, R.Wallace. 11th September 2005.
1. 15m 4a/4b. Climb the obvious stepped buttress until just below the sandstone rock band.
2. 20m 5a. Move up to the sandstone rock band and pull over a bulge. Continue up on good holds with limited protection into the corner and carry on to a cave. From here make the final hard but well protected moves on to the grassy gallery.

Back from the cliff edge, a line of small outcrops run south to almost meet the southern edge of the cliff at a large corner with a large boulder (abseil anchor) at its top.

Where the Taut Wave Hangs HVS 5a ***. R.Christie, B.Tosh, R.Wallace. 11th September 2005.
This fine route follows the corner with a deep off-width crack at its rear. Start from a ledge above the water.
1. 10m 4b. Follow the off-width to a ledge below a roof.
2. 20m 5a. Climb past the roof and stick to the right wall of the corner, stretching right to a crack for protection. Finish up a small chimney.

MID CLYTH, Over the Water:
Cellar Door 10m E1 5b **. R.Christie, A.Wallace, R.Wallace. 6th September 2004.
Six metres left of the arête of Friends in High Places is a deep capped corner. Climb the corner until a roof is reached at two-thirds height. Exit the roof to the right and make difficult moves up to a notch.

LATHERONWHEEL:
Notes from R.Anderson: A very good little cliff. On the approach cross the old bridge and follow the coastal path.

The routes on p384 starting with Sticky Fingers are all on what should be called Peninsula Wall, since they lie on the south facing wall of the peninsula which runs northwards from Big Flat Wall. Access is on foot down the gully on the north side of the peninsula into the dry bay with four stacks and around the end of the peninsula onto a non-tidal shelf, from which all of the routes from Sticky Fingers to More Noise start. A tidal cave/arch cuts right through the peninsula at the end of the shelf and to the right of this above the shelf are two arches, or caves.

Far East Arête should come after Reach for the Sky, which it appears remarkably similar to despite the difference in grades.

Coprolyte is the similar to the later route Pray and should be on p385.

The comment: "To the south of Coprolyte are two fine arches" is incorrect since the tidal through cave is to the south, or left of Coprolyte. With Coprolyte in its right place there are only two routes to its left before the end of the shelf and the tidal through cave. The comment should read: "To the south (left) of Footloose are two fine arches, or caves." The cave referred to in the description for Footloose is the right-hand arch.

Don't think Twice should only be two stars since the final short easy bit is not good and there is likely to be a vomiting Fulmar just to your left when you pull over after the steep bit! There is no proper belay at the top of this route and it might be better to belay on the ledge (Fulmar allowing) just below the top and then over the back of the grassy peninsula. This may also apply to some of the other routes here.

Freakers Crack is only worth one star, and between this and Pippet at the Post are two new routes. This area is generally best approached by abseil down Pippet at the Post from the large boulder on the cliff top to a non-tidal ledge.

Chance Encounter 15m HVS 5a. R.Wallace, B.Tosh. 14th May 2005.
Start 1m north of Freaker's Crack. Climb an overhanging crack to a bay. Easier climbing up a corner leads to a jutting prow that is turned to the left up another clean corner.

Note: R.Anderson stepped left to avoid some guano and climbed the centre of the wall to finish up short cracks (E2 5b).

Voodoo People 14m HVS 5a. R.Wallace, R.Christie, J.Malcolm. 7th June 2005.
The crack springing from above the right end of the ledge at the foot of Pippet at the Post.
Note: Repeated by R.Anderson, C.Anderson on 26th June 2005. Their name Light Work appears in *Scottish Rock Climbs,* as the earlier ascent was not known at the time.

Imperial Lather 15m E1 5a ***. R.Anderson, C.Anderson. 26th June 2005.
Just right of Pippet at the Post, climb a thin crack, then step right and steeply climb horizontal breaks to the top.

Belarusk 16m E1 5b *. J.Malcolm, R.Wallace. 8th June 2005.
Climbs the wall between Border Raid and Angel of Sleep without using the right-hand wall of Border Raid. Start up the mini chimney, move left and pull through the roof using the twin cracks. Follow the right-hand crack up the slab on to a narrow ledge, then trend right and pull over another roof to the top.

The Grey Coastline 15m VS 4b. R.Wallace, J.Malcolm. 15th May 2005.
Climb the Grey Coast alcove on to the wall above. Branch diagonally left and follow the crack past the big ledge and straight to the top (probably climbed before).

The Big Flat Wall (GPS – ND 18789 31771)
Note from R.Anderson: Routes are generally over starred, the climbing is good but the upper right side of the face has a grass ledge cutting across it occupied by gulls. It also weeps here. Cask Strength should be to the left of Macallan's Choice. The Other Landscape is probably only 4c. Laphroaig is probably VS 5a. Two Good Friends is eliminate and if removed from the equation Puffin Attack is probably worth three stars.

The next three routes start from the ledge of Primary Corner.

Soap on Tyre 16m VS 4c. R.Wallace, R.Christie. 17th October 2005.
Start up the right-hand wall of the corner and move up and right to stand on a good foothold at the base of the hanging arête. Delicately climb the left wall of the arête to a platform at the top of a crack. Climb past a big ledge to a bigger ledge below another hanging arête. Climb the wall just to its left.

Kelp Line 16m Severe 4b. R.Christie, R.Wallace. 17th October 2005.
From the ledge, traverse left round the arête to the base of V-cracks in the middle of the wall. Follow the right-hand crack to a platform on the arête. Continue to a grassy ledge and join Primary Corner for a short open corner, then move left to finish up a separate crack.

Thank Cod for Friends 16m HVS 5a. R.Wallace, R.Christie. 17th October 2005.
From the base of the V-cracks, delicately follow the thin left crack. At its top,

move up left into a large triangular niche, then up and left again to finish up a corner.

Stack Area:
Personalized Dwarf 12m Severe. J.Malcolm, R.Wallace, R.Christie. 31st May 2005.
Start on the seaward side of the wall to the right of Sunspot. Climb by a small alcove to a ledge below the main overhanging arête, then continue up the right-hand side of the arête.

Silly Blunt 12m VS 4b. J. & D. Preston. 29th October 2005.
The blunt arête left of Out of Reach. Climb the initial wall to a ledge. Continue up the blunt arête, using holds mainly on the right, to ledges at the top.

Yellow Streak 12m VS 4c. J. & D. Preston. 29th October 2005.
The steep recessed lichenous wall to the left of the blunt arête. Climb easily up to a large chockstone on the right. Finish slightly rightwards up the steep wall above. Escapable but a good direct line. Possibly a more direct line of the following route – Ed?

Dabble 10m Severe 4a. R.Wallace, S.Ross. 10th July 2005.
From the base of Out of Reach, start a couple of metres to the left up a step. Follow a right diagonal crack then up onto a ledge. Step left and pull round a flake to the top.

Dibble 10m Severe 4a. R.Christie, G.Milne. 23rd April 2005.
Left of Dabble, climb the sweeping crack and climb directly to finish up the arête.

Catching The Worm 12m Severe 4b. R.Wallace (unsec). 27th March 2005.
Climb a wide crack between the stack and the wall of Coaster into a huge niche. Move up left to climb the narrow chimney.

Bedrock:
Freddie Flintoff 12m Hard Severe 4b **. J.Lyall, J.Preston. 2nd September 2005.
The crack and wall just right of Bam Bam.

Rubble Trubble 12m VS 4b *. J.Lyall, J.Preston. 2nd September 2005.
Climbs the wall direct between Bully for Brontosaurus and Sorry Scorry.

Right Barney 12m VS 4c *. J.Preston, J.Lyall. 2nd September 2005.
Climb the wall right of Pebbles Dash by an obvious sidepull to gain the ledge at a slight ramp and go straight up.

Pebbles Dash 12m VS 4c *. J.Preston, J.Lyall. 2nd September 2005.
Climb the wall just right of the left arête (Thinking of Wilma) by flakes to a ledge and go straight up the top wall.

ORKNEY, Yesnaby, Qui Ayre Point, Point Wall:
An excellent wall of superb weathered sandstone, packed with lines. Most are

strenuous but well protected, particularly with small cams. All are close together but independent and their proximity does not detract from them. The wall faces due south. It is in an exposed position and the bulk of the routes require calm seas and a mid to low tide for access.
Descent: At low tide the base of the routes can be accessed by a steep little down climb from the west, left (looking in) from Half Buoy or from the East by The Crevasse descent then along the wave cut platform below The Tower. Easier, and so that a number of routes can be bagged, is to abseil. The routes from The Bends rightwards can be accessed at higher states of the tide by abseil with belays taken on tapering ledges below Tuttie's Wall etc.

The Fantastic Mr Fox 10m E2 6a *. T.Rankin, D.Fox. July 2005.
This route climbs the wall between Route 91 and Up tae High Doh. Start 2m left of Up tae… climb the wall direct using an obvious two finger pocket to overcome the blankest section (crux). Well protected.

Up tae High Doh 10m E1 5b ***. T.Rankin, D.Fox. July 2005.
Five metres right of Route 91 is another fine crack running the full height of the wall. A superb well protected pitch.

Billy Bean's Dream 12m E3 5c **. T.Rankin, D.Fox. July 2005.
Right of Deep Blue is a white calcite mark at one-third height on the cliff. Start below this and climb the steep wall direct to jugs just right of the mark, stand up right then step back left to follow superb breaks direct to the top always to the left of the stepped corner-line. Low in the grade.

The following routes can be accessed at higher tide levels by abseiling down near Tuttie's Neuk and belaying along the tapering ledge.

The Bends 12m E2 5c **. N.Morrison, D.Fox. July 2005.
Right again and at half-height on the cliff are two left facing overlapping corners. Gain these from below and right (the leftmost end of the tapering ledges) and finish direct from their top left-hand side.

Blue Crush 12m E1 5b *. N.Morrison, D.Fox. July 2005.
Right of the overlapping corners is a right-slanting crack running between horizontal breaks. Start as for the previous route. Lovely climbing.

Birdman 11m E1 5b *. N.Morrison, D.Fox. July 2005.
Right again and before the vague black crack of Tuttie's Wall there is a thin crack-line with a small triangular jutting block above a break at half-height. Climb to, then up the crack and the wall above.

Tower Area:
Standing Stone 20m E3 5c **. N.Morrison, D.Fox July 2005.
Climbs the cracks on the edge of the impending wall immediately right of The Quarryman. Climb through a niche into the cracks (common to The Big Swall), then continue up the edge. This soon leads to into The Quarryman for a rest of sorts. From the rest step back right onto the wall and forge on up the cracks to the top.

The Clett:
Note: The route in SMCJ 2005 is called Things Complete.

HOY, The Berry:
General Sheridan 245m XS. S.Sustad, M.Fowler (alt.). 10th September 2005. Takes the highest headland of The Berry. From the top of Beriberi walk north to a deep gully after 100m. Descend the gully (abseil required over a 15m steep section) to sea-level. Wade north (low tide essential), pass through an arch and continue over large slippery boulders until the boulders run out and the cliffs drop sheer into the sea. Swim 15m to pull out on ledges above high tide level. Traverse these to belay 6m right of an obvious corner just short of the crest of the buttress.
1. 20m 5b/c. Go up steeply, traverse into the corner and follow it to an obvious break.
2. 15m. Traverse horizontally left, drop down left again, then back up to a ledge.
3. 15m. Continue the traverse easily, then move up when possible to belay beneath two parallel cracks just left of the crest of the buttress.
4. 20m 5b. Go up the right crack for 3m, transfer to the left crack and continue to a break.
5. 10m. Go up and then traverse left for 8m on the next break. Move up to beneath red overhangs.
6. 20m 5b. Climb a short right-trending overhanging crack and continue up a groove line.
7. 30m. Continue up a groove on the right wall to a terrace. Trend up right to a block beneath a wide crack.
8. 40m. Climb the crack and easier ground above to below a red band.
9. 30m 5a. Climb a crack in the centre of a depression in the red band to belay on a break above.
10. 30m. Continue straight up to reach the left-bounding edge of the buttress. Climb the edge for 10m.
11. 15m 5a. Move right and climb a break to a fine finish.

SHETLAND, MUCKLE ROE
Da Kist 65m E1 **. M.Tighe, D.Lee, J.McClenaghan. 25th June 2005.
An excellent 50m stack of superb red granite off the west side of Muckle Roe (HU 652 293). From a small ledge at the north-west corner go up and left along airy off-balance ledges on the landward face until progress is barred by a gently overhanging wall with a diagonal crack. From runners in the crack, tension down and left to gain the central fault system, which leads to the fine panoramic summit. Though bone dry on the first ascent the central fault-line is the natural drainage line and could be very wet. Approach was made by fish farm boat, though a long swim is possible from good ledges on the shore opposite.

Picts Ness, Walls of Troll: (HU 2973 8681) Partly Tidal East Facing:
The spectacular red granite cliffs on the west coast of Muckle Roe mainly consists of poor quality rock. The Walls of Troll provide some good lines on weathered granite and an igneous plug in a sheltered geo.
Approach: From Brae follow the A970 west for 1 km and turn left onto the road for Muckle Roe. Follow this south almost to the end and take a track on the right 100m west of Narwood at HU 3261 6310. The track splits after 1km (this short

connecting section of track is not shown on the latest OS map). Take the left fork and follow this to park at HU 3092 6425 before the track descends steeply to a bridge. Contour from the parking space through Leftie Scord to Picts Ness. The walls and prominent hanging corner of the Troll Catcher are easily seen from the cliff top. All routes are gained by abseil and only affected at high tide when there is a large swell.

The Troll Catcher 35m Hard Severe 4b ***. R.I.Jones, J.Sanders. 13th June 2005.
The prominent hanging corner-crack of weathered red granite against a wall of igneous rock provides a great jamming crack for those with hands the size of trolls. For humans a couple of large cams (4 or 5) will help protect the lower section. Start 3m right of the corner and climb up to join the crack at 4m. Continue up the wall/crack to the top.

Who's Afraid of The Light? 30m HVS 4c. R.I.Jones, J.Sanders. 13th June 2005.
Right of the corner is a broken crack-line. Climb this on poor rock.

To the right of this route the wall of igneous rock deteriorates. The next wall of blackened granite provides good climbing on solid rock from ledges that run along the bottom of the wall. The first route starts 3m right of a hidden grooved chimney.

Hobbits For Dinner 20m Hard Severe 4b. R.I.Jones, J.Sanders. 13th June 2005.
Climb the wall just left of a small right-facing corner to a break at 5m and climb the crack-line above.

Troll Wall 20m HVS 5a **. R.I.Jones, J.Sanders. 13th June 2005.
Start 2m right of a short rightward slanting crack-line/break and below a thin crack-line that starts at the break. Climb the wall and crack-line to the top. Good balanced climbing.

Slapping The Troll In The Face 20m Mild VS 4b *. J.Sanders, R.I.Jones. 13th June 2005.
Start from the ledge at the bottom of the chimney. Step left onto the face and climb the wall on small broken crack-lines left of the two large crack-lines.

Bad Troll 20m Very Difficult. J.Sanders, R.I.Jones. 13th June 2005.
Climb the chimney to the two crack-lines on the wall and climb these to the top. A disappointing route up two good looking crack-lines.

All Trolled Up And No Where To Go 20m Difficult **. J.Sanders, R.I.Jones. 13th June 2005.
Climb the chimney and the short final wall.

Right of the chimney is another wall of clean granite with a slightly right-slanting crack-line up the centre.

Party Troll 20m Hard Severe 4b *. J.Sanders, R.I.Jones. 13th June 2005.
Climb the crack easily to a steep pull through a bulge at a hanging flake at two-thirds height and then to the top.

NESS OF HAMAR:
The coast around Riva Geo, Red Head and along to Silvi Geo provide a range of climbs up 20m which are being developed by local climbers, but the routes have not yet been written up. The following routes had not been tackled prior to the ascents listed below.

Approach: Red Head is best approached by parking just before the gate to the croft at The Berg (HU 3119 7606) and then contouring around the hills.

Medusa Wall:
(HU 2968 7442) Partly Tidal West Facing
The routes are only affected at high tide and with a large swell.

Snake Face 15m VS 4b. J.Sanders, R.I.Jones. 11th June 2005.
Start at the centre of the first wall on the left from the descent to the beach. Climb the broken crack-line and then the face direct where the crack-line slants rightwards.

The Gorgan 20m E1 5b. R.I.Jones, J.Sanders. 11th June 2005.
10-15m right of Snake Face is a hanging crack-line which is undercut with a lighter band of rock. Start below the hanging crack-line and climb to the small left facing overhanging corner. Pull around this into the crack and climb this to the top.

Medusa 20m HVS 5a *. R.I.Jones, J.Sanders. 11th June 2005.
Start 2m right of The Gorgan and climb up and rightwards to the base of the crack-line. Climb this to the top. High in the grade.

Dragon Geo:
(HU 2972 7432) Partly Tidal South-West facing:
Only affected at high tide.

Taming the Dragon 20m E2 5c **. R.I.Jones, J.Sanders. 14th June 2005.
The corner crack-line provides good climbing and an awkward crux at the top.

ESHANESS:
Goblin Cleaver 40m E2 5c ***. R.I.Jones, J.Sanders. 18th June 2005.
This route climbs a curving crack-line on an overhanging left-facing corner system in the north-west wall below the lighthouse and has very different character to the other climbs nearby. From the car park head west to a concreted pipeline north-west of the blow hole. Follow the pipeline to its end, then head directly north to the cliff top to the top of a corner-groove that forms the exit to the route. The route suffers from a small amount of seepage after rain at the crux. Abseil to a triangular ledge beneath the overhanging cliff face. From the ledge climb a rib to the hanging crack-line. Pull around into this and make difficult moves to easier ground and a final lay back crack to the top.

Aisha 35m E1 5a *. R.I.Jones, J.McClenaghan. 19th June 2005.
Climb the centre of the wall right of Atlantic Sea. Bold but never strenuous. A large rack helps creative gear placement!

Notes: Black Watch is VS 4c **, not HVS.
The Wind Cries… the description for this route seems to climb the same rib and groove/scoop as Mary?

Living the Dream 30m E3 5c. A.Wainright, A.Cave. 7th June 2005.
The chimney line immediately right of Cave Crack (Lost for Words?). Climb the groove in the left wall of the chimney, over an overlap, to reach and follow the chimney.

Aero Arête 30m HVS 4c. A.Long, P.Robins, B.Bransby. 7th June 2005.
The attractive slabby stepped arête, half-way between Black Watch (?) and the next wall. The route is a lot easier than it looks though quite bold. Abseil down to a sloping ledge above the sea on the slabby right wall. Climb the slabby right wall of the arête to a roof. Steep moves left through this with good holds, leads to a jug romp up the upper arête.

Team Specsavers 30m E5 6a. P.Robins, B.Bransby. 7th June 2005.
The next major zawn, and perhaps the last, to the south of Black Watch has a large 30m north facing wall with an arching roof at two-thirds height. The wall is bounded by a steep smooth corner, high up on the right above a ledge. This route climbs the centre of the wall, crossing the roof to finish up a short hanging groove on the right. Abseil to a small ledge, just above the sea, at the base of the right-hand of two cracks below the roof. Climb the crack and continue rightwards up an easy large flake. Move up to the roof and awkwardly left, then up to a rail leading through the roof, crux, and onto the upper wall. Easier but bold climbing leads up and right, aiming for the left-facing hanging groove and gear.

THE FAITHER:
The Faither (far point) is the most northerly point of land to the west of Ronas Voe.
Approach: From the parking spot for Warie Gill (HU 2460 8245) walk north to the headland.

Faither Stack:
(HU 2564 8590) Tidal South-West and North-East facing:
This fine 35m stack is hidden away from view by the surrounding cliffs. Access to the stack is gained by a 50m free hanging abseil from the cliff-top north-west of the stack to a wave washed platform, followed by a dash to the stack across a channel between waves up to mid tide. A 100m abseil rope is required as anchor points are spaced out.

Don't Even Think About Going To Spain 35m Hard Severe 4b **. J.Sanders, R.I.Jones. 15th June 2005.
Start to the left-hand side of the face below a right-slanting groove that starts at one-third height. Climb this and the groove to the top on good rock.

Cheshire Cat 30m VS 4c ****. R.I.Jones, J.Sanders. 15th June 2005.
Guaranteed to bring out a big smile in all who climb it. Climbs the centre of the face on excellent rock. Climb to a small left-facing corner, climb the wall to its right and the crack-line above. Step left into a shallow groove and then to the top.

Faither's Day 30m Hard Severe 4b. J.Sanders, R.I.Jones. 15th June 2005.
Climb the V-groove to the right of the wall, then traverse around on the south-east wall which is climbed to the top.

There is a poor quality line on the north-east facing wall which is best approached by abseil from the top of the stack.

It Never Rains, It Pours 35m Hard Severe 4a. R.I.Jones, J.Sanders. 15th June 2005.
Climbs the wall to the left of the large hanging left-slanting crack-line on poor rock. (Climbed in the rain while waiting for the tide).

Arched Wall:
(HU 2565 8590) Non-tidal South-West facing:
This is the wall opposite Faither stack which is descended by the line of the abseil for approaching the stack. Both routes can be climbed from the tidal platform as an alternative to a long jumar up the wall after climbing the stack. The wall is broken in its lower half by a black right-slanting ramp line and is made up of large pockets. A wide range of cams are useful.

Memory Games 55m VS 4b *. R.I.Jones, J.Sanders, P.Whitworth. 16th June 2005.
Abseil to a large ledge at the bottom of a right-slanting ramp/crack.
1. 20m 4a. Climb the ramp/crack to a large spike.
2. 35m 4b. Climb the wall to the left for 3m, then traverse along a ledge (possible belay) before making an exposed pull around the arête onto a wall. Climb large pockets up easier ground to beneath an overhang to reach a corner and climb the wall on the left to finish.

Sea of Change 40m HVS 5a ***. R.I.Jones, P.Whitworth. 16th June 2005.
Abseil to a small niche to the left and slightly lower than the start of Memory Games and just right of a left-facing corner. Climb the arête to another smaller corner at 12m. Step right back onto the arête and climb this in a fine position to a short steep groove. Climb this direct and the wall above to easier ground. Finish at the same short final wall as for Memory Games.

RONAS VOE:
Many other routes have been climbed by the Whitworth brothers. The crag is easily accessible by boat from Heylor, or by a long walk from the east. All the routes here are on granite outcrops set back from the sea.

High Crag:
The slabby upper tier.
Up on the Hill 10m Severe *. W.Moir, T. Whitworth. 23rd July 2005.
The obvious right-facing corner.

Up the Hill Backwards 10m VS 4c *. W.Moir, T.Whitworth. 23rd July 2005.
Takes the thin crack through the bulge left of previous route.

Low Crag:
The squat crag just off the beach.

Mussel Beach 10m E3 6a *. W.Moir, P.Whitworth. 23rd July 2005.
The central crack-line through a bulging nose. Go up right of the crack, then pull back left and up via twin cracks.

Right-Hand Crag:
Below and right of High Crag.
The Blade 14m E2 5c **. W.Moir, P.Whitworth. 23rd July 2005.
A fine route up the left-slanting crack-line.

Heylor High Water 10m E1 5b *. W.Moir, P.Whitworth. 23rd July 2005.
A crack left of The Blade, joining it at the top.

PAPA STOUR, Kirsten Stacks (HU 1525 6040):
Two fine 20m stacks guard the entrance to Kirsten Hole. The stacks are separated in places by only 10cms, but they remain two separate stacks.
Approach: Abseil from stakes to a tidal corner directly north of the stacks and swim to the platform on the west end of the west stack with the end of the rope. The second then relocates the abseil to a block opposite the stack to make a 40m abseil/tyrolean straight onto the stack. 100m rope is required. Retreat is by tyrolean from the top of the stack.

The Guardian 15m Very Difficult. R.I.Jones, S.Calvin, J.Sanders. 12th June 2005.
Climb the west arête direct. It is possible to step on the summit of the east stack from the west summit.

Bordie Head:
A good cliff made of hardened red sandstone, just west of Redbeard's through cave. A scramble down some ledges over to the west of the cliff leads to a big rock platform beneath the crag. Walking east beneath the crag, a step up gains a narrower ledge as the cliff rises in height.

The Forewick Stud 25m E5 6a. P.Robins, B.Bransby. 8th June 2005.
The HVS-looking line almost immediately as one gains the upper ledge. Climb onto a ledge on the left at 3m. Step right into a slabby groove and boldly shimmy up to a ledge on the right. Attack the steep crack above till a hard move left gains an easier groove and the top.

Holy Shit 25m E5 6a. B.Bransby, P.Robins, A.Cave, A.Wainright. 9th June 2005.
A steep line in the middle of the wall, leading to an obvious hanging flake on the upper wall. Climb up the wall, with a hard move to gain a small ledge beneath the steepening. Continue up on good holds, gaining the right-facing flaky groove. Continue up this to its top, then step up and rightwards to finish. Low in the grade.
Papa Don't Preach 35m E5 5c/6a. P.Robins, B.Bransby. 9th June 2005.
An amazing route, traversing left from the eastern end of the upper ledge to gain a hidden hanging sweeping slabby corner. From the end of the ledge, traverse boldly left for 7m, then go up to an obvious small ledge. Climb the short right-facing black corner above, crux, then step left onto a slab beneath the right-facing

continuation corner. Climb the slab and corner, in a wild position, until a steepening gains an upper corner and the top. Low in the grade.

The Nose Tirls of Nort Lungie Geo:
Deeper Darker 30m E5 6a. A.Cave, B.Bransby. 9th June 2005.
This is a huge and complex cave/geo, reminiscent of a giant Swiss Cheese and largely capped by rock, to the south of Kirsten Hole. A bridge of capping rock remains near the edge of the cave then it opens out before becoming mainly covered again. From the depths of the cave, a chimney extends some 20m across the centre of the roof to emerge through a small hole in the roof. The route can be gained by climbing down through a large hole, some 50m back from the coast. A ledge runs down the south side of the cave from which the route can be viewed. From the back of the cave, climb through a body-sized thread to gain the chimney. Climb up some way into the darkness to belay. Wriggle and shuffle outwards on mainly good features for 20m, heading for the small source of light. A very traditional and enjoyable outing.

WESTERWICK, Two Towers Stack (HU 2763 4210):
The stack has two distinct towers which are separate in only the largest of seas.
Approach: Abseil from stakes or blocks to ledges opposite the stack and swim the 7m channel to the stack and set up a 50m abseil/tyrolean on the connecting platform between the stacks. Retreat is by jumaring back up the tyrolean to the cliff-top.

West Tower:
Building Blocks on a Rockin' Top 15m VS 4b *. R.I.Jones, P.Whitworth, J.Sanders. 17th June 2005.
Climb the south-west arête on good rock for 7m, then step right and climb the corner to the top. Descent is by abseil.

East Tower:
Climbing with a Porpoise 15m Hard Severe 4a. J.Sanders, R.I.Jones. 17th June 2005.
Climb the stepped wall between the towers to a corner and climb the wall on the right to the top. The corner climbed direct is 4c. Descent is by an easy scramble down the east ramp.

UNST
A nice little crag on this small headland of granite, previously occupied by the MOD, right on the north-eastern tip of Unst. Park at the end of the road (some routes in the guidebook are found on the eastern coast down) and walk north through the ruined military units towards the coast. A small NE-facing (?) cliff can be found to the west of a small arch. The crag has an obvious finger crack running up the centre.

The Most Northerly Route in Britain 10m E5 6b. P.Robins, B.Bransby. 13th June 2005.
The obvious central finger crack. A bold start leads to surprisingly awkward and strenuous climbing, easing towards the top.
Note: Not quite the most northerly, since M.Fowler, C.Jones and A.Nisbet climbed the Outstack in 1992, albeit at a lesser grade (Easy).

NORTHERN HIGHLANDS CENTRAL

No routes here as the new guide should already be out.

NORTHERN HIGHLANDS SOUTH

No routes here as the new guide is due out soon.

CAIRNGORMS

LOCHNAGAR, Southern Sector:
Triangle Buttress 70m II. S.M.Richardson. 18th November 2005.
Start from the foot of the Red Spout and climb the left-trending ramp running across the front face of the buttress. Climb straight up over a steeper section and continue up the easier buttress crest to the top. The route is a Moderate scramble in summer.

Perseverance Wall:
Starburst 70m II. S.M.Richardson. 18th November 2005.
The first line on the second rib of Perseverance Wall. Start 15m left of Gale Force Groove and follow a groove-line chacterised with a steep left wall. Move right and finish up the final ridge near the top.

The Gift 80m II. S.M.Richardson. 18th November 2005.
The prominent curving right narrow gully line on the fourth rib. Follow the gully past a steep bulge at one-third height and finish right of the final tower. A sweet little route and one of the best of the easier climbs in the Southern Sector.

Temptress 80m III. S.M.Richardson. 18th November 2005.
The groove line up the centre of the fourth rib. Climb this over three bulges to finish just right of the exit slope of The Gift.

Perseverance Groove 80m II. S.Stronach, A.Lyons. 18th March 2006.
The gully bounding the left side of Perseverance Rib. Climb the gully to half-height (where a snow slope exits left) and continue up the line of the gully into a groove that leads back up and right to a ledge. Continue up a thinly iced slab for 10m and finish up an easy chimney to exit onto the crest of the rib.

Central Buttress:
The Finalist 100m V,6. S.M.Richardson, C.Cartwright. 8th January 2006.
The prominent groove in the centre of the face.
1. 50m. Start at the foot of Shallow Gully and climb straight up over turfy mixed ground towards the groove. Cross the diagonal faults taken by Magical Mystery Tour and Sciolist and climb up right of a smooth undercut wall. Step left across the wall and move up to easier ground below the corner.
2. 30m. Move up into the corner and make a difficult exit right at its top. Belay on blocks up and right.
3. 20m. Continue up grooves in the line of the corner to join the crest of Central Buttress.

Sgurr Nan Gillean and Am Bhasteir at dawn. Photo: David Ritchie.
Chris Cartwright climbing Ninus (III), Coire Bhrochain, Braeriach. Photo: Simon Richardson.

Eagle Buttress:

Where Eagles Dare 250m VII,8. G.Robertson, S.M.Richardson. 10th February 2006.

An outstanding route taking the vertical headwall at the top of Eagle Buttress. The climbing is sustained, well protected and sensationally exposed, and the second pitch is one of the finest mixed pitches on the mountain.

1. to 3. Climb Eagle Buttress to where the original line bears right. Move up to the foot of a broad left-slanting groove system that cuts through the lower half of the headwall.

4. 35m. Climb the left wall of the groove with increasing difficulty and step right into a short corner near the top. Move up this to reach a good ledge below the vertical headwall.

5. 35m. Starting from near the left edge of the wall, climb a right-slanting crack to reach the central crack system. Follow this to a good ledge just below the top of the wall.

6. 30m. Continue up the wall to its top then move right and climb a short corner-crack cutting in to the final ridge that leads easily to the top.

Scarface Wall:

Scarface Wall 140m VIII,8 **. I.Parnell, G.Robertson. 8th April 2006.

A superb exposed route, with varied and very sustained climbing, taking a natural line of weakness curving leftwards across the right wall of Raeburn's Gully. The final 60m are common with The Straight-Jacket. On this ascent, in good conditions, the Straight Jacket off-width held some ice, but the steep corner above it did not and was harder. Start below twin grooves at a point midway between the Scarface icefall and the cave pitch of Raeburn's Gully.

1. 25m. Place a high side runner in the base of the right-hand groove and make a thin traverse horizontally right past a crack to gain turf in a little right-facing groove. Go up this and step left to gain and follow a steep fault which leads to snow bay. Belay at the back of the bay below a tapering groove.

2. 25m. Climb a short way up the groove, then pull out left onto a ledge. Traverse left across the smooth wall to gain an easier groove which leads to another snow bay. Move left again to belay below a short left-facing corner sporting a wide crack in its slabby left wall.

3. 30m. Climb the corner with difficulty and continue on leftwards into a slot formed by a precarious block. From the top of the block, step down left to gain and follow a strenuous groove, then move up right to a spacious platform below a wide chimney-crack.

4 to 6. 60m. Follow The Straight-Jacket to the top.

CREAG AN DUBH LOCH, False Gully Wall:

Coon's Yard 40m E1 5b. R.J.Archbold, G.S.Strange. 25th May 1980. From the grass slope beneath The Gathering and The Quickening, go left up an obvious slanting fault and climb a left-facing corner to belay at a grass ledge below a grey wall (left of the prominent pink wall). Climb the grey wall to easy ground (1PA used on the grey wall due to onset of rain).

GLEN CLOVA, Winter Corrie:

Wild Cat Wall 180m V,6. C.Cartwright, S.M.Richardson. 27th November 2005.

Jonathan Preston on the top pitch of Compressor VI,6, on Aonach Beag. Photo: Andy Nisbet.

A direct mixed line up the centre of the cliff. Start 40m right of Diagonal Gully below a hidden left-slanting chimney-ramp.
1. and 2. 80m. Climb the gully over a chokestone to the Basin. Move up to the foot of the headwall shaped like a inverted triangle.
3. 40m Gain the headwall steeply from the left, then climb easier ground to the foot of the vertical final wall. Belay below a prominent off-width crack.
4. 20m. Climb the off-width and continue up the steep continuation crack to a good ledge below and right of a large sloping roof.
5. 40m. Continue up the right of twin corners above and exit on to a left-trending ramp that leads to a long horizontal ledge. A superb pitch.
6. 20m. Move right along the dwindling ledge to a break that leads to the top.

BEINN A' BHUIRD, Coire nan Clach:
Unnamed 80m II. S.M.Richardson. 5th February 2006.
The broader buttress right of Ribeye. Gain the crest from the left and follow it over a short ice step to a steep exit.

Garbh Choire:
Unnamed 175m E2 **. S.M.Richardson, I.Small. 15th July 2005.
An excellent route taking the right edge of the front face of Mitre Ridge. The third pitch is sensationally exposed. Start directly below the well defined pillar split by a crack that lies just left of the initial chimney of Cumming-Crofton Route.
1. 30m 5a. Scramble up to the crack and climb it through an overlap to a good platform on top of the pillar.
2. 30m 5b. The route continues up the slim hanging groove in the edge between the corners of The Sacrament and Cumming-Crofton Route. Move right, then back left into the hanging groove and climb it to exit on easier ground on the front face of Mitre Ridge. Continue easily up the edge to belay where Mitre Link Variation joins from the right.
3. 35m 5c. Go up to the foot of the First Tower and climb the right edge on hidden holds.
4. 20m Scramble along the ridge to the notch below the Second Tower.
5. 20m 5c. Climb the wall on the front face of the tower (to the left of pitch 6 of The Sacrament) past a prominent protruding flake. Strenuous and awkward to protect.
6. 40m. Scramble to the plateau.

BEINN BHROTAIN, Coire Cath nam Fionn:
The following were climbed in lean icy conditions and may bank out under heavy snow. They may have been climbed before.

A Minus Gully 150m I. M.W.Holland. 31st January 2006.
The large dog-leg gully on the right of Fingal's Butress gives an easy line to the summit dome. Follow easy-angled snow into an amphitheatre, then a large open right-trending ramp, finishing up a narrowing and steepening gully.

Skirmish 120m II. M.W.Holland. 31st January 2006.
Approx. 150m below the Beinn Bhrotain/Monadh Mor col a big ramp leads right below a short buttress to gain a snowfield below a larger buttress. The route takes

the gully on the left of the larger buttress and is seen as a right-trending ramp on approach to the corrie.

Finn's Tale 200m II. M.W.Holland. 1st February 2006.
A Y-shaped gully which leads up from the left side of the second basin right of the Beinn Bhrotain/Monadh Mor col (at NN 946 933).

BRAERIACH, Garbh Choire Mor:
She-Devil's Buttress, Left-Hand Finish 30m V,5. S.M.Richardson, C.Cartwright. 27th December 2005.
In lean conditions, She-Devil's Buttress can provide a worthwhile mixed route. If the final wall is unconsolidated, traverse left for 5m into an overhung corner and climb this to finish on the crest of the buttress directly below the snow prow.

Garbh Choire Dhaidh:
Note: O.Metherell and I.Parnell made a free ascent of Digeridoo on 29th December 2005 after belaying at the wedge of blocks.

Pea Soup 250m II. A.Nisbet. 3rd February 2006.
Roughly in the centre of the south-west wall of the corrie and left of two steeper buttresses is this shallow gully. Start up a lower continuation which ends with an 8m ice pitch, potentially quite steep and leading to snow slopes at mid-height. Move left to the main gully which steepens to finish with an easier angled ice pitch. A rib on the left is a likely break in the cornice.

Chewing' the Fat 250m II. A.Nisbet, J.Preston. 31st January 2006.
Right of centre on the south-west wall of the corrie are the two steeper buttresses under the plateau, the left being larger. Between the two is a groove and ramp which leads into a high bay. A lower shallow snow gully leads into the groove and ramp which in lean icy conditions may hold continuous ice. A break in the cornice on the left is essential.

Coire Bhrochain, West Buttress:
Molar 80m Severe. A.Nisbet. 13th July 2005.
The leftmost ridge on the West Buttress. It looks more impressive than The Fang from the corrie floor but turns out to be much less prominent and therefore a bit artificial. A direct line at about VS would be better.
1. 30m. Climb slabby ground near the crest to a steepening.
2. 50m 4a. Move left and back right on waterwashed slabs to gain the top of a wide crack which is just left of the crest. At a second steepening, move into the base of a V-groove on the gully wall, then immediately swing back out left on to the crest which is climbed to a final steepening. Traverse right and climb the gully wall to reach a final horizontal crest.

Powerpoint 250m II. A.Nisbet. 26th January 2006.
In lean but cold conditions, a low-angled icefall forms on the broken ground left of the main buttress. Climb this and finish up the gully between Molar and The Fang, sometimes passing under a wedged block.

CARN ETCHACHAN, Lower Tier:
Starting Pistol 100m IV,4. J.Lyall, E.Pirie. 2nd January 2006.
A line up the scooped depression on the far left of the lower tier. Start at the foot of Eastern Approach Route.
1. 35m. Slant up left past the corner of Far East, breaking up right at the first chance to belay on a snow shelf.
2. 30m. Move right and climb up rightwards by a narrow groove (avoiding the easy snow ramp on the right) to a ledge and block.
3. 35m. Go up left by icy steps to climb a turf groove, to the left of a loose blocky corner, and work up left to the Great Terrace.
Note: Finishing Line (SMCJ 2003) was climbed above and thought IV,6 (J.Preston agrees).

SHELTERSTONE CRAG:
Note: The note in SMCJ 2001 that G.Ettle and S.Koch climbed Citadel Winter Variation free at VI,7 suggests that this was the first free ascent, but the original ascent of this variation by R.Anderson was free. The grade is G.Ettle's opinion.

GARBH UISGE CRAG:
Feld Spur 100m III. J.Lyall. 3rd January 2004.
The spur right of Quartz Gully.

STAG ROCKS:
Ashes Fever 40m HVS 5a *. J.Lyall, J.Preston. 12th September 2005.
Start up the left-slanting ramp of The Troglodyte and make an airy traverse right into the large corner which is followed to an old peg. Move left across the slab and up the edge to gain left-slating cracks which are followed to the belay on Quartz Diggers Cave route. Two old pegs indicate a previous ascent or attempt close to this line.

COIRE AN T-SNEACHDA, Mess of Pottage:
Crack Pot 120m V,6. G.Ettle, J.Lyall. 2nd December 2004.
The buttress edge right of Opening Break. Start at the diagonal fault as for Honeypot.
1. 20m. Climb the initial diagonal break, then slant left to belay at the foot of the corner of Opening Break.
2. 50m. Step right onto a ledge, move right and up to a crack-line which is followed to easy ground and the base of the slanting fault of Opening Break.
3. 50m. Gain the buttress on the right by large blocks and slant up right to a flake-crack. Traverse delicately left and up the edge of the wall moving left round the edge to a steep finish. Easy ground to the top.

COIRE AN LOCHAIN, No.1 Buttress:
Open Heart 100m VIII,9 **. I.Parnell, G.Robertson. 10th April 2006.
This excellent and very strenuous route links the first pitch of Ventricle to the crux of Ventriloquist. Protection is generally good, but hard won in the initial groove.
1. 10m. Climb the initial overhanging crack of Ventricle, traverse right for a couple of metres, then pull up to a good ledge beneath an overhanging groove with an in-situ peg at its base.
2. 30m. Climb the groove with increasing difficulty to hard moves rightwards over the bulge and a welcome rest. Step delicately back left into the continuation

groove then climb this with sustained interest to a hard exit onto the big ledge. Traverse left to belay below the crux crack of Ventriloquist.
3. etc. 60m. Follow Ventriloquist to the top.

No. 4 Buttress:
Swallow-tail Pillar 70m VS *. A.Gilmour, J.Lyall. 7th September 2005.
The pillar between Deep Throat and Gaffers Groove. Start below a right-curving corner just right of Deep Throat as for Aqualung.
1. 20m 4a. Start up the curving corner then traverse out right and climb the rib to belay just right of where the pillar eases in angle.
2. 30m 4c. Move left and up a quartz-lined groove on the right side of the pillar, then cracks lead to an awkward mantelshelf ledge. Follow faint cracks up the middle to the top (block belay.)
3. 20m. Scramble up the easy gully or abseil down the line of Deep Throat.

Cut Adrift 105m III,4. J.Lyall, E.Pirie. 19th December 2005.
Follows the parallel fault to Torquing Heads, starting about 15m farther right.
1. 30m. Follow the narrow icy fault (or traverse in along an icy ledge 5m further right if the initial ice is too thin) and continue up to the wider blocky fault.
2. 40m. Continue up the fault, then slant up left to a short chimney. Exit right and go up a left-slanting corner to a ledge just above. The easy upper gully of Torquing Heads is just to the left.
3. 35m. Step out right, then go straight up to finish by a tricky crack in the final rocks.

SGORR GAOITH, A' Pocaidh:
Spyglass Gully 150m III. C.Cartwright, S.M.Richardson. 29th January 2006.
About 40m right of Pick Pocket, a well defined icy gully cuts up through the right side of the cliff. Climb this in three pitches to the top.

GLEN FESHIE, Creag an t-Sluic (NN 834 907):
A broken crag lying above the track contouring round to Lochan an t-Sluic but with a impressive large dark recess with a very steep back and right wall. A pinnacle marks the left side of the recess (Alt. 600m, North-West facing). Approach via Glen Feshie and the track leading from Carnachuin.

Fifer's Fall 70m IV,4 **. R.McMurray, C.McGregor. 6th March 2005.
The large, obvious icefall at the left hand side of the recess.
1. 25m. Climb the ice-fall trending left to belay in the side wall.
2. 45m. Step back right and climb the steep icefall direct until it eventually terminates in the heather above. Belay well back in rocks on the right. Ice screw protection throughout.

Rambler's Ruin 115m III. C.McGregor, A.Carver, M.Dean. 5th March 2005.
Start at a long obvious gully at the right-hand side of the cliff at the lowest rocks.
1. 45m. Climb easily up the gully to a short steepening. Climb this to a large sloping ledge below the steep icefall.
2 and 3. 70m. Climb steeply up the middle of the fall, continuing on slightly easier ground to the final bulge. Surmount this and follow the ice, now much easier, to its finish. The technical grade can be upped slightly depending on the line taken.

NORTH EAST OUTCROPS

Note from N.Morrison: "I would like to use the Journal to apologise for my mistake in failing to fully credit Mike Reed and Scott Muir for their work on the Rosehearty section of the North East Outcrops guide. Mike wrote a substantial section on Murcurry which I checked and edited, while Scott wrote many of the descriptions for the area to the east of Quarry Head which I checked and blended in with the other routes done in this area. Apologies to them and to anyone else who has not been fully credited for their part in the guide."

CLACH NA BEINN:
No.2 Gully III,4. I.Munro. 11th March 2006.
There were two tricky sections, one at mid-height surmounting a slight bulge and the crux was the final exit moves. The key seemed to be using the right wall, as the guidebook suggests for summer. Protection was superb the whole way.

LOGIE HEAD, Embankment 1:
Dennis 14m VS 4c. P.Hill, P.Griffin. 15th June 2003.
Follow the obvious diagonal fault from right to left, keeping feet in the fault-line all the way, finishing past Mousehole.

Autonomous Collective 14m Severe 4a. P.Hill, P.Griffin. 15th June 2003.
Follow the obvious diagonal fault-line from right to left, keeping your hands in the fault-line. Well protected and a good introduction to traversing.

REDHYTHE POINT, The Gully Buttress (NJ 576 672), South-East Face:
Ministry of Silly Walks 35m Hard Severe 4b *. P.Hill, P.Griffin. 1st September 2005.
From a platform at the base of the descent, traverse right no higher than the high-tide mark to belay at the foot of Rampage. Either escape up here (Very Difficult overall) or continue along the channel wall to a character-building hop-off at the far end (protectable). Calm seas desirable.

I'm Brian 10m Moderate. P.Hill, P.Griffin. 1st September 2005.
Just right of the descent is a chimney-corner. Follow this with little difficulty to the top.

And So's My Wife 10m Moderate. P.Hill, P.Griffin. 1st September 2005.
Start 3m right of I'm Brian and follow the pillar to the top.

North-East Face:
Cardinal Fang 10m Very Difficult *. P.Hill, P.Griffin. 1st September 2005.
From the base of Rampage, step left on to the grooved arête and follow this to the top.

Gully Wall:
Flying Circus 12m Hard Severe 4b. P.Hill, P.Griffin. 1st September 2005.
From a small ledge opposite the undercut base of the arête, make a bold move to

gain a small ledge and groove. Follow this and a subsequent groove to join Lobster Line at half-height.

REDHYTHE POINT, The Stack:
The Stack provides a few clean climbs, although the main point of interest is the crossing of the narrow channel separating it from the main crag. It also provides a good deep-water solo traverse at high tide mark above the channel.

Approach: From the stance at the bottom of Rampage on the Gully Buttress, a 3m channel needs to be crossed. A ladder is ideal, and a small flat platform allows one to be used. Alternatively, if an abseil rope has been used to access the Rampage stance a character-building leap of faith using the rope for support can be made. In calm seas, swimming across will most likely be the quickest and easiest method. There are adequate anchors on both sides with which to set up a rope for others to use when crossing. Descent from the top of the stack is via a scramble down the south-east arête.

Bridge of Death DWS 5b. P.Hill. 28th September 2005.
Start at the bottom of the huge crack splitting the main section of the stack, at the high water mark above the channel. Traverse left keeping low to the north-east arête. Either climb out or continue at a slightly higher level (care needed with the state of the sea) all the way round to finish at broken ground on the east face.

Mr Creosote 10m HVS 5a. P.Hill, P.Griffin. 28th September 2005.
This takes the obvious overhanging wall facing the channel. Start at the base of a huge crack and climb a series of scoops direct to the top.

Unladen Swallow 12m Moderate. P.Hill, P.Griffin. 28th September 2005.
Climb the arête starting at the crossing point. Staying left makes the trip more worthwhile.

Coconut 12m Moderate. P.Hill, P.Griffin. 28th September 2005.
On the south face there is a large pointed block leant against the wall. Start just right of this and go straight up clean rock to the summit.

Castle Aargh 5m Severe 4a. P.Hill, P.Griffin. 28th September 2005.
Around the corner to the right from Coconut (and past the descent arête) is a step down above an inlet. Above is a short clean slab of rock with a crack just in from its right edge. Climb the edge direct.

PASS OF BALLATER, Western Section, Middle Tier:
Cavemen Go Clubbing 15m E4 5c. A.Robertson (unsec). 2nd July 2005.
A line between Juniper Crush and Lucky Strike. Start 2m left of Lucky Strike at an obvious white streak and climb this to a good hold at 3m. Continue directly up to a slot (crucial Friend 2.5) under the overlap and surmount this (crux) using a sidepull and nubbin on the lip out left. Move up the slab to a large loose block (care) and a good wire next to the peg. Move up and right to a rest and gear on the big ledge of Lucky Strike. From the ledge foot traverse a shelf 2m leftwards until below a small triangular overhang. Climb this and the continuation groove above.

She's Not So Special 15m E1 5b. A.Robertson (back-roped). 30th July 2005.
Climb Lucky Strike to the ledge and then take the obvious corner straight above the left edge of the ledge (right of the Cavemen Go Clubbing finish). Hard moves gaining and leaving the obvious slot lead to a slightly dirty finish.

Western Section, Upper Tier:
Variation Finish to Dod's Dead Cat E3 6a. A.Robertson, Alasdair Robertson. 24th August 2005.
An interesting variation finish to this or Smith's Arête. From the resting ledge, traverse delicately left for 2m to a finger ledge on the slab (right of the right-hand finish to Peel's Wall). Climb the slab directly via a couple of tricky rock-overs. Low in the grade but harder than the original finish.

MINOR CRAGS, Black Crag (p 480):
The Rib 20m Very Difficult. D.F.Lang, Q.T.Crichton. 24th May 2005.
The most prominent arête ('broken ridge') right of the prow is right of Abernyte Corner and has a small rowan tree at its top. Start at a small overhung recess directly below the line of the arête. Move over a block and ascend a slight overhang to enter a groove. Step left onto a narrow edge and up this to finish. A pleasant little route with good protection.

HIGHLAND OUTCROPS

STRATHNAIRN, Duntelchaig, Seventy Foot Wall:
Kill That Crazy Frog! E4 6a. N.Duboust, M.Lee. 19th June 2005.
Left of Slings is a blank wall. Technical 6a climbing with a potential ground fall leads to the halfway break and a peg runner. Traverse the break right and finish on Slings.

Ping-pong 15m E1 5c. M.Lee, N.Duboust. 14th May 2005.
Some 3m right of Swastika is a cracked wall. Follow a right-hand crack to a large ledge below a short overhanging wall. Climb this using flakes and with difficulty over the lip. Easier to the top.

Pinnacle Crag:
Soixante 10m E1 5c. D.Moy, R.Beaumont, G.Andrew. 24th February 2003.
Start at the foot of Tapered Groove and go diagonally right up to the ledge on The Wall. Traverse left into the middle of the wall and go up via a thin crack to the top.

CREAG NA H-EIGHE (TULLIMET):
The crag is known locally as Tullimet.
The Wide Awake Club 15m E4 5c. D.Cassidy, A.Cassidy. 1997.
Takes the short crack-line on the right side of the steep wall of Sleeping Sickness. Bold but never desperate.

Culpable Homicide 20m E5 6b **. G.Lennox, K.Howett. 17th June 1999.
This climb is right of Hunt the Gunman, climbing through the main roof. Climb the overhanging wall past ledges to a large break directly beneath the largest section

of roof. Follow the holds through the roof, pulling out slightly right and up via slopers.

CRAIG A' BARNS, Polney Crag:
Cold Tips 10m E5 6c *. G.Lennox (solo). 13th May 1998.
Start up Hot Tips, then swing left to the obvious undercling. Stolen Ivy (SMCJ 2002) climbs the arête direct from this. For this route, make a long reach left to finish up Side Line.

Note: S.Holmes climbed the small buttress below large stacked boulders as a start to Pop (Very Difficult). Pleasant, but has been climbed before.

Upper Cave Crag:
Natural High 20m E7 6b ***. G.Lennox, R.Fielding. 14th September 1998.
This route climbs the arête left of High Performance, finishing up the slab right of Coffin Corner. Climb the wall below the arête, stepping right onto the ramp of High Performance. Move round to the left of the square-cut face of the arête (wires 3 & 4 in crack above). Make powerful moves to slap for a jug beside a peg. Clip this (the last runner) and move up the face to where it bulges. Swing round left onto the slab and step up tentatively for the top.

GLEN LEDNOCK, Ballandalloch Farm Crag:
Mighty Mouse 15m E6 6b **. G.Lennox. 4th June 1998.
Climbs the left arête of the crag.

Hong Kong Fuey 25m E6 6b **. G.Lennox. 22nd May 2004.
A direct line up the clean wall right of Solutions to a Small Problem. Place a side runner at the first bulge in Jungle Warfare. Start at a jug in the centre of the wall and climb up to the sloping ledge in the middle of the wall, bold and committing. Continue with interest to a good jug and better protection. Move up to the overlap and pull straight over on jugs.

Glen Lednock, Hanging Buttress:
Hard Shoulder 20m VS 4c. S.Campbell, C.Adam. 31st May 1998.
Climb a bold slabby rib at the right end of the crag to a stance and gear, then over a bulge to finish right.

Glen Lednock, Balnacoul Castle (Base Crag):
Strychnine 10m E3 5b *. C.Adam, J.Lennox. 14th June 1998.
Takes the obvious corner to the left end of Base Crag, bold.

Adrenaline 8m E2 5c *. G.Lennox (solo). 5th July 1998.
Climbs the steep arête down left from White Lines.

Glen Lednock, Diamond Buttress:
Diamond Blade 20m E6 6b ***. G.Lennox, C.Adam. 7th July 1998.
Climb the arête and move left to gain the obvious left-slanting crack (crux). Climb the crack and wall above slightly rightwards.

Sick Boy 8m E2 6a. C.Adam, G.Lennox. 15th July 1998.
From the recess left of The Branch, climb the shallow overhanging corner past a jammed block, with hard moves at the top.

Glen Lednock, Codgers Crag:
The following two routes are on the first crag on the left on entering the start of the glen. It is believed that the routes have since been retro-bolted by S.Muir.

Codgers Corner 25m Very Difficult. C.Adam, G.Lennox. 8th August 1998.
Climbs the left-slanting corner to a tree and step off right to another tree.

Stiff Rib 25m HVS 5a. G.Lennox, C.Adam. 9th August 1998.
Climbs the arête left of Codgers Corner. Start at the lowest rocks and finish up Codgers Corner after the first tree (bold).

BEN NEVIS, AONACHS, CREAG MEAGAIDH

BEN NEVIS, North-East Buttress, First Platform:
Green and Napier's Route 130m III. S.M.Richardson, C.Cartwright. 5th April 2006.
Follow the summer line, except avoid the lower slab by traversing in from the right. The climb coincides with Raeburn's 18 Minute Route high up and it has probably climbed in winter before but not recorded.

Secondary Tower Ridge:
The Italian Job 200m VIII,9 *. D.MacLeod, T.Emmett. February 2006.
A true finish to Italian Climb, taking the gully the whole way, through the huge overhang at the top. Climb the gully in three pitches to a belay right inside the cave (spooky!). Work up and left from the belay across the overhanging wall using thin hooking cracks. Once established in the groove above, climb this direct to the top. The top groove is bold but maybe easier if iced.

Number Two Gully Buttress:
The Hard Right Edge 170m IV,4. S.M.Richardson, C.Cartwright. 4th April 2006.
A pleasant mixed route following the exact right edge of Number Two Gully Buttress.
1. and 2. 80m. Climb the lower arête, first up snow, then through a couple of mixed sections to reach a fine snow arête that leads to a belay below the right edge of the headwall.
3. 30m. Climb a steep corner just left of the crest (this is 5m right of the groove-line taken by the Direct Variation), move left below a blank bulging section into a narrow scoop and follow this back right to the crest.
4 and 5. 60m. Continue directly up the crest (with interest at first) to the easier upper slopes.

The Comb:
Anubis 40m E8 6c ***. D.MacLeod. 31st July 2005.

The first route to breach the lower overhanging barrier on the front face of The Comb. The line is the thin intermittent crack running up the huge roofed prow right of the open book corner in the centre. It gives steep and potentially serious climbing in an amazing situation. Walk up the ramp of Pigott's Route and belay to the right of the line. Move up past some cracked blocks to gain the big diagonal fault (gear in suspect rock). Work leftwards across the roof to boldly climb the committing bouldery arête, eventually moving left to a good hold and gear in the crack. Climb the easier wall above to a no-hands rest in a niche. Continue up the line of the crack with further interest to gain big ledges at the foot of The Flying Groove. Descend by abseil or continue up V.Diff terrain to the plateau if desired. Cleaned on abseil, then led with no falls.

Number Three Gully Buttress:
Sioux Wall VIII,8. O.Metherell, I.Parnell. 1st January 2006.
A more direct start rather than taking the easy ramp of The Banshee gained the obvious belay niche. Pitch 2 (crux, very strenuous but well protected) was the steep wall up into a ledge at the base of the "obvious corner groove". Pitch 3 was the groove, with surprisingly good protection. From here the summer pitch 3 continues with a crack (looked very good but hard). Instead, a rightward line was chosen which proved fairly serious.

Thompson's Route Direct Finish 140m VII,7. G.Hughes, T.Stone. 16th April 2005.
A direct finish to Thompson's Route, taking the deep right-facing corner from the right end of the platform. Climb Thompson's Route for two pitches to reach the right side of the platform of No.3 Gully Buttress, and move up into the snowy bay below a deep right-facing corner, 10m left of Gremlins (90m). Climb the corner (sustained) to reach a block belay (25m). Step right and finish up cracks (30m).
Note: Climbed under snowed up rock conditions, but probably climbed before when the buttress was well iced.

Creag Coire na Ciste:
Avenging Angel 105m VII,8. **. N.Bullock, O.Samuels. 19th March 2006.
The innocuous and obvious system of corners, cracks and ledges in the scooped wall to the right of Darth Vader. The first 40m are common with Archangel. Four pitches of sustained climbing, the first two giving a warm up, the third tackling an overhanging off-width above a small cave, and the very steep wall above the off-width providing the crux on the final pitch. Start beneath a broken groove and left-slanting slabby corner on the left of the crag and at the lowest point.
1. 30m. Climb the groove and slabby corner moving right at its top into a steep corner. Climb this, pulling right onto a rib, which is climbed until another corner and steep wall, beneath a off-width flake is reached.
2. 25m. Climb the wall directly above and pull right onto the rib and large ledge. At the back of the ledge the overhanging open-book corner is climbed direct on perfect torques and edges to take a hanging belay on a ledge in the corner directly beneath the small cave and the very overhanging off-width.
3. 20m. Climb the corner directly to the niche. Fight directly up the overhang using various techniques before thrashing a way to the top. Belay to the right.
4. 30m. Left of the belay, the striking corner clearly seen from the start of the

route forms the final barrier. Move left from the base of the corner and climb two cracks in the deceptively steep wall. Pull onto a big ledge at the top of the left-hand crack. Finish easily and direct following a narrow gully.

South Trident Buttress:
Triton Corners 100m IV,5. C.Cartwright, S.M.Richardson. 3rd April 2006.
1. 40m. Start 25m right of Poseidon Groove (SMCJ 2004) and climb a short bulging off-width to gain a stepped corner system that leads up and right. Continue straight up to a good stance under a steep wall.
2 and 3. 60m. Step left and climb an icy gully to exit into a wide snow chute. Continue up this to the plateau.

STOB BAN (Mamores), South Buttress:
East Wing 180m V,5. D.McGimpsey, A.Nisbet. 26th February 2006.
A devious but spectacular line near the crest of the very steep East Wing. Start about 15m up South Gully at the highest ramp leading out left.
1. 35m. Work out leftwards to the crest, always keeping above steep lower walls.
2. 25m. Gain the highest ledge up thick moss, then traverse it leftwards to a vertical column of wedged blocks.
3. 10m. Climb the column to a ramp leading up right.
4. 30m. Climb the ramp to easy ground.
5. 80m. Climb the easy crest to the top of the buttress.
Note: Climbed in 'summer conditions' by D.McGimpsey, A.Nisbet on 30th January 2006 at VS, frozen but no snow. The column of wedged blocks would collapse unless frozen.

Banter 200m III. M.Edwards, D.McGimpsey, A.Nisbet. 24th February 2006.
The buttress right of North Gully, starting right at the toe and closely following the crest. It offered a short tricky move at a nose low down and higher up, some slabby ground which might become much easier under good snow.

MULLACH NAN COIREAN (Mamores):
A crag at NN 135 656 between Mullach nan Coirean and Stob Ban, facing north. The base is at 850m and the crag is 80m high with a very steep bottom 25m. The routes are purely snowed up rock climbing. There are some great moderate ridges there as well up to 200m long and about Grade II or III.

Captain Caveman 70m III,4. M.Brownlow, D.King, M.Pescod. 17th January 2006.
The obvious line on the left end of the crag passing several caves.

Not Bad for a Dad 80m VI,7. D.King, A.Turner. 27th November 2005.
An undercut chimney at the left end of the main section of cliff. Climb into the steep chimney with bold initial moves to an alcove (30m). Continue with tricky moves exiting the alcove to the top (50m).

Himalayan Shuffle 80m VII,8. D.King, A.Turner. 27th November 2005.
A central left-slanting crack-line on the front face of the crag. Bouldery starting moves involving a can-opener mantelshelf move, no protection for 8m and

sustained tenuous climbing with difficult protection leads to the right side of the same alcove as on the previous route. Move right from a big block to stand on a small pinnacle and go straight up to the top.

Kid Gloves 70m IV,4. M.Brownlow, D.King, M.Pescod. 17th January 2006.
The right arête of the crag.

Kindergarten Corner 50m VII,8. M.Brownlow, D.King, M.Pescod. 17th January 2006.
A right-facing corner on the right face of the crag finishing with a steep move left at the top. Easy to finish up the arête of Kid Gloves. This route gaves fantastic sustained climbing with good protection apart from the last 6m. The crux moves are getting off the ground and the move left at the top.

AONACH MOR, Coire an Lochain, North Buttress:
Perplexed 80m IV,4. P.Chapman, P.Andersen. 16th February 2006.
1. 35m. Follow the rightmost gully until it narrows at half-height and belay against the rock wall on the left.
2. 35m. Move left on a ledge and climb a short corner before stepping right on steep ground and climbing up past a spike. Trend leftwards over easing ground to a large block on the crest.
3. 10m. Follow easier snow to the cornice.

Ribbed Walls:
Twisted Blood 110m V,6. C.Cartwright, S.M.Richardson. 4th December 2005.
A interesting mixed route taking the unclimbed buttress left of Aquafresh.
1. 20m. Start 10m left of Aquafresh below a shallow gully and climb to a large sloping ledge.
2. 50m. Climb the right-facing corner-line in the series of stepped slabs above (crux, good intricate climbing), then exit right into the snow basin above. Junction with Aquafresh.
3. 40m. Aquafresh trends left from here and exits up the depression on the left. Instead move up to the base of the steep tower above and climb the left to right stepped groove line to its end. Finish up the left side of the exit bowl of White Shark.

AONACH BEAG, An Ghaidh Garbh:
Compressor 150m VI,6. A.Nisbet, J.Preston. 18th March 2006.
A direct ascent of the central groove on the SE side of Munro's Last Ridge (SMCJ 2003). Ice is essential and previous visits saw little. Heavy snow followed by a sunny day caused much melting into the deep upper groove and just sufficient ice formed. Two long pitches on wet ice and snow led to the deep upper groove. Enter it over a bulging chockstone and climb a steep, thinly iced and unprotected corner (25m). Continue up another iced corner to the easy crest (25m). A long way up the crest, over the Munro top and up to finish at the same place as NE Ridge.

An Ghaidh Garbh, Braxton-Hicks Buttress:
Note: Inducement (SMCJ 2004) is described as starting down and right of Catabasis but appears to be the obvious gully to the left of that route (?). The following route takes a line up the buttress right of the gully.

Ginger Peachy 100m III. S.Kennedy, A.MacDonald. 29th January 2006.

Start from the foot of the slanting gully bounding the left of the buttress. Climb icy slabs right of the gully into a corner system. Climb the corner and groove above to the upper snow slopes. No cornice on this occasion.

Jericho Ridge 150m III,4. R.Hamilton, S.Kennedy. 18th March 2006.
To the left of the 'Goblet' Buttress is a long easy gully. The gully is bounded on the left by a ridge with small pinnacles in the mid section. This route follows the ridge. Start below a snow bay dividing this ridge from another higher ridge to the left (the two ridges converge about 35m below the cornice). Follow the ridge by the easiest line to below a prominent tower on the left. Move up right of the tower to reach the top of an easy gully leading up from the right. Steep snow leads to the cornice which is overcome by a ridge well to the right.

Stob Coire Bhealach:
Rip Curl 125m IV,5 *. S.Kennedy, R.Hamilton. 30th January 2006.
The buttress immediately left of The Clare Effect contains a band of overhanging rock at just over mid-height. This route negotiates the band by an obvious break in the centre. Start at the foot of The Clare Effect and climb a narrow gangway up left (may bank out) then up to a belay at the foot of slabs leading to the band (40m). Take the easiest line up the slabs aiming for a point just right of the break in the band. Move left under the overhanging wall, then climb a steep wall (crux) leading into the break (35m). Make an exposed traverse out right on the lip of the overhang, then up into a left-slanting groove which is followed to the upper snow slopes and cornice (50m).

STOB COIRE AN LAOIGH:
Pentagon 50m VI,7. S.Allan, A.Nisbet. 16th April 2005.
A steep line up the wall which forms the left side of the rib left of Taliballan. Start as for Serve Chilled.
1. 15m. The short chimney and right traverse, as for Serve Chilled.
2. 20m. The wall above is overhanging so climb up left for 6m, as for Serve Chilled, before a short traverse right gains a ledge. Gain a second ledge. Steep moves slightly right, then back left over a bulge gain a shallow corner which leads to the base of a big left-facing flake-line, an obvious feature on the upper half of the wall.
3. 15m. Climb the flake-line, then a corner on the right to pass a smooth wall and finish back in the original line. Abseil descent.

Easy So Gully 150m I. M.W.Holland. 3rd February 2006.
At NN 238 731, to the right of the final hanging corrie west of the crags of Stob Coire an Laoigh, an obvious gully heads up right to emerge at the Stob Coire Easain/Beinn na Socaich col. One water ice section at the narrows, otherwise easy snow.

BEINN A' CLACHAIR:
Note: M.Holland on 7th December 2005, struggled to identify the Eiffel Tower-shaped buttress as described in the guidebook on the far right side of the corrie. The obvious feature of the corrie is a distinct ridge leading direct to the summit with a long gully on its left-hand side and a short ridge bounding the gully on the left higher up. The distinct ridge has a triangular buttress at its bottom. The right-hand side of the lower triangular butress was taken on turf until it steepened and

became more distinct, moving left at this point (obvious flake bollard) gaving access to turf and stepped grooves leading to the main distinct ridge, which was followed to the top. Suggested name – The Blackpool variation.

CREAG MEAGAIDH, Bellevue Buttress:
Bellevue, Bienvenue 150m V,5. C.Cartwright, S.M.Richardson. 1st January 2006.
1. 50m. Start at the foot of The Scene, climb a short snow slope, then a left-facing V-groove to reach a small snow bowl.
2. 50m. Move up and left across the bowl to gain a right-facing corner system.
3. 50m. Climb the corner to a long capping roof, traverse right below the roof for 5m, then exit up a groove to reach the final snow slopes.

BEN ALDER, Garbh Coire Beag:
Alderweiss 300m II. A.Nisbet. 17th January 2006.
The rib left of Culra Couloir. A stream runs down the centre of the lower half of the rib. Climb this on ice, although in full conditions, all but the lowest and top tier may bank out. From the top of the ice move right on to the crest at a slight col. Follow the crest to the top, sometimes slightly on its left. This is close to Grade III, but there are easier options further left. The cornice is often small here, as the top 20m is low angled.

Aldermen 250m II/III **. D.McGimpsey, A.Nisbet, J.Preston. 3rd January 2006. Approach as for Pat-a-Cake but head right to climb an iced corner left of an easy gully. This is Alderwand, but was gained from the left instead of direct. Alderwand now trends right but continue slightly left on ice to the terrace which crosses the face. Traverse left, then return back right towards a distinctive smooth wall which is left of Alderwand. Go left through a weakness to enter a long final trough of snow. The finish may form a large cornice; a slight ridge where McCook's Gully finishes might then be an option.

Smallville 250m IV,5 *. D.McGimpsey, A.Nisbet, J.Preston. 28th January 2006. Climbs the left side of the triangular buttress between McCook's Gully and Left Gully. Avoid the lowest tier and start at the base of the main gully line of McCook's Gully. The gully line goes left; instead go up an icy groove slightly right to the terrace. Continue straight up a steep groove (the left of three). This is the crux but could be avoided by traversing the terrace right and returning back diagonally left, making the route Grade III overall. Take turfy grooves leading right for about 60m, then break back left into a large bay below the plateau. Climb the right side of the bay, then a groove leading right onto the final crest of the buttress and a break in the cornice.

MONADHLIATH, Carn Dearg:
The crag is directly beneath the summit of Carn Dearg (NH 635 024, Alt 860m, North-East facing). It has five pillars separated by faults. Descend to the right or left of the crag depending on the cornice.

Soul Survivor 90m IV,4. J.Lyall. 10th February 2006.
Climbs the turfy fault between the first and second pillars from the left.. Direct entry to the fault is barred by an overhanging wall at its base. On the left of this wall two short ramps are followed on to a slight rib, then up to a ledge. Go to the

right end of the ledge and make very exposed moves right on turf, then go up into the fault which is followed to the top.

Cold Turkey 90m III,4. J.Lyall, D.MacDonald. 28th December 2005.
1. 30m. Climb steeply into the left side of the amphitheatre between the second and third pillars.
2. 40m. Slant up left on a narrowing ramp to the crest of the buttress and climb this by a short slabby corner.
3. 20m. Easily straight up to the summit cairn.

Cold Blooded 100m II. J.Lyall. 10th February 2006.
Start under the third pillar and slant up left to follow the faint gully between the second and third pillars, initially close to the right wall but moving left, then back right near the top.

Monadh Lisa 100m III. J.Lyall, D.MacDonald. 28th December 2005.
1. 50m. Climb the gully between the third and fourth pillars into an overhanging amphitheatre, then climb the turfy left wall to gain the edge.
2. 50m. Easier slopes to the cornice.

Arctic Monkey 110m IV,5. J.Lyall. 10th February 2006.
A line up the fourth pillar. Sart at the toe of the buttress and slant up left by ledges and walls to climb the left-hand of two left-leaning corners. Gain a ledge on the left side of the steep tower. Move steeply up right and climb the corner in the tower, then over the crest of a short ridge to finish up easier slopes.

CRC Gully 110m II. G.Clowes, J.Lyall, J.Marsh, S.Pavelin, J. & K.Penrose, J.Preston, N.Wells. 16th February 2006.
The easiest line on the face, taking the left-slanting gully between the fourth and fifth pillars, to join the easier upper part of Arctic Monkey.

Sink or Swim 110m III. H.Burrows-Smith, A.Rock, D.Parsons, N.Easton. 16th February 2006.
A groove line on the right edge of the right-hand ridge.

GLEN COE

BUACHAILLE ETIVE MOR, North Blackmount Buttress:

Note: A.Campbell thinks The Snake should be HVS 4c (not VS).

CHURCH DOOR BUTTRESS:
Note: Un Poco Loco was climbed by the summer start (VI,7) by S.McFarlane, A.Clark on 26th February 2006. Still VII,7 overall and sustained.

STOB COIRE NAM BEITH, Zero Buttress:
Zero Buttress 115m IV,4 *. S.Kennedy, R.Hamilton. 26th February 2006.
The buttress immediately left of The Corridors is characterised by a huge recessed area forming a prominent right-facing corner. Climb directly into the base of the corner, then traverse out right to the foot of the slabs right of the corner (25m). Traverse the slab diagonally rightwards to a large block on the right edge, overlooking The Corridors. Surmount the block and follow an open groove to a short wall (45m). Climb a steep slab just left of the wall, then mixed ground

before moving left on snow to finish by an easy groove (40m). Climbed in thin conditions.

AN T-SRON, East Face (NN 137 554):
Cornerstone 48m E1 5b *. S.Kennedy, T.Hamilton, R.Hamilton. 14th August 2005.
Follows the line of a prominent arête situated on a small buttress about 100m above the path which leads into the upper part of Coire nam Beitheach. Start 2m left of the arête and climb a steep wall trending rightwards to the edge. Continue to a grassy ledge, then climb a short slab on the right. Follow the edge to the top. Traverse off right some distance to descend.

GARBH BHEINN (ARDGOUR), North Face:
Too Cave to be Brave 220m III. D.Johnson, G.Macfie. 4th March 2006.
This mountaineering line starts from the lowest rocks. Climb the buttress for 50m before traversing left to a snow ramp. Follow the left edge of the north face for two further pitches to a large cave. From the cave, traverse left along a ledge. Climb two further pitches of snow to the top. Two finishes are possible, a left-hand snow slope or a right-hand chimney pitch.
Note: The above route does not fit the guidebook description for North Face, although it may be near.

ARDNAMURCHAN, Meall an Fhir-Eoin Beag:
Round to the the left of the main crag is a short vertical west facing wall with a diamond-shaped boulder at its base. Described right to left.

Jedi Crack 10m Hard Severe 4b *. J.Bankhead, G.Steven. 21st April 2005.
Follow the right-hand crack up a rough slabby wall and through a steepening.

Yoda's Crack 10m Severe 4a. G.Steven, J.Bankhead. 21st April 2005.
Just to the left is a wider, stepped crack.

Eruption 14m E2 5c **. J.Smith, R.Parker. 21st April 2005.
Left of the grassy fault is a vertical wall with a prominent T-crack. Climb the crack strenuously to a bold finish.

Split Shift 10m VS 5a. A.Halewood, J.Bankhead. 21st April 2005.
Climb the steep Y-crack left of the corner then finish more easily up the corner.

SOUTHERN HIGHLANDS

BEINN AN DOTHAIDH, North-East Corrie:
Heyerdahl 145m IV,5. E Brunskill, G.Macfie. 29th November 2005.
Bold climbing up the buttress crest left of The Skraeling. Start at the terrace below the main buttress 20m left of The Skraeling at a left-facing corner. Climb the corner to a poor belay below the slabby wall of the main buttress (30m, easy escape off left). Climb boldly up the wall slightly left of centre on spaced tufts to a ledge below a prominent finger crack in a wall. Make hard moves round the crest on the left to a good belay (15m). Climb up and right onto a huge triangular block and climb the steep walls above to reach a prominent groove system. Climb this to a belay in the Thor fault-line, where the angle eases (40m). Follow the fault-line rightwards to join The Skraeling near the top and easy ground (60m).

Thor 110m IV,5. S.Burns, D.Crawford. 27th November 2005.
To the left of The Skraeling (and Heyerdahl) are two obvious deep groove come gully lines. This route takes the right groove and follows a fairly direct line above.
1. 30m. Climb the deep groove, passing a bulge to reach easier ground. Belay at the foot of an obvious very narrow chimney slot in a snow bay
2. 40m. Climb the narrow V-chimney above and follow a turfy groove aiming for an overhanging left-facing corner above.
3. 40m. Climb the corner to gain an obvious rightward foot traverse leading round a short arête. Traverse right and then climb the centre of a turfy wall aiming for a notch in the skyline.

Unnamed 200m VI,6. I.Small, S.M.Richardson. 5th March 2006.
A direct mixed line up the steep left wall of West Gully, crossing the ramp of The Upper Circle.
1. 50m. Start 20m right of The Upper Circle and climb a steep groove over a turfy bulge to a ledge. Step down and right onto an icefall and climb this and the open corner above to a stance on The Upper Circle.
2. 50m. Move up and right into a deep cleft and climb this to exit on a ledge. Climb the right of two corners to the crest of the buttress.
3. 50m. Move up to an off-width crack splitting the crest; climb this and continue along the crest and down into the saddle of The Beechgrove Garden.
4. 50m. Move up and left to a gully line cutting the headwall above, and follow this to the top.

BEINN DORAIN, Creag an Socach:
Defenders of the Faith 85m IX,9 ***. D.MacLeod, F.Murray. 16th March 2006.
The overhanging wall left of Messiah. Start not far left of Messiah. Climb a turfy ramp to gain the foot of a line of overhanging thin corners. Climb these (poor protection at first) to a rest below a roof. Pull through and get established on the headwall (crux). Traverse right in an airy position to gain a hanging corner. Mantel onto a turfy ledge at its top and follow a turfy fault for another 30m to a good belay on the left at a detached block (60m pitch). Step left and climb much easier ground to the top (25m).

BEINN A' CHREACHAIN, Coire an Lochain, West Buttress:
From left to right (looking up):

Rubadub Ridge 90m IV,4. E.Brunskill, D.Morris. 4th March 2006.
The last buttress up the gully up and left of The Bells. Climb the crest of the buttress via the obvious groove system in two pitches.

Detroit Grooves 185m IV,5. E.Brunskill, J.Hall. 27th February 2006.
High up on the front face of West Buttress (to the right of The Bells) are three prominent parallel groove lines. This route takes the right-hand groove. Start near the top of the gully rock island below a pyramid shaped buttress split by a two-stepped icy groove. Climb the groove in two pitches turning the steps via the buttress on the left to a terrace below the three parallel groove lines (80m). Climb the right-hand groove to a fine cave (25m). Climb the left wall of the cave (crux) and continue up the steep corner-line above (30m). Continue up the buttress above to the top (50m).

Strings of Life 175m V,6. E.Brunskill, D.Morris. 3rd March 2006.
A good icy mixed route taking in the very steep tower which forms the right wall of the upper section of Detroit Grooves. Start at a prominent large icy recess 35m up the easy rightward-trending wide gully/ramp from the start of Detroit Grooves. Traverse a thinly iced slab up and left heading for a shallow groove breaking out left to the crest of the buttress (35m). Climb the crest of the buttress to the terrace and belay at a prominent icicle fringe 15m to the right of the upper groove of Detroit Grooves (45m). Climb the icy left-facing rocky corner and climb steep ground up and left to an inverted triangular shaped slabby recess. Traverse the slab left and climb up to below a cracked roof (30m). Climb up and right on small ledges to a small V-groove breaking through the overhangs. Climb up this to a good thread (15m). Climb straight up the buttress above to the summit (50m).

Bumblie Buttress 200m II. E.Brunskill, D.Morris. 23rd February 2006.
The crest of the buttress immediately to the right of So Where's the Window and Door Buttress, followed by easy snow slopes to the summit ridge.

Wallace & Gromit 250m III,4. A.Mallinson, K.Bromelow. 25th February 2006.
This route climbs the ice walls, chimney and shallow snow gully cutting up through the steep buttress on the right of the West Buttress. Start at the beginning of the obvious rightward-trending ramp at the lowest part of the face. Ascend the ramp to a prominent nose (30m). Traverse 10m right to bottom of ice walls and climb these, followed by steep snow, to an overhang below a chimney (40m). Climb the chimney and vertical rock/ice step above to the top of a gully (40m). Cross a snow bay to the base of the shallow steep snow gully (40m). Ascend the gully and broken rocks above to the ridge (100m).

BEINN TULAICHEAN, Creag an Sputan:
Rob Roy's Falls 70m II/III. D.Crawford, S.Mearns. 5th March 2006.
Approaching via Inverlochlarig (from Balquhidder), the parallel frozen waterfalls will be obvious up on hillside at 600-700m, on the crag of Creag an Sputan on the 1:25000 map. About 70m long at the steepest bits, but the burn flows right down to the base of the valley so could be as long or short as required. There is a left-hand line of a similar grade but too sunny on the day.

BEN LOMOND, B Buttress:
Roamin in the Lomond 140m IV,3. E.Brunskill, J.Hall. 28th February 2006.
This route takes in the prominent chimney-groove line towards the left side of B Buttress and is capped by a huge chockstone at three-quarters height. Climb easy slabs up to the bottom of the groove (45m). Climb the groove into a chimney and belay in a small cave formed by a chockstone (40m). Continue up the chimney into an open bay just below the huge capping chockstone (15m). Climb a left-slanting turfy groove to the top (40m).

C Buttress:
Endrick Corner 105m V,6 **. D.Crawford, S.McFarlane. 3rd March 2006.
The line is about 200m down and left of Lomond Corner and is identifiable as

being a direct line up the turfy buttress up through a prominent right-facing corner.
1. 40m. Start in a recess directly below the large right-facing corner. Go up and step left into a groove. Continue up turf to a steep wall leading to the main corner.
2. 40m. Climb the corner. Move right beneath the roof into a body width chimney and reach groove above (crux). Continue to a large ledge above.
3. 25m. Move left then right to a continuation groove through an obvious slot in the skyline.

BEN CRUACHAN, Meall nan Each (NN 055 317):
The main cliff, some 100m in height, is dominated by a band of overlaps at two-thirds height.

Steinway 100m E2 5b. S.Richardson, C.Cartwright. 22nd August 2004.
This natural line climbs through the band of overlaps on predominantly excellent red granite. The route starts to the left of the overlaps, climbing a groove to gain a right-trending ramp-line.
1. 25m. Climb the groove (slightly dirty) for 10m to gain the ramp-line. Follow the ramp sharply rightwards for 15m to belay as it runs out.
2. 20m. Step rightwards on to slabs, working right and stepping down under the overlap. Break through the overlap at a crack with a wedged block, then up shallow corners above.
3. 25m. Follow easier corners to the top.

Coire Chat, Noe Buttress:
In Cold Blood 85m VII,7. S.M.Richardson, C.Cartwright. 27th February 2006.
The steep groove left and parallel to In the Knoe. Sustained from start to finish.
1. 25m. Start 3m left of the left-facing corner of Fat Lip Fandango and make a difficult move onto an undercut slab. Move up to the wide cleft of Fat Lip Fandango and then traverse right to the good stance at the top of the first pitch of In the Knoe.
2. 25m. Follow the shallow chimney of In the Knoe for 10m then make a difficult move left into the base of the left-hand parallel groove system. Climb this with increasing difficulty to a small undercut ledge on the left.
3. 35m. Continue steeply up the groove to a terrace, then exit up an easy gully on the right as for In the Knoe.

Stob Garbh:
East Ridge 300m II **.
The prominent ridge on the left side of Coire Chreachainn. The easiest line avoids the steep lower nose by ascending easy snow on the right and cutting back to the crest soon after. Climb the next steepening direct or make a step right, around a corner to gain the broad snow field above. A narrow notch and short twisting arête complete a fine mountaineering route.
Note: An older guide gives the ridge Grade I. But a recent ascent by P. and J.Hageman thought there were a couple of sections which would merit Grade II, and the length and lack of escape would also point towards II.

ARRAN

A'CHIR:
Note: Lower Right Chimney (Severe 4b) should read: Start to the right of the chimney. Start up a thin slab, then follow a wide left-slanting crack to a ledge. Traverse left and climb the chimney.

Lower Right Flakes 40m Severe 4b. C.Moody, C.Grindley. 10th July 2005.
Climb Lower Right Chimney to the ledge, then follow flakes and slabs above.

CIR MHOR, South Face: Note: C.Moody notes that pitch 2 of Ne Parl Pas is missing from the Arran guide. Whether it had been done before or not (SMCJ 1990), it is independent and worthwhile.

Hammer, Pocket Slab VS 4b **. C.Moody, C.Grindley. 9th July 2005.
Climb pitch 3 to where it goes rightwards. Follow a line of pockets up slightly left, then back right. Climb straight up to join South Ridge. Much better than the original pitch 3. It seemed better to run together Pitches 1 and 2. Pitch 3 seems to go right following "a downward-pointing flake" rather than "a microgranite vein".

Anvil, Right Hand Start 30m VS 4c *. C.Moody, W.Hood. 15th May 1982.
Start right of Anvil Recess Start below two large overlaps. Go up to the first overlap and climb a scoop rightwards through it. Continue to the bigger second overlap, then traverse left to join Anvil Recess Start. Presumably, Fraser's Variation starts to the right of this pitch and not at Anvil Recess Start.

LOWLAND OUTCROPS

GLASGOW AREA, Dumbarton Rock:
Rhapsody 35m E11 7a **. D.MacLeod. 9th April 2006.
An exceptionally arduous experience in every way. This climb takes the true line of the Requiem crack, following it to the top of the wall. Start up Persistence of Vision to gain the ledge. Climb the main Requiem crack to where it fades and Requiem goes right. Step left (good shake out). Launch directly up the wall, climbing a thin flange to gain better edges in a thin horizontal (avoiding escape left). Traverse desperately right along the horizontal to regain the crack; get established in this (crux) and continue up the crack without respite to the top. F8c/8c+ climbing with the prospect of falling the length of the pitch from the final moves. FA headpointed, placing gear on lead.

Note: Some first ascent details from G.Latter:
Dumbarton Rock:
1980 – Mestizo, Physical Graffiti, Toto and Pongo; FFA (not 1985) all G.Latter.
1982 May. Cyclops FFA by D.Cuthbertson & Neil Cockburn.
1983 September. The Big Zipper FFA.
1984 April. Alpha, Beta.
1984 April 4. Gamma.
1984 April 15. Samora, Rising Power.

Auchinstarry Quarry:
1983 February 3. Dream Machine.
1983 February 24. Carouselambra.
1983 April 18. Blade Runner.
1983 September 18. Death is the Hunter.
1984 High Dive.
1984 October 16. Surface Tension.
1986 March 1. Surface Tension Direct.

Cambusbarron, Thorntons Quarry:
1984 July 31. Grace Under Pressure.
1984 August 4. Power of Endurance.

Carron Glen, Kamikaze Squirrel Crag:
Wise Eskimo 9m Severe. S.Macfarlane, J.Dyble. 10th May 2005.
Start right of the block at the left end of the crag on a low slab. Move rightwards up the left side of a semi-detached pinnacle and continue up an obvious right-slanting crack to a hilarious finish over the cornice of vegetation using the tree on the left. Ho, ho, ho!

Funbags 7m HVS 5a. J.Dyble, S.Macfarlane. 10th May 2005.
Start at the same place as previous route. Climb onto a block on the left and continue up leftwards under bulge to finish in a thin groove.

Death to the Greys 9m E1 5b. J.Dyble, S.Macfarlane. 31st May 2005.
Climb the slab and thin crack between the previous routes over a poorly protected bulge at half-height. Gear may be placed in the crack of Wise Eskimo. After a couple of hard moves, poor for the feet, finish more easily on the left of the tree.

Hippos in Space 9m E2 5c **. J.Dyble, S.Macfarlane. 31st May 2005.
Start as for The Carronade and move up to the overlap. Move out of the recess through the left side of the overlap to the slab using an obvious poor hold. Pull onto a sloping ledge and upwards to a crozzly double pocket on the right, great technical climbing. Finish straight up over an even more hilarious finish. Crampons and axes recommended for the finish!

Auf Wiedersehen Berg Heil! 10m HVS 5a *. J.Dyble, S.Macfarlane. 6th June 2005.
Carronbridge climbs the left side of the wide mossy scoop. This route starts to its right and climbs the crack in the left-facing short corner to a shelf. Continue upwards, place gear, then traverse the obvious narrow foot-rail leftwards to reach the arête. Continue upwards to yet another hilarious finish.

AYRSHIRE, The Quadrocks:
The Benny Hill Show 12m E4 6a. K.Shields. August 2005.
Takes the line directly to the right of The Arête. Top-rope rehearsal, then led on two small wires at half-height.

The Fatal Kiss 10m E4 6c. K.Shields. 21st March 2006.
Takes the line of the usually running watercourse between the Traverse Face Direct and The Nose. Top-roped, then soloed.

GALLOWAY HILLS, The Merrick:
White Rhino 180m III/IV *. L.Biggar, J.Biggar. 5th March 2006 (Left Variation). D.McNicol, A.Brooke-Mee. 5th March 2006 (Right Variation).
The obvious icefall which forms in cold but generally snow free conditions about 30-40m right of the Black Gutter. A first introductory pitch of 40m leads to a branch in the icefall. Both the left and right variations have been climbed from here to the top at Grade III/IV; the grade could probably be reduced to III by weaving between them. Poor rock gear so take ice-screws and warthogs.

The following two routes share a common start up a short gully to a snow bay about 100m right of the Black Gutter. They take twin icefalls to the left of the overhanging square black wall mentioned in the description of the Lang Scots Miles.

The Icicle Thief 175m III **. S.Reid, C.Wells. 16th March 2006.
1. 50m. After a steep start, easier snow leads to the foot of the main fall.
2. 25m. The icefall is climbed to a large spike on the left, about 45m below its top.
3. 50m. Continue up the icefall to exit right, and follow the ice ramp leftwards to easier ground and a poor belay (warthogs in turf).
4. 50m. Run the rope out to the top.

The Lonely Warthog 180m III/IV,3 *. J. & L.Biggar. 16th March 2006.
The right-hand icefall is called the Lonely Warthog for good reason, don't expect much more protection! Climb a short, easy angled icy gully to a platform (this pitch is also used to access The Icicle Thief). From here two pitches of narrow ice and/or turf, depending on conditions, lead to easier ground. Highlight of the route is a reassuringly large and chunky spike belay at the left-hand end of a square wall after the first protectionless 40m. Above these two pitches another 100m of easy angled ice, or Grade I snow, lead to the plateau.

Lower Icefall 50m II. C.Hossack, J.Biggar, ANO. 17th March 1996.
This is the short icefall near the right end of the crag, below Kenny's Folly and Chippy's Downfall.

CLIFTON CRAG, Dirl Chimney Area:
Dirl Chimney Variations 13m VS 4c **. S.Reid, C.Bunker. 4th September 2005.
A good way up the crag although not a new route. Start as for Monkey Business. Climb the corner-crack as for Monkey Business and struggle left into Dirl Chimney. Go up this a short way until it is possible to stride out left onto the lip of the overhang. Climb up leftwards to a big flake and mantelshelf to the top (as for Gramercy).

CLINTS OF DROMORE, Central Buttress:
It Tolls for Thee 40m VS 4b *. S.Reid, C.King. 5th February 2006.

A bold route on great rock. There are two large slabs on the left flank of Central Buttress, one above and left of the other. Start 10m up left from the start of Left Edge, just below where the grassy bank steepens into a gully. Climb steep cracks and pull out left onto the lower slab. Traverse left into its centre and climb straight up to a large heather ledge. Traverse left to the next large slab (Friend 3 near the start) which is climbed up the centre without further protection.

Jigsaw Buttress:
Just left of the Deep Nick of Dromore (and about 100m right of the Black and White Walls) is a tall slim broken buttress with some dead trees growing out of its left-hand side.

Jigsaw 50m VS 4c. C.King, S.Reid. 5th February 2006.
Start on the right side of the buttress, up a grass slope to the right of a large sloping roof. Gain a horizontal crack and hand-traverse leftwards above the lip of the roof to a ledge. Follow the ridge above to the left-hand and lower of two large grass ledges under the steep headwall. Climb the wall above (crux), just left of the rib. It looks possible to finish up the right-hand wall above the upper ledge at an easier grade – this would probably reduce the route to Severe.

Far Buttress:
This is the small buttress 100m to the left of the Black and White Walls. It has a large clean ledge high up in its centre, and a lower heather ledge on the right. The rock is a little friable.

Under the Far Away Tree 10m HVS 5a. S.Reid, C.King. 5th February 2006.
A route with a rather serious feel, and quite hard for the grade. Starting on the left side of the buttress, climb up into a shallow scoop and make a rising traverse rightwards to gain the large upper ledge with difficulty. Pull straight over the centre of the roof and finish up a short groove. The right-hand rib of this buttress has also been climbed (Very Difficult).

THE BORDERS, Craighoar (Lowland Outcrops p209):
This miniscule buttress is more like 10m than 12m, but the rock is excellent sandstone, dries almost instantly and the crag is easily reached from the M74. The existing routes are re-described and others added.

Hoars d'Oeuvre 20m HVS 5a. S.J.H.Reid, C.King. 26th January 2006.
A left-to-right rising girdle. Start just left of the arête, at a rock pillar with sloping holds. Climb this directly to a sloping ledge. Make a move up the arête, and step right (wire). Make a rising traverse rightwards (several levels are possible) to gain the sanctuary of the deep crack of Hoar Cleft. Quit this to traverse right as for Crooked Brae, but continue the traverse to the right arête, and climb this, moving leftwards to finish.

The Hoardinary Route 10m E1 5a *. S.Reid, J.Biggar, L.Biggar. 25th August 2005.
The left arête. Start just left of Silence of the Ram and climb up to a vague break

(runner up and right by the block on Silence of the Ram for the nervous). Traverse left to the arête and climb it.

Silence of the Ram 10m VS 5a * (2002).
The left-hand of three crack systems. Start just right of the lowest point of the crag and climb up to the crack which is followed past a large square block at half-height.

Scobie-Doo 10m HVS 5a (2002).
Takes the dark coloured wall in between the left-hand crack of Silence of the Ram and the central Hoar Crack. A steep and fairly sustained route. Climb directly up the wall passing the right end of a ledge near the top.

Hoar Crack 9m VS 4c (2002).
Start beneath the central right-leaning crack with a high thin vertical crack to its left. After a hard start climb up to the thin crack and finish directly up it or slightly to the right up the main crack.

Hoar Cleft 9m Hard Severe * (2002).
The right-hand crack, starting just left of the roof on the right half of the crag. After a hard start, climb directly up with a steep pull to finish.

Crooked Brae 9m VS 4c (2002).
Follow for Hoar Cleft for 5m, then traverse rightwards across the short wall above the roof to a vertical crack. Climb this to the top.

Hoar's Draws 9m HVS 5a *. S.Reid, L.Biggar, J.Biggar. 25th August 2005.
Starting on the right, climb up leftwards under the overhang on the right of the crag. Reach out rightwards over the roof to a good spike, pull up, and then climb the crack in the wall above (as for Crooked Brae).

Up and left of the main buttress is a promising looking area of easier angle rock – unfortunately it is a false promise. *Hoarible* (Mild Severe, S.J.H.Reid, C.King, 26th January 2006) takes the central rib starting via mossy slabs on the right, but is loose, unprotected and unrecommended.

GALLOWAY SEA-CLIFFS, The Lookout – Tombstone Slab:
The clean slab to the east of Lookout Slab. The rock and protection are not bad (for greywacke). The Tombstone climbs the main slab on the right.

The Old Grey Wacke Test 13m VS 4c *. S.Reid, L.Biggar, J.Biggar. 26th August 2005.
Climb the main slab on the left, crossing the overlap via a thin crack near the left arête, and finish via a left-facing groove.

The Long and Winding Road 13m Very Difficult *. J.Biggar, L.Biggar, S.Reid. 26th August 2005.
Climb the main slab via its right edge until it is possible to step right over the off-

width crack onto the hanging slab. Go up this and finish up the diamond shaped top slab via cracks on the right.

AUCHINSTARRY:
Whimper 10m Severe. A.Wallace. 15th June 2005.
Start up Scream, then gain and climb the parallel crack to its right. Stay strictly in the crack for a decent climb.

CAMBUSBARRON, Fourth Quarry:
Rubbatiti 10m F6c+. C.Pettigrew, T.Cooper. 5th June 2005.
This climbs the front face of the sarcophagus shaped pinnacle to the left of Chisel. Climb the slightly overhanging front face of the pinnacle to the lower-off.

FORESTHILL (NS 859 667):
This old dolerite quarry faces north and from the road appears wet and vegetated, but appearances are deceptive. The routes are on either side of the entrance and face south, west and east on mainly sound, clean rock with an assortment of slabby walls and well-defined arêtes. All the first ascents were soloed by A.Wallace above a bouldering mat; therefore only technical grades are given.

The crag is visible close to the working quarry at Cairneyhill, immediately south of the A89 Airdrie to Bathgate road. There is also a good cycle path running parallel to the road. Park carefully opposite the quarry without blocking the gate, and follow the muddy track (wellies or big boots advisable), 2mins. The quarry is on farmland but the farmer is fine with climbers visiting.

There are a couple of small bits of rock on the left as you enter, which could give a few short problems. Past this is a wee wall with a good sidepull, a flat hold at head-height and a horizontal break just above.

Love Kraft 4m 5b *
There are various ways to climb this wall but the best goes straight up the centre without using the sidepull or big hold. Pull on using tiny crimps and wee footholds to gain the break, then poor sidepulls help you get your feet high enough to teeter to the top. It's also possible but not as interesting, to jump for the break then dyno to the top.

Rarete 4m 5a. A hard pull, then direct up the arête.

Pop Gun 4m 4b. The groove immediately to the right.

Spud Gun 3m 4c. Right again, the crack is harder than it looks.

The bigger wall to the right is seamed by a horizontal fault.

Fern Face 5m 4c. At the left side of the wall gain the horizontal fault then reach up to slanting sidepulls. Balance up to more sidepulls then make a quick scary slap to the top.

Easterling 7m 4c. In the middle of the wall, climb stepped holds to cracks and an exit right to avoid loose dirty rock.

Frontier Town 9m 5a. Boulder up small holds to a good flat hold, then twin cracks.

Cowboys 9m 4a. The easy left side of the arête.

Injuns 9m 4c. The right side is harder.

There now follows a stretch of broken rock, which might give a few short climbs. A better buttress follows this, with a prominent overhang pierced by a borehole.

Rifle Barrel 9m 5a. Bridge up to undercling the borehole, then reach its top. Commit to a pull and a high-stepping mantel, finish easily.

Kings of the Mild Frontier 9m 4b. The left side of the arête gives a steady climb.

Guns 'n' Thistles 9m 5a. The right side gives more steady climbing, then it surprises with an awkward crux near the top.

Cap Gun 9m 4c. Climb the overhung corner onto a big ledge and finish up the cracks.

The west wing of the quarry starts with a short clean-cut arête.

Wild West 5m 4c. The arête climbed on its right side.

Gun Free 5m 5a. The left side is a little harder.

Free Guns 5m 4c. The groove is trickier than it appears.

Raygun 7m 5a.Use side holds to climb the arête to a jug and a finish up the right side of the hanging prow.

Bullet Ballet 7m 5c **. The excellent direct line up the centre of the steep slab. Pulling up on shallow pockets as you stand on a toehold gains a wee sloping finger edge. Latch the bottom of a sloping ramp then with a foot on a tiny inset edge, pull up and smear with your right foot. Gain a flat hold on the ramp (don't use the jug at the top) then a big shallow pocket and go straight up to swing directly up the hanging prow.

Bububububibibububu 7m 4c. The layback crack is finished via a slightly loose groove.

Skylarking 7m 5a *. Use a borehole to reach a small sloping slab and a wee edge above. Span right to gain the break and finish up the curving vertical cracks.

Bug In Brandy 7m 4a. Climb the chimney to an interesting contortion round into a finger crack.

The Big Express 7m 5a. A good eliminate. Climb the short speckled pillar to gain holds on the hanging arête, then a spike. Swing round onto the Skylarking face and finish up the arête without using the curving cracks.

To the left the rock becomes more broken and vegetated but the climbing is better than it looks.

Easy Day For a Laddy 7m 3c. Climb an open groove to easy ground.

Drums and Wires 7m 4a. Climb a short slab then head for a long slim jammed flake. Use the flake to climb the wall on its right.

The Somnambulist 9m 4b. A grassy groove leads to the left side of the flake.

Sgt. Rock 9m 4b. A slim pillar leads to a grassy ledge, then a thin groove.

Capt. Chock 9m 4c. A small slab onto the ledge, then a jamming crack containing a jammed stone.

Etc. 9m 4c. Climb a leaning orange wall onto a grassy ledge then a slab split by a horizontal break.

Extras 9m 5a. A short black arête is 3m to the left. Go directly over it onto a wee slab then follow a right-trending line.

Afterthought 9m 5a. The left wall of the arête is seamed with hairline cracks. Climb it directly without using the ledges on the left, to a finish up a vegetated crack.

Rosyth Quarry:
Andy's Leg 4m Font 4. A.Wallace. 11th December 2005.
A nice wee eliminate between Legover Groove and Andy's Wall. Wobble to the top of the zigzag crack then pick your own finish.

Pis Aller 5m Font 4. A.Wallace. 11th December 2005.
The left arête of Philistine without going into Drizzle. Start with hands on a ledge at head height then go up to inset edge on right. Follow the flake arête then balance over a rounded bulge to slap onto a sloping ledge, downclimb or finish up Philistine.

The route CND is described as climbing "The wall just right of The Waullie", but local opinion (and the diagram in the guidebook) seems to suggest it climbs the groove bounding the left side of this wall.

Gonnae No' Dae That 10m Severe. A.Wallace, R.Wallace. 11th December 2005.
A trio of mantels up the wall between CND and Hands Off gains a sloping ledge. Move right and climb a tiny inverted staircase forming a slim groove.

You J'st Took That Too Far 10m E1 5b. R.Wallace, A.Wallace. 11th December 2005.

Start two metres right of Hands Off, below an overhanging block. Climb the crack on it's left to ledges above it. Regain the crack then a step up and a long reach across a sloping ledge gains a better hold. Match on it then highstep and rockover to gain the top.

Shady Character 10m E1 5a. A.Wallace, R.Wallace. 11th December 2005.
Just right of Suspect Device climb a crack onto a ledge. A precarious rock-over leads to a suspicious layback crack then a short dubious wall.

Whithering Heights 4m Font 5. R.Wallace. 11th December 2005.
To the right again is a low overhang, sit start below this with your feet at the back and use a good sidepull on the right to gain flat lip holds. Up to wee crimps then hoop left foot onto lip hold, rockover and slap up left to a sloping ramp, then a big ledge.

FIFE, Limekilns, South Face of the Sentinel:
Stag Dubh 12m E1 5a **. J.Dyble, J.Shanks. 5th March 2005.
Climb between the crack-lines of Humbug and Kiln Dance without recourse to either route for holds or gear. Stay true to the rules (and route!) for maximum effect as the crack-lines draw closer together nearing the top. Unprotected and serious with the crux right at the top, but a rather good eliminate.

West Face of the Gellet Block:
DT's Direct Shaker Finish 10m HVS 5a *. J.Dyble, D.Monteith, I.McCabe. 24th April 2005.
Climb DT's until the point where the original route moves towards the right-hand crack. Continue straight up the left-hand crack on wobbly jams to finish direct. Probably done before.

DT's Direct Wobbly Start 10m E2 5b **. J.Dyble, S.Macfarlane. 6th November 2005.
Start directly below the right-hand finishing crack of DT's and climb very boldly up to an obvious blunt spike on the right. There is gear in a short crack to the left at 5m. A tricky move before the gear leads to an easier finish.

BERWICKSHIRE COAST, Fast Castle, Little Rooks Stacks:
There are a number of small fins of rock and two larger stacks. These are accessible by scrambling down the cliff.

West Stack (NT 8502 7085 Tidal):
A narrow channel and a short gendarme defend this 18m stack.

The Gendarme and the Shrew 35m VS 4c. R.I.Jones, J.Sanders, R.Benton. 11th December 2005.
1. 5m 4c. Step across the channel onto a steep wall and climb a crack-line. Scramble across a sloping block to the bottom of the stack wall.
2. 10m 4a. Traverse right along the landward face to the eastern corner of the stack.

3. 20m 4a. Climb the eastern face for 5m just right of the arête, then up rightwards on poor rock.

East Stack (NT 8510 7088 Tidal):
A 19m stack that runs parallel to the coast and has a grubby landward face. The western face has clean rock.

Big Dipper 20m VS 4b. R.Benton, J.Sanders, R.I.Jones. 11th December 2005.
Start from the platform at the western end of the stack. Traverse leftwards on to the west wall and climb the centre to easier ground and belay. The top is a gentle 5m scramble above this. On the first ascent a hold broke and the leader took a big dip in the sea, before completing the lead.

A small 10m land based stack on the beach to the east of East Stack at NT 8516 7088 has been soloed at Very Difficult (R.I.Jones. 11th December 2005).

East Brander Bay. Notes from C.Lesenger: suggested grades of The Bat Crack at Hard Severe, The Buoy Wonder at E2 5b and Cockle Shell Cracks at E1 5b.

Lumsdaine Groove 25m VS 4c. C.Lesenger, J.Davidson. 14th October 1995.
From the foot of The Buoy Wonder step across right to a good belay ledge and climb the groove.

Direct Start 30m HVS 5a *. C.Lesenger, T.Lauder. 29th March 1998.
Climb the crack left of Carapus through the bulge direct to the good ledge.

Tripwire 40m E1 5b. C.Lesenger, C.Berry. 25th August 1996.
Climb a vague crack-line up the steep wall 5m left of Cockle Shell Cracks to join that route at a sentry box. Follow Cockle Shell to the bulge and pull through awkwardly to gain the clean vertical crack. Finish up a short wall.

Ladywell Craigs:
These crags while facing north have some of the best rock in the area and lie about 600m west of Midden Craig. They can be approached from there at low tide, or from the quarry, cross into the field and follow the dyke downhill into another field to a makeshift metal gate above a grassy gully. Follow the faint track west for 200m then the fence north to the bottom corner of the field. Pass a prominent clump of gorse to descend between the two upper crags.

Ladywell Craig, Lower Crag:
This partly tidal crag is distinguished by a deep cave and undercut pinnacle to its right.

Free Wullie 20m E1 5b **. C.Lesenger, C.Brown. 23rd March 1997.
Start in a recess at the left end of the central slab and gain the left-hand of two thin crack-lines. Climb the crack to gain the sloping ledge with difficulty. Cut through the traverse of Speed Trap trending slightly right to good finishing holds.
Slot Machine 20m HVS 5a *. C.Lesenger, I.Macmillan. 22nd March 1997.

The right-hand dogleg crack starting just right of the recess. From the ledge finish direct up a slim right-facing corner.

Cold Start 20m Severe. C.Lesenger, I.Macmillan. 22nd March 1997.
The prominent ragged crack-line gained by a tricky wall.

Speed Trap 25m Severe. C.Lesenger, C.Brown. 23rd March 1997.
The right to left diagonal fault-line starting just left of the cave.

Ingleneuk 20m Severe. C.Lesenger, T.Lauder. 9th November 1996.
The wide crack springing from the cave.

Boot to Touch 20m E2 5b. C.Lesenger, G.Gray, T.Lauder. 20th April 1997.
Start just right of the cave and climb the slabby wall passing a sloping ledge to finish up the main crack-line. Scramble up left to belay.

Fox on the Rocks 20m VS 4c. C.Lesenger, G.Gray. 20th April 1997.
Climb the prominent left-facing corner to the top of the huge boulder, then step left to finish up an awkward crack. Scramble up left to belay.

Bowstring 15m Severe. G.Gray, T.Lauder. 20th April 1997.
Climb the juggy arête to join Shortbow at the huge boulder. Finish up that route.

Shortbow 15m Severe *. T.Lauder, C.Lesenger. 3rd April 1997.
Surmount a bulge to gain the bottomless corner bounding the left side of the pinnacle. Reach the top over an awkward chockstone.

Pinnacle Face 20m E2 5b **. C.Lesenger, T.Lauder, G.Gray. 20th April 1997.
Start below the right end of the overhang and climb a short wall till a traverse on the lip of the overhang leads onto the front face of the pinnacle. Step left and climb the face trending slightly left. Pull out right at the top.

Dying Breed 15m VS 4b. C.Lesenger, T.Lauder. 2nd April 1997.
Start at a jug on the arête right of Pinnacle Face and climb a narrow slab to an overhung niche. Step delicately right and follow a crack to the top.

Ladywell Craig, Upper Crag Left:
Above and to the right of the lower crag is a steep compact slate-like slab with two fine cracks. These were cleaned by someone unknown in 1997 and belay stakes placed above but not claimed. C.Lesenger and C.Brown climbed the right-hand crack on 5th October 1997 at 20m HVS 5b *. From the grassy ledge a committing move gains the base of the crack which is followed to the top.

Upper Crag Right (Green Slab):
This slab lies a short distance to the right at the same level.

Verdant Works 20m VS 4c. C.Lesenger, G.Brimlow. May 1999.

Start just right of the lowest point of the slab. Climb thin cracks direct to a grass cornice finish. Friend 3.5 and in-situ peg belay in the short wall above.

Microlight 15m VS 4b. C.Lesenger, G.Brimlow. May 1999.
Ten metres right is a narrow slab wedged between vertical grass columns. Climb the slab trending left then right via a shallow recess.

Burnmouth Area, Breeches Rock:
Early Days 60m VS. T.Blakemore, S.Thompson. 5th June 2005.
A descending traverse of the north face before climbing the east (seaward) face directly.
1. 20m A line of flakes lead to a diagonal descending crack. Follow this, then turn the corner to a large bay. Climbed at high water, the pitch may be avoidable at low tide.
2. 20m 4b From the right-hand side of the bay, follow a crack until it steepens (crux) to reach a large block on the ledge above.
3. 20m Continue up the arête in a spectacular position to the top.
Descend by abseil from an *in-situ* anchor.

Loose Breeches 35m HVS 4c. J.Sanders, R.I.Jones. 15th October 2005.
Climb the left-facing corner in the middle of the landward face to join the arête 5m before the top. Climb the arête to the top. Care must be taken not to dislodge the loose blocks on the left near the top of the corner.
Note: The stack is impressive as the guide states, but only 35m not 50m high.

Breeches Arch (NT 957 621 Non-tidal):
This stack lies just to the south of the main stack.

Gardener's Choice 15m Severe 4a. R.I.Jones, J.Sanders. 15th October 2005.
Climb the landward face by the right-hand arête. Vegetated.

Maiden's Stone (NT 966 603 Tidal):
Scotland's Last Old Man 20m HVS 4c. D.Rubens, G.Cohen, W.Jeffery. 2003.
The route was led despite the current guide saying it was top-roped. Climb the centre of the seaward face/leaning flake and then the wall above on the left on soft sandstone.

Linkim Stack (NT 928 654 Tidal):
Park by Hallydown Farm at NT 923 646 and follow the track to the coast and down to the beach.

No Gear Required 20m Severely Loose. R.I.Jones, J.Sanders. 5th November 2005.
Climbs the landward face. Descent is by simultaneous abseil.

The 1938 SMC Dinner. (See page 392).

MISCELLANEOUS NOTES

The W. H. Murray Literary Prize.

As a tribute to the late Bill Murray, whose mountain and environment writings have been an inspiration to many a budding mountaineer, the SMC have set up a modest writing prize, to be run through the pages of the Journal. The basic rules are set out below, and will be re-printed each year. The prize is run with a deadline, as is normal, of the end of January each year. So assuming you are reading this in early July, you have, for the next issue, six months in which to set the pencil, pen or word processor on fire.

The Rules:

1. There shall be a competition for the best entry on Scottish Mountaineering published in the *Scottish Mountaineering Club Journal.* The competition shall be called the 'W. H. Murray Literary Prize', hereafter called the 'Prize.'

2. The judging panel shall consist of, in the first instance, the following: The current Editor of the *SMC Journal;* The current President of the SMC; and two or three lay members, who may be drawn from the membership of the SMC. The lay members of the panel will sit for three years after which they will be replaced.

3. If, in the view of the panel, there is in any year no entries suitable for the Prize, then there shall be no award that year.

4. Entries shall be writing on the general theme of 'Scottish Mountaineering', and may be prose articles of up to approximately 5000 words in length, or shorter verse. Entries may be fictional.

5. Panel members may not enter for the competition during the period of their membership.

6. Entries must be of original, previously unpublished material. Entries should be submitted to the Editor of the *SMC Journal* before the end of January for consideration that year. Lengthy contributions are preferably word-processed and submitted either on 3.5" PC disk or sent via e-mail. (See Office Bearers page at end of this Journal for address etc.) Any contributor to the SMC Journal is entitled to exclude their material from consideration of the Prize and should so notify the Editor of this wish in advance.

7. The prize will be a cheque for the amount £250.

8. Contributors may make different submissions in different years.

9. The decision of the panel is final.

10. Any winning entry will be announced in the *SMC Journal* and will be published in the *SMC Journal* and on the SMC Web site. Thereafter, authors retain copyright.

Dunmore Hotchkis wearing the old Club tie. Photo: James Hotchkis.

Sgurr Nan Gillean. (see page 401).

The W. H. Murray Literary Prize (2006)

The winner of this years W. H. Murray Literary Prize is first-time contributor, Guy Robertson, with his excellent piece *Final Destination*, which appropriately closes the Articles section of this edition of the Journal.

To say that this is an account of the first ascent of a Grade VI climb on Beinn Dearg adequately describes the subject matter, but gives no real hint of the style of writing to expect. Guy writes with a unique style which, with his clever use of imagery and metaphor, paints word pictures that surprise and delight. He has the ability as MacCaig so aptly put it: "To see the extraordinary in the ordinary."

"… the unthinkable arrests them, their jaws dropped slack like a pair of wooden puppets. A mighty Gulf Stream fist had driven unchallenged across the great stand of pines through which they toil. And now, up ahead, great wooden bastions lay slain and slaughtered across their way…" Which, left to a less artistic pen, might read: "Some trees had been blown over and blocked their way." – I rest my case.

This year's 'Prize' was one of the closest contested to date with Julian Lines's history of climbing on the Shelterstone, *The Shelterstone Saga* running Guy very close.

"… full of passion, crystal crimping pleasure and climbing characters – more metaphors and similes than holds!"

"An excellent piece documenting and recording the climbing history of The Shelterstone."

Julian somehow manages to describe these climbs, at times move after nerve-stretching move, without losing the reader's attention. His sense of the joy of climbing comes across clearly even while employing a commitment that most of us can't even imagine.

"If you can't do these climbs, this is as close as your going to get."

Another piece which came in for praise from the judges was David Adams *Hot Ice* a futuristic fiction pre-figuring what 'Ice-climbing' on The Ben might be like in 2075.

"An original piece of 'cli-fi', far enough removed from where we are to be plausible (just)."

"Well the Ice-Factor is just down the road and there is still 70 years to go!"

Finally, a mention must be made of the innovative two-handed narrative *Maneater* by Ken Crocket and John Mackenzie

"An excellently crafted tale of exploratory winter climbing in the North-west."

A personal favourite – but perhaps too innovative for some.

Congratulations again to Guy and all the other contributors, and to all you budding authors out there, there's always next year. The winning article, as well as appearing in this year's Journal, can also be read on the SMC website.

Charlie Orr.

SCOTTISH WINTER NOTES

By Simon Richardson

THE 2006 winter season was when Grade VIII finally came of age There were more ascents of top-end climbs during 2006 than any winter before, and this was despite a very slow start to the season that only really got going with the first heavy snowfalls in early March. Before then, ascents were snatched as a result of brilliant timing, or by those fortunate enough to be in the right place at the right time and willing to take an opportunistic approach.

The first big route of the season fell to Jon Bracey, Rich Cross and Martin Moran when they made the first winter ascent of *Hydroponicum* on Beinn Eighe at the end of November. This takes a sensational line up a tapering undercut ramp in the centre of Far East Wall, creeps round the left edge of a big roof, then climbs a plumb vertical groove to the exit. Andy Nisbet climbed it in summer with John Allott in 1995 as a rather dirty E1, but it had already caught Moran's eye as a potential winter line. He tried it with Chris Dale in 1993, but had to make a fraught retreat from just below the crux section due to the onset of a massive thaw – so success more than 12 years later must have been very sweet.

"Jon made an outstanding on-sight lead of the crux pitch," Martin told me. "Protection and placements were hard to find, but having led *Daddy Longlegs* in the Northern Corries the previous weekend he was clearly in great form. From a hanging stance just above the roofs Rich led the difficult exit groove in the dark. We reckoned the overall grade to be VIII, 8 and another worthy addition to Scotland's mixed climbing Mecca."

The next big event was the first winter ascent of *Sioux Wall* on Number Three Gully Buttress on Ben Nevis. This was first climbed in the summer of 1972 by Ian Nicolson and George Grassam and is one of the finest HVS climbs on the mountain. High mountain rock climbs on the Ben are not in vogue nowadays, so it is rarely climbed, but *Sioux Wall* had entered the modern climber's consciousness as a futuristic winter climbing target. With winter standards rising year on year, it was only a matter of time before it was climbed, and sure enough on January 1, Ian Parnell and Olly Metherell brought in 2006 with a bang with the first winter ascent.

"On the evening of December 31, we walked up towards the Ben and camped about two-thirds of the way to the CIC Hut," Ian told me. "New Year's Day was warm and slushy so we walked up with little optimism into Coire na Ciste planning to have a go at *Archangel.* As we got higher we began to realise how white everything was, with soggy snow stuck to overhanging, as well as vertical aspects, so I persuaded Olly to switch to an attempt on *Sioux Wall*.

"We started pretty direct and I led the steep wall from the obvious belay niche to a ledge at the base of the 'obvious corner-groove'. This pitch was the crux. It was very well protected, but super steep, sustained and pumpy – like *The Vicar* on steroids! Olly led the corner-groove that had surprisingly good protection, and although there were more rests, it was still pumpy.

"Olly fell off, leaving his axes in the belay ledge – we both were climbing leashless – so he climbed up again to finish off this pitch. From here the summer pitch 3 continues with a great looking crack, but with half-an-hour of daylight left I chose a rightward line. I hoped it would be easier, but it proved fairly serious, particularly up high – with a foot of snow over very thin vertical ground lit by head torch." With two pitches of 7 and two of 8, *Sioux Wall* (VIII,8) is a welcome addition to the growing clutch of Grade VIII routes on the Ben. Parnell and Metherell's ascent was met with general acclaim.

"I'm very impressed," said Andy Nisbet, New Routes Editor. "This sort of route is moving up a grade from the !980s and 1990s. It's the sort of route we couldn't quite do, and there's a lot of scope in Scotland for this type of climb. Really it's the new routing future, although there's no danger of me running out of easier remote routes!"

New routes are often used as the gauge for progress in mountaineering, however sometimes second ascents are made in such outstanding style that they take on special significance. Guy Robertson and Pete Benson's repeat of *The Steeple* (IX,9) on the Shelter Stone Crag was such a climb, and illustrates how standards are also advancing on long and technically demanding routes. The first winter ascent of *The Steeple* fell to Alan Mullin and Steve Paget in a 24-hour push in November, 1999. It was an outstanding piece of mountaineering but the climb was marred by two points of aid and the early season nature of the ascent was severely criticised. A clean second ascent in full winter conditions therefore, stood out as one of the great prizes of Scottish winter climbing. After a series of blizzards in early March, the high Cairngorms crags were draped in fresh snow, which prompted Robertson and Benson to have a look.

"Conditions were generally superb," said Guy. "There was good snow-ice in places and the turf was like toffee. There was lots of snow, and every crack, niche and crevice was utterly blootered with the stuff. Overall it felt very wintry."

Robertson and Benson completed the route in an astonishing 12 hours and finished just as light was fading. They started up the gully and 'fine corner' of the original line of *Postern*, then went right to the Terrace and up the summer crux of *Needle*. They continued up *The Steeple* 'layback cracks', climbed the big Steeple Corner in a single pitch and finished up the '5a wall cracks'. The 250m.-long route had two pitches each of 7, 8 and 9 and the Steeple Corner was led in a single 45m. pitch by Benson. The 5a wall cracks provided the second crux and the only flaw to the ascent was when Robertson dangled momentarily from an axe leash round his neck when his right tool ripped while he was pulling onto the slab above the final crack. Fortunately, the left tool held.

"What a feeling," Guy enthused, "locked off in the final corner, the last gear out of sight, pummelling desperately at a foot-and-a-half of rime ice, the wind howling like a Banshee in my face and 1000ft. of air snapping at my feet! I was completely blown away by this route, and I doubt I'll experience the like again. The length, difficulty, variety and majesty of the big Shelter Stone routes are simply unparalleled."

Two days before *The Steeple* ascent, Dave MacLeod and Fiona Murray were gearing up below one of the last great problems in the Southern Highlands – the gently overhanging wall left of *Messiah* on Creag an Socach above Bridge or Orchy. MacLeod set off up a turfy ramp to gain a line of poorly protected overhanging thin corners. Hard moves through a roof led onto the headwall followed by a difficult traverse left to a hanging corner and an exquisite turfy fault that finished on the traverse line of *Golgotha.* This astonishing 60m.-long pitch was thought to be M8+ in standard and is one of the most impressive on sight leads ever made in Scottish winter. The second pitch was considerably easier and soon MacLeod and Murray were on the top celebrating *Defenders of the Faith* (IX,9) – the first time a Scottish winter route of this grade has been climbed completely free and on sight.

"It put up a good fight," said Dave. "It's a great line and is classic Southern Highlands climbing with some 'Thank God' bits of turf in some highly improbable spots."

Across on Ben Nevis, MacLeod and Emmett made a direct finish to *Italian Climb*. This well-known problem tackles the cave and overhang at the top of the initial gully where the original Grade III route goes right. The crux was a steep cracked wall with long reaches, followed by a serious groove-line leading onto the crest of *Tower Ridge*. The *Italian Job* (VIII,9) was climbed on sight and is currently the highest graded route on the mountain, although it is possible that the top groove will become easier when iced. Higher up in Coire na Ciste, Nick Bullock and Owen Samuels climbed a difficult route to the right of *Darth Vader*. *Avenging Angel* (VII,8) climbs the first three pitches of *Archangel* and then continues up a steep corner, offwidth and overhanging wall in the true line of the impending corner system. Bullock had a good run of routes with the second ascent of *Babylon* (VII,8) on Number Three Gully Buttress with Mat Helliker, and an early repeat of *Postman Pat* (VII,7) on Creag Meagaidh with Kevin Neal.

There are many new route possibilities in the Northern Highlands, but a winter ascent of *Pobble,* a summer VS on Lord Reay's Seat on Foinaven, was a clear target. The 160m. route takes a series of chimneys up the centre of the crag, and had been eyed up by several winter teams over the years. Foinaven does not hold winter conditions well, but it can be a very difficult mountain to reach when the roads are covered in snow. Malcolm Bass and Simon Yearsley tried the route in November, 2004, but had found mounds of graupel below the crag, with a totally black buttress above.

Simon said: "This time the forecast proved too much of a mid-week temptation. Conditions were predicted to be ideal with heavy snow fall, then continuous snow showers during the day to top up the snow cover on the crag which is east-facing and quickly stripped by the morning sun."

After an epic drive, involving blocked roads and disintegrating snow-chains, they left the car at 5.30am, cycled along the approach track and then used snow-shoes for the ascent to the crag. They started climbing by 10am, reached the summit at 9pm. and finally made it back to the road by 3.30am. after 22 hours on the move.

"The route packs a real punch," Simon said, "with a superb mix of strenuous, yet helpful chimneys, and technical delicate slabs, finishing on the summit of Lord Reay's Seat."

Overall the route came in at a sustained VII,7, with one pitch of technical 6 and five pitches of technical 7. In common with other Yearsley-Bass ascents, this route was the result of imaginative planning and dogged persistence, and the style of their ascent drew many favourable comments from a cross-section of Scottish winter activists. It just goes to show that it's not always cutting edge technical ascents that provide the greatest inspiration.

It stayed consistently cold through March and April and Ian Parnell took best advantage of the unusually good late season conditions by climbing two new Grade VIIIs in the Cairngorms with Guy Robertson, before returning a week later with Tim Emmett to solve a long-standing problem in the Northern Corries.

Parnell and Robertson's first objective was the natural line of weakness curving leftwards across the right wall of *Raeburn's Gully,* on Lochnagar. This very steep recessed buttress, to the left of the classic ice line of *Scarface*, is an awkward proposition as it is undercut at its base and needs a good build up in *Raeburn's*

Gully to allow a way through the initial overhangs. Three very steep mixed pitches led to a difficult finish up the final two pitches of *The Straight-Jacket* (VII,7), an unrepeated Nisbet-Spinks route from 1980.

"The route provided some tremendous and exacting climbing," Guy enthused. "The weather was wild and conditions were full on at times – yet another memorable adventure."

With three pitches of technical 8, *Scarface Wall* weighs in at a mighty VIII,8 and a worthy addition to a growing list of modern Lochnagar test-pieces.

After a day's rest, the pair went up to No.1 Buttress in Coire an Lochain in the Northern Corries and made the first ascent of *Open Heart* (VIII,9), a very strenuous route that links the first pitch of *Ventricle* to the crux of *Ventriloquist*.

"This route was very much Ian's baby," Guy said. "He'd been on it with Ben Wilkinson a few weeks previously. It was pretty buried on that occasion, and Ben fell off nearing the top of the crux overhanging groove, ripping all his gear and landing on Ian's head. Ian cruised it when we went back, and made a very impressive lead. I'd say it was roughly the same grade as *Daddy Longlegs*, but maybe just a touch thinner."

Two new Grade VIII routes in three days is an impressive haul by anyone's standards, but Parnell was back the following week for more.

Ian said:" I thought that weekend with Guy would be the end of the winter for me, but when I phoned up Tim Emmett to arrange a trip to Pembroke he was desperate to get back up North, so Easter weekend in Scotland it was. We opted for an attempt on *Never Mind* in the Northern Corries. Most of the hoar was stripped on anything steep, but that little corner of the Corries was thick with frost and under a fairly uniform coat of icy hoar 12ins. to 18ins. thick."

Never Mind, an HVS rock climb on the pillar between No. 3 and No. 4 Buttress in Coire an Lochain, has seen a number of determined winter attempts over the years and was regarded as one of the last great problems in the Northern Corries. On Easter Saturday Emmett set off up the narrow groove just left of the front of the pillar. This blanked out at a roof and crux moves led rightwards across a blank wall to a short wide crack leading up to a stance. Emmett took a 25ft. fall on the crux, lowered to a 'no hands' rest and then completed the pitch. Parnell followed and then swung round to an overhanging groove in the right arête of the pillar.

Ian said: "It was impossible to see any features beneath the hoar which looked like the mushrooms on Cerro Torre. This pitch was exceptionally hard work, continually digging while laybacking up the overhanging groove. I took a fall about 30ft. up when my feet popped off the typical Cairngorm rounded breaks. I lowered to the belay, pulled my ropes and had another go – digging for glory. This time I climbed about 60ft. of gently overhanging climbing with no rests, excavating my way diagonally right to a flake-groove on the right side wall. I trusted my axe to some poor ice that pulled and I took another sizeable fall. I made another 10ft. of progress and finally stalled at a blank slab that guarded the last six feet of climbing."

The following day, Parnell led the first pitch straight off, and Emmett made a clean lead of the top.

"One of Tim's axes pulled on the last move on the very crest of the tower and he almost fell," Ian recalled. "Both the cruxes, but especially the top one, felt very modern with no secure torques but very thin hooking and some trickery – the sort of things Tim has learned from his time on the competition circuit. Grading this sort of thing is difficult especially as it was under a massive amount of hoar and it's so short, but we're guessing IX 9. Tim thought it comparable with *Happy Tyroleans* – not as pumpy, but with a more technical crux and bigger fall potential."

Normally, ascents of new Grade VIIs make the headlines, but this season they were overshadowed somewhat by the harder achievements outlined above. On Lochnagar, Guy Robertson and I filled in an obvious gap by climbing the very steep headwall of Eagle Buttress to give *Where Eagles Dare* (VII,8). Robertson thought this one of the finest technical climbs on Lochnagar and its quality was confirmed by the second ascent team of Pete Benson and Ross Hewitt a few days afterwards. Over on the West, Chris Cartwright and I filled in one of the remaining gaps on Noe Buttress on Ben Cruachan with the first ascent of *In Cold Blood* (VII,7). This takes the obvious groove left of *In the Knoe*, and in common with the other routes on the crag it packs in very sustained climbing from the first move to the last.

Finally, Andy Nisbet showed his mettle when he visited the West Face of Druim Shionnach with Dave McGimpsey in the Western Highlands and came away with *Bowling Alley* (VII,6), the turfy fault-line up the face to the right of *Bow Peep.* The climbing was bold and exposed, and Andy's lead of the 40m. crux pitch was protected by a meagre three knifeblades and a couple of hooks.

As well as Robertson and Benson's second ascent of *The Steeple*, there were several other noteworthy repeats. *Darth Vader* (VII,8) on Ben Nevis saw repeats from Iain Small and Viv Scott; Rich Cross and Nick Wallis; Nick Bullock and Blair Fyffe, and is approaching modern classic status. Ian Parnell and Ollie Metherell visited Garbh Choire Dhaidh on Braeriach and came away with a rare repeat of *Digeridoo* (VII,6), eliminating the rest point in the process.

On Ben Nevis, Andy Turner and Duncan Hodgson repeated *Sioux Wall*, (VIII,8), climbing straight up at the top where Parnell and Metherell went right, therefore chalking up the first winter ascent of the complete summer line. Another remarkable ascent in the Cairngorms was Tim Emmett's third ascent of *Happy Tyroleans* (IX,10) in Coire an Lochain with Dave MacLeod. Emmett took a couple of short falls, but the route was despatched in remarkably quick time after an extremely late 1pm. start from the car. Over in the West, *Unicorn* (VIII,8) on Stob Coire nan Lochan was climbed by Ian Parnell and Steve Ashworth, and the recent routes on Ben Cruachan saw their first repeats with ascents of *Tainted Elixir* (V,6) and *Goldfinger* (VII,7).

There were many fine additions throughout the season, but in my view, the most interesting have a strong exploration focus. John Lyall discovered a 100m. crag directly beneath the summit of Carn Dearg in the Monadhliath. The cliff has five pillars separated by faults and John climbed the major lines with the best being *Soul Survivor* (IV,4), the turfy fault between the first and second pillars from the left, and *Arctic Monkey* (IV,5), a line up the fourth pillar. Across in the Cairngorms, R. McMurray and C. McGregor had a good find with the excellent *Fifer's Fall* (IV,4), a steep 70m. icefall on the previously unclimbed Creag an t-Sluic in Glen Feshie. MacGregor also climbed the ice line of *Rambler's Ruin* (III) at the right end of the crag. Farther west, Donald King, Andy Turner, Mike Pescod and Mike Brownlow developed the easterly corrie of Mullach nan Corean in the Mamores by adding a series of 80m. routes with pride of place going to the excellent *Kindergarten Corner* (VII,8).

Andy Nisbet and Sandy Allan had a fine discovery on Creag Loch Tuill Bhearnach, the crag containing Lapland Buttress, to the north of Loch Mullardoch, where they climbed the excellent *Lap of Honour* (V,6) that takes a shallow narrowing chimney on the right side of the crag. Andy returned later with John Lyall and added *Weary Wall* (III), an easier line up the south side of the buttress.

Finally, Brian Davison and I fulfilled a long-held dream in late April by making a girdle traverse of the Ben Nevis cliffs. We started at 5.30am. and climbed *North Castle Gully* to gain the top of *Castle Ridge*. We then headed over *The Castle*, down across mixed ground into Castle Corrie, up *Ledge Route*, crossed the Trident Buttresses, descended Number Four Gully, climbed North Gully, traversed across Creag Coire na Ciste, up *Thompson's Route*, down Number Three Gully Buttress, up *Green Gully*, down *Hesperides Ledge*, across Comb Gully Buttress, up *Raeburn's Easy Route* and left into *Glover's Chimney*. We dropped down from the Gap into *Observatory Gully* and had lunch at 12pm. We then headed off under Indicator Wall and across Observatory Buttress into *Point Five Gully*. Getting in and out of the Point was the hardest part of the day – poor snow and tricky route finding. We then, very carefully, made our way across *Hadrian's Wall*, *Observatory Ridge* and *Zero Gully* on spooky snow and thin slabs finishing up *Slav Route* to reach the crest of *North-East Buttress* at about 17.45pm. There was about 4000m. climbing in all and we graded the expedition V,4. Grades are, of course, irrelevant on a route like this, and the real crux was waiting several seasons for favourable snow conditions to allow fast travel over the easier sections. Who would have guessed that the 2006 winter, bare and dry until March, would finally come up trumps?

Mountaineering in South Georgia

MOUNTAINEERING on the sub-Antarctic island of South Georgia is reserved for a determined few. A trip there also requires one to trespass on one of nature's paradises; the island is home to millions of breeding birds and seals. Few expeditions visit the island's mountainous interior and most that do, follow Sir Ernest Shackleton's route. Yet the island has hundreds of previously unclimbed peaks and routes to be done, if the weather allows. Expeditions can find themselves pinned to their camps or snow-holes for days and weeks on end because of the island's ferocious weather. Stephen Venables famously spent most of one of his expeditions in a snow-hole unable to venture out. Weather windows that enable a mountaineer to climb to a summit can be fleeting, but the rewards can also be sensational.

Disused and rusting whaling stations are the only visible remains of what was, some 70years ago, the southern whaling capital of the World. Today, the surrounding seas are a whale sanctuary and no longer red with the blood of whale carcasses. In the small whalers' and sealers' cemetery beside Grytviken's silent whaling station, the Antarctic explorer, Sir Ernest Shackleton, lies in peace. His grave is overlooked by the interior he crossed in 1916 to alert the world to the plight of his ill-fated expedition. It rises steeply to a snow-covered mountain chain that forms the backbone of the island. Huge snow-white glaciers split the mountain chain and flow down to carve great blue ice blocks, with a thunderous roar, into the surrounding ocean.

Inaccessible, hostile, rugged and remote, with no permanent human population, the crescent shaped island lies in the cold stormy seas of the southern oceans that are rich in marine life. The long snow and ice covered island is some 170km. long and 40km. at its widest point. It rises up to 2934m. at the summit of Mount Paget. Antarctica is1500km. to the south and the Falklands are 1400km. to the west. It lies South of the Antarctic Polar Front (Between 35° 47' to 38° 01' West and 53° 58' to 54° 53' South) about 2150km. from Tierra del Fuego and 1390km. south-east of the Falkland Islands. Two steep mountain ranges form two-thirds of the island's backbone and rise to 2960m. at the highest point (Mount Paget) with some 19 other peaks above 2000m. More than 50% of the island is under permanent ice cover from an altitude of around 460m. on the north coast and around 300m. on the colder southern coast. Steep sided valleys and indented bays cut deeply into the island and offer sheltered anchorages, particularly on the northern coast and in the Drygalski Fjord granite complex at the south-eastern end of the island.

The island is part of the UK Overseas Territory of South Georgia and South Sandwich Islands and is administered by the Government of South Georgia and South Sandwich Islands (GSGSSI) from the Falkland Islands. GSGSSI was formed in 1985 as a separate British territory under a Commissioner. It had previously been part of the Falkland Islands Dependencies. The Commissioner has vested in him, legal, financial and administrative authority and responsibility for the governance of the island. A Government Officer represents him on South Georgia.

A tourist industry brings about 4000 people and a dozen or so yachts to visit the island each year. The Government is responsible for the island's environment and natural resources. Strict regulations protect the wildlife and plants ashore. The island's commercial fishery, which includes Antarctic krill, Icefish and Patagonian Toothfish, is managed by the Government in close conjunction with the commission for the conservation of Antarctic Marine Living Resources (CCAMLR). Scientists first based themselves on the island in 1882; today there are two permanent research stations manned by British Antarctic Survey staff.

Each year about three or four expeditions go to South Georgia to ski, climb or kayak during the island's austral summer. If any member of the club wishes to go on an expedition to South Georgia to climb or ski then the author would be very happy to help with advice. The island's website (www.sgisland.org) provides much background on the island and a web camera can be accessed that looks across the bay to Mount Paget and neighbouring peaks. A Government permit is needed to take an expedition there. An expeditions advisory panel, which the author chairs, has been established to provide expeditions with advice and help. The panel also processes expedition applications and advises the Government. But beware, as expeditions can have a large price tag! A support vessel, such as a yacht, is needed so that self-rescue could be achieved if necessary. This is because of the remoteness of the island and the lack of search and rescue facilities. There is no airfield or helicopter. It is some four to five days sailing back to the Falkland Islands.

In 2003-04 and 2005, the author led two British Schools Exploring Society expeditions to South Georgia. In 2003-4 the expedition was very fortunate to have settled periods of weather that enabled them to ski up into the island's interior and to climb four previously unclimbed peaks in the Wilckens Range. The peaks climbed were not difficult, as the young expedition members had limited mountaineering experience. In December 2005, a smaller second expedition was not so lucky and despite spending three weeks waiting for a weather window, none arrived and so their planned summits remain unclimbed. The 6000ft. peaks were in the Allardyce range. They did, however, gain valuable additional mountaineering and leadership experience. A visit to South Georgia is always a memorable experience not easily forgotten. The wildlife in the relatively unspoiled wilderness is stunning and the mountain scenery breathtaking.

David V. Nicholls

CAMPED OUT THERE IN THE COLD

The temperature was 50° below, near enough the same as when the man from the creeks stumbled into the din and the glare of the Malemute Saloon prior to the shooting of Dan McGrew. The two of us were 15° of latitude farther south in the rain shadow side of the Coast Range of British Columbia, somewhere between Lytton and Lillooet but on the other side of the Fraser River. On the east side of the mountains the valley bottoms are dry and covered with sage brush and cactus. The snow starts higher up where the peaks catch the weather systems coming in from the wild Pacific shore.

We left the car at the end of a long dirt road and started off through the sage brush. After a few hundred feet we entered an open forest of feral Ponderosa pine floored with a mere dusting of dry snow. About 1000ft. farther up the stately Ponderosa gave way to denser stands of spruce and deeper drifts of snow. After some hours of this difficult terrain we reached a mile-wide bowl on the upper mountain where the forest opened out into twinkling snowfields studded with dense clumps of stunted spruce. Once clear of the forest we could see our route, a long narrow ridge beginning at the end of the tree-line 1000ft. higher up on the right lip of the bowl. If we could reach the ridge bottom on the morrow we had a chance of a quick dash to the summit.

By now the sun was low over the western peaks and the plummeting temperature indicated that things were about to get serious. Under these conditions it is wise to bivouac early so you can see what you are doing. A temperature decades below zero is no friend of living things. We headed for a thick clump of dwarfed spruce to make a des. res. for the night. I remember the clump we happened on was particularly well-favoured; it had three taller trees at its centre and the space around them was protected by a dense hedge of smaller trees. The central space was snow-free and level. We settled down for the night in this protected micro-climate. Once we got our mats and sleeping bags out, a candle burning on a knife blade stuck into a tree trunk and the primus roaring we had a sheltered home and dined in comfort. Outside our nook the silence was deep and the stars glittered in a black, black sky. Something – hopefully a coyote or a wolf rather than something less tangible – howled from time to time from different locations in the surrounding forest primeval.

It was the first time we had tried out this type of bivouac. We were following the advice of a patient of mine, a Red Indian by the name of Murdo MacDonald, who had explained that this was standard practice among his people when out on a winter hunting expedition. He also gave me the helpful advice that if attacked by a bear you should get your back against a tree, hold your knife in your right hand point upwards and throw your left arm across your throat to protect your windpipe and great vessels. When the bear embraces you, its claws dig into the tree. Before its teeth can do too much damage to your left arm, you stab upwards under its rib cage into its heart. This is anatomically a plausible procedure and may even work. His camping advice was certainly sound but I never had the chance to test his technique for dealing with an uppity bear.

The next morning we started late. It was cold outside and a strong wind had got up. Our refuge fortunately remained sheltered. It was warm and filled with the comforting aroma of coffee and pine resin. We lay in our bags listening to the wind in the branches until the sun was well up in the bright blue sky. When we eventually did get going the wind cut to the bone and travel through the spindrift and deep unconsolidated snow was slow and painful. We could see long plumes of silver snow dust streaming from our ridge all the way to the summit. It must surely be snow-free up there and we prepared for a battle along a windy corridor to an inhospitable summit. To gain shelter from the wind for as long as possible we returned to the trees and gained the lee side of the shoulder leading to our ridge. The price of the lee was deeper snow and denser forest as we were nearer the Pacific slope.

At one point I emerged from a dense thicket into a clearing. A few seconds later I was facing an Indian pointing a rifle at me. Then two other Indians materialised also with rifles. They seemed vastly relieved about something but not half as relieved as we were when we learned that they were on the point of shooting us as deer. However, something about our progress was un-deer-like and had made them pause. They spoke little English but the message was the same as you get for spoiling the sport of a stalking party anywhere in the world.

We pointed uphill and asked: "Okay?" They gestured us on and we continued the struggle. That incident had been a close call. A lot of people are shot by mistake in the hunting season. In some areas farmers put white smocks on their animals with 'COW' or 'HORSE', as appropriate, written on the side in large black letters. We were lucky to encounter experienced hunters on their native heath. Townie palefaces usually shoot anything that moves or even rustles. All this showed our double inexperience: the woods are dangerous in the hunting season and the new unconsolidated snow of November is best avoided.

We continued on to the foot of the ridge but after leaving the trees we were full-face into the teeth of a frost-biting wind; the ridge was longer than it looked from below and in a couple of hours darkness would be upon us again. We lost fortitude; old Auntie Prudence took over; we turned back. We had started later than we should have due to weakness of character. We wisely retreated from the land of wind-scoured rock and tearing silver spindrift to descend a couple of thousand feet through the spruce to the kindly belt of whispering Ponderosa pine. Here we found a sheltered spot, floored with pine needles instead of snow. We made a modest campfire and after our bacon and beans reclined beneath bright stars twinkling in the vast sky above. My companion was moved to quote from *The Shooting of Dan McGrew*:

Were you ever out in the Great Alone, when the moon was awful clear,
And the icy mountains hemmed you in with a silence you most could hear;
With only the howl of a timber wolf as you camped there in the cold,…
While high overhead, green yellow and red, the North Lights swept in bars?–
Then you've a hunch what the music meant…hunger and night and the stars.

Okay, so we weren't hungry, there was no music, no moon, no aurora and the wandering thing that howled in the darkness the night before seemed to be elsewhere, but the rest of the *mise-en-scene* was present: there was silence and a sense of immense darkness.

Iain Smart.

Friday Climbs

Following on from Adam Watson's article last year on Climate Change, Mick Tighe gives his perspective on what this has meant on the ground.

WE CALLED them Friday climbs, and a favourite was *No. 6 Gully* on the west side of Aonach Dubh in Glencoe. You could be on the first pitch within an hour of leaving the van and back down by mid-afternoon for a pint in the Clachaig. It was an ideal way to finish an ice-climbing week, and in those days you could almost guarantee that there would be ice at that level.

Other low-level favourites were *Great Gully* on the Buachaille and routes such as *Rev. Teds* and *Peregrine Gully* in the Lost Valley. Now, 20 years on, there's not a bit of ice to be seen in these gullies, rock, heather and waterfalls rule the roost and canyoning is the new activity, with water pouring down the neck instead of spindrift.

On several occasions in the late 1990s and the early 'naughties' there has been excellent ice-climbing in Scotland – some have said the best ever – unfortunately, this climbing has almost always been above 3500ft., confining it primarily to Ben Nevis, Aonach Mor and the Northern Corries of the Cairngorms. The down side of this is that when conditions are good, large numbers of climbers converge on the few 'in nick' areas, somewhat detracting from the ethos of the mountains' peace, tranquillity and solitude. The Rescue teams have an easy time of it though, as they can run along the bottom of the climber-infested crags and wait for folk to fall off, without having to go looking for them.

There's no doubt that the freezing level has gone up and that a climate that already changed quickly, changes even faster now. Why this is we can only let the boffins fathom out, but for the guide/instructor who has pottered around the Scottish Highlands for the last few decades in the snow, times are a changin'.

The ice falls of Norway, Chamonix, and Canada beckon. Ryanair, Easyjet and their cohorts have entered the arena at just the right time (maybe it's a ploy – their jets contributing to global warming.)

Everyone has chucked away Pterodactyls and straight-shafted tools, and bought curved-shafted masterpieces for the glistening ice-falls of Mecca, where eyes are protected from the glare by sunglasses, instead of from the wind by goggles.

Pints of heavy, wee drams and fish suppers are now Pernods, Acquavits and Croque-Monsieurs. Interestingly, things are getting warmer in these places too, but it was colder on average to start with, and there has always been more snow and ice in these foreign climbs anyway.

It's early February, and as I write, there's a dusting of snow on the Nevis Range, but precious little old snow underneath. I'm about to depart for a week in the North West Highlands (Poolewe), where I had a week at the same time last year. *Hayfork Gully* on An Teallach had some old névé, which provided a good day, and we followed that with three excellent days rock-climbing at Reiff as there was no snow anywhere else in the North West.

Huts – Round 2

HAVING run between each of the SMC huts on consecutive days and mountain biked round them all in three days, I thought it would be pleasant to cycle round them on the road. I had not consulted a map but was considering a leisurely day between each of the huts, maybe covering the CIC and Lagangarbh in one day.

I was discussing the idea of cycling between the huts with Charlie Orr and Tom Prentice when one of them said: "What in a day?"

I can't recall who said it but I'm sure I managed to refrain from saying out loud: "Don't be stupid."

However they had sown a seed, and I got the road atlas out. Some quick calculations showed the distance was about 300 miles, and of course there was the CIC to visit.

A few years ago a friend had tried to break the Land's End to John o'Groats cycle record. He'd failed after 600 miles, but I found it astounding that the record stood at around 40 hours for the 800-mile route. These top cyclists can sure move and their endurance is phenomenal. I looked up the 24-hour endurance record, and at 520 miles it showed that the huts cycle route was feasible for a top cyclist – but what about me?

I studied the maps more carefully, trying to decide on the best route. There was obviously going to have to be some back-tracking to visit either Lagangarbh or the Raeburn. The Raeburn proved the farther from Spean Bridge and so that had to be a start or finishing point and the Naismith Hut would be the other end. During discussions someone suggested getting the Mallaig ferry and travelling through Skye on the way to Torridon. The route through Skye was appealing and only a few miles longer, though the thought of missing a ferry and being stuck weighed heavily against it. To do the round in 24 hours required averaging 15mph to allow a few hours for food stops and to run to the CIC.

I started my training, a combination of running and cycling. It seems to get more difficult every year to get into some sort of semblance of fitness and find the necessary time to do training runs. So as June arrived I had not run more than 10 miles in one go. I set myself a few targets to try and stimulate some interest. First was the 40-mile run round the 'Derwent Water Shed' route in the Peak district. Being a fairly flat route it allowed me to increase my mileage without too many hills to kill me off. At the end of the month a cycling trip round all the Lake District FRCC huts proved to be just more than 100 miles, but at 7.5 hours I wasn't keeping to my 15mph average. Still the passes were steeper in the Lakes than anything I'd encounter on the Scottish roads. A week later saw me slogging round the 15 Classic Rock Routes in the Lake District on a very hot day. Running between each route took just under 20 hours. The route felt harder than the 40 miles would have suggested and having to ease swollen feet into rock boots at each crag allowed a new level of discomfort to be reached. I'd considered the rock routes as a training run for the Bob Graham round but with blistered feet I wasn't sure I'd manage to do one that summer. A few weeks later with my toughened feet recovered and with a forecast of total cloud cover above the tops I set out for a solo Bob Graham round. The 72 miles. and 30,000ft. of ascent felt a lot easier than the Classic Rock Routes had a few weeks before. Without any stops, and blister free, I was round in 22 hours and feeling good. It was time to head to Scotland.

As the August days ticked by I kept watching the forecast and finally got what I wanted, gentle southerly winds, so I headed to the Raeburn. I usually try and get an early night before the long drive to Scotland but on this occasion I was up until 11pm. wall-papering the bedroom. I bet Lance Armstrong didn't have to finish the decorating before he was allowed to ride the Tour de France!

None the worse of wear for my DIY exploits I reached the Raeburn the next evening and got a few hours sleep before creeping out of the hut before dawn and cycling through the dark and low mist to Fort William and the golf course, my first stop. I'd managed my first 40 miles in two hours so averaging 20mph, one of the targets I had never managed during training, but which, with the gentle descent from the Raeburn Hut to the sea on the West Coast, I now achieved. With my bike hidden in some bushes and the first dawn light in the sky I headed up the Allt a' Mhuillinn past the path-building machinery. The shutters were open as I reached the hut at 6am and turned round to run back to my bike.

The rain poured as I cycled past Glencoe village but I'd dried off by the time I reached Lagangarbh. It felt good to turn round and head back down the valley into the rain and past the village again and I'd dried off once more as I reached Spean Bridge and stopped for breakfast at the Little Chef. I'd done 100 miles and run to the CIC, and my legs felt it. I'd done the section fast but at the expense of not eating or drinking enough. I felt better after the stop and started to time myself to take regular food and sips of carbohydrate drink from my bottles as I cycled along the A87. With August holiday traffic towing caravans to Skye I was glad to turn off onto the quieter road for Lochcarron.

A brief stop at the top of a hill allowed me to eat some rice pudding and refill my pockets with food then it was onward. I'd been making good time but now the road surface was poorer and the hills steeper but thankfully short, and my averages were slipping. I'd run out of drink as I approached Torridon so a brief stop at the toilets got me out of the midges and allowed me to refill my bottles and scoff the last of my rice puddings. I'd passed the 200-mile barrier.

This was all new territory for me, I'd never cycled this far before and had been unsure at the outset whether I could manage to do the route in 24 hours or indeed at all. By now my bum was sore but as long as I kept on taking in food I knew my legs could keep turning the pedals. As I passed Kinlochewe the re-surfaced road gave me a new lease of life and I increased my speed. The hill out of Ullapool felt steep but I was still able to cycle it. Less than 22 hours after starting out from the Raeburn I reached Elphin and the lights of the Naismith hut, I'd managed to average 15.5mph., something I'd never managed during my cycles round the Lake District.

Travelling north the previous day I'd phoned the hut custodian to check on a place in the hut, here was the spanner in the works, the hut was full. So after 288 miles. I did a U-turn in the road and cycled back to a welcome bed with friends in Ullapool. At least it was downhill, most of the time.

Brian Davison.

('Chapeau' – as the French would say– Ed.)

The Club Tie

MEMBERS might be forgiven for thinking that the present design of Club Tie is as old as the Club. But in fact the design of the tie has seen a number of changes, the most recent being the addition of thistles. This was done, as far as I can recall, by Graham Tiso more or less on his own hook, sometime in the late 1970s. It is difficult to see what was amiss with the previous design of crossed ice-axes on navy silk, but office-bearers are always apt to meddle – with the good as well as the bad.

It came as an enormous surprise to me to learn last year that the axes-on-navy tie was not the first Club Tie, and that the earliest design bore absolutely no relation to it. My enlightenment came while trying to identify images in the A. E. Robertson Collection. Many of these around 1930 showed members wearing a striped tie, the stripes being broad, equal and horizontal, and alternately light and dark. At first I thought that perhaps this was an old version of the Alpine Club Tie, but inquiry disposed of that idea. So, I was left with the obvious possibility that this strange tie design was our own.

My next step was to consult Club records. The Club Tie and Button were devised by a sub-committee consisting of Alexander Harrison and George Sang in 1925, and approved at the AGM in December. However, the Club records gave no indication of the nature of the design except that the tie was made from knitted silk (a suggestion to switch to woven silk was rejected at the 1926 AGM) and that it retailed at a bracing 6/6d.

I turned then to the list of members, hoping to find someone who joined in the 1930s or early 1940s and might remember the early tie, or possess an example of it. I wrote to the few qualified members and was delighted to get a positive response from Dunmore Hotchkis (j. 1930), the father of James Hotchkis, Secretary of our Trust. He sent me his tie (in excellent condition) for examination and photography, and later permitted James to photograph him wearing it. *(See opposite page 385).*

Finally, he generously decided to donate his tie, very probably the sole surviving specimen, to the Archives. As may be seen the dark bands are an orange-brown and the light bands are a mixture of sky-blue and light gold. The retailer was R. W. Forsyth (a defunct Edinburgh business) but the manufacturer is unknown.

Sometime later, probably in the 1940s, this design was discarded in favour of the axes-on-navy design, perhaps because the old design had nothing Scottish about it, and conveyed no indication of mountaineering. However, I have not been able to discover any account of this change in Club records.

Curiously, the Alpine Club have just undergone a similar tie-revolution, discarding their original yellow diagonal stripe on green silk in favour of an iconic snowy peak on blue.

I would be very interested to hear from any member who recalls the circumstances of our change of tie, and would greatly welcome a decent example of the axes-on-navy tie for the Archives.

Robin N. Campbell.

100 Years Ago

THE 17th Annual Meeting and Dinner took place on Friday, December 1, 1905 in St Enoch's Hotel, Glasgow, with John Rennie presiding. Treasurer Napier announced a balance of £201-19s.-3d., which together with the new Life Membership Fund (introduced in 1904) brought the Club's total funds to £382-8s.-3d., £360 of which was immediately invested in South Australia Government 4% Stock! Secretary Clark announced eight new members, including Harry MacRobert and Percy Unna, two deaths, four resignations and the death of the Honorary President Cameron of Locheil. Librarian Goggs rejoiced in the increase of books from 430 to 600, and the grant of £22 -10s. to buy a complete run of the Alpine Journal. There was discussion of the Club's Rules and it was remitted to Committee to revise these for the next Annual Meeting.

The New Year Meet was held at the Royal Hotel, Tyndrum and attended by 29 members and six guests. Easterlies brought fine cold weather and 'set the fires of life aglow'. Members exploited the railway system (fully functional throughout the holiday period) to make various ingenious expeditions of which the most enterprising was that of Goggs, whose party was dropped off at Gorton to return to Tyndrum via Bens Creachan, Achallader, a' Chuirn, and Mhanach.

The Easter Meet was a grandiose and complicated affair, masterminded by the ingenious Secretary Clark. Thirty-eight members and 11 guests were scattered through the inadequate accommodations of Glen Coe, at Ballachulish, Clachaig and Kingshouse, all gathering at Clachaig on the Saturday morning for a famous Club photograph taken by Robertson. Although the weather had been wonderful before the Meet, it broke down on the Friday, and remained poor. Nevertheless, some worthy expeditions occurred. Raeburn and Ling made a snow-assisted ascent of *The Chasm* on the Thursday, making their escape below the Cauldron by the South Chimney, or a variant of it (see *J*. 9, 149-51). On the Saturday, a strong party consisting of Goggs, Ling, Raeburn and Ullen were defeated by the Church-Door Buttress. On the Tuesday, Glover and Worsdell "had a good climb in one of the gullies on Stob Coire nan Lochan. They found some of the pitches difficult and had five hours of step-cutting". The evenings seem to have passed in unruly fashion. Clark in 'Memories of the Kingshouse Meet, 1906' *J*. 9, 105-17, describes an obscure game of Frogs invented by Raeburn, and won by Goggs, and – following some indoor climbing games – observed that replicas of the china dogs on the Hotel mantelpiece "may perhaps be obtained in Glasgow".

In the week following the Meet, Raeburn went to meet Robertson at Fort William on April 22, but Robertson was unwell and recommended a Swiss climber Eberhard Phildius to Raeburn as a replacement. On the 23rd Raeburn and Phildius climbed what we now know as *Green Gully*, in full icy winter condition. This route was described by Raeburn in roundabout fashion, and was lost sight of during the commotions of the War, so that when Jim Bell climbed it – and named it – in April 1938 he believed he was making the first ascent. See my 'The First Scottish Ice Climbers' *J*. 30, 48-56 for this and similar forgotten *tours de force* of the pre-War era. It may seem surprising to us, but for Raeburn in 1906 *Green Gully* was a commonplace ascent.

In May P. R. Parkinson, seconded by George Hely-Hutchison Almond, made what was probably the third ascent of the direct route on Crowberry Ridge.

In June, Raeburn and Goggs visited Coire Ardair. Goggs described their

Julian Lines on First Ascent of Flawless (E7 6c), Achmelvich. Photo: Andy Nisbet.

expedition in *J.* 9, 118-25, beginning with a paragraph in praise of Raeburn: "The fresh post of Honorary Guide [should] be established, and Mr Raeburn should be elected thereto. His qualifications are numerous: – First and foremost he is a bachelor, and can therefore be at the beck and call of every member of the Club; secondly, he never seems to mind what kind of climber is at the other end of the rope, his one object in life being apparently 'helping lame dogs up cliffs'; thirdly and lastly, his climbing skill – but to refer to this is a work of supererogation."

So Goggs summoned the Honorary Guide to Kingussie, and they set off for Loch Laggan Hotel on bicycles. However, Laggan Hotel was entirely filled with Home Secretary Gladstone and his entourage. They wheeled along to Aberarder but met with no better luck from the shepherd's wife, who didn't like the look of them, so they spent the night equipped only with jam sandwiches, on the floor of a hayshed. They climbed what they called A Buttress, now South Buttress or South Pillar, and entirely suppressed in modern guidebooks, but from Goggs's description it sounds like a decent route.

Meanwhile, Hugh Munro was enjoying 'Hot Nights and Days in the Mountains' (*J.* 9, 126-31), passing from Strathcarron to Skye where, unable to secure the services of John Mackenzie because he was 'permanently engaged to Mr A. E. Robertson', he was obliged to make do with his own company or the 'the two Miss Protheros, nieces of Mr Phillip'.

Nevertheless, he had several good days and finished up his visit with an ascent of the Pinnacle Ridge along with Robertson, his faithful retainer and nephew Archie, and Mrs Urquhart. The price for Munro's inclusion in the party was that he had to wait on top of the Third Pinnacle with Mackenzie to allow Robertson to photograph them from the fourth – a famous image. There was a more interesting day in store for Mackenzie, however. When Norman Collie arrived for a summer stay with Colin Phillip at Glenbrittle Lodge in early July, he went immediately to explore a pinnacle at half-height on the vast unexplored crag on the south side of Lower Coire Lagain. Collie had deduced the existence of this pinnacle from a photograph. Although he couldn't reach it, he saw enough of it to figure out a route, and the following day he and Mackenzie followed this contorted route to reach the fantastic pinnacle, named A' Chioch by Mackenzie, and to begin a new era of Skye climbing – the exploration of Sron na Ciche.

The 1906 Alpine season was mixed, but many members enjoyed good climbing. Douglas climbed the Pelvoux, Pic Sans Nom, Barre des Ecrins and traversed La Meije. Unna spent three weeks at Arolla and climbed the Ruinette, Mont Collon by various routes, the Dent Blanche, and traversed l'Evêque with Goggs. But the major effort, as usual, was made by Ling and Raeburn, who visited three centres in three weeks: Val Ferret, Oberland and Zermatt. In the first, they made the first ascent of La Mouche, a pinnacle in the Aiguilles Rouges de Dolent, and of the NE face of the Argentière. In the Oberland, along with Eric Greenwood, they traversed the Finsteraarhorn and the Schreckhorn, using novel methods of traverse in both cases. At Zermatt, they made the first British guideless ascent of the Zmutt arête, descending by the Italian Ridge: "The ridge was in very bad condition, plastered with ice and snow, and almost every yard had to be won by the ice-axe. Starting at 4am, the top was not gained until 3 p.m."

William Inglis Clark remained at home, and enjoyed a tour of Sutherland in his 10h.p. Humber car, inspecting Inchnadamph Hotel in preparation for the 1907 Easter Meet, and accompanied as usual by members of his family. They explored

Ama Dablan and the Tenzing Memorial. Photo: Sandy Allen.

Kathy Grindrod climbing the Grey Tower, Ama Dablan. Photo: Sandy Allen.

Quinag, and climbed an interesting route on Sail Garbh to the east of the Barrel Buttress before descending Y Gully to climb Y Buttress. The party then moved to Stac Pollaidh where they met C. W. Walker, and made an ascent of the West Buttress by the easiest line. Clark's description of his explorations on Stac Pollaidh (*J.* 9, 175-91) included a diagram obtained from Norman Collie, of a route made earlier by him. This route followed a line on the right flank of the buttress. Although the Clarks' ascent of the Western Buttress is acknowledged in modern guidebooks, Collie's route and the Clarks' efforts on Sail Garbh are ignored and allocated to others.

Robin N. Campbell.

Logan Aikman and the Jubilee Dinner, 1938

THE obituary for J. Logan Aikman, Club Secretary 1935–46, which I wrote for the 2003 Journal, lacked a photograph. This was not entirely due to the incompetence of the obituarist, but it was a serious omission which should be remedied. Although there are many excellent photographs of Aikman in the collection donated to our Archives, I feel that the one chosen is most appropriate, since it pictures him at the dizzy heights of his office, celebrating the Club's Jubilee after the stunningly successful campaign to acquire the lands of Dalness for the nation. Beside him, at the magnificent dinner, attended by 154 members and guests, sits President Unna, and although it is not a wonderful image of him, we have so few that it merits publication.

The image (opposite page 384) is a small excerpt from one of the two official Dinner photographs. A copy of the Table Plan has survived, and together with 'landmarks' provided by those who are easily identified, this information makes reasonably confident identifications possible across the gulf of nearly 70 years. In the centre of the picture, beaming, is the organizer of the feast, Secretary Aikman. Behind him, and at the top table, is Percy Unna, with Founder Gilbert Thomson, guest S. Bryan Donkin (CC, and AC Secretary), and Godfrey Solly to his left. On the far side of Table 4, the only person visible is the dapper CIC Custodian Robert Elton, directly beneath the head of Solly. On the near side of Table 4 is Aikman, with J. Phemister (guest) to his right. On the far side of Table 3 are (left to right) part of Norman Hird, Sir Hugh Rose (guest) of the paint business Craig & Rose, and W. Whyte (guest). Finally at the bottom of the picture (left to the right) are Alex. Harrison, R. H. Gwilt (guest) and Alec–Guinness–lookalike James G. Kyd.

Robin N. Campbell

Glover and Worsdell's Gully, April 1906. Was it SC Gully or North-West Gully?

AT THE Club's Easter Meet in April, 1906 in Glen Coe, Glover and Worsdell "had a good climb in one of the gullies on Stob Coire nan Lochan. They found some of the pitches difficult and had five hours of step-cutting (*J.* 9, 81-2)". Now, on the face of it, this looks rather like an ascent of *SC Gully*. Indeed, their climb is indexed in the Volumes 1 to 10 Index as the 'Central Gully of Stob Coire nan Lochan'. What else has several pitches and would have detained these swift and nimble fellows for five hours of step cutting?

However, Glover and Worsdell's effort is identified in modern guidebooks as the *North-West Gully* of Stob Coire nam Beith, a somewhat easier climb. In fact, the move to *North-West Gully* begins with Bill Murray's Glen Coe Guidebook in 1949. Murray's note suggests that the name of the mountain was misprinted in the 1906 Journal. It would be interesting to know how Murray came by this information, and where he got the idea that it was *North-West Gully*, rather than one of the several other possibilities on Stob Coire nam Beith.

There is only one earlier guidebook than Murray's – Harry MacRobert's *Central Highlands Guide*. MacRobert's guide was published in May 1934, before Pat Baird had written his account of the first ascent of *SC Gully* in the November 1934 Journal (he took five hours over it, oddly enough). But MacRobert mentions *SC Gully* on p. 80: "The gully between the South and Central Buttresses is steep, with most impressive rock scenery. The lower part requires some care. Under winter conditions the gully, which is about 600ft., gives a good climb."

So it is not at all clear whether Baird's ascent was the first. Perhaps he wrote to MacRobert following his ascent in March 1934, but if so, it is very odd that MacRobert doesn't mention Baird. The gully was investigated in September, 1931 by J. H. B. Bell (*J.* 19, 317), who descended it, and Bell's account seems to have been used by MacRobert in writing the guidebook entry. But Bell merely says that it "*should* make a magnificent ascent under snow conditions", and gives no indication of previous winter ascents. So far as the North-West Gully of Stob Coire nam Beith is concerned, MacRobert says nothing about it as a winter route, noting only that it was climbed September, 1931 by Campbell and Horne.

So this is another of the pesky mysteries of early Scottish climbing. Perhaps Murray was right, and had the information from a reliable source such as Glover himself. And it may be that when MacRobert remarked that "under winter conditions. [SC Gully] gives a good climb" he was merely carelessly converting Bell's speculation into fact. But Murray was not immune to error or bias: he overlooked Raeburn's ascents of *Crowberry Gully* in winter and discounted his ascent of *The Chasm*, "it has not been admitted as a first ascent…" and he buried MacRobert's all-but-the-last-move, 1910 winter attempt on the *Shelf Route* in a footnote. Glover and Worsdell were perfectly capable of climbing *SC Gully* in 1906, and might well have done so.

Robin N. Campbell.

ALLT NA MHUINIDH WATERFALL : WEST CLIMB

On the third day of the SMC Easter Meet at Kinlochewe in 1899 a new climb was made on a cliff within easy reach of the hotel.

In the report of the meet (SMCJ, 1899, V, 253-6) Hinxman wrote: "Inglis Clark reports enthusiastically of the cliffs of Beinn Mhuinidh, above the head of Loch Maree. He reached the top with Glover by a route a little to the west of the waterfall, and describes the climbing as excellent..."

In the same journal, under Excursions, Glover gave a more detailed account of the climb in which he made it clear that there were, in fact, three climbers in the party – two of whom were photographers.

The identity of the third climber has remained a mystery. In the current Northern Highlands climbing guide (1993, p.18) it is suggested that the unnamed climber was probably Ling.

However, in SMCJ, 2002, XXXVIII, 25-8, Robin Campbell correctly pointed out that Ling was on Slioch that day with Lawson. Campbell then went on to suggest that the mystery climber must be Douglas, dismissing all the other members present as non-climbers.

The definitive answer to this puzzle has been before our eyes for more than 50 years. In his obituary of Glover in SMCJ, 1954, XXV, 257-9, Ling wrote: "Together, we attended the Easter, 1899, Meet at Kinlochewe, in poor weather, but we had good climbs with H. G. S. Lawson on Liathach and Sail Mhor. Glover had a fine new climb by the Allt a' Mhuinidh waterfall with Inglis Clark and Gall Inglis."

So the unnamed climber on the West Climb was J. Gall Inglis – the same climber whom Campbell recently identified as being the photographer on the first winter traverse of the Northern Pinnacles of Liathach. A cursory flick through early journals also reveals that Gall Inglis did "A Climb on the Rocks of Corrie Sugach" with Inglis Clark (SMCJ, 1902, VII, 70-5).

There is surely a case for eventually making all our journals available in electronic form.

Noel Williams.

Where are the Summits?

Background:

THERE is a certain satisfaction in reaching the summit of a hill, touching the cairn and, weather permitting, taking in the view, recognising hills that have been visited before. For many hills, the approach to the summit is clear. You may pass a false summit or two, but perseverance pays off as you continue climbing with a narrowing horizon to a cairn when there is no more climbing to be done.

Some hills are not that simple. There isn't a well-defined peak, but rather a summit plateau or near-level ridge. Where is the true summit? For Ben Vorlich (Loch Earn), it is fairly simple: the path from Loch Earn leads to a triangulation column, but there is a cairn about 100m. away along a near-level ridge. It is easy to visit both (under normal weather conditions), but unusually the trig-point is higher than the summit cairn. A more intractable problem arises with Beinn a' Chroin (Loch Lomond to Strathyre). According to the current (1997) Munro Tables, the eastern top is the Munro, a well-defined conical summit on a north-south ridge. However, to the west of this summit there is an undulating plateau, a delightful area of knolls and lochans now established by the Ordnance Survey as having a 942m. peak, 2m. higher than the 1997 Munro. There are several knolls in the vicinity of the new 942m. spot height, so which is the true summit? This should be determined by walkers, ideally armed with a theodolite, visiting the summit plateau. However, if I go to check your observations, how do I identify the peak you are reporting as highest? As a walker, how do I identify the summit? The only cairns are between the knolls, the knolls themselves not suitable for retaining cairns. Elsewhere, Robin Campbell has reported difficulties in identifying which summit the cataloguer planned to list in "confusing places like the Saddle, the An Teallach ridge, or the awful Mullach na Dhearagain ridge with many small tops". The issues that this article addresses are identification of peaks and determination of a 'Best Estimate' list of summits. Additional information, including a picture showing the competing summits of Beinn a' Chroin and graphs depicting data in this article, is provided on the author's website[1] on which listings and the table of questioned summits are updated with new data.

History:

Munro's original tables (as quoted in the Variorum tables in Robin Campbell's *The Munroist's Companion* [2]) gave a verbal description of the position of the summit, for example 4.25 miles. S by E of Crianlarich for the Munro Beinn a' Chroin. This helps to identify the summit, but is not precise. Indeed, the Variorum tables quote the same description for the West top. The 1974 edition of the Tables was the first to give 6-figure grid references, which define the position of the summit to the nearest 100m. or so, identifying a block of land containing the summit. However, there are several knolls within the relevant block in the vicinity of the 942m. spot height on Beinn a' Chroin.

In 1974, providing the 6-figure OS grid references corresponded to the precision to which a walker's position could reasonably be defined. Over the last few years, two significant developments have occurred that enable a more precise location of summits to be determined. Firstly, traditional visual surveying of OS maps has been replaced by photogrammetry allowing precise determination of contours and hence heights. With these more accurate maps, our problem is to interpret them, especially in rocky areas where contour lines are discontinuous. Secondly, the development of hand-held GPS (global positioning system) receivers means that we walkers can accurately determine our position to the map with a precision better than 5m. on the summit of a hill, with a clear view of the sky. "GPS technology allows any person to know his location on the planet with accuracy never imagined before." [3] GPS measurements of altitude have three times the uncertainty of lateral co-ordinates, i.e. a range of +/– 15m. and therefore the figure from the OS map is taken as the definitive height.

Grid Reference Problems:

The OS grid references given for the location of summits represents the latitude and longitude on the spherical earth using a flat (Transverse Mercator) projection overlaid with a grid based on kilometre squares. In principle, a 6-figure grid reference defines the location of a point to within 100m. in both the easterly and northerly direction. However, there can be ambiguity. In deriving the 6-figure grid reference of a location, for example a summit, from an OS map, the map has 1km. (1000m.) squares, but the grid reference has a precision of 100m. The instructions provided on OS maps say that the user should first quote the Eastings by locating the vertical grid line to the left of the point and reading the large figures labelling the line... and then estimate tenths from the grid line to the point. If, for example, the summit is at or close to the centre of the square, the temptation is to quote the position as the mid-point, or five tenths. However, one logical aspect of the grid system is that as the grid reference of a point is increased in precision, the part already identified remains intact. Thus, on a 1:50000 scale map where the kilometre squares are 20mm. wide, the easting should be quoted as five tenths if the point is between 10mm. and 12mm. east of the kilometre grid line. Visual estimation of the tenths is unlikely to be reliable and should be measured, for example with a Romer, essentially a ruler graduated with grid scales. The alternative interpretations are depicted graphically on the author's website.[1]

Where does this leave the walker? Unless you know the criterion used by the particular editor of tables, a traditional 6-figure grid reference is uncertain by150m. east-west and north-south, corresponding to the 100m. of the grid square plus 50m. depending on whether the 'nearest' or 'truncated' grid reference is used.

Along the diagonal of the square (using Pythagoras' Theorum), this corresponds to a range of 225m. for the location of a reported grid reference, even with a well-defined summit. For an ill-defined contour summit, the uncertainty can be even greater. For Tables compiled using the 'nearest' grid reference, the deviation for a number of summits determined more precisely would average zero metres, whereas if the (specified) 'truncated' grid reference is used, the average deviation would be 50m. The average deviation, using over 200 GPS determinations, has been found to be 17m. for the 1981 tables and 43m. for the 1997 tables, for example, the 1981 tables were generally a 'nearest' estimate whereas the 1997 tables generally followed the OS instructions.

With 8-figure grid references, the location of a point is defined within a 10m. square; a 10-figure grid reference provides a precision of 1m. On a 1:25 000 scale map, available from the OS through the free Get-a-Map service,[4] estimating a grid reference to 10m. (0.4 mm. on the map) is possible with care. The walker on the ground with a commercially-available hand-held GPS unit can readily provide a 10-figure grid reference for a summit, reproducible to better than 5m. The inherent ambiguity is insignificant – the 1m. precision of a 10-figure grid reference corresponds to one side of the summit cairn or the other. Unfortunately, with this increased precision, other errors related to the map datum, or how the National Grid is defined, become significant.

Map Datums:

GPS units perform internal calculations using a spherical representation of the earth, the WGS84 (or World Geodetic System 1984) datum. The location of a point can be specified by quoting latitude and longitude expressed as degrees north and east on the WGS84 datum. However, this is not consistent with common UK practice, as the commonly used OS maps provide grid references that can be readily determined, whereas traditional latitude and longitude are more difficult to derive. There are, however, more fundamental reasons for preferring not to use latitude and longitude for a theoretical spherical earth. The following comments have been distilled from OS-supplied information on their website – The National GPS Network.[6]

One problem is that the location of a point as a latitude and longitude is not unique because theWGS84 map datum is dynamic. As continents move or earthquakes occur, WGS84 modifies its co-ordinates to maintain a net zero error at selected reference points. Partly because of these adjustments, the Greenwich observatory is now about 100m. from the zero meridian of WGS84.

A further problem arises from measurements of height. Britain is apparently in a trough. WGS84 would put the sea level about 50m. higher than present, so if adopted would, at a stroke, delete a hundred of the lower Munros. Climbs from the shore at Loch Brittle to the Cuillin would start from an altitude of 50m. below sea level.

As the WGS84 datum changes, the OS will modify their 'best' datum to take changes into account and generate a 'new' datum so that UK grid references remain essentially the same. With the OS datum, heights remain relative to local (i.e. Newlyn) sea level, albeit with some adjustments. Apparently, northern Scotland is still rising following the last ice age so our hills are still growing. Logically, the same map datum should be used for lateral co-ordinates and for altitude: the National Grid with associated OSGB map datum.

Deriving 8 and 10 figure grid references:
With care, it is possible to derive 8-figure grid references from maps if the summit is well defined, for example, by a trig point. However, the OS did not position trig points to mark the summit, but for map-making purposes. The trig point must be visible from the surrounding land and be accessible. Thus, for both Slioch and The Saddle the true summit is located on hidden but slightly higher ground behind the trig point. The location of the true summit on the map is ambiguous although it is readily identifiable on the ground. For Spidean Coire nan Clach on Beinn Eighe, the 972m. trig point is on accessible land below the knobbly 993m. summit of Spidean Coire nan Clach, a fact that may have denied Beinn Eighe a second Munro for some years. The trig point could not be the second Munro summit, being lower than Sail Mhor (981m.), but Sail Mhor could not prevail until it was established the land behind the trig point was at least 9m. higher than the trig point.

For summits with a trig point, OS listing tables [6] provide accurate location data. Often the trig point is adjacent to the summit cairn, or has been incorporated into a summit shelter or cairn, so the grid reference is 'good'. For Slioch and The Saddle, the trig points are now Deleted Tops whereas Gulvain's S. Top with the trig point is sufficiently distinct to have retained Top status. For at least five other Munros, the trig point is known not to be at a summit. These are listed in a table of questionable summits.[1] Of the 594 Munros, Tops and Deleted Tops, 93 coincide with trig points.

If a summit does not have a trig point, the location has traditionally been determined as a grid reference from OS maps. An 8-figure grid reference can be derived from the map, provided the summit point can be identified. By visiting the site, a 10-figure grid reference can be determined using a GPS unit with the advantage that a judgement can be made as to the precise location of the summit. By recording the grid reference as determined using a GPS unit a 'second opinion' can be elicited from others and once tabulated the 'correct' summit can be identified for walkers. Accordingly the author proposes that 10-figure grid references from trig point listings or GPS readings should be listed wherever possible for all summits in future editions of the Tables.

Verification:
For the committed Munroist, it is expedient to climb not only the Munros but also summits deleted from the current tables that may be reinstated in future editions of the tables, depending on the whim (or even the considered opinion) of future editors. Even if the summits are never reinstated, they are (usually) well-defined points and therefore useful locations to store on a GPS device as additional navigation points. The project to collect 10-figure grid references from hand-held GPS measurements applies to all listed summits, viz the Munros, Tops, Deleted Tops, the Corbetts and Grahams (including the Donalds) and Other Hills. The remainder of this article concentrates on the Munros, Tops and Deleted Tops, illustrating principles that apply to the other sets of summits.

Before consolidating the data, checks were applied to establish how more precise data improved the accuracy compared with the tabulated 6-figure grid references. Four sets of data have been compared, three from maps, SMC tables of 1981, as revised in the 1990 revision (SMC 81/90), the SMC tables of 1997 (SMC 97), 389 8-figure grid references summit determined by Gerry Bye[7] on routes he determined to the 284 Munros, plus 105 Tops that were on the route to the Munro summit. The other data set comprised over 200 waypoints determined on the ground using GPS units (10-figure grid references).

Taking the data sets in pairs, the difference in the grid reference was determined for each summit in both the easterly and northerly directions. To simplify the assessment, the two difference figures were converted to a single number using the Pythagoras relationship for right angle triangles to calculate a Root Mean Square (RMS) deviation.

The SMC 81/90 and SMC 97 tables give the same grid reference for most summits. Most other cases show a reduction of one unit in either or both eastings and northings in the newer tables, consistent with the different adjustments of 17m. and 43m. previously described. More significant deviations arose with three Tops: (a) Aonach Mor - Tom na Sroine (probably a typographic error in the 1997 tables) (b) Cairn of Gowal, the 1997 tables identifying a 991m. summit between the 1981 summit labelled as Cairn of Gowal (983m.) on the OS map and the 1012m. Cairn Bannoch) and (c) the 924m. Top Meall Glas Choire on Beinn Eibhinn, which has a comma-shaped 920m. contour, so predicting the precise position of the summit from the map is impossible. The author's website[1] graphically shows this analysis plus similar assessments for other sets of map-derived data.

Comparing GPS and SMC 97 data, the RMS deviation was generally less than 70m. This corresponds to the diagonal from the centre to the corner of a 100m. square, the maximum deviation expected when upgrading from 6 to 10-figure grid references. Some improvement, especially with respect to outliers, was obtained by using the Best Estimate figures for map data as described in the next section. The ill-defined Beinn a' Bhuird – South Top provided the greatest deviation to date, the quoted grid reference corresponding to a 1179m. spot height, the maximum 9m. above the 1170m. contour. A GPS reading (by Rob Milne) was taken at what, in the absence of a cairn, he judged to be at the highest point, 60m. away from the spot height but in a different 100m.x100m. grid square. This exemplifies the desirability of locating the summit on the ground and relating it back to the map through a GPS measurement. If the map shows a spot height, it is not necessarily at the highest point. With a 10m. contour interval, the position of the summit may not be accurate if the terrain within the contour ring is in reality asymmetric. For all grid references determined from the map, there is uncertainty as to the position of the true summit if there is only a contour ring.

For both Sgor Gaoith – Meall Dubhag, where the mapped 998m. cairn is at the extreme SW end of the 990m. ring contour, and Beinn Teallach (deviation about 130m.), a double summit with rocky outcrops 150m. apart, two GPS positions were quoted by the reporting walker, who felt unable to identify which was the higher. In each case, one reading was close to the tabulated position and one at an alternative summit. Deviations of over 120m. were recorded at two tops on the complex An Teallach ridge, Lord Berkeley's Seat and Corrag Bhuidhe.

Comparison of two higher precision data sets of 176 summits, GPS values and Gerry Bye's data, 150 points showed a positional difference of less than 50m. This provides a clear advantage in reducing ambiguity, but there are nine significant deviations of more than 100m. These include the Munros Cruach Ardrain, for which The Tables give the location of the SW summit whereas the description in The Munros Guide led two independent GPS users to the NE Top, and Eididh nan Clach Geala for which the OS map shows a spot height to the SE end of the summit ring contour whereas the Munros guide says the NW cairn is the summit.

For listings derived from maps, deviations inevitably arise where the map is ambiguous or confused. Often the presence of multiple summits has caused problems, when comparing GPS measurements and map data. A table showing these and other questionable summits is maintained on the author's website,[1] with comments about the source of the uncertainty. These summits should be revisited, preferably by several separate walkers charged with making a considered assessment, ideally using a theodolite and recording the location of the competing summits using a GPS. It would be useful if a permanent reference identification for each summit could be defined, agreed and included in future editions of the Tables.

'Best Estimate' Listing of Summits:

The process described in this section has been derived to provide the best available estimate of the location of summits expressed as 10-figure grid references. For each of the 594 Munros, Tops and Deleted Tops, the quoted grid reference is the first available in the following sequence :

(1) OS trig point grid reference (10-figure) where the trig point is believed to correspond to the summit (Munro, Top or Deleted Top), from Phil Newby and John Davis.[6] 54 summits.

(2) GPS reading (if confident about authenticity) to 10-figures, for 215 distinct summits with some duplicates provided by different walkers or the same walker on a return visit. Data have been obtained from Bergleiter (11 summits), Nigel Cliffe (5), Ken Crocket (8), Graham Hartley (51), Henry Marston (83), Doug Meiklejohn (2), Rob Milne (63) and Alan Shepard (23).

(3) An average figure derived from OS maps for all summits in the 1981/90 and 1997 tables based on the following sources, as available. By averaging the available figures, the consequence of the grid reference ambiguity (for 6-figure data) is reduced (325 summits).

* Gerry Bye's 8-figure grid references,[7] with zero as the last figure in the northings and eastings in the 10-figure grid references; both the original and updated versions were used to increase weighting.

* The SMC 1997 grid reference, expanded to 10 figures with a 43m. adjustment.

* The SMC 1981/90 grid reference, expanded to 10 figures with an 17m. adjustment.

* Grid references derived from maps by Alan Dawson and Brenda Lowndes[8] expanded with a 40m. adjustment

(4) Robin Campbell's Variorum Table,[2] generally the grid reference in the 1974 Tables, expanded to 10 figures by appending 40m. to the Northings and Eastings (not calibrated to determine offset). 49 summits, all deleted in later Tables.

(5) 10-figure grid references derived from the description in Robin Campbell's Variorum Table for summits only listed in the first two editions of The Tables and interpreted by the author from the OS 1:25000 map (Get-a-Map service[4]); 15 summits. Some are now known to be less than 914m. high, others are small knolls at the end of the summit ridge, and one is apparently below a small rise.

Where the Best Estimate derived from maps is quoted,[1] the analysis starts at (3) above.

For (1) and (2), analysis of the reproducibility of 47 duplicate OS trig point data and GPS measurements to date (either a trig point and one or two GPS readings, or two GPS measurements) is summarised in the following table. In calculating

Units: metres	Eastings	Northings	RMS deviation
Average	8.3	8.9	13.8
Std. Dev.	18.1	8.6	19.0
Maximum	116.0	58.0	129.7

the average and standard deviation (Std. Dev.), the absolute discrepancy was calculated, i.e. ignoring the minus sign for negative differences.

The greatest discrepancies corresponded to the previously mentioned cases where a walker took duplicate measurements on Beinn Teallach, and Carn an t-Sagairt Mor, both with difficult-to-allocate summits. Knight's Peak has a double-topped rocky summit, with two peaks about 20m. apart – distinct, but which is the true Top? Duplicate readings at the same location were generally within 10m. and more than half were different by less than 5m. – including Cruach Ardrain, for which the on-the-ground readings differ from the Tables. The significant deviations are listed in the table of differences on the author's website.[1]

In summary, my proposal is to list the location of each summit by on-the-ground measurements, using GPS measurements for Munros, Tops and Deleted Tops (as listed in Robin Campbell's Variorum in his Munroist's Companion), Corbetts, Grahams plus Donalds and Other hills included in SMC lists. Ideally, multiple readings taken by different walkers on different days should be combined, eliminating dubious readings and averaging the others. I am therefore appealing to fellow walkers to make a point of recording the location of summits that you visit, marking the location of each summit as a waypoint on a GPS unit and passing the relevant data on to me. The procedure required to acquire consistent data is summarised as follows:

At the summit, first look round to check that you are actually at the highest point. Then get a time averaged GPS reading of the summit location. Place the GPS on the summit cairn, allowing the unit to average the data for a few minutes (by pressing the Mark button and selecting Average) and press Enter. The waypoint identification code should be recorded as well as the name of the summit. Note if there is a trig point and its location. If there is a separate trig point, take an additional GPS reading at that for calibration purposes. When you are downloading the data to your PC (or alternatively recording it manually from the GPS unit) ensure that you have a consistent map datum and co-ordinate system, preferably the Ordnance Survey GB map datum and the British OS Grid as the Grid option. Other formats can be accommodated, e.g. latitude and longitude with the WGS84 datum, but the format should be specified.

Note: These instructions apply to the popular Garmin GPS12 model but the basic principles apply to other GPS units.

Please e-mail the author[1] with data files of your recorded waypoints with relevant information such as GPS unit model and download software package plus calibration points, especially trig points. I am also interested in routes with relevant information e.g. as described in SMC Munros Guide or otherwise.

The collected data will, of course, be available to the compilers of the next edition of the Munro Tables, for consideration as a reference source. Official publication of the lists is therefore seen as likely to be through the SMC. However, as an incentive to walkers to provide GPS data, it is planned to make data available to contributors through links from the author's web page.

References
1. Henry Marston: http://www.hmarston.pwp.blueyonder.co.uk or alternatively http://www.hmarston.co.uk Follow links to Munros and GPS for further information plus the photographs and graphs described, to contact the author from website for paper version of graphs and to submit data
2. Robin N. Campbell: *The Munroist's Companion*, SMC, 1999
3. Odilon Ferreira Jr, GPS TrackMaker, http://www.gpstm.com/
4. Ordnance Survey: 'The Get-a-Map Service', http://www.ordnancesurvey.co.uk/oswebsite/getamap
5. Ordnance Survey: 'The National GPS Network' http://www.gps.gov.uk/guide1.asp
6. Phil Newby: 'Phil's GPS Waypoint resource pages', http://www.36haroldstreet.freeserve.co.uk/waypoints.htm
7. Gerry Bye: GPS data from the SMC, from http://www.smc.org.uk/books/gps_data.htm
8. Alan Dawson and Brenda Lowndes: *The Hills of Great Britain and Ireland.* http://www.liv.ac.uk/SportsandRecreation/hillwalking/mountain.html
9. Alan Murphy: 'GPS Utility' software package, http://www.gpsu.co.uk/

In this article, the term Summit is used as a generic term for the top of any hill, whether Munro, Top, Deleted Top (i.e. a Munro or Top that appeared in earlier tables but are now excluded), Corbett, Donald, Graham or Other hill.

Henry Marston.

Letters To The Editor

The Lizard, Creag Ghlas

The Lizard was the first route on this crag. It was climbed by me and Dave Bathgate in 1967. It followed the best line on the crag, the right-hand edge of the slabby south-west facing front, which forms a pronounced rib in its lower part.

Some years ago, I noticed gross disparities between the description of this route in John Mackenzie's *Northern Highlands Volume 2* (p. 63) and the original description, given by me in the 1968 Journal. Pitch lengths were very different and the crux pitch was referred to as a 5a 'mossy groove'. I thought at that time that Mackenzie had simply nabbed our crux pitch and described it as his own 'Loop Variation', but since no diagram or photograph was provided in NH2 and because of the confusion created by Mackenzie's aberrant pitch lengths, I did nothing about it. However, last year I picked up a copy of the new compendium *Scottish Rock Climbs* and found to my disgust that our route had been omitted from it, whereas many of Mackenzie's inferior routes had been included. This was too much dissing, so I began a long and unsatisfactory correspondence with Mackenzie and the SRC editor Andy Nisbet.

It is 40 years since I visited the crag. I have made no return visit, and we took only one unhelpful photograph. Furthermore, my description of the route (being an outstanding natural line) lacked detail. This is the disputed portion: "A prominent rib divides the buttress into smooth slabs on the left and steep walls and grassy corners on the right. The route follows this rib. Climb to broad rock terrace in two pitches, keeping to crest (130ft. and 70ft.)".

However, I remember that crux pitch (our pitch 2) well, because of its severity. Dave Bathgate embarked on a curving mossy groove leading up to the left, encountered difficulty and proposed to use a piton. I suggested that perhaps the pitch might go straight up the crest and he came back down so that I could try it. The climbing on the crest was very thin and exposed, but the difficult moves were in the first 20ft. or so and after to-ing and fro-ing a bit I got up. In those days we had no numerical grades, in fact not even sub-divisions of the Very Severe grade, but Bathgate and I were “at the height of our powers” (his description, not mine) and the pitch was as hard as we could manage. Whatever it was, it was not a 5a mossy groove. Yet that is where Mackenzie and Nisbet have put us, and – so far as I know – that is where we remain! Our line (in their opinion) was too hard for us to climb, and therefore we must have climbed elsewhere. Perhaps our line was instead simply too hard for them to climb. However, I don’t think that is the case: they hadn’t looked properly – that’s all. The truth of this matter will not be resolved by correspondence between three decrepit old parties like Mackenzie, Nisbet and myself. It will be resolved by the sort of young, able, enthusiastic climber who ought to be editing our guidebooks.

Robin N. Campbell.

In regard to Robin's letter I find all this a little mystifying and obscure – Robin's many years of absence has added a patina of confusion, whereas I and others (including Andy) climb regularly on the crag.

The Lizard is far from the best line – it is a good line, but no better than several of the others done by various folk over the years. *The Lizard* does, I’m sure, follow the groove which today is mossy, but then may not have been; it is hard for the grade and Andy simply took his description from the SMCJ – so did I for the guide book. Andy and I have both done the 'Loop pitch' variant and it is simply that – a variant – and not the natural line, which is the groove, but (today) harder and cleaner.

However it is just possible that Robin and Dave had done the hardest route in Scotland in 1962 by several grades – not to be topped until Julian Lines came along. My feeling is that Robin's memory is somewhat displaced by the years and I think the fact that his route was left out of *Selected Climbs* really hurt Robin. I would have included it as it is quite up to the mark, and a bit of cleaning would soon restore it to the original pristine glory that it once was. With climate change, all routes on relatively low level crags on certain rock types moss over in time and unless they are climbed reasonably regularly then that is their ultimate fate, sad but true. Who knows what the truth is? We certainly never intended to do Robin down – or the route which I think is good – and remarkable for its time, but I do think if Robin would care to accompany me (and Andy) up it again he would see for himself that the line has changed somwhat after 40 years.

John Mackenzie.

Scottish Mountaineering Trust – 2005-2006

The Trustees met on March 11, June 10 and October 7, 2005.

During the course of these meetings support was given to the British Trust for Ornithology; NVA Organisation – Storr Footpath; the Jonathan Conville Mountaineering Trust; the New Routes Editor for a computer; the Dundee Mountain Film Festival; the Mountaineering Council of Scotland – Access and Conservation; Mr R A Lawes – postgraduate research into Scottish mountaineering; Lochaber Mountain Rescue Team – construction of new mountain rescue base; RSPB – field study evaluating the effects of wind farms on upland breeding birds.

The Trustees wished to express their great sadness and sorrow at the loss of one of the Trustees, Rob Milne. As Convenor of the Publications Sub-committee, Rob was a Trustee ex-officio. His contribution to the Trustee meetings were invaluable. His energy and enthusiasm will be sadly missed.

Bill Runciman retired as Trustee by rotation. His contributions were much appreciated. In particular, he was instrumental in the production and completion of the Scottish Mountaineering Trust leaflet (which has now been available for over one year).

The present Trustees are P. MacDonald (Chairman), C. J. Orr, A. Tibbs, R. J. Archbold, D. A. Bearhop, D. J. Broadhead, C. M. Huntley, P. V. Brian, A. C. Stead and R. Anderson. J. Morton Shaw is the Trust Treasurer.

The present directors of the Publications Company are R. K. Bott (Chairman), K. V. Crockett, W. C. Runciman, M. G. D. Shaw and T. Prentice (Publications Manager). R. Anderson attends Board Meetings as the new convenor of the Publications Sub Committee.

The following grants have been committed by the Trustees:

British Trust for Ornithology	£2500
Jonathon Conville Mountaineering Trust	£1222
New Routes Editor – computer	£300
Dundee Mountain Film Festival	£1000
Mountaineering Council of Scotland – access and conservation	£5000
NVA Organisation – Storr Footpath	£4000
R A Lawes post-graduate research	£4500
Lochaber Mountain Rescue Team – new base	£20,000
RSPB field study	£2500

MUNRO MATTERS

By David Kirk (Clerk of the List)

ANOTHER buoyant year of hill-going is compleat and I thank everyone who has written to me to register a Compleation, or Amend their original entry. I continue to enjoy and be touched by the anecdotes your letters contain. The total new Compleaters for the last year is 206, a fraction down on the last two years. The cut-off date by which letters had to be received for inclusion in this year's Journal was April 1.

With regards to the SMC Website, I would remind everyone of the Photo Gallery which Ken Crocket does so well to maintain. Please dig out that old final summit photograph, and send a copy (or the original along with a SAE) to Ken.

The List of this year's Compleatists are as follows. As before, the first five columns are number, name, then Munro, Top and Furth Compleation years.

3337	Eve Maguire	2005		
3338	John R. Reay	2005		
3339	Elizabeth McDonald	2005		
3340	Dave McGowan	2005		
3341	Diane Ball	2005	2005	
3342	Ron Ball	2005	2005	
3343	Jacqueline B. Wilson	2005		
3344	Conor J. Pittman	2005		
3345	David Cameron	2005		
3346	Henning Wackerhage	2005		
3347	Elaine Milner	2005		
3348	Philip Wilkinson	2005		
3349	W. Allan Wylie	2005		
3350	James Paris	2005		
3351	Adam Gordon	2004		
3352	Roy H. Smith	2005		
3353	Ken J. Milson	2005		
3354	John Rennie	2005		
3355	Richard J. W. Tibbetts	2005		
3356	Lynne Martin	2005		
3357	Peter Dyson	2004		
3358	Michael Willis	2005		
3359	Jon Baldwin	2003		
3360	Barry Baldwin	2003		
3361	David Stevenson	2005		
3362	David Hallam	2005		
3363	Mike Assenti	2005		
3364	Barry Davies	2005		
3365	Andre Hawryliw	2005		
3366	Anne Butler	2005		
3367	Greg Lowde	2005		
3368	Roger N. Winterburn	2005		
3369	Paul Armstrong	2005		
3370	Alistair Orr MacSween	1997		
3371	Kenneth J. Radcliffe	2005		
3372	Dave Sanderson	2005		
3373	Brian Richmond	2005		
3374	Alexander J. Bell	2005		
3375	Derek J.B. Reid	2005		
3376	David W. Coia	2005		
3377	Dave Saddler	2005		
3378	Alicia Murray	2005		
3379	Charles Dingwall	2005		
3380	Mike Killingley	2005		
3381	Jason Brooke	2005		
3382	Bruce Maltman	2005		
3383	M. Ian S. Hunter	2005		
3384	Michael Cowan	2005		
3385	Tony Hulme	2005		
3386	Elke Braun	2005		
3387	Freda Wyn	2005		
3388	Paul Beverley	2005		
3389	Graham Vaughan	2005		
3390	Raymond Quinn	2005		
3391	Roderick Dingwall	2005		
3392	Andrew Summers	2005		
3393	Jeffery Quinn	2005		
3394	Sheila M.C. Dall	2005		
3395	George Clowes	2005		
3396	Andrew V. Stachulski	2003		
3397	Ian J. Jackson	2005		
3398	Graham Milton	2005		
3399	George Philip	2005		
3400	Sheila Boettcher	2005		
3401	Tony Richardson	2005		
3402	Steve Turnball	2005		
3403	Patrick Hetherington	2005		
3404	Keith White	2005		
3405	Janet Yates	2005		
3406	Neil Yates	2005		
3407	Robin Hildrew	2005		
3408	Andrew K. Sparkes	2005		
3409	Willie Robertson	2005		
3410	Stephen Young	2005		
2411	Mairi Mackenzie	2005		
3412	Richard Kurzweil	2005		
3413	Graham E. Bothwell	2005		
3414	Paula Hudson	2005		
3415	Ivor Robert Brown	1996		
3416	Graham Johnston	2005		

3417 Paul R.T. Newby 2005
3418 Albert Krawinkel 2005
3419 John Linnell 2000
3420 Richard B. Moore 2005
3421 Frances Moore 2005
3422 Norman Easton 2005
3423 Trefor Beese 2005
3424 Allan Gall 2005
3425 Alan Best 2005
3426 David Sneddon 2005
3427 William Stevenson 2005
3428 Kenny Morris 2005
2005
3429 Glen Gordon Adcock 2005
3430 Jimmy Reid 1984
3431 Graham Hunter 2005
3432 Sheila Simpson 2005
3433 Bill Simpson 2005
3434 J. Michael Arrowsmith 2005
3435 Duncan Boyd 2005
3436 Roy Manuel 2005
3437 Mr K. McGregor 2004
3438 Hazel Holmes 2005
3439 Donald Wooley 2005
3440 Thomas Campbell McGee 2005
3441 Paula H. Carter 2005
3442 Alasdair Kennedy 2005
3443 Tom Tracey 2005
3444 Graham Russell 2005
3445 Peter J. B. Aldous 2005
3446 Janice Shepherd 2004
3447 Cameron Kerray 2005
3448 Christine Anderson 2005
3449 Tom Webster 1996
3450 Alexander J. Masson 2005
3451 Michael Bird 2005
3452 Mr L. Forster 2005
3453 Tony Smyth 2005
3454 John F. Davidson 2005
3455 Keith S. Bryers 2005
3456 Ronnie Taylor 2005
3457 Susan McIntyre Taylor 2005
3458 Colin Waines 2005
3459 David J. Downey 2005
3460 Bob Stewart 2005
3461 Tricia A. Chapman 2005
3462 Adrian W. Chapman 2005
3463 Bill Taylor 2005
3464 Keith Gliddon 2005
3465 Colin F. Morsley 2005
3466 Douglas Barnes 2005
3467 Muriel Barnes 2005
3468 John Henderson 2005
3469 Steven R. Poore 2005
3470 Robert J. Hughes 2005
3471 Graham Scott 1995
3472 Guy Froud 2005
3473 Stan J. Urbaniak 2005
3474 Gordon J. Liney 2005
3475 May Liney 2005
3476 Charlotte G. Turner 2005
3477 Bob Mayow 2005
3478 Peter Atkinson 2005
3479 Roger Heckingbottom 2005
3480 Richard Bridges 2005
3481 Rick Salter 2005
3482 D.R. Kerr Fraser 2005
3483 Reamonn Lenkas 2005
3484 Stephen Miles 2005
3485 Janice Angwin 2005
3486 Nick Train 2005
3487 Alban Hough 2005
3488 Sally Varian 2005
3489 John D. Smith 2005
3490 Paul Corrigan 2005
3491 Bruce McGorum 2005
3492 Angus Plumb 2005
3493 Andrew Lawson 2005
3494 Andrew Morlin 2005
3495 Tom Waugh 2005
3496 George D. Cruickshank 2005
3497 Richard Knight 2005
3498 Sally Chaffey 2005
3499 Rob Mackay 2005
3500 Les Meer 2005
3501 Andrew Spink 2005
3502 Jim Hawkes 2005
3503 Donald J. M. McIntosh 2005
3504 Jean G. Urquhart 2005
3505 Joyce Beaton 2005
3506 Alison Maddocks 2005
3507 Ken Maddocks 2005
3508 Robert E. Wright 2005
3509 Bruce Madden 2005
3510 Robert Fraser 2005
3511 Ina Jefferson 2005
3512 Irwin Jefferson 2005
3513 Lorna Kinloch 2005
3514 Cath Close 2005
3515 Catherine Jackson 2003
3516 Andrew Watt 2005
3517 Charles Pinkstone 2005
3518 Ron Bell 2005
3519 Alan G. Courtney 2005
3520 Neil Campbell 2005
3521 Philip Sydee 2005
3522 Robert Marshall 2005
3523 Jenny Hatfield 2005
3524 Euan Laing 2005
3525 Alasdair Baird 2005
3526 Michael O'Donnel 2005
3527 David May 2005
3528 Chris Hallows 2005
3529 Mr R. Y. Potts 2005
3530 Malcolm Davidson 2005

3531	Derek McAdam	2005	3537	Stephen Mitchell	1999
3532	Rob Fuchs	2005	3538	Robert Craig	2006
3533	Tim Burns	2005	3539	Maggie Kitt	2005
3534	Karen McLeod	2005	3540	Michael Gray	2005
3535	David Jeffery	2005	3541	Joan Rennie	2005
3536	Steve Clayton	2005	3542	Rosemary Queen	2006

As ever, the tales of the various triumphs and antics of this year's Compleaters form interesting reading.

One of the longest rounds I can remember was by John R. Reay (3338). He started in 1957, compleating in 2005. He compleated on Meall Chuaich with 24 people present. He was presented with a poem by 'the re-incarnate W. McGonagall'.

For John, father, uncle, friend – thanks are now due,
An introduction to the mountains was indeed down to you.
All toiled up the slopes with all their might and main,
But the top was always worth it except in cloud and rain.

There are not many with more than a 48-year round, although Charles Dingwall (3379) comes close. He did his first Munro in 1959, it was Ben Avon while on a course at the new Glen More Lodge. He had Ben Humble as his instructor and can still remember his remarkable stories. Charles completed on Moruisg also in 2005. Just a fraction shorter – Peter Aldous (3445) took 45 years with the last 206 in three-and-a-half years. He only has seven 4000m. Alpine peaks to go (all in the Mont Blanc area).

Also with a long round duration was Mike Killingley from Winchester. He wanted to complete on Carn Mor Dearg then traverse the arête to the Ben, his first Munro, and to do it exactly 30 years on from his first ascent. Unfortunately, his three sons had tickets to REM in London, so he was forced to go eight days earlier.

The greatest number of folk recorded on a summit this year goes to Ron Bell (3518) with '60 people and a piper' plus champagne on the Cairnwell, all on his 60th birthday – hence the reason the piper wasn't included in the 'people'.

Ian Jackson deserves a mention for getting 40 people onto his final hill. Luckily, he'd picked a Geal Charn. Sheila (3432) and Bill (3433) Simpson got 39 people up Ben Lomond on 'the worst day of the summer', as they became Friockham HWC's first Munroists. Trefor Beese (3423) took 32 folk up Sgurr a Mhaoraich at the end of May. During his summit celebrations, he was informed by his daughter that she was three months pregnant, and that he was to be a grandad. He was presented with a cake decorated exactly like the Compleation Certificate – right down to my predecessor Chris Huntley's signature!

Neil Campbell (3520) finished on Meall Buidhe in Glen Lyon, witnessed by 28 people, many from the Blantyre HWC. He feels he did his bit to bridge the Campbell/Macdonald feud, as he wore a Macdonald kilt for the day. Paul Armstrong (3369) took 29 people up Ben na Lap on June 4. On their way down, they met someone else, possibly Mike Assenti from Scone (3363), just about to compleat. R. Potts (3529) decided to invite everyone he had ever been up a hill with over his 45-year compleation period, giving them 15 months warning. He finished on Beinn Sgulaird with 25 friends.

As well as unusually-decorated cakes, other items have figured in gifts. Sheila Boettcher (3400) was given a glass engraving of A' Glas-Bheinn (her final summit) and a painting of An Teallach

John Baldwin (3359) and his dad Barry (3360) started and finished together,

Eric Langmuir. Photo: John Mallinson.
Bill Wallace. Photo: Malcolm Slesser.

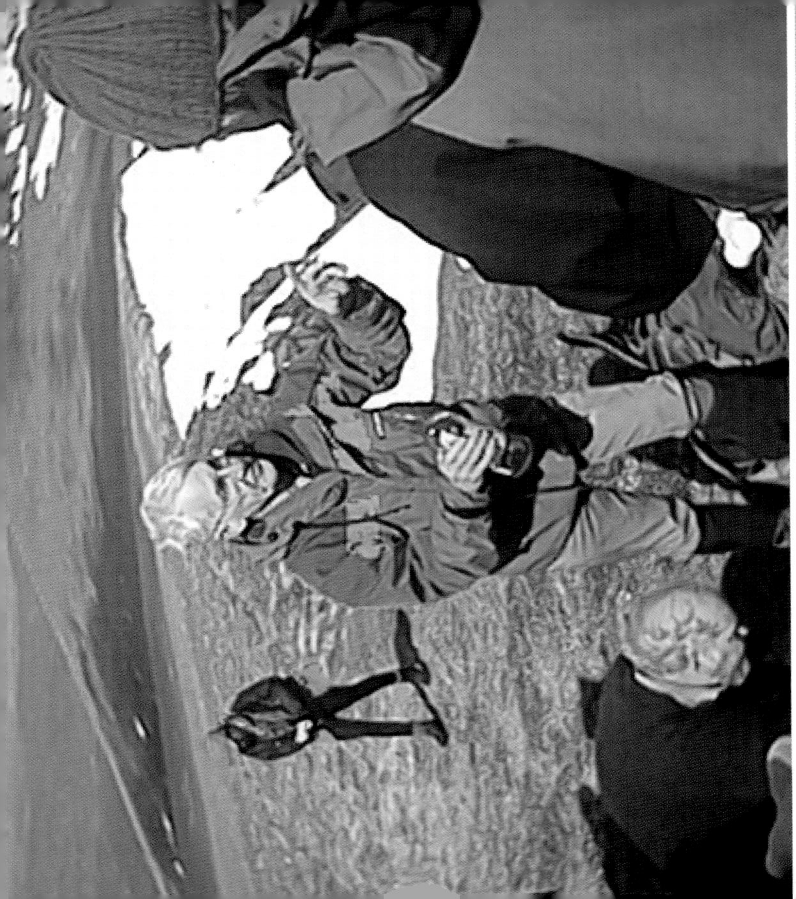

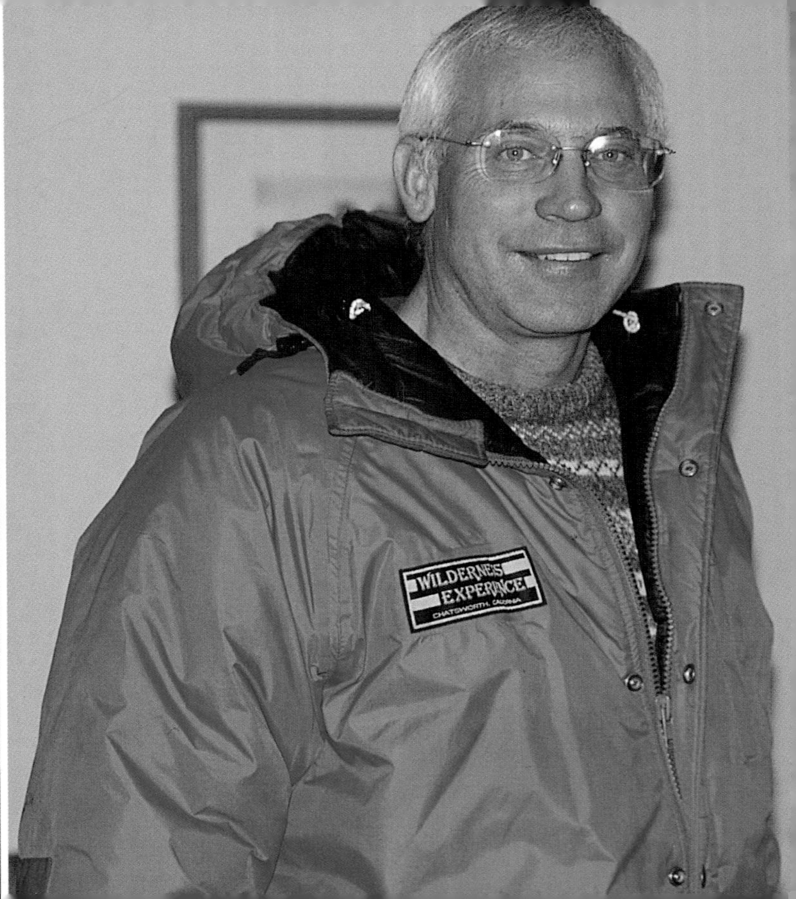
WILDERNESS
EXPERIANCE
CHATSWORTH

but it was only when they got round to writing to record their compleation several months later did they realise that their start and finish dates had been 13 years exactly apart – lucky for them they chose to register otherwise they might never have known this.

On the subject of first Munros, Gordon (3474) and May (3475) Liney only began when they took part in Gordon's father Les's (1473) last Munro. Reamonn Lenkas (3483) sold his ZX Spectrum to get enough money for his first boots and rucksack. His recent compleation on Beinn na Lap saw his party getting back for the train with only seconds to spare. A wonderful finishing trinity was achieved by Derek Reid (3375) and David Coia (3376), in a 24-hour trip (noon–noon) to Knoydart. After an afternoon doing Luinne Bheinn and Meall Buidhe, they camped at Mam Barrisdale and did Ladhar Bheinn the following morning, leaving the tent at 4.20am. Donald Wooley (3439) also completed his last two during a Knoydart trip – Luinne Bheinn followed by Meall Buidhe. Somehow or other he organised two pipers to play for him in the mist as he reached his compleation. Kenny McGregor (3437) also had pipes on top, and numerous people in kilts, on Ben More on Mull, while Rob Mackay (3499) was piped up Ciste Dhubh in October.

The most relaxed idyllic sounding compleation I heard of this year was by Duncan Boyd (3435) who wandered up Seana Bhraigh in the late afternoon from Coire Mor bothy after fishing in the loch. He rounded off the day with Highland Park, and did a similar thing the following day, but his chosen hill was the nearby Corbett, Carn Ban. Speaking of idyllic, Alan Best (3425) and his wife have an idyllic sounding life-style. They spend nearly all their time in their motor home, travelling round Europe 'biking, walking, climbing, skiing and ski-touring'. A three-month period in the Highlands saw his compleation on Binnein Mor.

The effort and expense that a lot of Munroists go to can always be seen in the distances which they have had to travel. Ann Butler (3366) took seven years, travelling each time from Plymouth – she plans a second round. Roy Smith (3352) and David Jeffrey (3535) travelled from Southampton (David took 41 trips). Nick Train (3486) took 52 trips from London. Elke Braun began while holidaying from Germany but made a move to Stirling to ease things. An interesting item arrived in my mail from Andrew Stachulski (3396) from Newton-le-Willows. It was his copy of the original J. Wilson Parker Munro Map. He'd also noted the various changes from each revision. Andrew too plans a second round.

On the subject of unusual things in the mail, I must thank Sally Chaffey (3498) for sending me a copy of 'Munro Mania – The Game of the Scottish Munros'. It proved very enjoyable at New Year. If anyone is interested in obtaining a copy from Sally, give her a call on 01773 825418. I don't imagine anyone will be writing to John Hughes (3470) however to get a copy of the photo he sent in – a full moon on the top of Beinn na Lap. John has only managed five Munros in the nude and wonders when a full round will be done in the Full Monty!

Statistics are always useful, if only to compare with our own experiences. Some similar sets were received this year. Richard Kurzwell (3412) took 870 hours, in 137 days, covering 2615km. and ascending 161km. (100 miles). Michael Arrowsmith (3434) took 113 hours 'away from the car' in 166 walking days, covering 2846km. and ascending 184km. Michael always started from a car and returned before dark each day. Richard Knight (3497) walked on 130 days, and covered 2543km. Robert E. Wright (3508) sent me a 24-page report of his trips. What jumped out was the number of different climbing and scrambling trips he had managed to utilise in his round.

Munroists often have tales of the interesting souls they encounter. Paul Newby

Ian Angell. Photo: Iain Cumming.
Rob Milne. Photo: Dave Cuthbertson.

(3417) recalls an unusual encounter with a Dutch Theoretical Physicist who repaired a 6-inch bike tyre split on Paul's bike with nylon cord, after first analysing the problem from first principles. Elaine Milner (3347), from Pudsey, Yorkshire had such adventures that she used tales from her round as anecdotes in school assemblies. Alison (3506) and Ken (3507) Maddock from Wales report a couple of encounters which slightly marred their round. The first resulted in them losing all their equipment from outside the Kingshouse. The second was a run-in with 'a certain misanthropic hostel warden who shall remain nameless' – answers on a postcard. A certain amount of bad luck befell John Davidson (3454), who cracked five ribs on the Horns of Alligin and took a headfirst dive while descending the Chalamain Gap, which still gives him recurring nightmares. Alistair Baird (3525) had been forced to take a year-and-a-half off, during his round, after breaking his leg at the end of a day's walking – in the Car Park! He decided to finally compleat on his namesake Sgurr Alasdair. Les Meer also suffered a rather unusual painful experience. He took a high voltage thump when ball lightening hit the top of Gleouraich – close to him. The elements were kinder on his final hill – he saw a double glory from Ben Lui. Les was the first member of the Hereford Mountain Club to compleat, and managed his last seven during the same trip north.

Inn Pinn stories did not feature quite as often in this year's letters. Alasdair Kennedy (3442) only had it to do by the year 2000. He then failed on it several times because of rain, wind etc. He finally succeeded on the only dry day on a ten day trip to Skye from The Wirrall. Euan Laing only reached the top of Beinn Fhionnlaidh after five attempts. His available time to compleat was running short as his fiancé is planning for seven kids. With a double failure on his last hill prior to compleation, Derek McAdam (3531) was so relaxed when he finally did Beinn Teallach, he felt he had floated up. In a summit group of 16, he had 11 previous compleaters.

I have to apologise to Keith Gliddon. In error, I gave Keith a number which I had already allocated. To correct the error, Keith accepted a later number.

AMENDMENTS

The following have added to their entries on the List. Each Munroist's record is shown in full. The columns refer to Number, Name, Munros, Tops, Furths and Corbetts.

1148	Colin Wilson	1993		2005	
1266	Joan Wilson	1993		2005	
2887	Michael O'Hara	2003		2005	
3293	Paul Ormerod	2004	2004	2005	
1747	Anthony Halhead	1997	2005	1999	
1981	Bill M. Edgar	1998	1998	2005	
		1987			1992
		1998			2005
634	Bill Miller	2004	1998	1991	
		1997			
1722	John Newman	2005	1999	2000	
		1980			
		1995			
216	Jeremy Fenton	2005	1984	1982	
1636	James A. Bennett	1996		2005	
660	Paul Gillies	1989	2005		
622	Robert Wilson	1988	2005	1995	
827	Pete Craven	1990			2005
1344	Pat Craven	1994			2005
2503	Grahame Downer	2000		2005	

		1994			2005
1295	William Beattie	1999			
1351	Margaret Beattie	1994			2005
		2000			
3141	Peter D. Cottam	2004	2002		
		1990			
763	Brian D. Curle	2005	1991	1991	
		1984			
341	J.F. Fedo	1988			
		1994			1999
1292	Julian P. Ridal	2005		1995	
2092	Steve Tompkins	1999	2001	2005	
3428	Kenny Morris	2005	2005		
		1992			
1126	Margaret Hendry	2003	2003		
		1992			
1030	James G. Halkett	2005			
1933	Dave Irons	1998	2005	2005	
2669	Brian Mucci	2001	2005		
2670	Alison Claxton	2001	2005		
		1998			
1942	Gordon J. McInally	2005			
		1997			
1780	Marion O'Connor	2005			
1660	John Kirkham	1996	1998	2000	2005
2641	Alan G. Duncan	2001		2005	
		1988			2005
755	J. Stanley Roberts	1988		1990	2005
599	James Taylor	1994			
660	Paul Gillies	1989	2005		
3463	Bill Taylor	2005	2005		
2182	Anne Morrison	1999			2005
		1985			1996
		1996			2005
384	J.M. Gear	2005	1985		
		1999			
2124	Chris Freeman	2006			
660	Paul Gillies	1989		2006	

As ever, people who wish to register a Compleation or an Amendment and who would like to receive return confirmation should send a letter with a stamped addressed envelope (A4 size if you wish a certificate for Munro or Corbett Compleation) to me. Please note, if you are asking for any more than one certificate, the 60gm. initial postage weight limit will be exceeded. I can be reached at:

Greenhowe Farmhouse,
Banchory Devenick,
Aberdeenshire,
AB12 5YJ.

Have a great day on the hill.

David Kirk
Clerk of the List

A Winter's Tale

Braemar before dawn cold bites,
fingers shaking and clumsy
there are tears in my eyes, it's the wind.
Walking in on iced tracks boots sliding
unyielding,
eyes widen as skies
become light, imperceptibly.
Apricot dawn warms cold shoulders of mountains
as we stumble through tussocks
spiky frozen Mohicans.
Dark deer, silent watchers dapple the hillsides
now still,
but tensing to flee.
Day is born, soundless and glorious
blue skies and look! Eagles, two eagles above us
guide our eyes to the ice climb, glistening alluringly.
All weariness fades as we gaze at the ice-fall
pure clean and clear, conditions are perfect.

Rhythm of movement, axe, crampon, pull upwards
ice water finds freedom through pick holes and ice-screws.
Armour-clad in its ice thrall
we can climb up its beauty,
frozen enchantment in motion suspended.
Axe, crampon pull upwards, axe, crampon
and onwards
last pitch
last belay
and hurrah, it's the top!

Dazzling white vistas unfold before us
but we shoulder our rucksacks,
it's a long journey back.
Descend, descend
endless tracks left by crampons
bear claws in the snow.
Terrain changing, its dark now
but the moon shines benignly.
Iced tracks snake enticingly, leading us homewards
boots heavy,
it's so far
to the car.
But is was great,
wasn't it?

Helen G. S. Forde.

IN MEMORIAM

ERIC DUNCAN GRANT LANGMUIR j. 1955

I FIRST met Eric when I arrived at the start of my first term at Fettes in early 1946. I was struggling to get a bulging suitcase up to my dormitory when Eric appeared and offered to help. So began a friendship that was to last just a few months short of 60 years.

We both left Fettes in 1950 and Eric went off to do his National Service in the Royal Artillery before going up to Cambridge to read Natural Sciences. His athletic potential became apparent when he won the army cross-country championship. I, in the meantime, had discovered a keen interest in hillwalking.

In 1950, having fallen victim to Munroitis, I set out from my home in Selkirk for the Cuillin on a three-speed Raleigh bicycle laden down with tins of food. I arrived several days later at Glenbrittle Youth Hostel feeling lucky to have survived the road from Carbost, which in those days was basically a boulder field interspersed with large and deep potholes. On the second day I was approached by a gent from Newcastle whose companion had to return home. He asked me if I could rock-climb, and if not, would I like to learn? I jumped at the chance, went to Portree that afternoon and had a cobbler knock clinkers and tricounis into my hillwalking boots and so I 'learned the ropes'.

Early in 1951 I was staying at Eric's parents' home in Glasgow when he asked me how I had spent the previous summer holidays. I told him that I had been rock-climbing on Skye. His face lit up. He said: "Toby (the nickname I acquired at school and which Eric used all the years that I knew him) I wish I'd known sooner. I'd love to rock-climb and I've been looking for someone to show me."

We agreed to go to Skye that summer. In the meantime, I had acquired a very powerful 650cc Triumph Thunderbird motorbike courtesy of my father for the then princely sum of £230. This was our transport for the Skye trip and later for many others. I would leave home in Selkirk after work on a Friday, head for Glasgow on the A8 (no M8 then), stop for a meal at Eric's then head off at top speed for Glencoe or wherever. Eric delighted in riding pillion urging me to go ever faster as we hurtled up Loch Lomondside. If you can imagine that road in the 1950s you will marvel, as I do now, that we survived these trips. But survive we did and that first summer we arrived in Glenbrittle complete with ex-WD carabiners, seven hemp slings, one hemp rope(!) and one new-fangled nylon rope.

By now I had acquired, in exchange for about two weeks' salary, a decent pair of nailed boots from Lawrie of London. We were ready! After a few introductory scrambles it was apparent that Eric had a natural ability and we set off for his first climb, which was *Cioch Direct*, graded severe. Three days later he was leading me up a very severe, the *Crack of Doom*. Apart from two very wet days we enjoyed perfect weather and were able to make full use of our three weeks to climb many routes. Eric never forgot that holiday and my getting him started on rock-climbing.

It was while we were in Skye that I first noticed Eric's amazing co-ordination of eye and body and his ability to cover rough terrain including scree and boulders at full speed. Had he misjudged he would have broken a leg, or worse, on many occasions. He must surely have broken the record for the descent of the Stone Shoot (in those days there were actually stones in it), including an apparently suicidal leap over a break at about the halfway point. I watched in amazement.

I also got a taste of Eric's mischievous sense of humour while staying at the hostel. We had, on a number of occasions, exchanged uncomplimentary words with a group of loud-mouthed individuals who were hogging the communal stove. The loudmouths had a greasy, malodorous, brown stew boiling on the stove, in what appeared to be a small version of a witch's cauldron. Since it was at the end of two days of heavy rain and the hostel's drying facilities were overwhelmed somebody had fixed a length of string above the stove on which numerous small items were hanging to dry. I noticed in particular a heavy woollen sock which was giving off an odour even more vile than the stew above which it was loosely and strategically placed. Eric and I exchanged glances. The guardians of the cauldron were in a corner, their brew unattended, noisily and otherwise occupied. Eric had also noticed the sock and a gleam came into his eye.

He said: "What do you think ,Toby?' I replied: "Go for it." Eric reached as if for something on the line and 'accidentally' knocked the sock into the cauldron. Panic! – the sock was floating on the mess but quick as a flash I used my spoon to push it under.

"You can chalk that one up," said Eric. We sat down to eat and to await the outcome. Ten minutes later we were treated to a volley of oaths and imprecations from the corner, where the group eventually dined on stale bread and jam, having dumped the contents of the cauldron into the burn. Half-an-hour later a spotty young man came round to ask if anyone had seen a black sock. We capped our evening by directing him to the unhappy group in the corner, who, we told him, had very likely seen a black sock. His fate at the hands of the group was not recorded.

Eric and I climbed some more in the Lakes and the Llanberis Pass and he introduced me to his friends in the CUMC, including Mike O'Hara and Bob Downes. In June 1954, Eric, Mike and I were at the head of Loch Etive to investigate a report that Eric's father had given of some rocks on Beinn Trilleachen that he had spotted when fishing on the loch and which might be of interest. They turned out to be much bigger than we had imagined. The angle looked deceptively easy but they were just about at the limit of friction. We were rather overawed since we did not have anything like today's rock shoes. Eric wore a pair of gym shoes while Mike and I wore vibrams. We decided to go for the easiest looking line and the result was *Sickle*, Very severe but vegetated and a disappointment. Next morning, Eric thought he spotted a promising line so we roped up and Mike started out in a determined manner. He led the first three pitches, including a short but brutish overhang. At this point he found himself on an expanse of slabs where holds were apparently non-existent. After several abortive attempts and some consultation, Eric took over the lead and eventually succeeded in climbing a difficult and exposed pitch and then led the rest of the route. Each time we thought an impasse had been reached Eric found the vital move to continue the climb. The route was far from obvious and it was a bold and brilliant lead for the time. We had discovered *Spartan Slab*.

Eric then continued to climb with winter routes on Ben Nevis and visits to the Alps and the Dauphine with other CUMC members. He spent time too at the Ecole Nationale de Montagne et de Ski in Chamonix with Geoff Sutton, Bob Downes (both CUMC) and Alan Blackshaw (OUMC) and in these summers he made several ascents. Notable among the climbs which he did was the first British ascent of the NE face of the Piz Badile along with Bob and Geoff. At that time it was regarded as one of the hardest routes in the Alps.

Although I did not accompany him on these Alpine trips we still found time for Scottish outings together and I am glad to say that his sense of humour remained undiminished. I by now was the proud owner of a small Standard convertible in which we were driving up Glen Ogle on one memorable occasion with the top down. We were stuck behind a large lorry loaded with three outsize cylindrical steel tanks which were new and empty. A clear straight appeared but the driver made every effort to prevent me from overtaking. I floored the accelerator and Eric pulled out his piton hammer from the pile of equipment at his feet, stood up, and as we passed he gave each tank in turn a resounding clout. The resulting noise became a mighty echo which reverberated all around the glen. The lorry driver was totally mortified and we were laughing so much that it took me all my time to avoid an oncoming car.

After graduating from Cambridge, Eric spent time in Canada as a geologist and there he met Maureen Lyons whom he married in 1957. Shortly after this our paths diverged and I headed for New Zealand and a career abroad while Eric returned to London to teach for a short time before turning to his career in the education and practice of outdoor sport with his appointment at Whitehall Outdoor Centre in Derbyshire in 1959. He remained there until his appointment as Principal at Glenmore Lodge in 1963. He presided over the centre as *the* place in Britain for winter mountaineering and continued to improve his own skills. In skiing he gained the top qualification of the British Association of Ski Instructors and in later years became the honorary president of BASI. He was himself caught in an avalanche while out on a rescue and it inspired in him a lifelong interest in avalanche research. He was one of those who was active in setting up the avalanche reporting system in Scotland. Later he was appointed Chairman of the Snow and Avalanche Foundation of Scotland. It was for his work in this and in Mountain Rescue that Eric was appointed MBE in 1986 and was made a member of the Royal Society of Edinburgh. When at Glenmore Lodge he first published his book *Mountain Leadership*, later *Mountaincraft and Leadership* which is the official handbook of the Mountain Leadership Training Board of Great Britain. It has become the 'Bible', widely known simply as 'Langmuir', for all who would go safely among the British mountains and especially for those who must be responsible for others.

His career then took him to Edinburgh in the interests of his children's education. First he was appointed senior lecturer at Moray House, setting up an Outdoor Education programme there. In 1976 he moved on to become an Assistant Director in the leisure and recreation services department of Lothian Region. In this post he had responsibility for all countryside matters which included Hillend Ski Centre and Port Edgar on the Forth. He was also involved in establishing the Pentland Hills country park. It was from this post that he retired in 1988.

I followed my career briefly back to London and then on to Santa Monica in California. We remained in touch over the years and when I retired in 1994 and returned to the UK I was welcomed as warmly as ever by Eric when I visited him in Avielochan and was able to admire the house designed by his son, Roddy. He still sought new and exciting experiences, and when I told him that my own house in LA had been trashed by an earthquake he claimed he was envious as he had always wanted to experience an earthquake.

It was now that we were in closer touch again that I was able to suggest that we should attend an SMC dinner as between us we had a total of 100 years of membership and only I had put in one appearance at such a function in all those years. To my surprise Eric agreed and he was surprised and delighted to be introduced for the first ascent of *Spartan Slab* in its 50th anniversary year. He held an ambition to attempt it once more in 2005 but sadly this was not to be.

On my way to the dinner we had time for a short outing and Eric, as ever, was full of vigour and good spirits and bounded over a seven-foot deer fence with no bother at all. I struggled a bit and when I complained and asked his advice on my arthritic knees Eric's response reflected the philosophy of his life. "Toby, you just have to keep going." This he did to the end of his life. In July and August he competed in two separate orienteering events with runs on six days in each. In August he was fell walking in the Lake District, completing three days' walking across country with an impressive descent down the steep screes from Dore Head into Wasdale in the company of his old friend and colleague John Cook. It was therefore a real shock to hear that he had become very ill but he was able to summon up the strength to thank me for my friendship over the years and especially for having introduced him to rock-climbing. For my part I was able to tell him in all sincerity that I regarded his friendship as a privilege. It was only three days later that the phone call came to tell me that Eric had passed away with his partner, Marion, and his children at his side.

How can I summarise such a full life and such a personality? It is given to very few of us to spend our life doing what we love best. Eric not only managed this but in doing so introduced the pleasures and skills of the outdoor sporting life to so many others.

His list of achievements is formidable: Cambridge, Whitehall, Glenmore Lodge, senior administrator in Lothian Region, first and first British ascents, significant contribution to avalanche research and to Mountain Rescue, MBE and FRSE and of course the classic 'Langmuir' read by so many, the list could go on.

The two major setbacks in his life, the loss of his wife Mo in 1980 and of his sister Marjorie in 1998 who both shared his love of the outdoors, and both to cancer, were borne with a quiet resolve.

My own personal memory of Eric is not a fixed picture but a kaleidoscope of many mental snapshots from the past – the boundless and infectious enthusiasm for everything that he did: mad motorcycle rides at all hours, boulder-hopping and scree-running, his inspired lead on *Spartan Slab* and so many great climbing days with Eric and his friends and his ever cheerful sense of humour. Now that Eric is gone from among us I shall miss him deeply. One could not wish for a better companion in all seasons on rock and hill.

I extend my deepest sympathy to Marion and to Eric's wonderful family.

John Mallinson.

Eric Duncan Grant Langmuir FRSE was born in Glasgow May 3, 1931, the second son of Dr James Langmuir OBE. Twenty-odd years later his home at 30 Buckingham Terrace became a haven for a procession of passing climbers.

He died on September 18, 2005, aged 74 and richly fulfilled, at his unique and uniquely hospitable home with its wonderful views of the Cairngorms. He died peacefully, surrounded by family, and still able to join in an impromptu ceilidh in his bedroom on the final day. His funeral in Inverness on September 24 was attended by about 300 people, family, friends and colleagues gathered from throughout Britain, paying their respects and fulfilling Eric's own recipe for the best way to express one's support in a bereavement: "I really think if you can possibly manage it, the best thing is to be there." Well we were there, with many more there in spirit, but ,of course, a lot more than mere physical presence is implied in Eric's remark.

Eric loved fireworks, despite getting a nasty injury once when discharging a rocket from a bottle held in hand. His family had put together a spectacular display for his entertainment that final weekend but events moved too fast. Instead, on the evening of the funeral, the inhabitants of Speyside were treated to a pyrotechnic celebration of a life well-lived.

Educated at Glasgow Academy (1936-1940), he was evacuated during the war, first to Achiltibuie, then Callander where he attended McLaren High School (1940-1943) moving on to Fettes College, Edinburgh (1943-1950). He did national service in the Royal Artillery (1950-1952) and was commissioned in May 1951. He went up to Peterhouse, Cambridge in 1952 and in 1955 (MA 1959) he graduated with an honours degree in Natural Sciences (Geology, Zoology, Physiology). Subsequently, Eric was certificated by the General Teaching Council of Scotland.

Eric's interests lay in outdoor pursuits, covering cross-country running, potholing, canoeing, sailing, skiing, rock-climbing, hillwalking, mountaineering, conservation, adventure education, orienteering and above all the pursuit of safety while taking controlled risks - because the rewards justify those risks. Toby Mallinson, old Fettes friend and climbing companion of nearly 60 years, was witness to Eric's claim to have made a five minute run down the 550m. Stoneshoot on Sgurr Alasdair in the Cuillin (in the days before 1952 when it still had stones in it), and has commented on his phenomenal coordination of eye, limbs and balance. Bob Downes (Cambridge Mountaineering 1956, p.18) wrote: "To try and race Langmuir downhill is the surest lost cause in mountaineering." During his National Service he won the army cross-country championship.

We first met at the opening meeting of the Cambridge University Mountaineering Club in October 1952, finding that we were in the same college and beginning a friendship of 53years duration. Eric in due course became president of the Cambridge University Mountaineering Club in its 49th year and he was present at the CUMC's centenary dinner in 2005. He was an active member of a substantial group of revolutionaries who wanted to see women admitted to full membership back in 1953 (Heavens, was life really that stuffy?). He was a member of the Alpine Climbing Group, the Climbers Club, the Scottish Mountaineering Club, and an honorary member of the Club de Montagne Canadien.

Eric and I were able to stay in college for all three years. We were both addicted to western films and rarely missed one at the cinemas in those days. These visits were frequently followed by 'shoot-outs' in our rooms, hands hovering, lips curled, bananas protruding from hip pockets, to determine who was the fastest banana east of Madingley.

Cambridge colleges in the 1950s operated a 10pm curfew policy, backed by the requirement to wear gowns after dark, and enforced by proctors, bulldogs, porters and high walls topped by rotating spikes. Our tutor (who was still addressing me as Langmuir two years after Eric graduated) drew our attention to the undesirable discrepancy between the small number of occasions on which we were signed in late and the large number of times when one or both of us were seen about town after 10pm.

This warning was soon followed by the setting of a trap. Eric, climbing in by the *voie normale* over the spikes at the rear of the college (2m., S., 4a. if not wet or pursued) about midnight was pounced upon by a posse of porters hidden in Gisborne Court and herded down into the narrow alley leading to the bicycle storage, which terminated in a 15ft. wall topped by spikes. "We've got you now, Sir." "May as well give up, Sir." floated respectfully but triumphantly up to me in our rooms, to be replaced by an alarmed "No, Sir. Don't do it, Sir." as Eric, in silhouette and with gown flapping like Batman, bridged quickly up between the walls of the alley and leapt over the spikes into the street. Eric appeared an hour or so later up a drainpipe, tapping for admission on our third floor window which overlooked the college gardens.

Eric had quick and intuitive reactions. At a camp in St. Moritz during the 1954 CUMC Alpine meet, I recall being woken by a shriek in the small hours, to find

Eric naked in the snow outside his tent (and sleeping bag) after an instant reaction to a vivid dream about an avalanche. Prophetic in hindsight.

One December night in 1954, Bob Downes, Eric and I were bivouacing under a large boulder near Steall in Glen Nevis. The roof slanted down and eventually met the thickly bracken covered floor. Eric drew the berth with least headroom. We were wakened in the night by a blood-curdling scream – and Eric had disappeared! – shades of Halloween. During the night he had wriggled and slid down an unsuspected and gently inclined slot between floor and roof, waking to find his arms pinned in his sleeping bag and the boulder pressing against his face.

His speed of reaction was certainly needed on the CUMC meet of 1955 in the French Alps. Carrying coils and moving fast on easier ground during an attempt on the *Sialouze Arete* on the Pic Sans Nom, his companion, Ted Maden, was swept away in a major rock fall behind him. Eric jammed himself into a crack, arrested the fall after some 30m. then marshalled his injured companion down to safety in a further 15hrs. of intense concentration.

After graduation, Eric was employed as a field exploration geologist with British Newfoundland Exploration (1956-1957) and in Northern Ontario, British Columbia and Alaska with the Mining Corporation of Canada (1957-1958). One product of this was a trio of bear stories.

He was awakened one morning by the thunder of a highly adjacent gunshot, to find a dead bear just outside his tent. A few days later while mapping in the bush he was approached by the sounds of yet another bear and took off at cross-country speed (Not adequate against bears and there was no companion to outrun.), eventually shedding rucksack, map-case and spare clothing in search of speed and made the shelter of the camp and the welcome presence of the rifle. He was joined soon after by a perspiring colleague bearing an urgent message, his rucksack, map-case, etc. Then there was the face-to-face meeting with a bear when both fled in opposite directions...

After his return from Canada he was employed as a science teacher at Wimbledon Independent Grammar School (1958-1959) before being requested by Sir Jack Longland, Everest mountaineer and Director of Education for Derbyshire, to take up the post as Principal at the Whitehall Centre for Open Country Pursuits run by Derbyshire Education Committee (1959-1963), where among others he employed as instructors Joe Brown and Bob Downes. After Whitehall he was appointed Principal at Glenmore Lodge National Outdoor Training Centre at Aviemore, (1964-1970), then on to the newly-created post of Lecturer, soon promoted to Senior Lecturer in charge of Outdoor Education at Moray House College of Education, Edinburgh (1970-1975) and finally the post of Assistant Director of the Recreation and Leisure Planning Department of the Lothian Regional Council which he held until his early retirement to enjoy life in 1988. In this latter post he was involved in setting up the Pentland Hills Country Park, developing the Port Edgar marina and sail training establishment on the Forth, and had responsibility for the Hillend Ski Centre, Britain's largest artificial ski centre and ski training establishment. Ever youthful, ever fit, Eric achieved a reputation in the Recreation and Leisure Planning Department for physical prowess, demonstrated by his ability to run up the stairs of the office from the ground to the sixth floor much faster than anyone else. Junior members of staff learned to jump to the side when he was trying to beat his own record.

Enjoying life after 1988 included being appointed to the Countryside Commission in 1990, serving a term on the NE board when that organisation became Scottish National Heritage and being a member of the Cairngorm Working Party 1991-93, entering a minority report with John Hunt, reserves manager for the Royal Society for the Protection of Birds, rejecting the voluntary partnership structure as a means of delivering good management, and playing an important role in the eventual foundation of the Cairngorms National Park, contrary to the initial inclination of the Government in Westminster.

From the earliest days his career was deeply involved with the improvement of instruction and technique with the particular aim that young people should be able to 'Adventure in Safety'. He was a member of the original Mountain Leadership working party in England 1962-1964 and launched a parallel scheme for Scotland in 1964. He gained extensive practical experience as leader of the Glenmore Mountain Rescue Team 1963-1969 and as rescue co-ordinator in the Northern Cairngorms during the same period. He was a member of the Mountain Rescue Committee of Scotland from 1964 and its chairman from 1968.

There is nothing to beat holding a falling body to arouse an interest in such otherwise dry physical matters as acceleration, kinetic energy, momentum and the resolution of forces. But the truth stressed by Eric is that hazard in the mountains comes from many sources and the majority of incidents have nothing to do with spectacular falls. Good equipment, fitness, foresight, careful planning, awareness of risk, good map-reading and route-finding skills, a watchful eye on the weather and a hyper-charged imagination are all essential parts of the armoury.

He studied avalanche prognosis and avoidance both in the Cairngorms and in Switzerland with Andre Roch, later setting up Scotland's first avalanche warning programme and laying the foundation for the Scottish Avalanche Information Service. In the course of one search for an overdue party of schoolchildren he and his party were swept 600ft. in an avalanche, and were dug out only 'at the true blue stage' as he put it wryly.

How many lives have been saved through Eric's work and how much grief avoided? Impossible to estimate, but I have heard rumour of two expert estimates suggesting that the avalanche studies alone may be saving as many as 30 lives a season in these days of greatly increased access to the hills. How much exhilarating adventure has been enjoyed in safety by young people as a result of his work?

His book *Mountain Leadership*, later *Mountaincraft and Leadership*, is the official handbook of the Mountain Leadership Training Board of Great Britain. It was first published in 1969, then extended and revised in 1973, rewritten and revised in 1984 and again in 2004. It has become 'the Bible', widely known simply as 'Langmuir', for all who would go safely among the British mountains and especially for those who must be responsible for the safety of others. The book has never been out of print and has sold over 150,000 copies – it was available in three shops in Aberystwyth when I checked last week.

The educational activities entailed the exercise of a high level of organisation and responsibility which he did not always extend into his leisure activities. One never, for example, entrusted him with carrying the party's supply of condensed milk or Kendal Mint Cake up to a hut – and there are rumours of weekly postal deliveries of succulent Chelsea buns from a Cambridge confectioner to Aviemore.

Once on a ski holiday with his wife and John Peacock he presented his passport, only to have it returned with the wry observation that it was usual for the passport to contain a photograph – he had prised it off the previous winter to meet the more immediate need for a photograph on his ski pass. Those were the days when one could still talk one's way through such minor embarrassments (I've gone through Orly with my passport still in Edinburgh) and the French were particularly understanding.

Eric relished slide shows with characteristic and uninhibited narcoleptic delight – if he was still awake after the third slide, the material was earth-shattering. During his years with Lothian Council, Eric achieved a reputation in the department for a propensity to fall asleep at inopportune moments, often at senior staff meetings when, from the 'chair' John Cook would see his head begin to roll forwards and do his best to keep him awake before his colleagues noticed. Eventually he gave up trying.

In 1957, he married Maureen Lyons, a Londoner whom he met in Canada when she was working for the Canadian Film Board and there are four children, Catriona (now a journalist), Roddy (an architect, who designed Eric's retirement home), Moira (a geologist and now a DTI inspector) and Sean (now a ski coach in Canada).

Maureen died of cancer in 1980 and her ashes were scattered by the family in the mountains they all loved. It was a shattering blow but Eric enthusiastically took on the extra housekeeping and parenting roles in addition to all his other activities, and discharged them with distinction. The three younger children were brought up in a ski-rich environment and all became expert ski racers who represented Britain internationally. At the time of his death he was delighting in his eight grandchildren. His partner Marion MacCormick, an enthusiastic orienteer (of which more below) joined him in 1989.

Eric brought to his hill-walking the cross-country expertise and the map-reading and route-finding skills which were later to blossom in his orienteering career. He was a hard act to follow. I recall four outings in particular, the first two in the early summer of 1953 when a party of six, comprising Ted Wrangham, Roger Chorley (the two drivers on Ted's Jaguar), Dave Fisher, Geoff Sutton, Eric and I departed the Climbers Club hut at Helyg, drove to Fort William and climbed Ben Nevis. Departing the summit in the small hours of the morning we hastened to the Lake District, climbed Scafell, and arrived in Lancaster with enough time in hand for dinner at a good hotel. Then on to Pen-y-Pass and up Snowdon to arrive at the summit also in the small hours of the morning but comfortably inside the 24 hours from departing Ben Nevis, the first party to achieve this. The same party had earlier crossed the Rhinogs from Maentwrog to Barmouth (it's in *Big Walks* – just try it sometime).

The third was at New Year 1956, when a party which included Eric, sister Marjorie, Geoff Sutton, Bob Downes and myself climbed Suilven from a base on the Achiltibuie road in an all-day and part-night round trip, across the grain of the country and through a couple of rivers – guess who came first on all three occasions. The last was in 1999 when Eric and I walked into Carnmore for a three-night stay, only his second and probably my last visit to the barn. Returning from an ascent of A'Mhaighdean by way of Fuar Loch Mhor (during which Eric had run rings around me like an enthusiastic sheepdog) we were put in our places by an encounter with a silver-haired grandmother well into her Eighties – carrying a good sized rucksack and en-route from Poolewe to Sheneval in the day (19miles. 500m. ascent and descent and two river crossings for the uninitiated). Self esteem was restored the following day by our meeting with a discerning young climber at Kernsary who elevated Eric to the status of living legend and made our day, week, year, whatever. Over a celebratory lobster dinner in Ullapool that night we agreed that the young climber had a great future in politics or public relations.

One of Eric's most endearing characteristics was his modesty; he simply shunned pomposity. Well usually. John Cook and Eric had joined Chris Brasher for the evening at the Three Shires Inn in Little Langdale when a young man came across the crowded bar to them with an autograph book in his hand. It was assumed, of course, that he was heading for Chris, always recognised and in demand for his autograph, when, to their surprise, he headed straight for Eric and very politely asked if he would oblige. Eric, looking a little puzzled but quite pleased, duly did as requested with a smile. The young man studied the signature and then blurted out: "Why, that's rubbish! You mean you're not Bobby Charlton." (the resemblance was quite marked).

Eric was a pioneering rock-climber in Britain until family responsibilities curtailed his activities – and responsibility was ever the name of Eric's game. 1954 saw the start of serious exploration of the climbing potential of the Trilleachan Slabs at the head of Loch Etive (although Robin Campbell tells me of an attempt made in the 1890s). Eric's attention had been drawn to the slabs by his father, an enthusiastic fisherman, mine had been aroused in the course of a camping trek along the south shore of Loch Etive in the spring of 1952. December 1953 saw the two of us washed out in a tent at the head of Loch Etive, but in the summer of 1954 we made multiple visits and attempted several of the obvious lines. Subsequently, the Etive Slabs have become a climber's playground. *Spartan Slab*, the 190m. VS route first ascended on June 13, 1954 by a party led by Eric Langmuir is in the four star category and ranks today as one of the most popular climbs in Britain.

Later that year found Eric at the base of the notorious Scoop on what is now the route *Hammer*, searching assiduously for a hold – any hold – while perched precariously on the shoulders of Bob Downes, who was equally precariously perched on my shoulders, I standing on the last positive hold some way above the piton belay. We had the wrong technique, it was a deceptively easy-angled slab but a steep learning curve; faith and friction or 'nutless guts for gutless nuts' (R. Campbell) are required.

Eric also had a hand in the early exploration in 1955 of Minus One Buttress on Ben Nevis (*North-Eastern Grooves*, VS. again, with Bob Downes and myself) which ultimately contributed to and resulted in the composite route of *Minus One Direct* (E1. 4 star quality, assessed in the latest guide as an outstanding climb and one of the finest of its grade in the country). In 1961 with Joe Brown he began the exploration of the wings of Dinas Mot in the Llanberis Pass, creating a highly regarded HVS. route, *The Mole*.

Eric's best season in the Alps was in 1955 when, after the club meet in La Berarde and the excitement already mentioned, Alan Blackshaw, Bob Downes, Geoff Sutton and he went on to the Ecole Nationale de Montagne et de Ski in Chamonix. Highlights were ascents of the South Face Direct (ED) of the Punta Gugliermina, and the first British ascent of the North Face of the Badile (ED), significant contributions to the post-war renaissance of British alpine climbing.

In October 1991, at the age of 60, he joined an expedition to the Bhutan Himalaya where he made several first ascents, including that of Wohney Gang, 5589m. with George Band.

Eric was a Grade 1 Ski Teacher with the British Association of Ski Instructors and a member of the British Ski Instruction Council, becoming its Honorary President in 1993. In 1964, together with John Disley, John Peacock, Peter Steele and a guide, he made one of the earliest traverses of the Haute Route by a party of British mountaineers.

With his partner Marion MacCormick he began a serious, and as ever fiercely competitive, interest in Orienteering following his retirement. Together they set up the local Spey Valley Orienteering Club. He was the main organiser of the Scottish Orienteering Championship in the Spey Valley in 2003. He was the winner in his age class of the Scottish six-day event in Lochaber 2001; was British National

Champion in his age class in Northern Ireland 2002 and competed in international events. In 1973 the Royal Society of Edinburgh sought to broaden its membership base in Scottish life beyond the dominantly academic. When Eric's name was suggested at Council it received instant recognition and support around the table. He was elected a Fellow in 1978 for his pioneer work on avalanche prognosis in Scotland and for his publications and personal contributions to outdoor education and safety in the mountains. He was awarded an MBE in 1986 for his contributions to safety in mountaineering and adventure training, but he had greater and far more highly valued rewards – the total respect and affection of the outdoor and mountaineering communities. His enduring monument, however, is the strength and cohesiveness of his family, a tribute to his parenthood and an indication also of just how sorely he will be missed. In 1999, Eric had the rare experience of reading notices of his death issued by post and via the web site of the Royal Society of Edinburgh and was able to assure friends that the reports were 'greatly exaggerated'. The error was understandable – his sister Marjorie Langmuir was a doctor practicing in Aviemore until her death the previous year, who also received literature from the Royal Society of Edinburgh. When her clinic wrote to the Society requesting that Dr Langmuir of Aviemore be removed from the mailing list, it was assumed that it referred to Eric.

The man had fantastic energy and drive, celebrating his arrival in the 70s in 2001 with an ascent of Mont Blanc in the company of friends. That same year he made a traverse of the Cuillin Ridge in the company of Andy Munro and his children Moira and Roddy. These are two expeditions which mountaineers 40 years his junior would have prized. Optimistic plans were afoot for a 50th anniversary ascent of *Spartan Slab* in 2004 by the original team, to be led by daughter Moira (I suspect that at least one of us could no longer have cocked his leg above his right ear as required on the third pitch). Only four weeks before his death he spent three days with John Cook walking vigorously over the roughest Lakeland fells, still impressing his companions with his downhill technique over screes.

We had a 20-minute telephone conversation the day before he died, marked by a deep appreciation of all the good times enjoyed, characteristic realism and a mutual absence of stiff upper lip.

Goodbye, Eric old friend. You did all things well and it is my privilege to have known you.

Mike J. O'Hara.

IAN R .ANGELL j. 1981

On January 14, 2006, Ian Angell died from a head injury sustained after a fall while hillwalking on A' Chrois at Arrochar. He was 66 and his death stunned all those who knew him.

Mountaineer, alpinist, rock-climber, ice-climber, ski-mountaineer, skier and hillwalker, Ian was all of these because of his love and enjoyment of the great outdoors. Ian was excellent company while pursuing any of these activities.

He was born on the January 18, 1939, just a few tense months before the Second World War and was brought up in Sheringham in Norfolk, an area not renowned for its hills, although Ian claimed to have climbed Beacon Hill (105m.) the highest point in Norfolk. He never knew his father who was tragically killed in an industrial accident when he was two years old. His mother was a council clerk who later ran a tobacconist and confectionery shop in Sheringham High Street.

Ian was educated at King Edward VII Grammar School in Kings Lynn and seems to have started climbing when at school as, it is rumoured, his initials can still be found at the top of the bell tower, reached at night from the dormitory and along the roof. His first recognised rock climb was in 1956 on the Idwal Slabs and the following year he attended a rock-climbing course run by Hamish McInnes.

On leaving school Ian went to Rugby College of Engineering, and while there worked as an apprentice electrical engineer at the AEI works in Rugby. He achieved a Diploma in Electrical Engineering in 1962 (aged 23) and was a Member of the Institute of Electrical Engineers. While a student in Rugby he was a founder member of the Rugby Mountaineering Club.

In 1961, as 'a slim 22-year-old student', Ian did a solo ascent of the Hornli ridge of the Matterhorn in 3 hours 25 minutes. a post-war record. As befitted his modesty he was astonished and possibly embarrassed that the event became national news on the front page of the *Daily Sketch*. In a dispatch from Zermatt the headline read: "Mad dog Ian climbs it solo!" The report quoted the Zermatt Chief Guide Godlieb Perren, "a splendid effort which only an Englishman would dare. He is a first-class mountaineer". His mother was also quoted: "He's climbed the Matterhorn? Oh my goodness that's quick! I feel terribly proud. He does a lot of climbing, but he's never done anything like this. At least not that I know of..."

However, trips were not without incident and while skiing from the Valsorey Hut, up the Plateau de Couloir on the High Level Route in the mid-1970s he was avalanched. Frantic digging by various parties, including a following German team, revealed a cyanosed, lifeless form, but swift, effective resuscitation restored him in what one companion described as, the nearest thing he had seen to the resurrection. Interestingly, Ian restarted the tour only 24 hours later, having recovered from both the trauma and hypothermia, and the group successfully finished in Zermatt.

Ian was devoted to his wife, Shirley, who was also a climber and a successful author who wrote the definitive history of the Pinnacle Club. On page 178 she relives the first time she set eyes on her husband to be, which was up a tree outside the Vaynol Arms in Snowdonia! "Later he danced the polka with me up and down the road. It was love at first sight."

He lived in Cumbria where he worked for the UK Atomic Energy Authority. He established many new rock routes in the area, publishing a guidebook to St. Bee's Head and a number of articles about the crags. As was typical, the articles he wrote not only listed the established climbs but also directed others to areas where new climbs might be found. Both Ian and Shirley were members of the Wyndham Mountaineering Club, based around a school in Egremont which had a climbing wall. He was also a member of Wasdale Mountain Rescue Team. In the late Seventies he moved to Ayrshire to work at Hunterston.

Ian qualified in 1978, at the age of 39, as a British Mountain Guide. However, it was not something he publicised, although he always took great delight in reminding climbing partners that he was entitled to a free pass when skiing or climbing in the Alps. He served as treasurer for the British Mountain Guides in the late Eighties and early Nineties.

Ian retired from the UKAEA in 1996 and more recently he successfully ran his own independent business working in various Nuclear Power stations. This gave him more time to head for the hills and in recent years he successfully climbed all of the VS rock routes on Buachaille Etive Mor and achieved his ambition of a winter ascent of *Orion Direct.*

Bell ringing was another activity Ian enjoyed. Starting in 1962 in Markfield, Leicestershire but mainly in Irton, West Cumbria, he was an enthusiast for nearly 25 years. Ringing was less frequent in Largs as there was no tower nearby, but whenever he was back in Cumbria he would try to visit Irton and join in on practice nights; he enjoyed these visits and would comment that it was as if he had never been away. Despite the absence of bell towers in Largs he put his climbing skills to good use by carrying out maintenance work on many church towers, most recently at the Cathedral of the Isles on Cumbrae.

Ian always retained a boyish enthusiasm for the hills and continued to plot and plan his trips for the coming years with youthful vigour and anticipation. His easy going manner and quiet nature masked a steely determination when it came to getting up climbs. He kept himself very fit and was always a willing companion. He led generations safely up classic routes they would otherwise not have managed. However, he always remained modest and unpretentious with no airs and graces. His phone calls and his conversations were always short and to the point, not much time for small talk, and would go along the lines of: "Hey Ho are you coming out to play?" It was little wonder he had such a wide circle of climbing friends. In recognition of his contribution to UK mountaineering he was made an honorary member of both Rugby Mountaineering Club and Wasdale Mountain Rescue Team. He became a member of the Fell and Rock Climbing Club in 1972 and from 1976 until 1980 was assistant warden at Brackenclose, the club hut in Wasdale.

In 1981 Ian joined the Scottish Mountaineering Club and played a full and active part in Club activities. He first served on the committee from 1983 until 1988 and then as a Trustee of the Scottish Mountaineering Trust. In 1998 he became the Club librarian. With his fondness for mountaineering books and journals, this was a role he enjoyed. With it came a lot of hard work; however, he approached this role with characteristic vigour and the club benefited from the long hours he put in to catalogue and organise the library. Without doubt, he has left it in good condition and will be a hard act for anyone to follow. Ian was a willing contributor to work parties at huts and was one of the stalwarts during the construction of the Raeburn hut at Laggan. His name was always at the top of the list when volunteers were needed.

As a worthy and valued member of the SMC Ian had a lifetime of achievement in the mountains – extending from the local outcrops close to the many places he lived, to the debilitating heights of the Himalaya such as Mera Peak. He was generous with his time, taking people out and showing them the ropes whether it was on his local crag near Largs, the Quadrocks, or on the higher mountain ridges. Over the years he climbed with many in the SMC and most of the Glasgow JMCS, showing his youthful enthusiasm and sense of fun. Friends would regularly receive post cards from him detailing his exploits and those fortunate to receive these, will appreciate that they normally took some time to decipher.

Perhaps it was a skill developed working for UKAEA but he always impressed with his ability to organise. He loved adventure and 1992 saw the first of his visits to the Staunings Alps in East Greenland, to enjoy ski-touring, climbing and living in Arctic surroundings. He returned in 1994 and again in 1996, achieving first ascents on each visit and naming one Shirley's Peak after his wife. He enjoyed these Arctic trips and in 1996 he also visited Spitzbergen, where he freely admitted that his characteristic calm was finally disrupted by the discovery of polar bear tracks all around his tent. But it did not put him off. He was busy planning his return to Greenland to go ski-touring this year.

Ian cared passionately about the mountain environment and was dismayed by the recent proliferation of radio masts and wind turbines. He objected to the wind turbine erected at the CIC hut and because of his high principles was not slow to

Elly Moriarty. Photo: Robin Campbell.
Karale Glacier, East Greenland, April 2005. Photo: Peter MacDonald.

tell the Club. He believed that the only responsible approach was to take only photographs, leave nothing but footprints and he took great care to ensure he left no trace of his visits to wilderness areas.

He enjoyed a good few laughs over the years both as the subject and perpetrator of many jokes. People were never slow to pull his leg about his fancy light-weight skis and bindings and the unique skiing style which he had perfected. It was called "a stem and a wheech". This obviously touched a nerve and, of course, backfired. When in the Alps and trying to follow him down a steep descent in soft snow with a heavy sack on, Ian had adapted his technique for such conditions but others had not. Those that ended up in a heap were admonished with the comment: "Now, you've been spending too much time on the pistes young fella-me-lad, you must learn to stem and wheech." This anecdote captures the essence of Ian and his interaction with the mountains. Ian was effective. Over the years he climbed to high standards both in summer and winter. There are few classic routes in Scotland he had not done. His enthusiasm amazed. Normally, if he was repulsed on a route he would be back up at the first opportunity, often with another partner for another crack at it. He didn't like unfinished business.

When Ian moved into semi-retirement he decided the time was right to do the Munros. Previously, he had steadfastly refused to become a Munro Bagger. As was his style, once he decided to do it, the routes and outings were planned to maximum effect and in April of 2005, he was joined on Sgor Gaoith in Glen Feshie, his final Munro, by a group of more than 50 family and friends. Such was the man that nothing was left to chance. To ensure there were no surprises on the day, Ian reconnoitred the route to within a few metres of the top beforehand. For once, the weather behaved and he was cheered on to the summit as Golden Eagles flew below over Loch Einich. It was his day and a grand event, celebrated in style both on the mountain and also later in the evening down in Kincraig.

Ian was also very involved in the local community and church, though he rarely spoke about his Christian Faith. It did allow him to show his concern for those who were less well off. At his death he was chairman of an effective group which had successfully lobbied to make Largs a Fair Trade town and he was a member of Largs Churches Together. At the funeral on the January 25, seldom has a church been so overflowing as family, friends and colleagues paid their last respects. Ian is survived by his wife, Shirley, and sons, Timothy, Adrian and Stephen. He also took great delight in his grand-daughters, Bethany and Megan. He had a wide circle of friends who climbed with him over many years. They will all cherish memories of excellent days on the hill, with a fine man of the mountains.

Ian died from a simple fall while doing what he loved, in the hills. The inquest report suggested his injuries were such that he died instantly, a finding which may bring some comfort to those who knew him.

C. M. Jones.

I FIRST met Ian Angell in 1987 when we were building Raeburn on a very tight budget and we had to wire the hut ourselves. Bill Duncan as custodian elect, and also as an electrical engineer, organised things and his first choice was Ian followed by Dougie Niven as the architect and me as Convener of Huts.

We gathered in the chill of the hut in bitterly cold conditions one Saturday morning and laboured until about seven in the evening, when we retired to the Loch Ericht Hotel for a meal on the club. We dossed in the hut and, in the morning, continued pulling and labelling hundreds of metres of cable, finishing the job late that day. Having had my own house re-wired, and bearing in mind the complexity

Doug Lang (top figure) and Bob Richardson climbing the Lilias Icefall, Cogne, Italy. Photo: Des Rubens.

of the Raeburn, it is not unreasonable to suggest that we saved the club around £2000 – not bad value for four meals and petrol money.

I met Ian again at Raeburn during my custodianship when he turned up at a work-party and asked for a job. At that time, the Achilles heel of the hut had been the water supply, which usually froze in very cold weather and considerably reduced the amenity of the hut. The problem seemed to be a section of pipe which came out of the burn before going underground via the original pipeline. I explained to Ian that I wanted a trench dug and the pipe buried and, handing him a pick-axe, I left him to it. Ian was always a good work-party member as you could give him instructions, leave him to it and know that the job would be done properly. Not all work-party members can work without direction. Those who can are doubly valuable. Several hours later, Ian reported the job done and the water supply has not frozen over in the last three years – Thanks Ian.

Gerry Peet.

WILLIAM WALLACE j. 1958

FEW people can have been more determined to make the best of their lives and skills than Bill Wallace, our past president. In a progression from high standard rock-climbing, through expeditioning to club ski-racing and then ski-mountaineering he excelled in all of them. He was a true mountaineer. Bill died suddenly, abruptly, of heart failure on the February 25, 2006, descending from the Rotondo Hut towards Realp on the final leg of a week's ski-tour organised by his close friend, Dick Allen. It was the sort of finale he would have wished for; a little too soon for his friends and family.

Bill's mountaineering debut is lost in the mists of time. He was in the Edinburgh JMCS in the early 1950s, and a frequent figure on the week-end mountaineering bus. As one would expect of an essentially kindly individual, he guided lots of beginners to their early climbs. Indeed there was a didactic streak in him. He had phenomenal stamina. It is recorded that he and Hugh Simpson (then a member) and Bill Brown made all the 4000ft. peaks and tops in Scotland in one 44-hour excursion, still, as far as is known, the record. They made a particular point of never treading on a road, and crossed the A9 by walking under a bridge!

After qualifying as a chartered accountant he worked in London, climbing mostly with the London JMCS, with the usual harrowing drives to North Wales. He gave up his London job in 1958 to organise an expedition to Peru with Myrtle Emslie (of Edinburgh) and Hugh Simpson, then in the Antarctic. They obtained MEF funding and sailed for Lima, where all three met up. Without any support from donkeys or porters they climbed seven peaks, including the first British ascent of Huascaran, 6768m.

He found a job in Scotland and settled near Helensburgh. It was here that I met him and forged a climbing partnership that was to last the rest of his life. He took belaying the leader very seriously. I never felt safer than when with Bill. He was a bolder climber than me. He only fell off once. It was while exploring a virgin crag in Glen Lednock. He dusted himself down and returned to the fray and made the passage. In those days it never occurred to us to record a 40m. route.

Bill knew his Scotland backside forwards. To the end of his days he could recall the height of every Munro, most Alpine peaks and many Himalayan ones. He had a remarkable feel for geography, which made for excellent route-finding. Though equipped with artificial hip joints sometime in the 1990s he continued to be a long distance, fast hill-walker. He may well have climbed all the Munros, but such tick-list climbing never appealed to him.

Bill took time off again to join Hugh and Myrtle Simpson and Roger Tuft on Hugh's stress analysis experiment. The party was to man-haul a sledge across the Greenland ice-cap, more or less on Nansen's route. Urine samples taken each day provided the data. It was a bold trip, and very arduous. The scientific conclusion was that people adapt to physical stress. Surprise, surprise.

After his first hip replacement the surgeon apparently had said that he should calm down, give up rock-climbing, skiing and squash. He temporised. He gave up squash and continued to ski like a demon. On an alpine down-hill ski holiday if he failed to descend 7000m. of down hill per day he felt he was wasting his money and time. He was looking forward eagerly to 2007 when he would be eligible for a free veteran ski-pass at the Trois Vallees.

In 1996 he retired from Tiso's where he had been financial director. With his time now his own, he stravaiged far and wide: Nepal, Spain, Majorca, the Alps, Greenland, Spitsbergen, US, Lyngen (Norway), and a long trip to South Africa, Botswana and Namibia with his wife, Maureen. He participated in two Himalayan treks, being one of only two who made the 5800m. summits.

More for social reasons than any other he now began to take golf rather too seriously for his friends' liking. Nonetheless, he kept climbing. Considering that he had difficulty bending to lace his boots, this makes his climbing all the more remarkable. High steps were out and delicate little movements were all he could manage. Yet he maintained his ability to do severe routes. In his Seventies he led *Agag's Groove*. I was with him when he made the 14-pitch south ridge of Cayre de Cougourde in the Maritime Alps. In 2005 he was exploring virgin rock in Glen Ceitlin. He was a true mountaineer with a fine eye for the route, and the boldness to overcome unexpected obstacles.

In the 1960s Bill joined the Glencoe Ski Club and was successful in club races, but the call of the tops became stronger and he took to ski-mountaineering, much of it with me. Often there were just the two of us. We were acutely tuned to the dangers involved. On one tour when it thawed from beginning to end, we came to the Scatta Minoia (col) and deliberately created an avalanche to make the descent safe to Vanina. That trip finished with an ascent of the Blinnenhorn via a soggy couloir first on skis then on foot and then we whistled down the Gries glacier leaping crevasses. The list of his ascents are too numerous to record here. The following give a flavour of his climbing taste: Mont Blanc on skis from the Grand Mulets (solo), Barrhorn (3610m.) on skis, the Corde Molla route on Monte Disgrazia, East ridge of the Zinal Rothorn, the North ridge of the Piz Badile. We both loved steep skiing, and perhaps one of the most exhilarating, which I shared with him, was the descent of Sron na Creise east face in spring snow.

We both got caught up in a Robin Chalmers project to make a film of crossing Scotland coast to coast. When asked how much he wished to be insured for in case he broke a leg, he said: "Ñothing, but insure me for being in the helicopter."

David Bathgate, Ian Nicolson and Hamish McInnes were advisers and assistants to the camera crew. David made a painting of the event that hung for ages in the Kingshouse bar and later in the White Corries tea room.

Bill made an immense contribution to our club. He represented us on the Glen Brittle hut committee for many years. He was treasurer from 1976 to 79, and he took over the arduous role of secretary from Donald Bennet, holding the reins of the Club for 10 years, 1979-88. He was elected President in 1988. It was in his time that the Club voted in women members. He chaired the Centenary Dinner. He was co-author of the SMT ski-mountaineering guide.

Bill's passion for mountains and wild places naturally drew him into the John Muir Trust. From 1988 to 2001 he was a trustee, and much of that time secretary and treasurer. It was typical of the man that though he held views often quite at variance with the Trust, such as the Slattadale hydro scheme and nuclear power, he let these issues slide over him, helping out in the Trust's affairs wherever he could. Nigel Hawkins, the director, said of Bill that he was always the quiet, assiduous worker behind the scenes, keeping the Trust on the rails.

I cannot be alone in feeling that it has been a privilege to be his friend and climbing companion.

The love where death has set its seal
Nor age can chill, nor rival steal

Malcolm Slesser.

KNOWING full well that others have greater claims and greater knowledge of Bill's undoubted character and considerable all-round mountaineering skills, I also wish to remember him, however briefly.

I think that I first met Bill at a JMCS meet on Gunpowder Green under the shadow of the Great Herdsman of Etive. We were callow youths, when a 120ft. of nylon laid rope, a dubious hemp sling, one rusty ex-WD carabiner and maybe a pair of vibrams made up the highly improbable equipment of the day.

Even then, Bill seemed to live in a rarer atmosphere than any of the others; that he was destined for greater things was soon to be demonstrated in the bigger mountains across the world. Annoyingly, he didn't seem to mind climbing in foul weather. Suffering to that degree always seemed to me exceptionally bad for the character – but then, what would Lord John have made of that. Doubtless he would have heartily approved of Bill's activities in those far off days.

Later on, in our Thirties and Forties, opportunities arose for us to climb together fairly regularly. By this time, Bill had mellowed some what; he seemed more relaxed and didn't seem to mind the indecision of a dithering companion – his patience seemed inexhaustible. I must say that I was pleasantly surprised by this, as I knew him to be highly competitive, as many who played against him in other sports knew to their cost. There were other frailties, but then, I like to think that he knew them better than anyone else.

Recounting any of our many exploits now seems inappropriate; sufficient to say that they are there in that mysterious and wonderful landscape of the mind.

I climbed with Bill more than any other member of the club or indeed, any other mountaineer. I shall remember his enthusiasm, his obvious enjoyment of the mountain scene and of course, his whole-hearted enjoyment of life itself. He was an excellent companion on the hill, a good friend, and I owe him a great deal.

Douglas Niven.

ROB MILNE j. 1988

ON JUNE 5, 2005, Rob Milne (48) suddenly collapsed and died of a heart attack on the way to the summit of Everest (8848m.), just below the Balcony at 8450m. There were three doctors on the summit team with him and Rob had shown no signs of any problem prior to this, so it was completely unexpected. Rob's ascent of Everest would have been the final peak in his quest to climb the Seven Summits.

The summits he had already climbed being: Denali, North America (1980); Carstenz Pyramid, Oceania (2001); Aconcagua, South America (2003); Mount Kosciuszko, Australasia (2003); Kilimanjaro, Africa (2003); Vinson, Antarctica (2004); Elbrus, Europe (2004). Those of you who are sharp may have spotted that there are seven names here. The reason being that there is some debate as to whether Carstenz Pyramid, on which he climbed a new route with Steve Sustad, is in Australasia, or not, so Rob being Rob, he climbed them both.

Rob was born in Montana in 1956. His parents moved to Colorado and that's where he started to climb. He soon found that the grander mountain environment was to his liking and he quickly progressed to the bigger ranges. In 1975 he made the first ascent of the North-East Ridge of Mount Vancouver in the Yukon and a few years later some fine ascents in the Kitchatna Spires in Alaska.

It was sometime around 1979, when Rob came to Edinburgh to complete a PhD. in Artificial Intelligence, that I first met him. There had been word of a young American who was quite a handy ice-climber after a string of good ascents on the Ben. Rob took to the Scottish Winter scene like a duck to water and somehow we ended up climbing together. Our first route in January 1980 was *White Elephant* (VII 6) on Creag an Dubh Loch. Since then we had climbed together every year and in March 2005, shortly before heading off to Everest he proudly announced that we had climbed 100 winter routes together. Among many significant ascents were the *West Buttress Direttissima* (VII, 8) on Beinn Eighe, *Inclination* (VII, 8) and *Ravens Edge* complete (VII, 7) in Glen Coe and the opening up of the Southern Highlands with *Deadman's Groove* (VII, 7) on the Cobbler. In the Cairngorms classics such as *Deep Throat* (V, 6) and *The Hoarmaster* (V, 6) were established. We also made a number of significant repeats here such as *The Migrant* (VI, 7) and *Postern* (VI, 6).

Rob was the stabilising influence in our climbing partnership, laid back is perhaps a better word. I was more focused about specific objectives. I don't think Rob would have minded if I said that I was the stronger climber, particularly since I trained more on indoor walls and spent all season rock-climbing. Rob was mountain fit though, and by that I mean his body was more suited to deep snow and long winter days out. Often I would bemoan my lack of hill fitness and a little extra from the Anderson hardware rack would be taken into the Milne rucksack.

To some extent Rob just wanted to go and climb and have a good time. I generally played my cards close to my chest and kept my objectives to myself. It's not that I didn't trust Rob, I just knew of his enthusiasm to share what he had been up to, and as a result it was easier for me to keep quiet. It's also easier to fail on something when no-one knows what you wanted to do in the first place. We would often end up going climbing somewhere 'For a look', without me really telling Rob what the objective was. There were times when we would arrive at a cliff and I could see him looking around at the unclimbed bits to see what he might find himself on. Needless to say, this meant there were a few occasions when he found himself standing at the foot of some hard-looking objective with little time to psych up for it. Rob took it all in his stride though, as usual.

Interestingly, my enthusiasm for the rigours of Scottish winter climbing was not quite of the same magnitude as Rob's, so I was not the only one with whom he climbed. As a result there are many others who enjoyed his company on the hill. He certainly had boundless energy and enthusiasm and when the conditions were not good for climbing he would go off hillwalking. Rob had compleated all the Munros and their Tops and was set to complete the Corbetts and the Donalds in the same year that he completed the Seven Summits.

In his early years in Scotland, Rob joined 'The Jacobites', no doubt in his quest for partners. He wrote two articles for their Club journal, both repeated in 2005 following his death. The first was *On Top of America* and described his ascent of Mount McKinley in Alaska with Brian Sprunt, who was subsequently killed on the North Face of The Matterhorn. The second was *Up and Down the Ben* and described his third ascent of *Galactic Hitchhiker* and his rapid descent of *Pointless* while attempting the second ascent with Pete Myles. This enforced descent came about when Pete's feet popped off on a bulge 30m. up the second pitch while he was leading.

Remember the experimentation with extra wide leashes for shoving your bent arm through to facilitate the placement of ice-screws in order to avoid hanging on aid? Well, what happened next was a good example of a learning process, for all of us at the time. Pete's wrists slipped through his leashes and despite an heroic effort to hang-on by two fingers he left both axes behind and hurtled groundwards, ripping out what gear he had, before pulling Rob and the belay off. Both were deposited onto the slopes at the base of the route down which they cartwheeled for some distance.

They came out of it remarkably unscathed and to quote Rob: "I believe I hit my head so was not harmed." Following this incident, and by way of illustrating Rob's determined nature, he went back in the Spring after the snows had melted to find the camera that he had lost during the fall. He painstakingly traversed back and forwards up the slopes beneath the route and actually found the camera, together with pieces of equipment that others had dropped. However, like the name of the climb he had been on it was pointless, for both the camera and the film had been ruined.

In 1980 he climbed Denali and the North Face of the Eiger. In return for his PhD. he then gave the US Military back the years they gave him. This reduced his climbing somewhat but while back in the US he was part of a top American team including Galen Rowel and Andy Embick, which opened everyone's eyes to the potential of Karakoram granite with the first ascent of the beautiful Lukpilla Brakk spire.

Rob became the Chief Artificial Intelligence Scientist at the Pentagon and when he returned to Scotland he used his skills to establish a new business, 'Intelligent Applications'. Dr Milne became one of the leaders in the AI and software engineering fields, gaining a string of recognitions and awards. He was a fellow of the British Computer Society, a Fellow (and past President) of the European Coordinating Committee for Artificial Intelligence and a Fellow of the Royal Society of Edinburgh. He also held some 14 professional posts, and as well as having more than 50 academic and scientific published documents to his name, he had made more than 50 conference presentations around the world, mainly by invitation.

Rob was not just a mountaineer. However, no matter where he was on his regular business and conference travels around the globe it figured in has plans and he would always manage to squeeze in some climbing. It was on such a trip that he climbed Mount Kosciuszko in Australia. There were times when he did more climbing abroad on business trips than I did on climbing trips.

Rob was a member of both the American Alpine Club and the Alpine Club. More importantly though, he was a member of the Scottish Mountaineering Club. I am pretty sure that as with the Alpine Club, Rob attended every SMC dinner when he was in this country, which is actually quite a feat for I admit to having only attended a handful in a longer period of time.

Rob became involved in the Club's affairs, taking on the role of Convener of the Publications Sub Committee, as well as a Trustee of the Scottish Mountaineering Trust. He also became the Editor of the SMC's Hillwalkers' Guidebooks and was one of those behind the acclaimed 'District Guidebook', *The North-West Highlands*, as well as a CD Rom to The Corbetts, the Second Edition of *The Corbetts* book and the publishing of e-books through the SMC's website. His involvement in our publications ideally combined his business talents with his climbing skills and his in-depth knowledge of the Scottish Hills. It never seemed out of place that an American, albeit one with dual nationality, should be so involved in the affairs of a club such as the SMC, so steeped in history and tradition. Rob will be a hard act to follow and he will be missed by many.

Rab Anderson.

JAMES 'ELLY' MORIARTY j. 1959

BY NAME Big Elly, Big Jim or whatever, he was certainly larger than life. From the quiet unassuming presence of later life few would ever imagine the remarkable exploits of his dicing with death on roads and mountains at the extreme end of survival. He was one of the Currie lads with whom I was greatly taken, their composite skills in climbing, drinking and uninhibited style of life, quite novel at that time, but decidedly a foretaste of future generations.

Elly took up apprenticeship as an engineering fitter and, with this assumed mechanical know-how, bought his first motor bike, alias old heap. In the first week of ownership Dougal almost wrecked the machine and himself, so Elly inherited the mantle of driver and began an unenviable trail of destruction, with him regularly stepping out of wrecked cars like the Terminator of later sci-fi films. As he only earned an apprentice wage, most of these cars belonged to friends, but it says much for Elly's magnetism that they all remained life-long buddies. It seems his early days of faith in running down to chapel from the Cobbler corrie stood him in good stead, for he surely lived under a guardian angel in surviving these spectacular write-offs. One simple story illustrating this was when driving home ultra-late he fell asleep at the wheel of his mini, drifted across the main road and rammed a large concrete lamp standard. This, of course, woke him up. You or I would have the steering wheel embedded in our chest but he still had a firm hold of the wheel, now bent round the column like a calzone. Then, on getting out to assess the damage, the upper half of the concrete standard fell on top of his mini and completely destroyed the cabin. One other tale, to close this car destruction phase of youth, was his success in landing a sporty high speed buggy on top of a tree!

Whilst he had a hard-worked angel, he in turn was guardian to Haston and saved him during many vulgar pub brawls and altruistic escapades on the mountains. For example, to further their education we took them to the Alps in 1959, beginning in the Dolomites with successful ascents of a brace of north walls in Cortina, then down to Civetta where I gave the Currie lads a description of an

ED on the Valgrande, whilst we went of to do the Solledar (my interest in history). They managed to climb the wrong hill and spent much time achieving nothing, returned to camp frustrated and thumbed through the route notes to select one of the hardest climbs in the area. Their story is well recorded in climbing annals, not so well known is that on waking from a very unpleasant summit bivvy Elly thought he was hallucinating, instead, he was covered in snow. They were outrageously underclad but he had the benefit of greater body mass and pummelled Dougal back to life to start their epic return to safety.

In testimony to his strength, during his mountain-school days, with a client much of his own age, he went rock-climbing in the Lost Valley and enjoyed a day doing the face. The client pleaded to experience leading, which he accomplished well but came off, unfortunately breaking an ankle. Elly stabilised his injury and lowered him from the face, tied the lad onto his back and, in numerous knackering sessions, stumbled all the way down the Lost Valley gorge and up to the main road where he thumbed down a friend's van and delivered the casualty direct to the Belford. He thought his schooling days were done for and all sorts of legal doom about to fall, for the lad's father was a big-wheel in the Navy. However, instead, he was greatly impressed with his son's account of the prodigious effort of it all, to the point of embracing smelly Elly and calling him a hero, which of course he was – and a very relieved one at that.

I had gone by thumb to Glencoe, Ronnie and Elly were to follow later in an old Singer Le Mans hot-rod wreck to meet up on The Ben. Lifts were not forthcoming and I ended up just north of Kinlochleven, in darkness and contemplating a bivvy, when I heard the roar of the Singer growling across the loch and the lads singing – but no lights. All was revealed when they nearly ran over me – the wiring had gone, they had no lights but decided to don their head-torches and had driven like that all the way from Stirling. Mind you, it did improve with my third torch.

Elly had a wild sense of fun, not too funny if you were the butt of the humour. For example, on a late night in Lagangarbh he hard boiled all the eggs and blackened all the oranges from the food lockers and returned them to their containers. The confusion and puzzlement of the victims trying to crack eggs into the frying pans and solve the black oranges mystery was gratifying to say the least.

However, this fades into insignificance when compared with the time he enticed a group of fellow boozers to try and beat the record for the number of people in a phone box (a craze at the time). All eight of them, if I remember correctly, made it, then Elly whipped a sling and a krab round the box and walked away, leaving them severely contorted and gasping for air, to the point where the box moved off its base and some kind passer-by relieved their stress.

The name 'Elly' was given by his early peers, an abbreviation of elegant, for he was ever in balance on the rocks. That, in combination with his power, allowed him to enjoy most contemporary 'moderns' of the day and supplement them with a few fine examples of his own.

More than just a climber, he was 'all things to all men' with a vital interest in the wider aspects of life, and harvested many lasting friends across a wide spectrum of society. It seems impossible that our 'not so gentle giant' has gone, like a great oak felled in the wind, without so much as a word or the big spade of a handshake, his downfall a rapid worsening of a chest infection. Patently, his guardian angel had gone off duty, a serious dereliction of service, for Elly still had lots to surprise us all. We never know what's around the corner and can only be thankful to have shared his life and the stimulating adventures of bygone years.

Jimmy Marshall.

PROCEEDINGS OF THE CLUB

The following new members were admitted and welcomed to the Club in 2005-2006.

Stephen Ashworth, (27), NT Campsite Warden, Langdale, Cumbria.
Nick Carter, (35), Mountaineering Instructor, Aberdeen.
John C. Hine, (45), IT Consultant, Perth.
Niall McNair, (26), Occupational Therapist, Edinburgh.
David V. Nicholls, (56), Royal Marines (Rtd.), Tayport, Fife.
Vivian Scott, (24), Research Student, Edinburgh.
A. G. Scott Stewart, (35), Account Manager, Stewarton, Ayrshire.
James R. Thacker, (27), Mountaineering Instructor, Sheffield.

The 0ne-Hundreth-and-Sixteenth AGM and Dinner

The fickle snows of early winter were reduced to a few well-washed remnants as we gathered at Fort William for the 116th. AGM.

The early arrivals were able to watch Graham Little's excellent and intriguing slides of his recent trip to Pakistan – ironically idyllic in view of the recent devastation wrought on that part of the world. Donald Ballance also gave an interesting account of his traverse of Iceland. Other incidental entertainments available during the afternoon were a video-tape made at Ling on the occasion of the re-fuelling/ 50th.anniversary party and the outline plans for the proposed CIC extension.

There was a time when the AGM resembled a Blackcock lek with much display of opinions and flurries of motions and amendments. Nowadays we are more mature or civilised, or there is, thanks to our efficient Office-bearers, nothing much to get het up about. And so the AGM went smoothly with only the odd flicker of flame from ancient animosities. Financially, the Club seems to be in good health at the moment.

We have avoided having to pay retrospective tax but this liability will be incurred in future. The CIC extension proposals at last got under way with general agreement to seek outline planning permission for a 6m. x 6m. extension to replace the present porch and to include toilets, kitchen area and drying room. This particular saga still has a long way to run. One issue raised was the location of the printing of the Club's guidebooks. Charlie Orr's appeal for a Scottish printer was countered with the hard economics of printing abroad.

The campaign against the proposed high pylon transmission line was mentioned by Dave Broadhead and evoked general support.

The pre-Dinner piping was of a higher standard than we are accustomed to as the piper was not a Club member. The meal was of a high standard for these things. Colin Stead addressed the Club with due mention of the various adventures of Club Members during the year. Gordon Ross gave his usual rendition of the Club song, accompanied by Robin Campbell on surely the worst keyboard in the west. 'Dark Lochnagar' was also rousingly sung, continuing what has become a Club tradition.

The 'Toast to the Guests' was proposed by Gill Irvine – the first time this has been done by one of our lady members. (Gill is Andy Nisbet's GP - it has been said that that is a full-time job in itself.) She made a fine job of it with special mention of our Guest of Honour, Sir John Crofton of Crofton-Cummings fame and some medical renown. (Sir John is a lively ninety-three.) Ian Mitchell responded for the Guests with a lively and humorous speech although he made the mistake made by many Guest speakers before him by introducing a smidgeon of lavatory humour. The SMC doesn't go in for that kind of thing, at least not at its Dinners. After the speeches had concluded the Members got on with what they are good at – conviviality and conversation.

R.T. Richardson.

Ski-mountaineering Meet 2006.

Members present: Calum Anton, Donald Ballance, Bob Barton, Robin Chalmers, Ewan Clark, Neil Craig, Graham Dudley, Dave Howard, Colwyn Jones, Ann MacDonald, Peter MacDonald, Ken Moore, Tim Pettifer, Chris Ravey, Bob Reid, Brian Shackleton, Malcolm Slesser, Iain Smart, Anthony Walker.

The SMC ski-mountaineering meet was held on February16/17/18 2006. The venue was the well appointed Corrie Odhar House and The Chapel, both on the Corrour Estate which is on the eastern shores of Loch Ossian at an altitude of 390m.

The venue promised plenty of access to local Munros for skiing, and so it proved; Beinn na Lap, Sgor Gaibhre, Carn Dearg, Chno Dearg, Ben Alder and the ridge of Beinn Eibhinn, Aonach Beag and Carn Dearg – one excellent 5 star route from the SMC ski-mountaineering guidebook.

On the Thursday evening the advance party drove in through rain, then sleet as they reached the high point at 430m. on the land rover track which finally led to the estate buildings. Access to the meet was along a 12 mile mile land-rover track/ estate road from the A86 Laggan road near Moy Lodge and people were advised to use a 4x4 vehicle in case of snow and potholes. Otherwise snow chains and a shovel might be needed. Helicopter access is possible, as this is how the estate owners arrive, or so I am told. But prior permission is required to land on the estate. Seaplanes have also landed on Loch Ossian. An alternative (if the road was blocked) was by train to Corrour station and a pleasant, flat walk or ski along the shore of Loch Ossian to the house, or more energetically taking in Beinn na Lap en route.

On the clear, sunny Friday morning there was a light frost at the lochside with the mountains pristine white above the 550m. contour. Carrying skis up to 500m. next to the Allt a Choire Chreagaich they continued on skis south over the bealach of Mam Ban then up the wide west ridge of Sgor Gaibhre (955m.) a new Munro for some. From there they headed south to the delightfully and unusually named Meall na Meoig (868m.) of Beinn Pharlagain, a new Corbett for everyone. There was excellent snow especially on the north face of Sgor Gaibhre and by the end of the day there were trails of carved turns all over the place. An excellent day out.

Friday night saw the remaining members arrive from across Scotland, and further afield. The Chapel has been converted in the style of a 1950's ski lodge and, as the more mature members were billeted there, it was an education to experience them in what must be their natural habitat. Overnight the temperature fell to -5 celsius.

Next morning the 19 members and their guests scattered from Corrour. Nine ascended the ridge of Beinn Eibhinn (1102m.) – living up to it's name of delightful hill – in superb conditions with diminishing numbers continuing along to Aonach Beag(1116m.), Geal Charn(1132m.), a descent to Bealach Dubh and a final ascent of Ben Alder(1148m.). There was great snow cover on the plateau and it felt like skiing in true Alpine conditions with virtually no wind and golden sun. Having the ski-tracks of another party to follow off the summit of Ben Alder gave a speedy descent and a return to the cottages just after dusk. A total round of 22km. and 1400m. of ascent. Ben Alder and adjacent peaks saw a number of ski ascents while others drove to Corrour station and climbed Leum Uilleim(906m.). Five members walked directly east up the Uisge Labhair from Corrour then skinned up Ben Alder via the NW Shoulder from Beallach Cumhann. They also enjoyed the snow over the plateau and all agreed it was like skiing in the Alps, with virtually no wind, sunshine, fantastic views and great scenery!

The descent off Ben Alder was pleasant and variably challenging, depending on the skis being used. Snow quality ranged from light powder, packed powder through to wind crust. On returning to the Bealach Cumhann, three traversed the high ground over Beinn Chumhainn(901m.), Meall a Bhealaich(865m.), Sgor Choinnich(929m.) and Sgor Gaibhre. The best snow of the day was on the North slope of Sgor Gaibhre. A memorable descent on great snow with the orange sun slowly dipping below the horizon, before finishing on the patchy snow of the valley floor.

On Sunday morning the 19 members again left from Corrour. Carn Dearg (941m.) was quickly ticked by a party of two and they passed a group of five continuing on to Sgor Gaibhre. This group of five had headed up Carn Dearg via Coire Creagach. It was a windier day with more cloud, but surprisingly good visibility. However, the tops were not so pleasant for hanging around, much better to keep moving. They descended Carn Dearg via the North Slope into the Coire Creagach on great powdery snow tucked up in the corrie steeps. Excellent skiing and the best of the trip. A long climbing traverse across the north slopes via Mam Ban led back to the summit of Sgor Gaibhre where once again they enjoyed another good ski down the north face and back across the patchy snow and hummocky lumps of Allt a Choire Chreagaich to Corrour lodge. It has to be said the conditions for skiing were pretty good. The powder on Sunday on the north slope of Carn Dearg was described as being as good as any in the Alps!

Beinn na Lap(937m.) saw a heroic mass ascent by the five experienced members of the group. The estimated combined age of the party was 350 years and they enjoyed magnificent views from the summit. Others drove up the road to go to Meall Garbh(977m.) and ChnoDearg(1047m.).

Colwyn Jones.

Easter Meet 2006 – Kyle

The meet was held at Kyle Hotel and a late Easter promised good clear days with fresh snow on the hills. With a wide range of temperature and a few sunny spells, the cold westerly wind brought rain and sleet higher up the mountains. Members still ventured onto the hills over a wide area, ranging from Skye to Affric and Torridon. On Sunday evening Malcolm Slesser and Jane King, who had sailed from Oban, joined members at the hotel and afterwards entertained on their boat.

Members explored new areas and climbs including Ben Sgritheall, Sgurr an Airgid, The Saddle via the Forcan Ridge, Moruisg, Beinn na Caillich, Beinn Dearg Mor, Beinn Dearg Bheag, Sgurr Gaorsaic, An Staonach, Garbh-bheinn and Belig, Other areas included the Quiraing, Coire Lagan and Glen Carron at Coulags through to Torridon via the Bealach na Lice.

Those present: President Colin Stead, Robin Campbell, Brian Fleming, Peter MacDonald and guest Calum Anton, Malcolm Slesser and guest Jane King, Iain Smart, Bob Aitken, Dick Allen, Paul Brian and guest David Stone, Dave Broadhead, Robin Chalmers, John Fowler and guest Helen Forde, John Hay, Bill McKerrow, and Roger Robb.

Dick Allen.

JMCS REPORTS

Glasgow Section: Although membership has reduced to 96, the newer members are taking an active part in the club, and meets are well attended. Weekend meets are held fortnightly on average, and the Ibrox climbing wall is visited weekly by a number of members. There are regular pub meets in the West End, which allow weekend plans to be made, and which serve to introduce new members to the club.

The club was blessed with some excellent winter conditions in 2005 and members reported a successful string of winter ascents.

The club meet at Easter to Elphin heralded the start of the rock-climbing season with four days of climbing at Reiff, Ardmair, and Camas Mor, a mass ascent of the Old Man of Stoer, and some memorable evenings. Summer saw some good dry conditions and equally good ascents - *Cougar, Vampire* and *Goliath* on the Dubh Loch and a highly productive trip over the border to Scafell - most notably *White Wizard, Ichabod, Hells Groove, Saxon, Dyad* and *Centaur.*

Officials elected: *President,* Claire Gilchrist; *Secretary,*Jeremy Morris; 38b Queen Square, Glasgow G41 2AZ. *Coruisk Hut Bookings*, John Fenemore; 7 Campsie Road, Lindsayfield, East Kilbride G75 9GE. www.jmcs.org.uk

Jeremy Morris.

Perth Mountaineering Club (JMCS Perth Section)

Wind, crawling and horizontal precipitation seem to have been recurring themes of the year's meets. It was not an unusually wet summer by any standards but it seemed that the gods were not smiling on the Perth Mountaineering Club. That said, club members showed great resolve in going out in all weathers. The April meet was a case in point when, despite severe conditions, 13 hardy members climbed nine Munros and several Corbetts between them during a weekend based at Strawberry Cottage in Glen Affric.

The summer backpacking meet to the Trotternish Ridge in Skye was similarly afflicted.

The disappointing conditions meant that little winter climbing was done during the club meets. However, one couple did manage an ascent of *Central Gully* on Ben Lui on a February day meet, and a group of three traversed the Five Sisters Ridge in icy conditions in March. Also worthy of note was the ascent of *Tower Ridge* on Ben Nevis by the Nicolls in August.

The meet based at the Ling Hut in late August was blessed with a rare clear day on the Saturday enabling those attending to reach some of the more remote hills by bike – hotly pursued by clouds of midges by all accounts!

With many of the active club members now having completed their Munros, some meets have been more geared to Corbetts, such as the successful meet to Resipole in Ardgour. A day meet to Glen Lyon in September also presented the opportunity to tackle the Ben Lawers hills from the north, thus avoiding the crowds, and providing a new perspective to these well known favourites.

The annual dinner meet in November, 2004 was held at the outstanding venue of Mar Lodge. Some sixty members attended to celebrate the Club's 75th Anniversary with, in particular, the welcome presence of some of the Club's more senior members. The weekend was generally very cold and bright so there were ample opportunities for working up an appetite before the festivities.

Officials elected: *President,* Irene MacGregor, *Vice President,* Donald Barrie, *Secretary,* Sue Barrie, Glensaugh Lodge, Laurencekirk, *Aberdeenshire, AB30 1HB 01561 340673, Treasurer, Pam Dutton, Newsletter Editor,* Des Bassett, *Meets Convenor,* Beverly Bain, *Committee Members,* Chris Hine, Phil Taylor, Ray Lee.

London Section: A varied meets list and a range of activities characterised a year in which several members were active abroad. The traditional January President's meet took place in a damp Bethesda with a sprinkling of snow on the tops and this was followed by a well-attended Scottish meet first at Jock Spot's and then at the Raeburn Hut, from where routes were climbed on Creag Meagaidh and in the Northern Corries in less than ideal winter conditions. The more sensible members headed south to the Ecrins, for short walk-ins and sun burned quality ice-climbing.

There were successful meets in Pembroke and at Stanage, which saw a large proportion of the club active on the rock, climbing a variety of classic routes, in between visits to the Lake District and North Wales.

Of special note was the five-week trek by John Steele, Barbara Gibbons, Trevor Burrows, Andy Hughes and Rod Kleckham in the Everest region that culminated in ascents of Mera and Island Peaks. A similar trip is planned to the Annapurna region in 2007. The year ended as it had started in North Wales, where 32 members enjoyed a very pleasant club dinner at Plas y Nant and unseasonably fine weather, with climbing on warm rock at Tremadoc, and scrambling on the ridges of Snowdon, taking in great views for this time of year.

Officials elected: *Secretary,* Chris Bashforth; *President,* John Firmin; *Hut Custodian,* Rod Kleckham; 01252 721 049; *Treasurer,* Dave Hughes; Meets secretary, Dan Calverley, 01457 856 826.

Chris Bashforth.

Edinburgh Section: Membership is currently 82 including a number of new and associate members. Rock climbing, winter climbing and hill walking are the most popular activities, with ski-mountaineering and mountain-biking also being pursued by members.

The section continues to hold Wednesday evening meets indoors during the winter months at the Heriot-Watt University climbing wall and outdoors during the summer at local crags around Edinburgh. Ratho Adventure Centre is now the wet weather alternative during the summer months and Alien Rock is also popular with members.

May 2005 brought good weather and a well attended meet on Arran, camping at the Glen Rosa site. Despite the time of year a few midges were present but this did not stop a number of classics being climbed including *South Ridge Direct*, *Souwester Slabs*, *Arctic Way*, *Pagoda Ridge*, *Mosque* and *Blank*. Successful meets were also held in the Lake District and North Wales.

Winter meets started in December with Inbhirfhaolain in Glen Etive and Muir of Inverey in January. Winter conditions had not really arrived but members made use of the time for some Munro-bagging.

Our Annual Dinner saw us back at the Atholl Arms Hotel in Blair Atholl. A good meal was followed by a memorable after-dinner speech by the SMC's Malcolm Slesser.

Our huts continue to be popular with the Smiddy in particular experiencing a rise in demand. The section's long association with Jock Spot's near Newtonmore came to an end on April, 30, 2006 with the termination of the lease.

The joint SMC Eastern section/JMCS slide nights continue to be well supported by both clubs. The venue is now the South Side Community Centre at 117 Nicolson Street, Edinburgh, at 7:30pm on the second Tuesday of the month, from October to March.

Officials elected: *Hon. President*, John Fowler; *Hon. Vice-President*, Euan Scott; *President*, Brian Finlayson; *Vice-President*, Patrick Winter (also Meets Secretary); *Treasurer*, Bryan Rynne; *Secretary*, Neil Cuthbert, 25 Plewlands Gardens, Edinburgh. E-mail – (secretary@edinburghjmcs.org.uk; *Webmaster*; Davy Virdee, *Smiddy Custodian*; Helen Forde, 30 Reid Terrace, Edinburgh; *Ordinary Members* – Susan Marvell, Stewart Bauchop.

SMC AND JMCS ABROAD

Europe

COLWYN JONES REPORTS: Ann MacDonald, Brian Shackleton and myself spent a week ski-touring in Switzerland leaving the UK on April 16. Flying to Zurich, we met fellow SMC member Mark Litterick and spent the next day skiing in Andermatt in low visibility and high avalanche risk. Heavy rain next day dictated moving via Davos and St Moritz (both closed for the season) to the fine Diavolezza Hut (1973m.). The avalanche conditions restricted skiing to on, or close to the piste which was excellent powder. We snatched an ascent of Munt Pers (3207m.) as a consolation during a brief window in the weather, then had to return to the perfect powder on the quiet pistes again! With the main goal, the Piz Bernina too dangerous to attempt and an outbreak of cabin fever, we headed east, to the end of the railway line at Scuol in the Engadine. There we met Swiss locals Anya and Kobe who reported a good forecast which meant a late night trek up to the excellent Chamanna Tuoi hut. In glorious sunshine next morning we had a superb trip to the summit of DreilÑnderspitze (3197m.) then an equally good ski down in super spring snow.

Next day, with faces liberally smeared with sun tan cream, Piz Buin (3312m.) was the summit reached with another fine ski descent back down to the hut. Then back to the valley floor ready for an early morning train journey back to Zurich. The result was a week of poor weather early on, excellent powder and with two excellent ski-touring days to finish.

BOB RICHARDSON reports: This year Beaton's Annual Ice Circus went to Italy in early February. Four SMC members (Jim Beaton, Doug Lang, Bob Richardson and Des Rubens) and four others (Bill MacMillan, Wendell Martin, John Orr and Duncan Walker) negotiated the labyrinth of Geneva Airport and went to the Scottish ice-climber's second home at Cogne.

Based at the excellent Hotel La Baume in Valnontey we spent a week enjoying the varied ice routes in the area. This year the conditions were thinner than usual with only a few of the routes at Lillaz being present but Valnontey provided enough ice to keep us occupied until the weather broke on the last two days.

This area is well known to the ambitious ice-climber but I can recommend it to the more mature as well. The scenery is pleasant, the woods abound in tame chamois, ibex and langlauf skiers. More importantly, the approaches are relatively flat and the routes well provided with rappel chains. A variety of routes were climbed with Des and Wendell searching out the more testing, e.g. *Parti Droite* while we less ambitious enjoyed a number of routes at around Scottish 5. The highlight of the trip was the atmospheric *Cascade de Lillaz*. If you haven't been, sharpen your picks, get some good ice-screws and go.

COLWYN JONES reports: Four SMC members enjoyed a fine spell of settled weather for ski- mountaineering in the Monta Rosa area. After an easy flight to Geneva, Ann MacDonald, Colwyn Jones and Mark Litterick met in Saas Grund on April, 13, 2006 to celebrate Easter by eating lots of pizza.

The Hohsaas lift was used early next morning to reach the 3200m. contour. The normal route up the Trift glacier on the NW face of the Weissmeis (4017m.) was heavily crevassed and the chosen ascent route was up a steep, broad gully at the right side of the glacier. They continued up the normal summit route after reaching the west ridge and eventually achieved the summit in windy conditions, with most enduring a background headache. The descent back to the Gletscherpiste was initially hard wind-blown snowpack, but there was a softer snow in the gully which allowed a splendid ski descent before reaching the well groomed, patrolled runs. Next morning, the three attempted to ascend the Alphubel (4206m.) from Saas Fee. They reached Langflue on the first uplift and had skinned up to a height of 3900m. before the increasing cloud and wind strength forced a retreat through the crevasses in a whiteout. Increasing cloud in the afternoons was typically experienced each day of the trip.

Brian Shackleton arrived early that evening and next morning on the April, 16, all four attempted to climb the angular Fletschorn (3996m.). In a light cover of fresh snow they branched off the Weissmiespiste, climbing through the morraine to reach a height of 3200m. before high winds caused them to abandon the ascent. On the positive side this allowed a prolonged, pleasant lunch in the Saas Grund ski area and an early arrival at Tasch later that evening.

On April,17, they celebrated the end of Easter with a busy ascent of the Breithorn (4164m.) in splendid conditions and even better views. They then skied over the frontier to the excellent Ayas Hut (3420m.). Next morning they climbed Castor (4228m.) by the West flank and the superb airy North ridge. A guided party, attempting the ridge in what can only be described as traditional style, delayed the ascent. The ridge was so narrow they had mounted it à cheval and the guide was attempting to haul his two be-straddled clients up the ridge. Their use of alloy crampons and lightweight touring axes proved ineffective on the hard blue ice of the summit ridge, hence this traditional technique. However, it allowed Colwyn, who was leading, plenty of time to cut a line of buckets on the side of the ridge and place ice screws for solid protection. On finally reaching the summit there was no breeze and fantastic views in all directions.

After another comfortable night in the Ayas hut, the few centimetres of fresh snow which had fallen overnight provided a fantastic ski down to St. Jacques. After a short walk down through the pinewoods to the village, they caught the bus 2km. down the road to Frachay. There the ski uplift over the Col de Bettaforca to Stafel allowed them up to 3200m. for an awkward traverse over to the Rifugio Citta di Mantova (3400m.).

The Mantova hut provided another good base and on April, 20, they skied up to the Col de Lys from where they climbed both Zumstein (4563m.) and Signalkuppe (4554m.) with splendid views in all directions. There was a reasonable fall of new snow next day and the threatening cloud farther south dictated a frantic early morning dash over to the Monta Rosa hut (2795m.) via the Col de Lys (4248m.) as the weather closed in behind them.

Next morning they returned to Zermatt via the Gorner Glacier and home.

Paklenica – Croatia

Heike Puchan and Brian Whitworth report: The Stirling-based Anglo-German section of the Glasgow JMCS had been looking for a venue for the traditional early summer trip when the latest edition of *Klettern* popped through the letterbox.

Only a couple of pages in, after the adverts for the sauerkraut flavoured dehydrated meals, was a rather striking full page spread of a huge cliff – 1500ft. high, or rather 500m. to give it its full euro-measurement, and half-a-mile long. Might be worth a trip, we thought. All very inspiring but what the heck is it? Where is it? And, will it be full of Germans?

Turns out that the cliff was 'Anica kuk'in the Paklenica National Park. Turns out that it is in Croatia. And, yes, to the third one. A bit of web-surfing turned up flights from Edinburgh to Zagreb for £200, including a stop in Frankfurt. Perfect chance to pick up all one's favourite German delicacies from the underground supermarket – Brezels and Bratwurst, mmm. A hire-car was also pre-arranged for a bit less than the standard euro rate, and so with our freshly ATM'd Kuna (beavers tails – the traditional Croatian barter currency), we were off. A couple of hours down the new autobahn, with only Germans and Austrians for company, led us with great ease to Starigrad Paklenica, a strange little post-communism holiday resort on the coast, about 100km. North of Split. Some dodgy English on the websites had led us to believe there was camping in this place, along with bears, vultures and snakes. While we never saw the wildlife, a quick look around suggested that almost every back garden seemed to be a campsite, and so with great reluctance we checked ourselves into the garden closest to Dinko's, the local bar – a full 50ft. away.

An evening on the local pop was comfortably light on the wallet at one euro a pint, although less so on the ears, as the resident famous Slovene mountaineer demonstrated his horse-like burping impressions. I believe he has since been rescued off Nanga Parbat communicating solely in 'horsish'.

The following week made a pleasant change from the usual Scottish 'drive for two hours to climb for 30 minutes before it rains'. The main climbing area, Velika Paklenica, lies less than two miles from the village. So you drive up to the bottom of the gorge, hand over your 10 beavers for park entry (less than £10 for the week) and decide whether you can be bothered to walk more than five minutes to get beyond the heaving throng of Germans that beat you to the gorge sport climbs – anything from one to five pitches – or are you feeling brave enough to scale a route on the mighty 'Anica kuk'.

Being trad-heads at heart, we generally favoured the long walk in, all 45 minutes of it, to the big cliff. Climbs up there require gear. Ignore any comments about 'bolted'. All the big routes we did were bolted to Croatian standard rather than the efficient German standard, so if you like 5m. run-outs between 'haken' with the difficult bit always just before a bolt, this is the place for you.

We did two of the famous trilogy of routes on the cliff. *Mosoraski* was a pleasant ramble up several pitches before a slippery F5+ crux pitch pops you out near the 2500ft. summit. The other, *Velebitaski*, was a bit more full on with the F6a+ crux falling admirably to Scottish winter ethics (get up it, anything goes). This was definitely the best longer route we did, following the easiest line up some very steep terrain. The other long local classic of *Domzalski* on the elephants-bum-like Stup was also enjoyed, notably for its under-graded slippy, slabby crux.

As the week wore on the temperatures got hotter and hotter. Consequently, the starts got more and more Alpine to enable climbing in the cool of morning. Paklenica is a great location for most of the year as there is always a sunny side and a shady side

When the heat gets too much there is always swimming. The gorge itself has a picturesque burn flowing down it with some great swimming spots, ideally situated at the end of a tiring descent down the back of 'Anica kuk'. By the time you have dried out, you will be back in the village, which is only a short ice-cream away from the coast. Just bring some flip-flops for the pebble beaches.

The village has a couple of supermarkets selling everything you could need including sun-cream, flip-flops and cold drinks, mainly aimed at the visiting, beach-lining hordes from the Austro-Prussian empire. However, there is also a climbing shop for those forgotten essentials, like gear!

The walking looks lovely, although we never got around to it. There was just too much climbing to be done.

But whatever you do, if you go to Dinko's, avoid Humar. He burps like a horse.

Drygalskifjord, South Georgia. Photo: David Nichols.
On the Neumayer Glacier, South Georgia. Photo: David Nichols.

Greece – Mount Olympus

Dave Broadhead reports: Mountaineering objectives and family holidays seldom overlap in our household, until last year (July 2005) when we decided to visit Greece. Friends of Moira's in the LSCC were very enthusiastic about their ascent of Mount Olympus (2917m.) earlier in the year, and with some careful persuasion our teenage offspring were gradually won over to the idea.

We arrived in Litohoro (305m.) on a Saturday evening, and were lucky to find a hotel room. Situated at the foot of the Enipeas River gorge with the Olympus massif towering behind, this pleasant little town is easily reached by car or public transport. Next morning we drove another 18km. to the end of the road at Prionia (1100m.), the start of the mountain trail. A steady three-hour climb up through pleasant shady woodland took us to Spilios Agapitos, Refuge A (2100m.). Perched on a ridge in the trees, this proved a perfect spot to spend the afternoon relaxing or exploring the neighbouring corries.

The Greek version of an alpine start proved very civilised, and we had no difficulty in starting the next stage of the climb at 7.30am. next morning, ahead of most other parties. Soon out of the trees, the scenery started to open out as we gained height, giving us a better appreciation of the geography of our surroundings. In the absence of a map we were simply following the sign-posted path, grateful for the excellent weather. Much of the massif is a Cairngorm-like plateau, cleft with deep corries. Our goal, Mytikas (2917m.), the highest summit was like a bit of the Cuillin grafted on, with a few hundred metres of easy but interesting scrambling leading to the top, which we reached at about 10.20am. Superb views all around, but cloud was already starting to build up, and we were happy to stay ahead of the guided parties that were appearing. Requiring no specialist equipment, (I did the whole climb in shorts and trainers, with a fleece and long trousers for the cool of the evening at the hut) I would recommend this short trip to any keen hill-goer on holiday in Greece.

John Steele reports: In July 2005 four London JMCS members held a pre-trek training meet in Kandersteg. Peaks climbed were Stand, Frundenhorn, Blumisalp and the fine snow/ice face of Morgenhorn. Members: Steve Gladstone (Leader), John Steele, Barbara Gibbons and Trevor Burrows.

Greenland

Colwyn Jones reports: Four SMC members – Ann MacDonald, Colwyn Jones, Chris Ravey and Jim Thomson, headed off to The Roscoe Mountains in Liverpool Land, North East Greenland. 'The Delectable Arctic Playground.' (Slesser, SMCJ, 2001).

"A Gruffalo, what's a Gruffalo?" I naively asked. Chris and Jim looked shocked.

"What's a Gruffalo? Don't you know? He has terrible tusks, and terrible claws and terrible teeth in his terrible jaws!"

"I think I can see some," said Ann looking at the three of us. Gruffalos featured heavily on the trip, being blamed for every mishap by the two fathers, Chris and Jim. Reading about Gruffalos in children's storybooks most evenings, doesn't mean they exist.

In our Global village, access to north-east Greenland is now fairly routine.

On Friday, July 23, 2004, Ann and Colwyn flew from Glasgow international airport on a routine Icelandair Boeing 757 flight to Keflavik. They caught the 'Flybus' to Reykjavik where the damp atmosphere seemed to presage conditions later in the trip, it was raining heavily and Colwyn had guaranteed Ann a fortnight on the Arctic Riviera. The hotel was full of young Icelanders who, it seems, gravitate to Reykjavik for weekends of binge drinking. Their noisy carousing allowed Ann and Colwyn to note that it stayed light all night.

Next morning, a Fokker 50 flew from Reykjavik domestic airport to Kulusuk,

Looking east to Vagakallen from the summit of Haveren, Lofoten Islands. Photo: David Ritchie.

NE Face of Middagstinden (Scottish V,5), Lofoten Islands, Climber Neil McGougan. Photo: David Ritchie.

the airport that serves Tasiilaq in the Ammassalik district of Greenland (formerly Angmagssalik). The flight took two hours, ending on an alarmingly short runway at Kulusuk. They disembarked, admired the skin of a polar bear which had been shot nearby and then walked around Kulusuk village for an hour glancing nervously behind them every few steps. They re-embarked and in less than two hours the Fokker landed at Constable Point at around 5pm. The helicopter was busy ferrying locals to the settlement at Ittoqqortoormiit (Scoresbysund) so they found their air-freight and got the tent pitched on the tundra just to the north-east of the airstrip. Collecting the hired gun from the airport manager was straightforward, he was too busy to instruct them on how to use it. However, the thought of employing it as a rudimentary club against an inquisitive polar bear is a strong motivator to develop one's amateur weaponry skills. The evening was spent introducing Ann to the flammable – or otherwise – combination of the MSR stove and Jet A1 fuel. The steady, but cool, breeze deterred mosquitoes as the party enjoyed the beautiful Arctic sun, which didn't quite set.

Overnight they heard three birds; the quacking of some unidentified duck, a Snipe humming and finally a Sandpiper. Some Ravens were also flying around enjoying a prolonged breakfast. Unable to afford to pay for the airport to open on the Sunday they spent the day walking along the sandy Fjord shore with its amazing profusion of timber and detritus. The plastic detritus was all Danish or Greenlandic from the writing, and the presumption was that it had floated round from Ittoqqortoormiit. Back at the tent the helicopter pilot was out practising his golf and supervised firearms training was later successfully undertaken. The forecast for Monday was poor and the golfing pilot mentioned flying was unlikely the next day, which was a pointless discussion as it turned out.

On Monday, it did rain for most of the day but it offered the chance to rest, unwind from the frenetic pace of civilisation and adjust to Arctic time. The mosquitoes had been out the night before and the first medical emergency arose. Ann had a very swollen left parotid gland, and the differential diagnosis included mumps, although comparison of serology during the acute and convalescent phases was not locally available. However, it was just some impressive, though superficial swelling, caused by a mosquito, or perhaps a Gruffalo bite. Tuesday, July 27, was wind and rain again. Hopeful signs of clearing weather arrived, then left, but a Fokker 50 arrived from Reykjavik later in the day as Constable point has a low visibility landing system.

Wednesday, July 28, and they were rudely awakened by early helicopter flights. Three came in from Ittoqqortoormiit. It was a beautiful morning. After breakfast and two days stuck in a tent they took two of the older resident husky dogs for a walk up a hill to the north-east of the airfield. It was a lovely Arctic summer's day with stunning views, but lingering too long over said views, they were still on the hill when Chris and Jim's flight arrived.

After hurried packing it was their turn and all four were flown due east over Hurry Fjord in the Bell Jet Ranger to the Roscoe mountains on the South Hans Glacier, some 15 minutes. away (readers should note the names are those suggested in Slesser's 2001 article). Landing initially on a very crevassed area which was flat (The low tail rotor on Jet Rangers apparently, means a nervous pilot) they tried a second time and disembarked, but had to rope up and carry all food and gear to a more benign area. Civilisation flew off and they got established but found their food supplies had been pilfered. Most of the cakes were missing, it might have been a dog with a sweet tooth, but there were more plausible two legged culprits.

Next morning was again a stunning day and they walked from basecamp, climbed over a problematic bergeschrund to a steep gully leading to West Col. (GPS 1195m. N. 70° 40'27.2" W. 021° 59'02.2"). Fine views to the coast dictated a lunch stop and they then headed south over jumbled rocks to the summit tower of Tvillingerne (The Twins). A short pitch of difficult climbing got them to the highest easterly point (1445m. aneroid, 1447m. GPS. N. 70° 40'15" W. 021° 58'52.1".) There were good views to the south and across Hurry Fjord. To the east the pack-ice still guarded the coast. Leaving the summit at 16.00hrs after finding an empty jar of marmite hidden under a cairn, the weather came in with heavy cloud in the evening and the rain started as they got to bed at 23.00hrs. They had bagged the first peak in this 'delectable Arctic playground,' 1000m. of scree and 30m. of rock!

Rain overnight, but it finally stopped at 14.00hrs. though it was still too windy to sit out. The rain continued intermittently for the remainder of the afternoon and evening with Gruffalos idntified as the likely cause. Saturday July 31 and the sun was on the tent by 07.20hrs. They went to the head of the South Hans Glacier to the Col de Pisse then traversed to the moraine on the south side of the Grete Glacier to lay in a food dump for the planned return to the coast.

On Sunday, August 1, they were again awakened by the heat of the sun on the tent at about 07.30hrs – not a bad way to start the day. The wind was much lighter with a clear view down to the sparkling blue waters of Hurry Fjord. Camped on the ice they were using ice-screws to secure the tents. However, as they might need them for climbing they spent a short time making Abalakov anchors to hold the tents down. One person tried to screw a nice new sharp Black Diamond ice-screw through his ice-chilled finger. However, the cold didn't seem to reduce the impressive, profuse bleeding. Within a short time the ice was stained pink around the tents, raising speculation about the acute sense of smell of polar bears. However, keen to get up another peak, they set off with the reassurance that as his finger was still bleeding he was clearly not empty, yet.

They all returned to West Col and scrambled up the easy, but worryingly, loose peak to the north of the Col. They are not sure of the name of the peak but it was 1420m. aneroid, GPS 1412m. N. 70° 40'42.3" W. 021° 59'11.5". It had a large flat summit area with a vertical drop off the north-east face and the rock looked like it was better quality. Again the views were stunning in all directions. There is no doubt about the beauty of the Arctic. They returned to camp over the deteriorating bergschrund to find the food had been raided. Was it a polar bear or a Gruffalo that had broken open the cardboard food boxes and helped themselves to the tastier morsels? They found only Raven footprints.

Next morning, the Ravens returned, no doubt spying for the Gruffalos. They were just getting the rifle ready when the birds flew off. Deciding to strike camp, abandon the blood stained ice and head over to the food dump, it was a late start with heavy packs via the Col de Pisse on a glacier walk to camp 2 at the head of the Grete Glacier (780m. N. 70° 30'24.2" W. 021° 56' 36.3").

Despite the appalling weather, blamed on the Gruffalos, the two highest peaks in the Roscoe Mountains were climbed. Farther south the peaks were poor for climbing, being largely composed of loose scree when approached as described. It might be an Arctic ski-mountaineering paradise in the Spring and if we can avoid the Gruffalos, it would be worth returning to check it out! All in all, an easy way to access Arctic mountaineering, and when the conditions allowed, the views were stunning.

Reference

Slesser M. 2001, A Mountaineer's Guide to the Roscoe Bjerge, SMCJ, vol.192, pp.731-735.

Greenland – Rytterknaegten

Peter MacDonald reports: As reported in last year's Journal, Bill Wallace and five others were in the Karale Glacier region of East Greenland in April 2005. For some of the party it was their second attempt to reach this area: the first, fondly referred to as the SMC Kulusuk Airport Expedition 2002, had been thwarted by bad weather and logistical problems.

At first, it looked as though that experience was to be repeated, but this time we did reach our destination, and in the few days of good weather explored the great expanses of the Karale. This magnificent cirque is dominated by one peak, Rytterknaegten (2020m.), a superbly shaped spire reminiscent of the Matterhorn from certain angles, or of the fantasy mountain at the start of Paramount films. It was first climbed as long ago as 1938 by a Swiss party including, Andre Roch, which made many other first ascents including Mount Forel ,the second highest peak in Greenland. The mountains here are generally less suitable for ski ascents than those of the Roscoe Bjerge, where our group had been in 2003, and the route out more strenuous as we discovered when the weather closed in again – but that's another story! We all felt immensely privileged to have witnessed such scenery and for those of us who are now left, it was also a privilege to have been with Bill on his last trip to Greenland.

Himalaya – Ama Dablam

Sandy Allan reports: I led the 'Team Ascent' Ama Dablam Expedition during Autumn 2005.

The team comprised of six, Kathryn Grindrod (SMC member/Sport Scotland Avalanche information service observer), Dr Janis Tait, Dr Alistair Meikle, Chris Cookson and Rob Sturdy. We climbed the mountain by the South-West Ridge.

Departing the UK on October 16 we flew to Kathmandu, Nepal and then on to Lukla on October 20. Rather than going direct to Ama Dablam base camp we trekked towards Everest base camp and Kallipatar and then over the Kogma La (5535m.) in order to assist acclimatisation. We arrived at Ama Dablam base camp (4800m.) on October 30, with everyone in good spirits. After a rest day we carried equipment to Camp1and returned to Base Camp. On November 3, the team ascended to Camp 1, spent the night there and then ascended to the Yellow Tower, traditional site for Camp 2 and returned to Base Camp. Finally, on the 6th the team all set off for a summit attempt, staying at Camp 1 and then Camp 3 and attempting the summit on November 8.

All the team members got to Camp 3 (6400m.) Dr J. Tait and Rob Sturdy ran out of energy at about 6500m. and turned back to Camp 3 at around 8.30 am. Myself, Kathryn Grindrod, Chris Cookson, Alistair Meikle, Sonam Sherpa and De Nima Sherpa (Sirdar) all summitted between 10am and 10.30am in cold and windy weather. All members returned back to Camp1 that same evening, returning safely to Base Camp on November 9. We would like to thank, *Mountain Equipment*, *Patagonia* and *Rab Down Equipment* for their support.

This was Kathryn Grindrod's first ascent in the Himalaya, and my second ascent of Ama Dablam, having climbed the South-West ridge during a winter ascent in 1999.

JOHN STEELE REPORTS: In October 2005, five London JMCS members visited the Everest region of Nepal. Starting from the roadhead at Jiri, a two-week approach was made to Mera base camp and the peak climbed shortly thereafter.

Due to heavy snow a retreat was made into the Solu Khumbu and the tourist route followed to Dingboche. Several days later Island Peak was climbed from high camp. Members: John Steele (Leader), Barbara Gibbons, Rod Kleckham, Trevor Burrows and Andy Hughes.

This was a private expedition manned exclusively by people from the Nepalese village of Salle (whom we support). If you are planning a trip, contacts can be made at dantamang@yahoo.com and bluesky@mail.com.np.

Australasia

JOHN STEELE REPORTS: Barbara Gibbons and I spent most of March 2004 in Tasmania. Our main exploration was a 10-day trek across the Central Highland region.

We followed the Overland Track, starting at Cradle Valley and finishing at Derwent Bridge (Lake St. Clare). Peaks climbed along the way were: Cradle Mountain, Barn Bluff, Mt. Oakleigh, Mt. Ossa (the highest) and Acropolis.

Other forages were made to Mt. Anne in the South, the remote South-West Track and the Totem Pole sea-stacks on the rugged south-east coast. Tasmania is a truly beautiful, wild and remote island where conservation is paramount. A fantastic trip.

Africa

DEREK PYPER reports: In February, 2006 along with Hugh Spencer of the Etchachan Club, I visited the Ruwenzori Mountains in Uganda where we spent 10 days walking from hut to hut in the most appalling conditions either of us has experienced. It rained every day which turned a wet place – at the best of times – into an overall bog.

It proved quite exhausting walking, or teetering, for miles over deep bogs on 'paths' of slim, smooth and slippery branches where the penalty for a false move was unthinkable.

Mount Speke (4890m.) was climbed in mist, rain and later snow – no view.

We will never moan about Scottish bog-trotting again.

REVIEWS

High Endeavours – The Life and Legend of Robin Smith: Jimmy Cruikshank. (Canongate, 2005, hardback, 374pp. ISBN 1 84195 5589, £26.99).

Some can climb, some can write but only a very few can do both at the highest level. Robin Smith was one of that few. As one of the greatest mountaineers Scotland has ever produced, and especially in the context of its current political, literary and artistic renaissance, his biography is long overdue.

This is a many-sided and rich book written, or as he modestly says 'compiled' by Smith's school friend and companion on his early climbs, Jimmy Cruikshank. My profound impression is that this is a labour of love. Cruikshank, an amiably self-effacing biographer, has assembled a massive number of sources and has spoken to and corresponded with a huge variety of people who knew Smith. From this mass of testimony, painstakingly gathered over many years, there emerges a fascinating study of a unique young man.

High Endeavours is divided into three parts: the first, comparitively short, deals with his early life and influences and takes us through Smith's schooldays and on to university. The second and longest part covers what we might call Smith's mature period including all the famous Scottish climbs and his best documented ascents in the Alps. The third part deals with the expedition to the Pamirs on which he met his death.

The meat of the book is in Parts I and II. In these Cruikshank sensitively traces the birth and growth of a singular personality. His father, we learn, died when he was young. His mother was a remarkable woman: free thinker, English graduate. The deep bond between Robin and his mother runs like a motif through the book. Constantly, wherever he is travelling, we see Smith sending his mother a stream of letters and cards, (one can't help wondering if Haston and co. seeing Smith scribbling away in some remote mountain hut realised what he was writing; letters to mother one suspects, were not high on the agenda of the Currie Boys). But Robin was sent away to school, at first in Crieff.

Here he was taken under the wing of Bee MacNeill who thought him "...loveable..., sensitive, friendly but happy on his own or in the little dream world that he liked." [1]

Apparently, he liked to walk by this kindly lady on nature walks. On one occasion when Robin had been clowning, Miss MacNeill "asked him if the other boys were not laughing at him and he said 'yes' but I could see from his grin that he couldn't care twopence". [2]

How perceptive she was. How well Cruikshank has done to quarry this out. How brilliantly MacNeill's observation suggests the showman and writer's love of an audience.

Then it was on to Edinburgh and that school of hard knocks George Watson's. Here he met Cruikshank who observed his early unhappiness at first hand: "... big-eyed twitchy glances swivelling nervously between teacher and floor." Robin, we are told, eventually "blended in with wary caution". [4]

Watson's, one supposes, fulfilled its primary function of crushing the crushable and forcing the spirited to rebel. Robin, of course, rebelled. The shy new-boy, towards the end of his school career, became the leader of the 'Scottish Chaoserians' (pronounced choss) and swept the polls in the school's mock general election. By contrast, the account of his stay in the 'bughut' (boarding house) run by the infamous 'Butch' Fleming is much darker and Cruikshank has provided excellent sources both in terms of the testament of contemporary pupils and, notably, Donald Scott who represented the more enlightened brand of young teacher then starting to replace an authoritarian generation.

Part I of *High Endeavours* gives us a vital insight into the early influences which shaped his personality and this journey of discovery is continued in Part II which substantially tells the story of Smith: climber, writer, and student of Philosophy.

There is no need for me to detail Cruikshank's thorough treatment of Robin's climbing career, it's all there: the climbs with Haston, the wonderful week with Marshall, the *Walker Spur* with Gunn Clark, the epic on the Fiescherwand with Goofy, *Yo-Yo, Shibboleth, Big-Top, The Needle...* they're all there for the reader's admiration and enjoyment. In some cases Cruikshank has provided accounts of the climbs from Smith's and also from his partner's perspective and this works well, notably in the 'alternative' accounts of Jimmy Marshall and Goofy. Cruikshank makes a compelling case for Smith's inclusion in the highest rank of Scottish mountaineers, but this biography does so much more than that.

Striving and seeking seem to lie at the heart of Smith's mystery. He wanted success in so many fields: climbing, writing, Logic, Philosophy. He was seeking enlightenment, but I think Cruikshank's work suggests (no more than this) that there is a deep psychological longing for the approbation of the father-figures he found in his world; deep down he had a need to belong in their world and to be recognised as belonging.

There are perhaps four or five men who stand out from this biography as fulfilling, in different settings and at different times, the father-figure role: Archie Hendry (nicknamed 'Papa' at Watson's), Jimmy Marshall, Willie Stewart (one of Robin's lecturers in Philosophy at Edinburgh), Geoff Dutton and finally, John Hunt. Now, it would be quite crass to to suggest that any of these men, in any sense, took over the role of Robin's deceased father – that is not suggested. At the same time it seems insensitive to deny that there is an element of fatherliness in these relationships, doubtless greater in some than in others, but present in all, and, crucially, sought by Smith.

Hendry it was, whose sharp tongue and sardonic manner hid a kindly streak, who gave Robin that vital early chance. (How many young lives have been shipwrecked for want of it?) How important it must have seemed that someone from the adult world beyond the family took him seriously. This is well attested in Smith's diary which Cruikshank uses to good effect.

The relationship with Marshall was somewhat different and undoubtedly a more equal one (indeed they got arrested together by the polis in Fort William!), but there still seems to be the fatherly echo. Marshall is constantly referred to as 'the Old Man' in Smith's famous article on that week on the Ben [5] and perhaps there is a deeper meaning in it than even he imagined. Marshall had a wild streak and perhaps acted as a half-way house between the untamed tiger-cubs of the Currie Boys – Haston et.al. – and the caustic fatherlieness of Hendry, but again we have the independent voice of Robin Campbell which also bears witness to Marshall's quazi-paternal qualities in the contemporary climbing scene. [6]

Geoff Dutton and Willie Stewart, in very different ways, also seem to have had a fatherly hand on Smith's shoulder. Dutton, as newly-appointed editor of this

Journal, had the task of encouraging Smith to contribute. In Cruikshank's book it is he who makes the most determined effort to appreciate Smith the writer: "...he calmly achieves his most cathartically black effects without a single oath. But these effects were built up by brains, imagination, wide reading and sheer hard work; he would sometimes write me several versions of a sentence, before its rhythm satisfied him." [7]

Smith is revealed as a highly conscious artist who "forwarded meticulously crafted barbs and stings..." [8] Dutton modestly denies knowledge of Smith the man and Smith the climber, but, in his writing "... we moved together..." [9]

Willie Stewart had the unenviable task of prizing Philosophy essays from Smith the undergraduate: "Dear Robin, All joking apart, I *want* your Leibniz essay – and in reasonable time...". But he didn't want it in order that Smith could scrape through the course, but rather to justify the awarding of "a class medal and the Hutchison Sterling Prize". [11] Smith was not only a talented writer, but a promising young philosopher. There are revealing expressions of affection in Stewart's letters to Smith. "I was very glad to get your letter. I liked your egg shaped angels. (I like you too also)."[12] This letter actually closes, "Love Willie." [13] Stewart notes "Robin's ability to attract Guardian Angels...". [14] In a letter to Cruikshank written much later, Stewart says: "Whether Robin regarded me as a father-figure is difficult to tell."[15] Of course what is going on at a deeper level in one's life is not obvious at the time, but Cruikshank's work helps us to appreciate that there was a pattern here.

I have claimed that the meat of this book is in Parts I and II. Here are the famous climbs, the notorious incidents, the rebelliousness, the bad behaviour, copying the Currie Boys and all that. Cruikshank ably guides us through a wealth of material while wisely leaving us to pass judgment. He certainly doesn't flinch from exploring the more controversial aspects of Smith's behaviour, and he reminds us that Smith was by no means universally popular during his lifetime.

The third part of *High Endeavours*, concerned almost exclusively with the expedition to the Pamirs, is a somewhat odd coda to the book. Increasingly, the biographer's voice fades out and we are left with a series of lengthy quotations from Cruikshank's sources. There are two ways of looking at this: one can, with some justification, say that Cruikshank is employing his habitual modesty and allowing his sources to tell the story themselves. On the other hand, this is, after all, Cruikshank's book, ought he not to tell the story? The reader must decide.

In any case, I wondered if the story of the expedition needed to be told at such length? What do the initial arguments about the aims of the expedition and who to include in it tell us about Robin Smith? Is a whole chapter on Wilfrid Noyce[16] really necessary?

However, the crucial act of character revelation in Part III for me is the insight we are given into Smith's relationship with John Hunt the expedition leader. To Smith, Sir John – the leader of the successful Everest Expedition, army officer – must have seemed the quintessential establishment man; a type against whom he had been prone to rebel. As the increasingly factious wranglings about who was to go on the expedition reached their climax, Smith, still let us remember, hardly more than a student, wrote a letter to Hunt in which youthful spiritedness bordered on sheer cheek. Hunt, wise and tolerant, chooses not to slap him down as perhaps he deserved, but writes him a carefully reasoned reply in a very man-to-man tone. It seems to me of the essence of Smith that he instantly appreciates Hunt's fairness and courtesy and acknowledges that his own letter had been 'impetuous'. [17] His reply reveals a subtle shift of feeling. Here is another of Smith's 'Guardian Angels' at work. There is a delightful vignette, recorded by Hunt, at the expedition training weekend at the CIC, in which Robin "... lay cosily in his sleeping bag" and watched "with what I took to be cynical appraisal, as I busied myself sweeping up the mess on the littered floor." [18] But Hunt passes the test and later in Russia writes: "Derek, Robin and Wilf are wonders of selfless labour in the common weal." [19] From Bee MacNeill to John Hunt, wisdom and kindliness seem to have been qualities to which Smith always responded.

The sad conclusion to Smith's part in the expedition is recorded in detail through the eyes of those who were there. In order, however, to recapture the essential Smith, one should look back to the concluding chapter of Part II: a sparsely written, characterful account by Davie Agnew of Smith's last climb in Scotland – *The Needle* in the Cairngorms. This piece takes us back to where Smith has his being. As he and Agnew are waiting for a lift on their way from Clydeside to Rothiemurchus "across the road ... was a band of gypsies, camped in a field beside a wee burn." [20] The image powerfully suggests Borthwick's *Always A Little Further* [21] and it is to the tradition of work like that and of men like Murray and Patey, that Robin Smith's life belongs.

Canongate have produced the book very pleasantly: the type is a good size, the 32 photographs are well chosen and the index is useful. The text seems free from serious errors but I noted a howler on p.8 (*Sir Hector* Munro indeed!) and is it really "*moster-wheel* " in line 7 of Smith's poem quoted at the start? With so much of Part III dependent on quotation, surely detailed references, particularly to published works, should have been given in chapter notes at the end.

I do not think that this will be the last biography of Smith, but Jimmy Cruikshank has set a high standard. All who come after will have to be thouroughly acquainted with this work. He has also discharged a debt of honour – and love – to a friend.

P. J. Biggar.

References

[1] *High Endeavours* p. 2.
[2] p. 3.
[3] p. 4.
[4] p. 4.
[5] *The Old Man and the Mountain,* R. Smith SMCJ, 1960.
[6] *Bringing Up Father* R. Campbell, EUMCJ, 1968-69.
[7] *High Endeavours* p.145.
[8] p.145.
[9] p.145.
[10] p. 72
[11] p. 72
[12] p. 74
[13] p. 74
[14] p. 73
[15] p. 76
[16] pp. 230-234
[17] p. 268
[18] p. 271
[19] p. 271
[20] p. 227
[21] *Always A Little Further*, Alistair Borthwick, Faber and Faber, London, 1939.

Seton Gordon's Scotland – An Anthology:- Compiled by Hamish Brown, (Whittles Publishing, 2005, hardback, 329 pages, 25.00. ISBN 1-904445-22-5).

This is a very special book; a real celebration of the writings of that most influential and kindly of Highland gentlemen, Seton Paul Gordon, CBE. FZS. MBOU.

The naturalist, photographer, hillwalker, historian, folklorist and piper was born 120 years ago, three years before the founding of the SMC, yet lived until three years after Hamish's celebrated mountain walk. Tempus fugit!

There was certainly plenty of candidate material for the anthology; 27 books totalling nearly 6000 pages and two million words, plus legion articles from many publications and the contents of the Seton Gordon archive at the National Library of Scotland.

Hamish has done Seton's works and memory proud, compiling 120 extracts on a wide range of topics into 14 themed sections, each with a short introduction. We get sections on, for example, The Cairngorms, The Outer Hebrides, Hill Days, and Ways That Are Gone; and topics as diverse as, The Collection of Cairngorm Stones, A Day At The Peats, Christ's Birds, and Berries Of The Hills. Some of the extracts are quite lengthy, others, no more than 100 words or so. All, however, contain that magic born of the writer's deep knowledge of, and passion for his chosen subjects. As Seton's biographer, Raymond Eagle pointed out: " The uniqueness of his writing lay in his ability to transport the reader so that they saw the world through his all-discovering eyes."

Hamish once described Seton as ' the grand-master writer on The Cairngorms', the area he wrote most about, therefore it is fitting that the preface is by Adam Watson, Seton's star pupil. Like Eagle, he marvels at "… the power and wonder of his written word." And that "… the reader easily imagines standing beside him when they look at the scene together."

Although Seton was no mountaineer, as in the purist's definition, he was a hill-walker of formidable ability, totally at home on the highest of bens or longest of glens – and in all weathers. Witness these words from the extract 'At The Pools Of Dee': " I had walked across from Aviemore to Braemar to assist in the judging of the piping at the Braemar Gathering and, as I was expected to do the same thing at the Kingussie Gathering the next day, it was necessary for me to return through the Lairig Ghru very early the next morning to reach Kingussie in time."

Throughout the anthology there are Seton's wonderfully simple, yet evocative descriptive phrases such as , 'the mutter of thunder', 'the faery light of the glowing sun' and the 'careless grace' (of an eagle over An Teallach).

As well as loving the flora, fauna and history of his native land Seton was also a great 'people person', with a keen sense of humour – never malicious, but slightly impish. This comes out in 'Those Sorts Of Situations' within the 'A Vanished World' section: "I chuckled to myself when an acquaintance rang me up one day to tell me he had seen three eagles perched on telegraph poles." Also, on the skills of the piper not rated too high locally: "… he had scarcely walked off the platform when one of the audience yelled at the top of his voice, 'Sit doon ye ….' At once the chairman was on his feet and called out in stern and disapproving tones, 'Who called the piper a ….?' Came the answer instantly, in the broadest Scots 'Fa caa'd the …. a piper?"

Adam Watson states, in his forward to the 1979 reprint of Seton's 'The Immortal Isles': "Others whom I know had a spark lit in them by Seton Gordon's writings and went on to become naturalists and writers themselves. And others unborn will have this magic in the future." Hamish lists in his foreword some of those influenced by Seton; Adam of course, Desmond Nethersole-Thomson, David Stephen, Tom Weir, Mike Tomkies, Don and Bridget Maccaskill and Jim Crumley. Modesty will have prevented him directly associating himself with this august gathering, but he should be up there for surely what Seton did for Adam and others, Hamish has done, in turn for quite a few of his irreverent band at Braehead School and all of us who relish his mountain travel writings.

Seton Gordon would enjoy this book, recognising Hamish as a kindred spirit. He would also take quiet satisfaction from the following words – which he could have written himself – from *Hamish's Mountain Walk,* as proof that his spark will never be extinguished: "The hills are peopled with all these past memories, enriching, encouraging. How could I possibly be bored? Oh, can I plead for the taking of the heritage in full; do not be a specialist, the mountains are worth so much more. Read and look, and go to the very end. It is all joy." Just like this book!

Ian Hamilton.

The Mont Blanc Massif - The Hundred Finest Routes: Gaston Rebuffat, (Baton Wicks, hardback, 239pp, ISBN 1-898573-69-7, £25.00)

I can still remember the first time I opened a copy of Rebuffat's *Hundred Finest Routes in the Mont Blanc Massif,* well over 25years ago. I was a first-year student smitten by climbing, with a notion to visit the Alps that summer. Turning the pages of Rebuffat's book I immediately knew that Chamonix was the place to go. The photographs showed a new world of fairy-tale peaks and Rebuffat's evocative prose added an intoxicating romanticism. The sequence of routes, from simple climbs in the Aiguilles Rouges to the *Central Pillar of Freney,* put in place an alpine apprenticeship that I, and hundreds of others, have subsequently followed.

Thirty years after its publication, Rebuffat's route selection stands the test of time. Climate change means that some of the ice routes are best climbed in spring, winter or autumn, and one or two routes such as the *Bonatti Pillar* have suffered devastating rockfall, but what aspiring climber does not want to climb the *Walker Spur*, the South Face of the Fou or the North Face of Les Droites?

For many years the English translation of *The Mont Blanc Massif* has been out of print, but it has now been republished by Baton Wicks. Inevitably, it carries the Ken Wilson stamp of authority. The picture reproduction is superb and considerably better than the original. Small portrait pictures of key first ascensionists have been added at appropriate places in the text and an appendix, at the end of the book on new developments, gives modern grades and updated guidebook notes on many of the climbs.

All in all it's a superbly handsome book and cannot fail to inspire both the accomplished alpinist and new hand alike. Now, when am I going to get around to climbing the Peuterey Ridge....?

Simon Richardson.

Scotland's Mountain Ridges: Dan Bailey. (Cicerone, 253pp., full colour, ISBN 1-85284-469-8, £17-95).

This is a first-class production from the Cicerone Press concentrating on the experience of Scrambling, Mountaineering and Climbing on the best ridges in the Scottish Mountains in both summer and winter.

"Surely every mountaineer loves a good ridge? Threading a bristling gendarmed spine; inching around an extravagantly fluted cornice; balancing along a stone tightrope in the clouds – these are some of the finest things a climber can get up to…"

Not many would disagree with these sentiments expressed in the introduction to this lavishly illustrated book which covers territory ranging from the walking and scrambling of An Teallach to the vertical challenge of Eagle Ridge on Lochnagar. Here we have extracts from OS maps, diagrams and inspiring photographs which simply invite fireside planning, assuming that is, that you've either – not yet reached, never desired to reach or, more than likely, past, the stage that you want to scare your self to death every week-end. Although, thinking back, Eagle Ridge was not exactly a dawdle was it?

Gair Swanson

OFFICE BEARERS 2005-2006

Honorary President: William. D. Brooker

Honorary Vice-Presidents: Douglas Scott, Gerry S. Peet

President: A. Colin Stead

Vice-Presidents: David J. Broadhead, Brian R. Shackelton

Honorary Secretary: John R. R. Fowler, 4 Doune Terrace, Edinburgh, EH3 6DY. **Honorary Treasurer:** John A. Wood, Spout Close, Millbeck, Underskiddaw, Keswick, Cumbria CA12 4PS. **Honorary Editor:** Charles J. Orr, 28 Chesters View, Bonnyrigg, Midlothian EH19 3PU. **Convener of the Publications Sub-Committee:** Rab Anderson, 24 Paties Road, Edinburgh, EH141EE. **Honorary Librarian:** Vacancy. **Honorary Custodian of Slides:** Graeme N. Hunter, Church House, Gill Croft, Easingwold, Yorkshire YO61 3HH. **Honorary Archivist:** Robin N. Campbell, Glynside, by Fintry, Stirlingshire, G63 0LW. **Convener of the Huts Sub-Committee:** William H. Duncan, Kirktoun, East End, Lochwinnoch, Renfrewshire, PA12 4ER. **Custodian of the CIC Hut:** Robin Clothier, 35 Broompark Drive, Newton Mearns, Glasgow G77 5DZ. **Custodian of Lagangarbh Hut:** Bernard M. Swan, 16 Knowes View, Faifley, Clydebank, Dunbartonshire, G81 5AT. **Custodian of the Ling Hut:** William Skidmore, 1 Kirkton Drive, Lochcarron, Wester Ross, IV54 8UD. **Custodian of the Raeburn Hut:** Heather Morning, Duach Mills, Nethybridge, Inverness-shire, PH253DH. **Custodian of the Naismith Hut:** William S. McKerrow, Scotsburn House, Drummond Road, Inverness, IV2 4NA. **Committee:** Donald J. Ballance, Adam Kassyk, Alex Runciman, Ann Macdonald, David M. Nichols, Chris R. Ravey, Campbell Forrest, Gillian E. Irvine, Clifford D. Smith

SMC Internet Address – http://www.smc.org.uk SMC e-mail: smc@smc.org.uk

Journal Information

Editor:	Charles J. Orr, 28 Chesters View, Bonnyrigg, Midlothian EH19 3PU. (e-mail: charliejorr@hotmail.com).
New Routes Editor:	A. D. Nisbet, 20 Craigie Avenue, Boat of Garten, Inverness-shire PH24 3BL. (e-mail: anisbe@globalnet.co.uk).
Advertisements:	D. G. Pyper, 3 Keir Circle, Westhill, Skene, Aberdeen AB32 6RE. (e-mail: derek@pyper.fsbusiness.co.uk).
Distribution:	D. F. Lang, Hillfoot Hey, 580 Perth Road, Dundee DD2 1PZ.

INSTRUCTIONS TO CONTRIBUTORS

Articles for the Journal should be submitted before the end of January for consideration for the following issue. Lengthy contributions are preferably typed, double-spaced, on one side only, and with ample margins (minimum 30mm). Articles may be accepted on floppy disk, IBM compatible (contact Editor beforehand), or by e-mail. The Editor welcomes material from both members and non-members, with priority being given to articles of Scottish Mountaineering content. Photographs are also welcome, and should be good quality colour slides. All textual material should be sent to the Editor, address and e-mail as above. Photographic material should be sent direct to the Editor of Photographs, address as above.